Bisexuality in the Ancient World

Bisexuality in the Ancient World

Eva Cantarella

Translated by Cormac Ó Cuilleanáin

YALE UNIVERSITY PRESS

NEW HAVEN AND LONDON · 1992

Copyright © 1992 by Yale University
English language translation © 1992 by Cormac Ó Cuilleanáin

Reprinted 1993
First published in paperback 1994

Original edition *Secondo natura* © 1988 by Editori Riuniti, Rome

Set in Sabon by Best-set Typesetter Ltd., Hong Kong
Printed and bound in Great Britain by Biddles Ltd., Guildford and Kings Lynn

Library of Congress Cataloging-in-Publication Data
Cantarella, Eva.
[Secondo natura. English]
Bisexuality in the ancient world / Eva Cantarella.
p. cm.
Translation of: Secondo natura.
Includes bibliographical references and index.
ISBN 0–300–04844–0 (hbk.)
ISBN 0–300–05924–8 (pbk.)
1. Homosexuality, Male—Rome—History. 2. Homosexuality, Male—
Greece—History. 3. Bisexuality—Rome—History. 4. Bisexuality—
Greece—History. I. Title.
HQ76.2.R6C3613 1992
306.76′5′09376—dc20   92–11566
                             CIP

A catalogue record for this book is available from the British Library.

Frontispiece Lovers: from a red-figured Attic cylix,
c. 500 BC. Yale University Press Art Gallery.
Gift of Rebecca Stoddard.

Contents

Contents

Preface

It often happens that an author does not choose a topic; rather, it is the topic which chooses its author. That is what happened to me.

The theme of this book forced itself on my attention over the last few years, as I continued my efforts to understand the key points in the development of the female condition in classical antiquity. As my research moved onward, I gradually realised that male homosexual relations were so widespread, in both Greece and Rome, that they must necessarily have had an impact on the way in which women were loved. And I became aware, at the same time, of how imprecise and misleading it is to speak of 'homosexuality' with reference to the ancient world.

The Greeks and the Romans — leaving aside the profound differences between their two cultures — experienced relationships between men very differently from the way in which they are experienced (with exceptions, obviously) by people who opt for a homosexual existence today. For the Greeks and Romans (again allowing for exceptions), homosexuality was not an exclusive choice. Loving another man was not an option falling outside the norm, a different or somehow deviant decision. It was just one part of the experience of life: the manifestation of an impulse which could be either a matter of feelings or of sexuality; during one's lifetime this would alternate and interweave (sometimes simultaneously) with the love of a woman.

That is why the title of the present book, unlike some others dedicated to the same theme, refers to 'Bisexuality in the Ancient World'. In writing it, I set out from the observation outlined above, and tried to clarify a series of problems for my own benefit. Each of these problems seemed to me fundamental to a better understanding not only of the sexuality, but also of the entire culture of Greece and Rome.

In the first place: what were the psychological, social and cultural mechanisms which determined male sexual choices, directing them, in different circumstances, towards women or towards other men? Incidentally, the fact that I speak only of male choices need cause no surprise: the possibility of having experiences of either a heterosexual or a homosexual kind was allowed (at least theoretically) only to men.

A second problem: was the choice of homosexuality completely and absolutely free, or was it subject to rules, and thus to some extent constrained, if not indeed coerced? More precisely, was it available to all men, whatever their social and legal standing and whatever their age? And, within a homosexual relationship, was the choice of the active or passive role left up to individual inclinations, or was it determined by the participants' status and age?

Lastly, the Greeks and Romans gave ample space to male homosexual love, considering it an absolutely normal alternative to heterosexual love. What were the consequences of this (apart from the men's relationships with women) for their value judgements, their customs and their law? If taken as a model of the good life, bisexuality is an approach which can leave deep marks on a culture, playing a very considerable part in determining its character. To be convinced of this, all one has to do (to take one example) is think of the famous and much-discussed problem of the social function of homosexuality in Athens.

In Athens, homosexuality (which as we know was really pederasty, in the sense of a sexual relationship between an adult and a young boy) held an important position in the moral and political formation of young men, who learned from their adult lovers the virtues of a citizen. Relations between men and women, obviously, could not be immune from the repercussions of a mentality shaped by the exaltation of exclusively male virtues, permanently marked by a 'sentimental education', which allowed very little space for the possibility of viewing the heterosexual relationship as anything more than an instrument of reproduction for a group of citizens, who would subsequently be educated, according to their fathers' values. If the pinnacle of love, the expression of the highest feelings, the possibility of showing the noblest part of oneself, lay in the relationship between men, how would heterosexual relations be experienced by a Greek? And on the other hand, how would women react to this state of affairs? How did they accept their role, how did they experience their relations with men, what did they expect from them?

The first difficulty that arose, logically and historically, in dealing with these problems, was the question of cause and effect. Should homosexuality be seen as the outcome of a way of living which, by shutting women up within the confines of their houses and denying them all education, rendered them not only inaccessible but also highly undesirable as partners except in a purely material or physical sense? Or was it the other way around: was homosexuality the cause of their segregation, of their exclusion from the life of the mind, and of their earmarking for a basically reproductive role (always assuming, of course, that one is considering 'respectable' women rather than courtesans or prostitutes)?

My initial interest in male homosexuality was thus, in a sense, merely a means to an end, subordinate to other research objectives.

As time went on, however, there was a shift in my centre of interest: I began to become curious about the rules of the homosexual relationship in itself, the meaning of this relationship which was so important in the mentality and customs of society, so minutely codified in the rules of 'courtship' which lovers could not ignore, so carefully considered in legal rules, and above all, so variously evaluated by public opinion. For alongside the exaltation of homosexual relationships in philosophical works (or at least some of those works) and in certain judicial pronouncements, one also finds homosexuality being grossly ridiculed in comedy.

The philosophical sources themselves, moreover, are anything but straightforward: sometimes they seem to exalt the spiritual aspect of the relationship and reprove the physical manifestations of love. But the literary sources, graffiti and iconography irrefutably demonstrate that physical relations formed an integral part of pederasty – and that these relations included not only intercrural intercourse but also anal intercourse, contrary to the argument recently put forward by K.J. Dover. As I continued my attempt to identify the meaning of these loves, their practical modes of expression, and the differing values attached to them by popular culture, I also found a steady increase in the number of sectors within Greek culture which, in my opinion, could not be comprehended without an understanding of homosexuality.

For a start, how are we to interpret certain laws which refer not only to private but also to political life (for example, the ban on political involvement by men who have prostituted themselves), without a knowledge of the sexual ethics underpinning those laws? How can we understand Plato without identifying the features of that Eros which is one of the dominant themes in his philosophy – one might almost say its underlying theme? How can we hope to comprehend the artistic manifestations of Greek culture without a full understanding of the feelings which inspired the poets, or the erotic models expressed by figurative art? To say nothing of the problems – different but no less fundamental – that arose in connection with the Roman world.

Although less visible, and certainly (one might say) less publicised, homosexuality was widespread in Rome too, and despite what is usually maintained, it was by no means an 'imported product' (specifically, a habit introduced and propagated by contact with Greek culture). On the contrary, it was an indigenous custom, and as such was regulated by a code of sexual ethics completely different from the one that inspired Greek pederasty. Yet this does not mean that there were no analogies between Greek and Roman homosexuality.

In both Greece and Rome, as the most recent studies have correctly argued, the fundamental opposition between different types of sexual behaviour was not the heterosexual/homosexual contrast, but the active/passive contrast, the former category – activity – being characteristic of the adult male, while the latter – passivity – was reserved for women and boys. This meant that, in both Greece and Rome, disapproval and ridicule were directed only at the passive adult male.

Too many hasty equivalences, however, have been advanced on the basis of these undeniable analogies, thereby distorting the completely different perspectives within which Greeks and ·Romans experienced and viewed such loves. The homosexual relationship, in Rome, did not fulfil the function of educating young males which it held in Greece. It was no coincidence, then, that in Rome the passive partner in the relationship, at least as a rule, was not a free youth but a slave. This detail is by no means unimportant, and it allows us to identify the mechanism (more social and psychological than sexual) which induced Roman males to have such frequent relations with persons of their own sex that it came to be considered absolutely normal.

The young Roman male was educated, from his earliest years, to be a conqueror: *tu regere imperio populos, romane, memento*, writes Virgil. To impose one's will, subjugate everyone, dominate the world: this was the watchword for a Roman. And his sexual ethics, when one looks closely, simply expressed an aspect of his political ethics. Subjecting women to his desires was not enough for a Roman. In order to satisfy his exuberant and victorious sexuality, and show it off to his peers, he also had to subject men – so long as they were not other Romans, of course. How could a boy become an invincible, dominant male if he had been forced to submit to another man at a tender age? That is why the Romans used to sodomise slaves (or, where available, defeated enemies), and not young freemen.

But at this point another problem arises: if the rules of indigenous homosexuality were as I have described, how then can one explain the flowering, more or less from the Augustan period onwards, of love poetry dedicated to boys who were not infrequently – against all the rules – of free status or even of noble lineage?

Alongside the traditional interpretation, which held that for the Roman poets, love between men was simply the transposition of a Hellenistic literary model, another hypothesis has been gaining ground in recent times: that this poetry was inspired by real passions, expressing the pangs of love that flourished frequently and genuinely and therefore provoked anxiety and happiness, jealousy and despair which did not differ from those called forth by love for women. Besides Lesbia, for example, Catullus is thought to have loved Juventius no less passionately, and sincerely desired 'the honey of his kisses'.

I believe that the love affairs between men sung by the Augustan poets were real, at least in the sense that they reflected the existence, in contemporary Rome, of homosexual relationships which were no longer an expression of social and sexual oppression, but a manifestation of romantic love, conducted according to the canons of Greek pederasty. The Greek model, in short, really had begun to influence Roman culture by this point: and adult males, by this period, along with their traditional 'servant' love affairs, were now experiencing affairs of the heart, courting and exalting the lovely, recalcitrant youths who, just like their Greek counterparts of similar years, kept their suitors sighing by behaving with 'feminine' flirtatiousness.

Changes in homosexual behaviour were not of course confined to this: as the years went by, more or less from Caesar's time onwards, the ruling class began blatantly to break the rule whereby adult males must always confine themselves to an active role; and the middle class, reassured by this example, followed the new fashion.

But the mass dissemination of a custom so inimical to ancient principles could not be tolerated. So we find legal repression coming into play at this time. Whereas during the Republican period the law had taken very little interest in the problem (with the exception of a certain mysterious *lex Scatinia*, the contents of which are much debated), from the third century onwards a series of imperial constitutions began to lay down penalties of increasing severity, first against passive homosexuals and then against active ones. Was this change due perhaps to the influence of Christian morality? Or was it (as recently argued by Paul Veyne) for reasons internal to pagan society? This too was a problem which I felt it indispensable to tackle and to try to understand in greater detail.

In this context – and despite the difficulties caused by scarcity of information – I have also attempted to comprehend the role of female homosexual love in both Greece and Rome, its degree of diffusion and the needs to which it responded, in different situations and at different times.

Lastly, I have tried to understand how both Greeks and Romans experienced the alternation of homosexual and heterosexual loves, the meaning and function of that alternation, whether there were differences in how men and women were loved, and whether bisexuality (as is often argued, with particular reference to Greece) was really the recognition of a sexual freedom – at least for men – which was later lost.

Stimulated by the desire to answer these and many other questions, in the present book I set out to provide, if not an exhaustive picture, at least a useful instrument for a better understanding of a 'different' aspect of love. 'Different' obviously, not because it was deviant, still less perverse, but because it was experienced differently at different times, and evaluated according to rules linked to lifestyles which, with changing eras and changeable situations, underwent profound modification and took on different degrees of importance, function and significance. Starting out as an effort to gain a more detailed understanding of some aspects of the female condition and relations between men and women, the book has evolved into an attempt to understand the choices, thoughts and affections of all those people (men and women alike) who laid the basis for our civilisation, and who, consequently, have inevitably contributed, through the mediating influence of time, to the direction of our own choices, our values and affections.

Eva Cantarella

Publisher's Note: Acknowledgement is made to the following for permission to quote copyright material from the sources indicated.

Penguin Books Ltd: *The Poems of Tibullus*, translated by Philip Dunlop (Penguin Classics, Harmondsworth, 1972).

Oxford University Press: *The Poems of Catullus*, English translation by Guy Lee (Oxford, 1990).

PART ONE

Greece

1

The Beginnings, the Greek Dark Age and the Archaic Period

The Problem of Origins and Homosexuality as a Form of Initiation

No sooner had it emerged from the so-called dark centuries of its history, beyond the period that once used to be called the Greek Dark Age, than Greece began to speak of love:

> Once again limb-loosening Love makes me tremble, the bitter-sweet, irresistible creature.

wrote Sappho.[1] We owe the first description of the inevitable pain of love, then, to a woman: more precisely, to a woman who loved other women. And her verse at once reveals two features which the Greeks attributed to this feeling. The first was its inexorable nature. It is not by chance that Love (Eros) was a god armed with bow and arrows: nobody could escape his wounds.[2] The second was the absolute indifference of Eros to the sex of his victims. Just as he had entangled Helen and Paris, so Eros bound Sappho, one after another, to Gongyla, Agallides, Anactoria, and the loveliest pupils in the circle which under Sappho's guidance studied dance, music and singing – in other words, the culture which Greece set aside for women, before the rules of the *polis*, the new form of city organisation, excluded them from all participation in the life of the spirit and the mind. But I will come back to this: my purpose here is to point out that whereas in the view of the Greeks (given the indifference of Eros to this problem) a love relationship could take shape without distinction, according to circumstances, between persons of different sexes or persons of the same sex, that did not mean that all loves were equal: depending on the circumstances, love had profoundly different characteristics and functions.

What, then, were the characteristics and functions of homosexual love? While one of the first pieces of evidence about this type of love relates to love between women, the kind of homosexuality with which I will be mostly (though not exclusively) concerned will be male.

3

After Sappho, in Greece, love between women was no longer the subject of poetry. How could it have been any different, when one considers that with the strengthening of the bonds of citizenship, women had been relegated to a reproductive role, excluded from all forms of education, and consequently from the use of language? In the centuries of the city-state, female homosexuality disappeared, as a socially visible and significant custom. And, at the same time, male homosexuality came out, in a manner of speaking. I shall focus my attention on male homosexuality for two reasons: the greater possibility of following its history through surviving documents, and the fundamental role which these documents show that it played in the life of the *polis*.

But was it only after the formation of the city that the Greeks took to loving other men, and more particularly boys? Male homosexuality in Greece, in fact – or at least its most socially and culturally significant forms – was, in practice, pederasty, and was extremely widespread. The problem of its 'origins' remains open.

Erich Bethe, in a celebrated article in 1909, raised the veil of silence which had covered up this embarrassing question. At the same time, however, he offered scholars of the ancient world (who were very reluctant to admit this 'defect' in a people whom they had mythologised and taken as a model of rationality) an excuse which was immediately accepted, and served for years as a sheet anchor. Homosexuality, in his opinion, was not a Greek custom. It had been imported into Greece by the Dorians, the conquerors from the north.[3] But after a few decades, dissenting voices began to be heard. In 1950 H.I. Marrou wrote: 'It was bound up with the genuine Hellenic tradition as a whole: German scholarship is mistaken in regarding it, as it frequently does, as a peculiarity confined to the Dorian race.' More precisely,

it is one of the most obvious and lasting survivals from the feudal 'Middle Ages' [i.e. the Homeric Age]. In essence, it was a comradeship of warriors. Greek homosexuality was of a military type. It was quite different from the inversion which is bound up with the rites of initiation and the duties of a priesthood.

This type of inversion is now the subject of ethnological study in all the many forms in which it appears among 'primitive' peoples.... It is not difficult to find parallels to the Greek type of love – parallels not far removed from us in space and time: the proceedings in which the Templars were involved; the scandals which broke out in the Hitler Youth movement in 1934; and the practices which I am told grew up during the last war in the lower ranks of certain armies. In

4

my view, love between men is a recurring feature of military societies, in which men tend to be shut in upon themselves. The exclusion – the utter absence – of women inevitably means an increase in masculine love – as for example in Moslem society – though here, it is true, we are under the conditions of an entirely different civilisation and theology. The phenomenon is more accentuated in a military milieu, for here, with the glorification of an ideal made up of masculine virtues like strength and valour and loyalty, with the cultivation of a distinctly masculine pride, there goes a tendency to depreciate the normal love of a man for a woman.[4]

Marrou was undoubtedly correct in saying that homosexuality was widespread in Greece even before the 'descent' of the Dorians: but was he right when he made it into a custom and ideology linked to the shortage of women? I think not. In fact, as already explained, women became inaccessible for the Greeks only when the first written laws, codifying their role as reproducers of the citizen body, established that they were to carry out this role segregated within the walls of their households. But during the Homeric era, in a situation when rules of a customary kind were a great deal more fluid, women had not yet been closed up within their houses, even in the physical sense (at least in Athens). Although destined for a future as wives and mothers, women in Homeric society were free to move around, within the city and outside, both before and after marriage. Nausicaa, in the *Odyssey*, goes with her handmaidens to wash her clothes in the river bed, and when she sees Ulysses, shipwrecked on the coast of Scherie (the island where her father Alcinous is king), she welcomes him without fear, and invites him to present himself at her father's court, even thinking that he might be a welcome suitor for her hand.[5] This last idea was one which girls living some centuries later would have neither the occasion nor the nerve to entertain, subjected as they were to the will of a father who promised them in marriage to an unknown man while they were still children. The same situation obtains in the *Iliad*: in time of war, at the moment of greatest danger to the city, Andromache leaves her house, runs on to the walls of Ilium, urges Hector to think of her and their little son, and begs him not to endanger their life by abandoning them to the sad fate of widows and orphans.[6] It was only from the eighth or seventh centuries onwards that women became really inaccessible to Greek men.

The origins of homosexuality must therefore be sought elsewhere. The most recent research in this area directs our attention to a time further back than the Homeric period: to the tribal past of Greek society, where the organisation of the community (not yet political) was based, in the first place, on divisions according to age categories.

In societies organised on this basis (and this is true both of ancient societies and of the dwindling but still surviving tribal societies of today), the progression of an individual from one age category to the next is accompanied by a series of rituals (the so-called rites of passage). The structure of these, apart from certain local variations, is as follows: to be accepted into the higher age category, the person being initiated (rites of passage are initiations, just like the 'mystery' rituals) must spend a period of time far away from the community, living outside the rules of civil existence, often in a state of nature. He must, in short, go through a period which ethnologists call 'segregation', accompanied by death symbolism, represented more or less realistically, which some-times precedes segregation, sometimes follows it, and is sometimes symbolised by it. And at the end of this period he is reborn to a new life, as a member of the higher age category.[7]

Having said that, let us return to Greece: the existence of rites of passage in Greece, before the age of cities, was demonstrated by scholars such as Jeanmaire, Gernet and Brelich. More recently it has been confirmed – leaving aside significant differences in approach and method – by the researches of Vidal-Naquet, Bremmer, Patzer, Lincoln and Sergent. And homosexual love between a man and a boy, in Greece as with other populations in a tribal condition, clearly has its roots in these rituals.[8]

In the different areas of pre-city Greece, boys learned the virtues which would make them into adults during the period of segregation, living in the company of a man, who was at the same time an educator and lover. These are the remote origins of Greek pederasty. But what proof – or what evidence – can be adduced in support of this assertion?

In the first place, there are numerous myths which, more or less explicitly, refer to homosexual love affairs: the affair between Zeus and Ganymede, for example, or Dionysus and Adonis, Poseidon and Pelops, Apollo and Admetus, Hercules and Jason, or Apollo and Cyparissus. These different myths, as has been shown by Bernard Sergent, share a common structure as myths of initiation.[9] The homosexual relationship forms part of a narrative showing the transformation of a youth into an adult through the performance of a heroic gesture or – frequently – through death, explicitly or implicitly followed by the resurrection of a new individual designed to replace the adolescent, who has disappeared as such, within the category of adults. And in this context homosexual love always plays the essential role of an educational instrument, capable of transforming the boy into a man. But that is not all: Strabo reports, drawing on Ephorus,[10] that in Crete adult men, known as 'lovers' (*erastai*), used to kidnap the adolescents whom they loved (*erōmenoi*) and take them away outside the city, for a period of two months (the period of segregation), during which they conducted relationships specified in minute detail by the law, which laid down their mutual duties. At the end of this period, before returning to the city, the lover presented his beloved with a military kit (the sign of his entry into the adult community).

In Sparta, furthermore, according to Plutarch's account, when boys reached the age of twelve they were entrusted to lovers chosen among the best men of adult age, and from these they learned to be true Spartans.[11]

And finally we have the celebrated 'graffiti' of Thera (today called Santorini), a series of inscriptions discovered at the end of the last century on a rock wall not more than 70 metres from where the temple of Apollo Karneios once stood. Hiller von Gaertringen, who found them, dated them to the geometric period. Later, Carpenter dated them to the sixth century.[12]

Why should these inscriptions be of interest to us? Because they have kept a record of pederastic love over the centuries, beyond the slightest possibility of doubt. In one inscription, to take a single example, we read clearly: 'here Krimon had anal intercourse with his *pais*, the brother of Bathycles'.[13] At first sight, this could be nothing more than 'indecent wall-scratchings', as they were defined by H.I. Marrou.[14] But several factors make one think that this is something quite different: the sacred location where the inscriptions were made, and their frequent references to 'courotrophic' divinities (that is, the gods charged with the education of young people).

How can one avoid thinking, on the basis of these considerations alone, that far from being 'indecent wall-scratchings' what we have here are ritual inscriptions, designed to celebrate the completion of initiation ceremonies? Further factors can be added, which are anything but negligible: the precision of the personal references, in particular, and the tone of the inscriptions. Why should Krimon be so anxious to let us know that he has sodomised the brother of a certain Bathycles, unknown to us, but presumably a prominent person in the community? If it had been a casual encounter, he would probably have shown more discretion. And, above all, he would not have called the friend of a moment 'his *pais*' (his boy). Obviously, the inscriptions preserve the record of an important, not to say institutional, moment in the life of the young boy: the moment of his initiation, the concluding stage in a period of his life which, to be considered definitively and publicly

7

superseded, demanded that he should have had a pedagogical-amorous relationship with an adult over a certain period of time, including a sexual relationship. This last circumstance, in fact, is fairly surprising to us, and we naturally feel obliged to ask the reason for it. Why on earth should anal intercourse among the Greeks – as among other people who were very far from them in time and space – be considered part of the process of formation of an adult man?

According to Erich Bethe (who supports his hypothesis by comparing Greek practices to those of other 'primitive' populations) the sexual relationship was considered necessary on the grounds that it could transfuse the manly virtues into the boy through the sperm of his lover; in fact, the Greeks not infrequently used the verb *eispnein* (*inspirare*)[15] to denote this type of relationship, and used the nouns *eispnēlos* and *eispnēlas* (*inspirator*)[16] as a synonym for lover.

This is a possible explanation, although it is certainly very difficult (not to say impossible) to prove. Besides which, at least one other theory, recently maintained by Eva Keuls, should be borne in mind. Anal intercourse, according to Keuls, is an act which humiliates the person undergoing it, and symbolises in a very obvious way the submission of the younger person to the older: in other words, it is an act of 'enculturation'.[17]

But I believe that (quite apart from the impossibility of formulating any reply other than a mere hypothesis) it does not create any problem if we leave the question open. What is sufficient for our purposes is the observation that Greek homosexuality, at its origins, was connected with initiation. Submission to a sexual act with an adult (or, in some cases, a sexual relationship with him) was an indispensable social prelude to the birth of an individual who, from that moment on, would assume the manly role in its full sense: that is to say, he would abandon the passive role and would assume the role of a husband with women, and that of the 'lover' with boys. We will return to this view, to clarify and develop it, during the course of the following pages. It will reveal its fundamental importance when we go on to discuss the issues of love between men in the history of the city.

The Homeric Poems

Before moving on to the era of the cities, it will be useful to refer briefly to the long period during which the Greeks, following the collapse of the palaces and their Mycenaean civilisation, organised their community life around some types of association and institutional forms which, after a preliminary phase of great 'fluidity',[18] gradually consolidated themselves and built up solid authority in certain areas, finally giving rise to the emergence of political organisation.[19] These centuries (extending between the twelfth and the eighth century BC) have often been called 'dark' by historians, for two different reasons, and with two different meanings: on account of the lack of information and documents revealing the conditions of life in that era, and on account of the supposed state of impoverished backwardness into which Greece had fallen (hence the term 'Greek Dark Ages').

But in fact these centuries are not 'dark' at all, in either of these two senses. Recent archaeological discoveries have brought to light the existence of dwellings and urban settlements which, while they cannot compete with the opulence of the Mycenaean palaces, still bear witness to living conditions which were more than respectable.[20] And the modern interpretations of the Homeric poems (which historians today no longer consider as documents representing Mycenaean life, but as texts describing the life of Greek social organisations in the centuries between the collapse of the palaces and the complete formation of the *polis*) have thrown new light on a period which is thus no longer 'dark' even in the sense of 'unknown'.[21]

But this does not mean that the attempt to understand whether, during these centuries, homosexuality was a widespread custom – and, if so, whether it was socially accepted or censured – is by any means a simple undertaking. It is often observed that neither the *Iliad* nor the *Odyssey* contains references to this type of love.[22] But, on closer inspection, this assertion leaves quite a few questions unanswered.

In the first place, Homer describes male friendships of such emotional intensity that one inevitably thinks of bonds much stronger than simple solidarity between comrades in arms. The friendship which it is almost obligatory to cite at this point is that of Achilles and Patroclus – a relationship so strong that Achilles, after the death of Patroclus, declares that he has only one aim in life: after avenging his friend, to lie with him in the same grave, for ever, united with him in death as he had been in life. This relationship, then, is very different from the one which Achilles had with Briseis, the slave-concubine whom Agamemnon had stolen from him when he was deprived of his own slave, Chryseis. Female slaves were interchangeable companions: as we can see from the behaviour of Agamemnon, who immediately consoles himself for the loss of Chryseis by replacing her with another woman.[23] The link between Achilles and Patroclus, on the other hand, was irreplaceable: and in this connection the speech of Thetis, the hero's mother, to her despairing and inconsolable son, is of considerable significance. Achilles, says Thetis, must carry on living, and having forgotten Patroclus he must take a wife 'as is proper'.[24] A rebuke, perhaps? Proof that Thetis disapproved of her son's homosexual love? At first sight, one might think so. But on closer inspection things look very different. What emerges, in reality, from Thetis' words is that the bond with Patroclus was the reason why the hero had not yet taken a wife: confirmation of the amorous nature of their relationship. But the mother's exhortation to her son to carry out his social duty at last is not – despite this – an absolute condemnation of his relationship with Patroclus. Rather, the speech seems like an invitation to accept what the Greeks saw as a natural law: on reaching a certain age, one had to end the homosexual phase of life, and take on the virile role with a woman. And for Achilles, now, this age had arrived. If disapproval can be discerned in Thetis' words, the reproach is that her son has carried on too long in the phase of homosexual love owing to his infatuation with Patroclus.

Homer presents a theme which is not uncommon in Greek literature, which we will also find in authors from the later period, such as Theocritus, and which returns in the Roman poets, from Catullus to Martial. But the pointers to a love affair between Achilles and Patroclus (given that we are talking about pointers, certainly not about proof) do not end here.

In a recent study of this topic, some passages from Homer have been highlighted which would make it very difficult to think of the relationship between the two heroes as a simple friendship between comrades in arms.[25] When his friend is dead, as I have already pointed out, Achilles no longer has any reason for living: over and over he wishes that he had never been born, declares that his only desire now is to die, and seems to threaten suicide. And he does not confine himself to expressing his sorrow by groaning and covering his head with clay, as is normal for Homeric heroes. At the beginning of the nineteenth book, Thetis finds him 'stretched out on Patroclus', desperately embracing his corpse, in an attitude which is not at all in keeping with most displays of mourning in Homer.[26]

So it is not difficult to read the story of a love affair behind Homer's words. The ancients, for good reason, had very few doubts about this. In a fragment of Aeschylus's *Myrmidons*, preserved in Plutarch's *Amatorius*, we read about Achilles' explosion in a desperate cry of jealousy before the corpse of his dead friend, accusing him of having betrayed their love:

> You have not respected the august purity
> of your thighs [*mērōn*], despite our kisses.[27]

10

One of the lost dramas of Sophocles was entitled *Achilleōs erastai*, 'The Lovers of Achilles'.[28] Aeschines, finally, in his oration *Against Timarchus*, speaks of the two heroes as a pair of lovers,[29] as does pseudo-Lucian.

In antiquity, the only detail subject to dispute was this: in the famous couple, who was the lover and who was the beloved? According to Athenaeus (as well as Aeschines and Aeschylus) the *erastēs* was Achilles.[30] Plato, in his *Symposium*, maintains, on the contrary, that the *erastēs* was Patroclus.[31] The iconographic tradition seems to accept this interpretation, as shown in a celebrated vase kept in the Staatliche Museen in Berlin, which represents Achilles binding up the wound of his friend, and shows Patroclus with a beard, the symbol of his greater age.[32]

Leaving aside these diverging opinions,[33] what is interesting is to note the widespread conviction, in antiquity, that there was a love relationship between the two heroes: this shows, at the very least, that in the Classical era it was natural and inevitable to think that such an intense friendship between two men should also include a sexual bond. And this is certainly not without significance.

Apart from the case of these two heroes, there are other arguments which support the hypothesis that homosexuality was widespread in the Homeric world. Bernard Sergent observes (picking up an observation by Dumézil) that Telemachus, on reaching Pylos, is welcomed by King Nestor, who puts him sleeping beside Pisistratus, his only son who is as yet unmarried, while Nestor himself sleeps in the marriage-bed beside his wife.[34] In other words, Homer compares Telemachus and Pisistratus to a married couple. This happens more than once: in Sparta Telemachus again sleeps with Pisistratus, who has accompanied him, while Menelaus sleeps with Helen,[35] so that Athena, when she appears to Telemachus to exhort him to return to Italy, finds the two young men lying together. And Telemachus, when the goddess moves away, wakes up Pisistratus, 'touching him with his foot'.[36]

Homosexuality, then, although it does not appear explicitly, seems to emerge from the poems, while remaining in the background of the story, to some extent hidden, or at least in shadow. But why – if all this is true – does Homer (or the rhapsodes who go under this name) display such remarkable reticence in talking about the subject?

Sergent advances one (admittedly hypothetical) explanation: they did so because relations between men in Homer are not pederastic – neither concerned with initiation, as they had been in the previous era, nor with instruction, as they were to be in the later era. These are relations between people of about the same age. They are in fact 'trivially' homosexual entanglements, and as such they are reproved.[37] This hypothesis must be evaluated, even though it is clear that a number of doubts inevitably remain, owing to the scarcity and uncertainty of the documentary evidence.

The Age of Lyric Poetry: Solon, Alcaeus, Anacreon, Theognis, Ibycus and Pindar

While the voice of poetry celebrating love between women fell silent for ever after Sappho, love between men went on being celebrated. The first testimony of this type of love (some years prior to Sappho's poetry) comes from an unexpected figure: Solon. This is a personage almost removed from the human dimension by the legends which have surrounded his life from antiquity. *Diallaktēs kai nomothetēs* (as well as archon), the sources define him:[38] judge and legislator. In fact he was the man who, at a moment of profound economic and social crisis, managed to mediate the contradictory interests of the warring classes, and gave Athens a corpus of laws which survived through the centuries. But before he was a 'judge and legislator', Solon was a man: and as such he too was inevitably a victim of Eros: in Plutarch's biography, for example, he falls victim to the charms of his young cousin, Pisistratus.[39] Opening a completely unexpected vista on his private life, some auto-biographical verses have come down to us, with phrases which allow us to see, behind the austere image passed on by a tradition whose only preoccupation was to offer a model of public virtues, the feelings of a man who, during the course of his long life, knew – like all others – the temptations of love:

> Till he loves a lad in the flower of youth,
> Bewitched by thighs [*mērōn*] and by sweet lips.

So writes the great legislator.[40] And while it is true that thighs and lips can obviously be either male or female, it is equally true that, coming from a Greek, the reference to thighs is extremely significant: in general, the thighs desired by a Greek were those of a boy. This can be seen, beyond the shadow of a doubt, in the works of poets who (from Solon's time onwards) entrust the stories of their loves to verse: from Alcaeus to Anacreon, from Ibycus to Theognis to Pindar.

We know little about Alcaeus; legend has him desperately in love with Sappho: 'sweet smile, violet hair'.[41] The tradition records his loves for his companions, from Melanippus to Agesilaidas, from Bacchis to Aesimidas, from Dinnomenes to Menon.[42] It is to Menon that Alcaeus dedicates two verses revealing an interest which, more than friendship, looks like a sentimental attachment: 'I request that charming Menon be invited, if I am to enjoy the drinking party.'[43]

But now we come to Anacreon, whose evidence is both more explicit and more copious.

One of the recurrent themes in the poetry of Anacreon, born about 570 BC on the island of Teos, opposite the coast of Asia Minor, was his desire for boys: 'I long to enjoy the fun of youth with you, for you have graceful ways', he says to one of them,[44] and to another: 'Come, pledge me, dear boy, your slender thighs.'[45]

His lovers are numerous, from Bathyllus[46] to the Thracian Smerdies,[47] to Cleobulus, his greatest love: 'I love Cleobulus, I am mad about Cleobulus, I gaze at Cleobulus.'[48] To conquer Cleobulus the poet calls on the aid of Dionysus: 'Give Cleobulus good counsel, Dionysus, that he accept my love.'[49] But these loves are not always happy. Sometimes the desired youth may resist:

See, I fly up on light wings to Olympus in search of Love; for [the boy] does not wish to enjoy the fun of youth with me.[50]

Anacreon then decides that he will love no more: 'Once again I went down to Pythomander's to escape Love.'[51] But it is no use fooling oneself. Love is always stronger:

Once again Love has struck me like a smith with a great hammer and dipped me in the wintry torrent.[52]

So many boys loved, so many verses for them. Anacreon is certainly not wrong in writing that 'for children might love me for my words: for I sing graceful songs and I know how to speak graceful words'.[53] And Bruno Gentili rightly observes in this connection that 'there is a certain symbolic value in the account by which the poet, asked on one occasion why he wrote songs for young boys and not for gods, responded: "because they are my gods"'.[54]

Less explicit than Anacreon, but no less clear, is the attitude of Ibycus, born at Reggio into a noble family in the sixth century BC, and correctly identified in the *Suda* as 'most ardent in ephebic love':[55]

Euryalus, thou scion of the delicious Graces . . . darling of the lovely-tressèd Muses, surely thou wast the nursling of Cypris and tender-eyed Persuasion amid flowers of the rose.[56]

We now move on to consider Theognis, born between 544 and 541 at Megara, on the Greek isthmus, author of a collection of 1,388 verses in two books. The second book, dealing with pederastic love, reveals the poet's passion for young Cyrnus:

Listen to me, boy, you who have bent my heart:
persuasive and welcome are my words.
And try to understand me:
for you there is no need to do what is not pleasing to you.[57]

This is one of the exhortations to his beloved, followed by an ironic invitation:

Love me for a long time, then go with others, you liar,
you are the opposite of faithfulness.[58]

And here, inevitably, comes suffering:

I suffer, boy, and you must not excite my heart
lest your love bear me away
to the kingdom of Persephone. Pay heed to divine anger,
and to what the world says: be merciful.[59]

But the boy resists:

Boy, how long will you flee me? I search for you,
I follow you: I wish I could reach the goal.
You have your terrain, you have; but you are arrogant, proud,
and you run away: you are cruel as a hawk.
I beg for mercy, stop: for you will not long have
the gifts of the goddess girded with violets.
You know that the flower of the longed-for age is more fleeting
than a race track. And you know,
savage boy, loose the bonds, so that you two may not
have to face the torments of the Cypriot goddess,
as I do with you: watch your step, and don't be dominated
by childish perversity.[60]

Haughty and arrogant, this Cyrnus. And a traitor too:

I saw you in silhouette, and your deception has not escaped me,
boy. You have grown intimate
with them; and this love of mine you have left, despised:
and yet, you were no friend of theirs, beforehand!
And I, who codded myself you were my faithful
companion! Very well, have yourself another man.
I have done right, and am cast down: as for you, may no one
ever again consent, when they look on you, to love you.[61]

Then love comes to an end:

I love him no more, the boy: I've kicked out all that pain,
I have happily survived the harshest sorrows,

14

I am free of the passion of lovely Aphrodite.
For you, boy, nothing more from me.[62]

The poetic output of Theognis also includes a body of reflection
which could be called theoretical: comparing the love of boys and the
love of women:

The boy makes friends: with a woman, there is no such thing
as a reliable lover: he makes love with whoever he meets.[63]

Whatever may happen, Theognis has no doubts:

Loving a boy, having him, losing him, all are fine,
Easier to discover than enjoy him.
Endless woes come from this, endless good:
There is something fine even thus.[64]

And here we are at last at the threshold of the so-called 'Attic' age
of Greek literature: with Pindar, born in 519 BC at Cynoscephalae,
in Boeotia, and author of some very beautiful verses dedicated to
Theoxenus, which, as Bruno Gentili writes, 'faithfully reflect the aristocratic ideal of ephebic love'.[65]

At the right moment, my heart,
you should have gathered loves in youth;
but who from the pupils of Theoxenus
looks at the sparkling rays
and does not tumble into desire,
in steel and in iron has tempered
his black heart with a cold flame;

He does not honour bright-eyed Aphrodite,
or with violence bustles after cash
or enslaved to female impudence
drags himself along a frozen path.
But for the love of her
I am undone in the grip of the rays
like the wax of the sacred bees,

when I see in the fresh limbs
of young boys the grace of love.[66]

Here is immediacy of inspiration, which makes perfectly clear the
erotic transport that the Greeks felt for people of the same sex; but the
verses of the lyric poets also add the ability to transmit – without
needing to make explicit statements of principle – the meaning of these
loves, the cultural value they had, and the rules of the sexual ethics to
which they had to conform.

Love, they reveal, bound an adult to a boy who was loved, in the first place, for his beauty: and beauty, for the Greeks, went hand in hand with virtue.

Although it was an erotic relationship, the relationship with a boy was not purely sexual: it was closely linked to social qualities, convivial rituals, encounter, where the *pais* was not merely the object of desire. He was a personal companion who learned with the lover, and from him, to enjoy in the right way and to the right extent the pleasures of life: song and dance, wine and love. This, inevitably, was enough to make homosexual love superior to love for women, who could not be companions for one's social existence (unless they were dancers, flautists and courtesans: these are the female figures found in lyric poetry). Finally, for a boy to be loved was a sign of honour, proof of excellence, confirmation of his virtues. A person who was loved, in short, need fear no reproof if he accepted the offers of his lovers. If he rejected them for some time this was only in order to be more desirable, to be provocative, to augment his reputation and emphasise the excitement of yielding.

In a society which had already become exclusively masculine, these were the features and rules of homosexuality during the archaic age. We shall try to see whether these features and rules vary over time, when we come to analyse the evidence from the Classical age.

2

The Classical Age

The Etiquette of Love. How to Conquer a Boy: The Social Rules of Courtship

In Athens, for a boy to have a homosexual relationship with an adult was considered not only acceptable, but also, under certain conditions, socially approved. We read in paragraph 139 of Aeschines' oration *Against Timarchus* that the laws of the city forbid a slave to be the lover of a free *pais*: 'A slave shall not be the lover of a free boy nor follow after him, or else he shall receive fifty blows of the public lash.'

But this ban, Aeschines comments, does not apply to free men. Quite the contrary. The law does not forbid the citizen to love, to associate with, or to follow after a *pais*, and the boy himself will not only avoid blame on this account but will use the opportunity to show evidence of his propriety. In what sense? To understand this, it is necessary to bear in mind that in Athens courtship was regulated by a prescribed etiquette, which a man who loved a boy was absolutely forbidden to neglect.[1] And where there are rules of etiquette, it is obvious that one is neither outside the law nor outside the bounds of socially accepted behaviour. Rather, one is within a sector of social life which requires attention, and on account of its importance and delicacy, deserves – or rather demands – to be handled in the way which the community believes correct at any particular time and at any particular moment.

But what were the rules of courtship in Athens? The first and most comprehensive of our sources of information is Plato.

It is well known that when Plato speaks of Eros, he mostly, not to say exclusively, means homosexual love.[2] A first, irrefutable proof of this comes from the *Symposium*. There are two types of love, says Pausanias in this dialogue: the first is the one inspired by Aphrodite *Pandēmos*, and this is 'common' love; this is the love which inspires men of little worth, who give their affections without distinction to women and boys, and who are more in love with bodies than with souls. The

17

second type is inspired by Aphrodite Urania and, unlike the first, is not lascivious: this is the feeling of those who love boys. It is not difficult to distinguish it from 'common' love: a person inspired by 'heavenly' love does not choose boys who are too young and as yet without discernment, but only those who are already close to puberty, and thus to the age of reason. The noble lover does not pay court to little boys and then abandon them as soon as he finds a new love object more desirable than the last. He loves his boy in a stable manner, courts him with perseverance, and tries to show the serious nature of his intentions in every possible way. Nobody who loves after this fashion will be considered ridiculous on account of his behaviour, or incur blame for it. On the contrary, the nobility of his intentions will also ennoble his voluntary enslavement to his beloved.[3]

It would be hard to ask for more explicit statements. Paying court to boys is not evil in itself; it becomes evil only if the courtship is inspired by a purely physical desire, and the observation of the rules of courtship guarantees the goodness of the sentiment.

This, then, is the etiquette governing lovers. But how should the beloved behave? For him too, there were very precise rules. First of all, the object of affection should start by resisting the courtship, running away from the lover, showing himself stubborn, difficult to win over, almost incorruptible. But how far should he take this game? According to some writers, he was supposed to resist to the bitter end, never 'submitting' to the wishes of the lover. For example, David Cohen picks up a phrase of Alvin Gouldner, to the effect that honour was a 'zero-sum' game, in which the lover won by obtaining the favours of the beloved, while the beloved won by refusing him those favours.[4] But if that were the case, what would be the point of courtship, other than a useless sado-masochistic manoeuvre?

It has often been said – and Cohen points this out – that courtship in Greece was redirected towards boys on account of the unavailability of women (which is probably true in the Classical period, at least in part). And it has also been observed that the rules of the game in pederasty were the same as those of heterosexual courtship in traditional societies.[5] This last observation seems to me not only correct but extremely significant. The rules of heterosexual courtship envisage as a final outcome (at least potentially) the capitulation of the woman. The woman's honour does not consist in refusing always and everywhere, but in yielding at the right moment: in some societies – the more hidebound – at the moment of marriage; in other, less traditional societies, at the moment of betrothal or declaration of serious matrimonial intentions. But in all cases the capitulation of the woman is envisaged: a system of courtship which is destined to fail is an absurd game. Even the most stylised, almost 'ritual', forms of courtship, apparently an end in themselves, conducted (so the story goes) without any hope, have a sexual objective which is in some way attainable. Let us take, for example, the case of medieval courtship: an extreme case, certainly, but precisely on that account particularly significant. The woman loved and courted, in the Middle Ages, was the wife of another: theoretically, then, an unattainable prize. But in practice? Undoubtedly, *amour courtois* was more cerebral and stylish than heartfelt. By paying court to a lady the lover improved himself, expressed the noblest part of himself, educated himself to higher feelings. Seen from this angle, medieval courtship was the opposite of pederastic courtship, which served to educate and improve not the lover, but the love object. But that is not the point. What is interesting is the simulated uselessness of courtship, for the 'courtly' lover lived and celebrated his love as though it were without hope.[6]

Reality, however, did not always match the theory. *Amour courtois* was 'productive' even if the effects produced did not always, perhaps, fall to the advantage of the troubadours. It would seem that they often served, more or less deliberately, the purposes of others: more precisely, the purposes of their beloved ladies who, celebrated by the troubadours, acquired a reputation capable of attracting numerous lovers.[7] And the higher the rank of these lovers, the more benefits the troubadours reaped from the situation. With undoubted exaggeration, but also perhaps with a dash of realism, it has been written that the troubadours were 'high-class pimps' compensated by the 'unattainable' women whom they celebrated with some minor erotic favours, and with some of the gifts with which those ladies were showered by their chosen lovers.[8] Perhaps this may have happened from time to time in practice, although it would certainly be not merely reductive but mistaken to suppose that this was the nature of 'courtly' love in the Middle Ages. What is of interest here, in any case, is another aspect of the question: even the most 'stylish' system of courtship in Western history, the most explicitly hopeless and useless one in theory, was in practice sexually 'productive' (never mind how, never mind who benefited).

Let us return to pederastic courtship. Why on earth should the Greeks, alone among the nations of the world, have identified and codified a courtship system of such absurdity that its rules prevented the *erōmenos* from ever yielding, on pain of losing his reputation? Obviously, the Greek boy too needed a way of yielding honourably. And in fact this way did exist. The Greek boy lost his honour only if he showed himself impatient and eager concerning his lover's choice. If he

19

gave in at the end of a lengthy and serious courtship, having made sure that his lover's intentions were not only sexual, the situation was different: far from being blamed, the boy deserved honour and consideration.[9] I do not believe that this can be refuted on the basis of Plato's observation (once again, in Pausanias' speech in the *Symposium*), that the Athenian *nomos* on love (and by *nomos*, here, he clearly means accepted behaviour) both encouraged the lover to court the beloved, yet required the beloved to resist this courtship.[10] To resist, as we have seen, meant testing the lover before yielding. That is what Pausanias is trying to say, when he says that the rules of love in Athens are complex and ambiguous.[11] He makes this point explicitly: there are some cities, he observes, where love between men poses no problems: either it is always allowed (as happens in Elis and in Boeotia), or else it is always frowned on (as in Ionia). But in Athens the law of love is more complicated, so much so that it is not possible to understand it at once: on the one hand, it encourages courtship up to the point of excusing a lover who swears falsely, while on the other hand it demands that fathers should protect their sons from those who wish to court them, placing them under the control of teachers. Hence, one might imagine that the love of boys is something base; but this would be mistaken. Love is ugly only when it is 'common'. When it is inspired by noble sentiments, it is beautiful; and when this is the case, it is no shame for a boy to yield to his lover. Anyone who thinks that yielding is dishonourable is thinking only of vulgar loves.[12]

This is an explicit piece of evidence, which makes it hard to imagine that boys were forever engaged in the pointless game of diehard resistance imagined by some scholars. It could be objected that Plato is a very special type of source, and that his opinions might very well not represent the Athenian mentality. Against this, one can easily recall another, completely different, piece of evidence which, unlike Plato, certainly reflects public opinion: the one with which I started in approaching this topic. I mean the evidence of Aeschines. We are dealing here with a legal orator who, by profession, wrote speeches with the precise aim of persuading the citizens sitting as judges in the popular tribunals of the justice of a cause. Those people were not particularly educated, often came from the countryside, and belonged to a background which certainly did not make them likely to hear and accept sophisticated interpretations designed (as some people think the Platonic dialogues were designed) to justify, for the purposes of a minority which practised it, a generally unacceptable custom (which, again according to certain people, was the position of pederasty).[13]

Speeches in court had to win the assent of the average citizen and avoid shocking his susceptibilities: what is said in these speeches about the love of boys cannot therefore be anything other than an expression of popular morality. What, then, does Aeschines say about pederasty?

As we have already seen, after referring to a law which forbade slaves to be the lovers of free boys, or to pay court to them, on pain of fifty lashes, Aeschines observes that the law does not prevent a citizen from loving a free-born boy, associating with him or following after him. He further observes that the boy not only suffers no dishonour from the fact of being courted, but on the contrary gets an opportunity to show his propriety.[14] What Aeschines has to say, essentially, can be taken together with what Plato said, corroborating it and receiving corroboration from it: a boy (Aeschines, like Plato, insists on this point) can honourably have a relationship with an adult, if he has chosen a good lover on reaching the age of reason.

There is complete coincidence between what Plato writes for an intellectual public and what Aeschines writes for a public made up of average citizens: and no less significant than this is the consideration of the context in which Aeschines places his comments on pederasty.

His objective, in the speech against Timarchus, is to get the court to rule that Timarchus has lost his political rights because he has prostituted himself (we shall return to this topic of male prostitution). But in doing this, Aeschines is anxious to make it clear that he has no intention of condemning all instances of love between men.

The substance of his speech is this: I do not want the defenders of Timarchus to accuse me of 'wanting to open up an epoch of hateful barbarity',[15] by maintaining that I want to heap infamy on anyone who has a lover. In order to discredit me, they will remind you of couples of noble and famous lovers like Harmodius and Aristogeiton or, in other times, Achilles and Patroclus, thereby insinuating that I do not recognise the value and importance of these loves. In order to make my charge against Timarchus seem inconsistent, they will further recall that I too have loved boys, and have written erotic poems for them. Very well, I do not deny my loves, I admit that I have written erotic poems, and I further declare that I still love boys. I do not denigrate honourable love affairs: I condemn (as the law condemns) only mercenary loves.

That is what Aeschines says. But there is more. After praising at length some couples among ancient lovers, the orator moves on to celebrate some more recent love affairs. He recalls the names of some boys that the jurors knew well, and who were celebrated and respected precisely because, on account of their great beauty and virtue, they had been much loved:

You know, fellow citizens, Crito, son of Astyochus, Pericleides of Perithoedae, Polemagenes, Pantaleon, son of Cleagoras, and Timesitheus the runner, men who were the most beautiful, not only among their fellow citizens, but in all Hellas, men who counted many a man of eminent chastity as lover; yet no man ever censured them. And again, among the youths [*meirakia*] and those who are still boys, you know the nephew of Iphicrates, the son of Teisias of Rhamnos, of the same name as the defendant. . . . Again, Anticles, the stadium runner, and Pheidias, the brother of Melesias. Although I could name many others, I will stop here, lest I seem to be in a way courting their favour by my praise.[16]

How can one think that public opinion was hostile to pederasty, when one considers not only the approach adopted in this speech, but especially the list of young 'loved ones' living in Athens at that time, identified by name, surname, and family connections, with the aim of publicly celebrating their virtues?

The risk that Aeschines was taking – and knew that he was taking – by accusing a male prostitute was that his adversaries, in complete bad faith, could get the jury to believe that he was a hypocritical scourge of public morals, a man who, while himself engaging in love with *paides*, wanted at the same time to condemn Timarchus merely because he had taken a number of lovers – something which was unacceptable to the Greeks. Hence his praise of celebrated homosexual couples, and of virtuous 'love objects', whose praises Aeschines is almost forced to sing in order to prove that he is not against pederasty in itself, but only against the deplorable conduct of Timarchus, who had prostituted himself.

The conclusions, at this point, seem inevitable: pederasty (so long as it was not 'common') was neither forbidden by law nor socially reprobated. And this first conclusion leads us to a further problem, currently the focus of quite a lot of debate. What were the forms, the expressions, the physical manifestations of the love of boys?

How to Love a Boy: Erotic Manifestations in the Pederastic Relationship

At the end of the courtship the *pais* yielded to the lover, establishing with him a relationship which, if the love was 'well chosen', was first of all spiritual, intellectual and educational by nature. But, equally certainly, it was also erotic: the terminology in this area is perfectly clear, starting with the use of the verb *eran*, alongside the nouns *erastēs* and *erōmenos*.

As early as Homer, the word *erōs* indicates sexual desire,[17] and the verb *eran*, from the time of its first appearance in the seventh century BC, is regularly used in a consistent manner to indicate the physical perception of love,[18] not infrequently used alternately with *epithumein*, another verb from the vocabulary of desire.[19]

Equally significant is the use of the verb *charizesthai*, which, referring to the love object, alludes to the behaviour with which he satisfies the sexual desire of his lover.[20] *Charizesthai* (which means gratifying, satisfying, making happy) has, in turn, a very clear sexual connotation. In describing the first woman, Pandora, sent by Zeus among men to punish them for their impertinence, Hesiod is explicit: Pandora is a *dolos amēchanos*, a guile which cannot be withstood. And she is this because she has 'the mind of a dog' and a deceitful character, because she carries lies and crafty speeches in her heart. Despite all this, she appears to men as a beautiful, irresistible woman, equipped with all the instruments of seduction. Pandora, in short, is a sexual snare, and among the weapons which make her into such a trap the first is *charis*, the grace which seduces and which inspires desire.[21]

Between the lover and the beloved, then, a relationship of a sexual kind is established. That this is the rule in pederastic relationships emerges with clarity precisely from the account of an exceptional and very famous case in which this does *not* happen; and the absolute strangeness of the fact emerges, in a very clear way, from the account that one of the protagonists, Alcibiades, gives of it through Plato's words.

In the *Symposium*, Alcibiades recounts in detail his attempts to persuade Socrates to love him:

> I allowed myself to be alone with him, I say, gentlemen, and I naturally supposed that he would embark on conversation of the type that a lover usually addresses to his darling when they are *tête-à-tête*, and I was glad. Nothing of the kind; he spent the day with me in the sort of talk which is habitual with him, and then left me and went away. Next I invited him to train with me in the gymnasium, and I accompanied him there, believing that I should succeed with him now. He took exercise and wrestled with me frequently, with no one else present, but I need hardly say that I was no nearer my goal.... So I invited him to dine with me, behaving just like a lover who has designs upon his favourite....[22] When the light was out and the servants had withdrawn ... I nudged him and said: 'Are you asleep,

Socrates?' 'Far from it,' he answered. 'Do you know what I think?' 'No, what?' 'I think that you are the only lover that I have ever had who is worthy of me, but that you are afraid to mention your passion to me. Now, what I feel about the matter is this, that it would be very foolish of me not to comply with your desires in this respect, as well as in any other claim that you might make either on my property or on that of my friends. The cardinal object of my ambition is to come as near perfection as possible, and I believe no one can give me such powerful assistance towards this end as you.'[23]

But Socrates evades his advances and Alcibiades moves from words to action:

Without allowing him to say anything further, I got up and covered him with my own clothes – for it was winter – and then laid myself down under his worn cloak, and threw my arms round this truly superhuman and wonderful man, and remained thus the whole night long. . . . But in spite of all my efforts . . . I swear by all the gods in heaven that for anything that had happened between us when I got up after sleeping with Socrates, I might have been sleeping with my father or elder brother.[24]

This is certainly an unusual case, and the tone adopted by Alcibiades reveals this beyond all shadow of doubt. Whether Socrates really kept to this type of behaviour, with Alcibiades and other young men, is another matter. The story could be the expression of Plato's wish to present the figure of Socrates as being different, detached from the desires which tormented the rest of humanity, an idealised personality, to be contrasted with the unquestionable degradation which not infrequently, during that period in Athens, attended pederastic relationships, thus allowing part of public opinion to attack them as an infamous and dangerous custom. But we will return to this later on. What is worth noting here, apart from the question of Alcibiades' truthfulness, is the tone of indescribable amazement with which he recounts his adventure, and his certainty that his hearers will feel a surprise just as great as his own.

But having said all this (in other words, having noted that pederasty was partly a physical bond), there is another problem, which has recently given rise to quite a lot of debate. What exactly was the type of physical relationship that bound the lover to the beloved? How exactly did the beloved 'satisfy' the lover?

It has recently been maintained that Athenian sexual morality did not envisage sodomy in the pederastic relationship. According to the findings of Sir Kenneth Dover, anal intercourse (which never appears when intercourse between adults and *paides* is depicted on vases) seems to be reserved for relations between adults. The numerous representations of pederastic relationships describe the two successive moments of courtship and sexual union in a very particular form. In the courtship phase, the *erastēs* is represented in the position which Beazley defines as 'up and down': in front of his beloved, with one hand he brushes his face, with the other his genitals.[25] At the moment of union he is once again standing in front of the *erōmenos*, but this time with his penis between his thighs.[26]

Does this finding necessarily mean that anal intercourse was socially prohibited in the case of *paides*? Might one not assume that the iconography represented images better suited to highlighting the affective aspect of the pederastic relationship, almost as if to point out and emphasise the importance and nobility of this relationship, contrasting it with the purely physical one which linked two adult lovers? Another quite relevant consideration springs to mind, when one thinks about the iconography of heterosexual relationships: in this case too, penetration is only represented when the woman is a courtesan. Relations with 'respectable' women leave out all reference to the sexual act. Would anybody dream of thinking, on this basis, that Greeks had sex only with courtesans, and not with their wives?[27]

I believe that, to confirm the hypothesis that anal penetration was normal in pederastic relationships, it would be helpful at this point to look once more at lexical analysis. The verb which most frequently indicates the moment when the boy yields to the lover is, as we saw, *charizesthai*: but often, to indicate this moment, two other highly significant verbs appear – *hypourgein* and *hypēretein*, 'rendering service' and 'serving as a subordinate'.[28] If the ethics of pederasty envisaged intercrural intercourse as the only form of sexual satisfaction for the lover, why speak of the beloved 'submitting'?

But the most significant confirmation of the hypothesis we are seeking to verify comes from the graffiti of Thera. More than once in these graffiti we read specific references to anal intercourse. In the inscription that we already looked at, for example,[29] Krimon, the lover, to describe his intercourse with his beloved uses the verb *oipein*. This verb occurs five times in the inscriptions, and in the Dorian dialect (as shown by its meaning in the code of Gortyn)[30] it means the male sexual act performed either on a male partner or on a female partner: which inevitably means that when used with reference to homosexual intercourse, it indicates anal penetration. In the light of this consideration it really becomes very difficult to imagine that a custom of such antiquity and with such major traditions (even though, over the centuries, the memory of its institutional value was lost) could not only have been lost but have become an infamous practice.

To say nothing of the continuous references to buggery in the comedies of Aristophanes, who was undoubtedly a highly individual author, ferociously hostile to the spread of love affairs between men. By his time these had lost the features which once made them into an expression of nobility, not to say excellence in politics and morals, and the poet now saw these affairs as one of the causes, or at least as an unmistakable symptom, of Athenian decadence. But it is worth pointing out here that what Aristophanes condemns, in homosexuality, is not the practice of anal intercourse itself, but the wrong use which is made of it, on account of the moral degeneration of the Athenians, the immorality, opportunism and mercenary nature of their relationships. To prove that sodomising young men was not in itself considered negative, there is clear evidence in the homoerotic poetry collected in the *Greek Anthology* and, in particular, the series of verses written in the twelfth book, in which, among others, we find compositions by some poets who lived at a time not far removed from Aristophanes, for example Dioscorides and Rhianus, both of whom lived in the third century BC.

In these verses, as has been correctly pointed out, no feature of the charms of the beloved boys seems to be as erotically attractive to lovers as the anal area, which is often described through metaphors of such a romantic kind (however mannered this might be, like the rest of the poetry of the time) as to signal unmistakably not only the lack of any social interdiction, but also the absence of all vulgar connotations when thinking about anal penetration.[31]

Sometimes called a rosebud,[32] sometimes compared to the sweetest of fruits, the fig,[33] other times again equated with gold,[34] the anus (*prōktos*) is at any rate (together with the hinder parts of the beloved's body in general) irresistibly attractive:

> The Hours and Graces shed sweet oil on thee, and thou lettest not even old men sleep. Tell me whose blest darling thou art and which of the boys thou adornest. And the backside's answer was, 'Menecrates' darling',

writes Rhianus.[35] And Dioscorides:

> Love, the murderer of men, moulded soft as marrow the backside of Sosarchus of Amphipolis in fun, wishing to irritate Zeus because his thighs are much more honeyed than those of Ganymede.[36]

Nor could it be said that these poets lack explicit links between the attractiveness of this part of the body and its sexual function:

26

There has come to me a great woe, a great war, a great fire. Elissus, full of the years ripe for love, just at that fatal age of sixteen, and having withal every charm, small and great, a voice which is honey when he reads and lips that are honey to kiss, and a thing faultless for taking in. What will become of me? He bids me look only. Verily I shall often lie awake fighting with my hands against this empty love.

Thus moans Scythinus.[37]

And what can Strato be talking about, if not anal intercourse, when he confesses, after a night of love with Philostratus, that he 'was incapable'?

Yesterday I had Philostratus for the night, but was incapable, though he (how shall I say it?) made every possible offer. No longer, my friends, count me as your friend, but throw me off a tower as I have become too much of an Astyanax.[38]

In the light of these pieces of evidence, so diverse and far from each other in time and yet so consistent, how could it be thought that the pederastic relationship did not envisage (and should not envisage) anal penetration of the *pais*?

To finish with this point, I believe that it was absolutely normal throughout the course of Greek history for a boy to 'submit' to his lover, and that this did not necessarily involve any loss of honour. Honour, certainly, was at stake: but it was lost, as we have seen, only by *paides* who yielded without respecting some rules of what might be called a procedural nature. These rules were established on a social level by the etiquette of courtship; they have already been described, and on examining the evidence, despite everything that has been said on this topic, we find these rules confirmed and clarified by the provisions of the law.

The Laws on Pederasty. Two Stages, Two Cities: Athens and Beroea

We have seen, in relation to courtship, that in Plato's *Symposium* Pausanias, explaining the complicated and inscrutable nature of ephebic love in Athens, alludes to the fathers' practice of having their sons escorted by pedagogues who are charged with monitoring and controlling them. This habit shows how frequent were the more or less legitimate attempts at courtship, and the worries felt by fathers that their sons might have lovers. The existence of these worries, which affected not only fathers but the entire community, is confirmed by the analysis of legislation on *paides* (traditionally attributed to Solon),[39] reported once again in the oration *Against Timarchus*:

> The teachers of the boys shall open the school-rooms not earlier than sunrise, and they shall close them before sunset. No person who is older than the boys shall be permitted to enter the room while they are there, unless he be a son of the teacher, a brother, or a daughter's husband. If any one enter in violation of this prohibition, he shall be punished with death. The superintendents of the gymnasia shall under no conditions allow any one who has reached the age of manhood to enter the contests of Hermes together with the boys. A gymnasiarch who does permit this and fails to keep such a person out of the gymnasium, shall be liable to the penalties prescribed for the seduction of free-born youth. Every choregus who is appointed by the people shall be more than forty years of age.[40]

What other reason could there be for this type of law, if not the protection of *paides* from attempted seduction (or at least from some of these attempts)? Nor, when one examines the evidence, was Athens the only city whose laws had this aim. During the Hellenistic period the law on schools in Beroea, a city in a different and faraway area – Macedonia – reveals interesting and unmistakable analogies with the so-called laws of Solon, helping to clarify further their meaning and scope, showing, among other things, that protective legislation (as in Athens) was not directed to preventing all pederastic relationships, but only those which could prove dangerous for the *paides* on account of the low quality of the lovers involved.

Forbidden lovers: *unworthy, infamous,* neaniskoi *and schoolmasters*

Engraved on the two sides of a stele, the law of Beroea (which can be dated to about the middle of the second century BC) contains, exactly like the law of Solon, a list of those who could not come into the local gymnasium: slaves, the *apeleutheroi* (slaves who had been freed), their sons, the *apalaistroi* (a term with an uncertain meaning, which appears here for the first time, and which probably indicates those who could not carry out the gymnastic exercises, on account of infirmity or physical weakness), the *hetaireukotes* (male prostitutes), those who carried on commercial activities (obviously considered people of a lower social class), drunkards and lunatics.[41]

A recent interpretation argues that these prohibitions in the law in Beroea were intended to prevent any homosexual relationships,[42] but I cannot see that a reading of the text allows any such conclusion. When one thinks about it, the adults who were forbidden to go into the gymnasium in Beroea were only a limited group of people, whose company could be particularly dangerous to young people. The concern in Beroea was to prevent only those relationships which, on account of the unworthy nature of the lover, would have made pederasty vulgar and anti-educational. And this is confirmed by a further provision of the law, on the basis of which another category of dangerous lovers was identified within the gymnasium: the *neaniskoi*, who were forbidden to speak to the *paides*.[43]

But who were these *neaniskoi*, and why, for the *paides*, would it be dangerous to associate with them, not only in Beroea? In Athens too, the law on *paides* specified 'which *neaniskoi* can frequent these premises [meaning schools and gymnasia]', and how old they had to be.[44] In Athens too, then, the *neaniskoi* were seen as requiring special attention from the legislators. At this point, there is a pressing need to identify fairly precisely who these people were. A first indication for this purpose comes from the provision in the law of Solon just mentioned.

Obviously, if not all *neaniskoi*, but only some of them (identified by their age) were entitled to frequent schools and gymnasia, this means that people started being *neaniskoi* at schoolgoing age, and continued as members of this category for an indeterminate period, even after moving beyond that stage. But once again this definition remains too vague: to specify the terms of the question, we have to undertake a brief survey of the Greek terminology of age.[45]

The interest which the Greeks took in this terminology, and the importance which they attached to it, can be clearly seen from even the briefest glance at the works dedicated to this topic by the Alexandrian grammarians and lexicographers, more particularly (leaving aside the survey by Pollux) the treatise *Peri onomasias hēlikiōn* by Aristophanes of Byzantium. The list of terms reviewed by Aristophanes is long and detailed, especially the terms indicating ages before the attainment of majority.

Brephos, writes Aristophanes of Byzantium, is the newborn baby. *Paidion* is the baby who sucks mother's milk: presumably, therefore, a child under the age of two, three or four years, when he starts to walk and becomes a *paidarion*. *Paidiskos* is the child in the stage immediately following, and he stops being such, and is termed *pais*, when he goes to school (six or seven years old, then). Later again, he is called a *pallax*, *boupais*, *antipais*, *mellephēbos*, and finally, at the age of eighteen, *ephēbos*. The older ages are measured by the terms *meirakion* (or *meirax*), and then *neaniskos*, *neanias*, *anēr mesos*, *probebēkōs* (also called *homogerōn*), *presbutēs* and lastly *eschatogēras* (decrepit old man).

Therefore, in this list (which is of a later date, but can still be seen as a useful point of departure) the *neaniskos* is a young man who has reached the age of majority (which occurred at eighteen, when young men were called ephebes). Given that in Athens military service as ephebes lasted two years, it is likely that a *neaniskos* was a boy who had reached the age of twenty.[46] This hypothesis is confirmed by a statement from Diogenes Laertius, according to whom Pythagoras divided the ages of life into four periods (corresponding to the four seasons of the year), defining a *pais* as somebody who had not reached twenty years of age, *neēniskos* between twenty and forty, *neēniēs* a man between forty and sixty, and *gerōn*, finally, over this age.[47]

Let us now check this information against the previous era, to see what semantic shifts have taken place. Even within a terminology which usually stays much the same, like the vocabulary of age, such shifts cannot be ruled out. When does the term *neaniskos* appear?

Unknown in the vocabulary of Homer, Hesiod, Pindar and the lyric poets, *neaniskos* is clearly a word that arises in the course of a process of enrichment and gradual specialisation of the terminology of age, which can be plausibly dated during the course of the fifth century.

Although tradition speaks of a lost *fabula* by Aeschylus, with the title *Neaniskoi*,[48] the term does not appear in the tragic writers. But it does crop up, with notable frequency, in the plays of Aristophanes.

In *The Acharnians* the elders complain against the city, which allows them to be mocked, in legal disputes, by *neaniskoi* advocates.[49] The *neaniskoi*, given their ability to speak before the courts, must be adults. In this example the term has the meaning later attributed to it by Aristophanes of Byzantium. But that situation does not always prevail.

In Aeschines, for example, we read of an orphan brought up by the city until he had reached adulthood. The story is not particularly striking in itself, considering that the education of war orphans was one of the tasks of the city which, as Plato says, took the place of dead fathers by educating their sons;[50] but in this case, the orphan brought up until reaching adulthood is defined as a *neaniskos*.[51]

To sum up: in some sources one is a *neaniskos* in the last years of *paideia*, before becoming an ephebe. In other sources, however, the condition of *neaniskos* arises only after the age of majority has been reached. But how long does it last? On the basis of some evidence, it would seem that we could say: up to twenty-five or thirty years of age.

Agis IV, for example, governed Sparta between 245 and 241 BC, when he was aged between twenty and twenty-four, and Plutarch defines him as a *neaniskos*.[52] Or again, the poet Agathon, born between 447 and 442, won the drama competition in 417–416, that is to say, when he was aged between twenty-five and thirty, and Plato defines him as a *neaniskos*.[53]

This term, then, belongs to everyday, non-technical language, and indicates an age which takes in the last years of minority (during which in a technical sense one is a *pais*) and the first years of majority (during which, technically, one is already a *neos*). It is no accident that the spoken language introduced this term, almost as if to correct the excessive rigidity of the technical contrast between *paides* and *neoi*. The changeover to young manhood is a moment to which social consciousness and the law attach particular importance, identifying it, one might say, as the watershed between irresponsibility and responsibility. Once majority has been reached the young person is able to think, and is fully able to make up his own mind; consequently he acquires, in the eyes of the law, the ability to act.

The vocabulary of the Greeks is crystal clear on this topic: born without wits (*aphrōn*), the young male at the age of eighteen or twenty began to reason (*phronein*).[54] In other words, he started to know and observe the rules of community life, and to distinguish between right and wrong.[55] Consequently, he was registered in the *lēxiarchikon grammateion*, acquiring full entitlement to civil and political rights. But, obviously, the eighteen-year boundary was a threshold set in abstract terms, which did not imply an immediate jump from emptyheadedness to wisdom; that would be impossible. And the *neaniskoi*, straddling these two psychological and intellectual periods of life, are sometimes described as wise young men, already fully capable of *phronein*, and sometimes as impatient young scallywags, incapable of restraining themselves and controlling their instincts, given to pointless showing off and wishing at all costs to have their way without respecting the rules of common sense.

A further consideration must be added here: the difficult and delicate change from *paideia* to youth was more difficult and delicate in Greece than elsewhere. It has already been pointed out that in Greece before the city-state, the attainment of adult status meant a change in sexual role, from the passive to the active. This rule clearly signals that during this period the fundamental contrast between different types of sexual behaviour was not the heterosexual-homosexual dichotomy but the active-passive one (the active role belonging to the adult male, and the passive one to boys and women). Sources from the age of the cities clearly confirm that this ancient rule (leaving aside the transformations caused by the shift from a tribal to a political society, and the fact that the rule was by now divorced from its original meaning) continued to inform the sexual morality of the Greeks.

It was still true in the age of the city-state that at the point of reaching adult age a boy had to face the problem of switching his sexual role: no longer *erōmenos*, but now *erastēs* – no longer the beloved, but the lover. It hardly needs stating, however, that in practice such a changeover could not take place between one day and the next. On the one hand a minor, already close to the eighteen-year-old threshold, might be tempted to take an active role with *paides* of a younger age: in Xenophon's *Symposium*, to take just one example, we read of Critobulos who 'while still an *erōmenos* nevertheless desires the other youngsters'.[56] On the other hand, it could happen that after reaching the age of eighteen a boy might continue to be a passive partner in a homosexual relationship. In the light of these considerations I think it is possible to understand the provisions on the *neaniskoi* contained in the law on *paides* attributed to Solon, and in the law of Beroea.

In the eyes of the law, the attainment of adulthood was marked by reaching the age of eighteen (to which were added two years of military service). However, society knew that in real life, the shift from the passive to the active sexual role did not happen from one day to the next, nor even from one year to the next. It was a process which inevitably lasted for a number of years: the years, roughly, between fifteen and twenty-five. Consequently, the Greeks considered that young men in this period of their lives (the *neaniskoi*) were people in an uncertain and ambivalent state, at the same time *paides* and *neoi*, and thus simultaneously irresponsible and reasonable, and in the sexual field simultaneously passive and active. All of this meant, obviously, that they could not make good lovers. The law recognised and, so to speak, codified their particular status, taking care to prevent them seducing their younger companions.

Unworthy adults and hotheaded youngsters were not the only seducers whom the *paides* had to fear. Day in, day out, they were exposed to the wiles of those who in theory were supposed to educate them and who, instead, took advantage of their position to attempt approaches of all kinds: their masters.

Aeschines knows this situation very well, and denounces it harshly: schoolmasters, he says, earn their living by the respectability of their behaviour. But although they know that any bad conduct on their part could ruin them, they frequently yield to temptation, to such an extent that legislators are forced to distrust them, and prohibit boys remaining in school between sunset and sunrise.[57] Fourth-century Athenian schoolmasters, then, were a bad lot. But were they the only ones? Obviously not.

During the Hellenistic age a series of epigrams went on complaining about a disturbing state of affairs in the schools:

You want payment too, you schoolmasters! How ungrateful you are! For why? Is it a small thing to look on boys and speak to them, and kiss them when you greet them? Is not this alone worth a hundred pounds?[58]

This is what Strato asks the teachers of his time. And he addresses one of them, Dionysius, with heavy-handed irony:

How, Dionysius, shall you teach a boy to read when you do not even know how to make the transition from one note to another? You have passed so quickly from the highest note to a deep one, from the slightest rise to the most voluminous. Yet I bear you no grudge; only study, and striking both notes say Lambda and Alpha to the envious.[59]

To say nothing of the gymnastics masters, who suffered stronger temptations and obviously had very bad habits:

Once a wrestling-master, taking advantage of the occasion, when he was giving a lesson to a smooth boy, forced him to kneel down, and set about working on his middle, stroking the berries with one hand. But by chance the master of the house came, wanting the boy. The teacher threw him quickly on his back, getting astride of him and grasping him by the throat. But the master of the house, who was not unversed in wrestling, said to him, Stop, you are smuggering the boy.[60]

Once again the speaker is Strato, who elsewhere offers an epigram describing the athletic techniques used by an unknown but dedicated trainer:

A. '...take your adversary by the middle, and laying him down get astride of him, and shoving forward, fall on him and hold him tight.' B. 'You are not in your right senses, Diophantus. I am only just capable of doing this, but boys' wrestling is different. Fix yourself fast and stand firm, Cyris, and support it when I close with you. He should learn to practise with a fellow before learning to practise himself.'[61]

And lastly, once again from the *Greek Anthology*, here is Automedon guying the instructor Demetrius, with heavy nudges about the night-time exercises which Demetrius most likely performed with his pupils:

Yesterday I supped with the boy's trainer, Demetrius, the most blessed of all men. One lay on his lap, one stooped over his shoulder, one brought him the dishes, and another served him with drink – the admirable quartette. I said to him in fun, 'Do you, my dear friend, work the boys at night too?'[62]

The reason for the law: protecting pederasty

After identifying the dangerous lovers, the ones to be avoided by all wide-awake *paides* concerned for their reputations, we can now draw some conclusions from this long but necessary account of the legal provisions governing pederasty.

Should we agree or disagree with the view which holds that Greek law (especially in Athens and in Beroea, the two cities whose laws have come down to us) harshly opposed and possibly punished, without distinction, all types of pederastic relationship?

Only one provision among those examined so far could induce us to draw such a conclusion: the provision contained in the law attributed to Solon, which, in the form which has reached us, punished by death all adults (with the exception of the schoolmasters' closest relatives) who were caught on school or gymnasium premises. But it is highly debatable whether such a provision really existed in Athens.

The law attributed to Solon is reported by Aeschines with some obvious inaccuracies. For example, the choreguses to whom he refers (those charged with bearing the expense of the choirs of *paides*) were not designated by the people, as he states, but by the tribe, as Aristotle explicitly tells us.[63] What we have, then, is a document which is undoubtedly fundamental to an understanding of Athenian law in relation to pederasty, but only, so to speak, in its fundamental lines, as an indicator of trends and social values. Having said that, it cannot be taken literally and accepted as true in all its details. Among the details which are clearly unacceptable we may place his reference to the death penalty for all adults caught in premises reserved for *paides*.

We know with certainty that in practice the gymnasia were regularly frequented by people who were already well into manhood. To prove this point, it will be enough to recall the encounter between Socrates and Hippothales, in the first pages of the *Lysis*.

Plato recounts that Socrates was on his way to the Lyceum when he met Hippothales and Ctesippus, surrounded by a group of lads, on their way to a recently opened gymnasium, where they intended to spend the day. 'Our pastime chiefly consists of discussions,' says Hippothales, inviting Socrates to join the group. And Socrates agrees, but first he asks who is the handsome boy (*kalos*) who has aroused his friend's interest. 'Each of us has a different fancy,' Hippothales replies. Socrates presses him: 'And who is yours?'

This story is quite instructive. Adults used to spend a large part of their time at the gym, with the very definite aim of ogling and courting the prettiest young boys, in particular the beautiful Lysis, with whom Hippothales is in love to the point of being the butt of friendly irony on the part of his friends. They say that poor Hippothales, in fact, 'raves like a madman'[64] over Lysis, spending his time admiring him as he does his exercises in the gymnasium. This is a fairly clear proof of the fact that the rule reported by Aeschines does not exist. Another considera-tion can be added to this, leading inevitably to the same conclusion.

Let us admit, for a moment, that the rule in question might really have been enforced. We should then have to conclude that Athenian law reproved pederasty in itself, independent of all considerations con-cerning the quality of the lovers and the type of relations which they established with their *erōmenoi*; and that the law opposed them to the point of establishing the death penalty for anyone who had tried merely to pay court to a boy.

How can we reconcile this type of attitude, not only with the sources, from which it emerges that judicious courtship was allowed, but also with the absence of any law in Athens punishing pederasts (unless, as we have seen, the lover was a slave)?

Apart from mercenary relations (the punishment for these will be dealt with later), Athenian law only punished homosexual relationships imposed through violence; moreover, even in that case the sanction was not death, but only a fine. We read in Lysias that 'if anyone forcibly debauches a free adult or child, he shall be liable to double damages.'[65] The hypothesis that any adult would be put to death merely because he had gone into a school or a gymnasium is thus unthinkable. In all probability, Athenian law confined itself to prohibiting certain par-ticularly undesirable adults from entering those places. This seems to have been the rule in other Greek cities, as the law on schools in Beroea confirms. But before concluding on this topic, one final question arises: why should Aeschines, in reporting the text of the law on *paides*, falsify the extent of one of its provisions?

After what we have seen of the oration in which this law is cited, the distortion cannot be too surprising. Aeschines wanted the tribunal to view Timarchus as a male prostitute, with all the consequences of that. But as we have seen, he was running a twofold risk: on the one hand, his adversaries might paint him as a repressive prude, who condemned homosexuality in all its forms; on the other hand (at the age of forty-two, when he wrote this oration, he was a convinced, enthusiastic and incorrigible *erastēs*) his enemies could paint him as a hypocrite, a corrupter of youth, lascivious and loose in private, but a scourge of unconventional behaviour in public. A tricky position, from which he could escape only by showing that he merely wanted to condemn homosexuality of a mercenary or unworthy kind. He had to show that he was well aware of the rules of sexual ethics, which condemned degenerate homosexuality but defended the freedom of high-flown relationships. Hence his line of attack, which consisted (with regard to the first possible accusation of his adversaries) in praising more or less famous lovers, whose love was not only respectable but worthy of admiration; while (with reference to the second charge) showing that he was perfectly aware of the rules designed to prevent the degeneration of pederasty. Among these latter rules, in an excess of zeal, he inserts the legal provision which has just been discussed.

A non-existent provision, then. However, in all probability, no juror would be aware of this: in Athenian trials, it was the responsibility of the parties involved to inform the jury of the laws in force. And given that jurors did not know the law (they were drawn by lot from among the citizens, without any specific competence being required), it was anything but rare for legal orators to modify the laws for their own purposes, sometimes inventing them out of the whole cloth.[66]

To conclude: Athenian law was undoubtedly interested in the problem of pederasty. Considering it as a phenomenon which could be either highly formative or very dangerous to young people, depending on the individual case, Athens was careful to guarantee, as far as possible, that the life of the *paides* should be carried out according to rules which would prevent non-educational, vulgar love affairs. But it did not go beyond that, leaving the citizens entirely free to engage in 'licit' love affairs with consenting *paides*, on condition that they had reached the age which would make them capable of choosing a good lover with their eyes open. This brings us closer to a problem that has already been mentioned several times: the age for love.

The Age for Loving and the Age for Being Loved

The preoccupation returns constantly in treatments of pederasty, whatever their origin: the beloved must be of a suitable age. This is stated not only by Plato, who makes it one of his conditions for distinguishing 'heavenly' from 'common' love. In attempting to convince the jury that his attitude to pederasty is the correct one, rigorous but not repressive,

Aeschines returns to this topic insistently. The law attributed to Solon confirms that the legal system shared society's preoccupations. But nobody ever tells us what this age was: neither Plato, nor Aeschines, nor the law on *paides*.

What, then, was the age of the *erōmenoi*? H.I. Marrou, in his *History of Education*, maintains that this age extended from fifteen to eighteen years.[67] On the basis of a passage in Aristotle, who writes in the *Politics* that for three years, before their ephebic stage, boys did not practise gymnastic exercises,[68] Marrou writes that 'between the boy's primary-school days and the ephebia there thus was a period for which, in the "old" education, no provision had been made. It was an unsettled time, a "difficult" age, in which he tended to get involved in unsavoury love affairs.'[69]

But leaving aside all discussion of this alleged institutional vacuum (M.P. Nilsson, for one, does not believe in it),[70] are we quite sure that the correct age for starting on being loved was fifteen? That *erōmenoi* were often younger emerges clearly from the literature of love which, although referring to a later historical period than the one we are dealing with here, contains very valuable indications. The *Greek Anthology*, in fact, not only demonstrates – without the shadow of a doubt – the continuity and vitality of pederotic poetry, but provides valuable information on the social rules governing this type of love, which included, in pride of place, the question of the suitable age:

> I delight in the prime of a boy of twelve, but one of thirteen is much more desirable. He who is fourteen is a still sweeter flower of the Loves, and one who is just beginning his fifteenth year is yet more delightful. The sixteenth year is that of the gods, and as for the seventeenth it is not for me, but for Zeus, to seek it. But if one has a desire for those still older, he no longer plays, but now seeks 'And answering him back'.

Thus Strato.[71]

Just a few years, then, for being loved – the years between twelve and seventeen. At this age, when the beard and body hair sprouted thickly, boys stopped being desirable:

> Thy beard will come, the last of evils but the greatest, and then thou shalt know what scarcity of friends is.[72]

Thus Strato threatens a reluctant boy who does not give in to his flattery. Beard and body hair: these are the dangers. A real obsession, for the *paides*, and a constant source of blackmail in the hands of their suitors, when the beloved played the waiting game too long:

By Themis and the bowl of wine that made me totter, thy love, Pamphilus, has but a little time to last. Already thy thigh has hair on it and thy cheeks are downy, and Desire leads thee henceforth to another kind of passion. But now that some little vestiges of the spark are still left thee, put away thy parsimony. Opportunity is the friend of Love.[73]

So writes Phanias. And Julius Diocles, writing of Damon who is playing hard to get:

One thus addressed a boy who did not say good day. 'And so, Damon, who excels in beauty, does not even say good-day now! A time will come that will take vengeance for this. Then, grown all rough and hairy, you will give good-day first to those who do not give it you back.'[74]

Speaking of Heraclitus, by now hairy beyond repair, Meleager warns the son of Polyxenus:

Heraclitus was fair, when there was a Heraclitus, but now that his prime is past, a screen of hide declares war on those who are behind-mounters. But, son of Polyxenus, seeing this, be not insolently haughty. Even on the buttocks too there is a Nemesis growing.[75]

The *paides* feared them so much, these horrible inevitable hairs, that they tried to hide them from their lovers after they had sprouted. Strato writes:

Why are you draped down to your ankles in that melancholy fashion, Menippus, you who used to tuck up your dress to your thighs? Or why do you pass me by with downcast eyes and without a word? I know what you are hiding from me. They have come, those things I told you would come.[76]

A cruel anonymous writer sneers at Nicander, now inexorably hairy, once as lovely as a god:

Nicander's light is out. All the bloom has left his complexion, and not even the name of charm survives, Nicander whom we once counted among the immortals. But, ye young men, let not your thoughts mount higher than beseems a mortal; there are such things as hairs.[77]

Lastly, here is the pitiless Asclepiades, brutally rejecting the offers of a *pais* who is no longer desirable:

Now you offer yourself, when the tender bloom is advancing under your temples and there is a prickly down on your thighs. And then you say, 'I prefer this'. But who would say that the dried stubble is better than the eared corn?[78]

Only a great love, apparently, made it possible to go on loving a boy even after his splendour had faded:

I caught fire when Theudis shone among the other boys, like the sun that rises on the stars. Therefore I am still burning now, when the down of night overtakes him, for though he be setting, yet he is still the sun.[79]

Thus Strato, speaking of Theudis.

Not infrequently it happened that lovers, just as they threatened reluctant youths by reminding them how short was the time for love, reassured those who had yielded and now feared abandonment on reaching 'retirement age'. Strato makes a solemn promise to Diodorus, who loved him:

Now thou art fair, Diodorus, and ripe for lovers, but even if thou dost marry, we shall not abandon thee.[80]

A sailor's promise, perhaps? Strato (no differently from others, probably) made copious use of such promises:

Even though the invading down and the delicate auburn curls of thy temples have leapt upon thee, that does not make me shun my belovèd, but his beauty is mine, even if there be a beard and hairs.[81]

Thus he promises another young man, swearing eternal love for him: a love, in short, like the legendary love of Euripides for Agathon, whom the poet loved all his life, justifying his choice by saying that 'even the autumn of the fair is fair'.[82] And, besides, it appears that Socrates too loved boys who were getting on in years, at least when they were as beautiful as Alcibiades. As we read in Plato's *Protagoras*, the philosopher, faced with the mockery of a friend who pointed out that Alcibiades, whom Socrates contined 'to pursue', was by now irredeemably bearded, reproved his friend by saying to him: 'But you are not a follower of Homer, then. Homer says that a youth is most seductive at the moment when his beard begins to grow!'[83]

We are now dealing with exceptional, or at least marginal, cases. As a rule, the age for being loved was very short. Seventeen, as we saw, was the furthest limit. The perfect age was sixteen, the year 'of the gods', as Strato called it;[84] for Scythinus, 'that fatal age', which makes him fall head over heels with Elissus 'full of the years ripe for love';[85] perhaps the age to which Plato alludes when he says that the love inspired by the

Heavenly Aphrodite is directed towards boys who are 'near' growing a beard.[86]

But the most delicate problem regarding the age of love objects was not so much the upper limit as the lower one: 'That an immature boy should do despite to his insensible age carries more disgrace to the friend who tempts him.'[87] Here again the writer is Strato, who obviously did not give in to the charms of the very young (or at least that is what he would have us believe):

> My neighbour's quite tender young boy provokes me not a little, and laughs in no novice manner to show me that he is willing. But he is not more than twelve years old. Now the unripe grapes are unguarded.[88]

Obviously, loving too young a lad was considered much more disreputable than loving one who was too old. Going beyond the upper limits of age, in short, was more a question of personal taste than anything else. To ignore the lower limits, on the other hand, was reprehensible. And the minimum age, Strato confirms in this epigram, was twelve: those twelve years at which, as we have seen, he felt it was justified to start 'enjoying the flower'.

Over time nothing had changed, and in the different areas of Greece the rule was evidently the same: in Sparta, as we know, boys were entrusted to their lovers at precisely twelve years of age – which, for the Greeks, was much less childish than in our society today.[89] For proof of this, one merely has to think of the age at which girls were given in marriage. Although the philosophers indicate a slightly older age as the ideal, in practice Greek girls got married at twelve or thirteen, which means as soon as they had reached puberty.[90] The tone in which philosophers speak of the question is quite significant. By saying, as Plato does, that girls should not be married off before the age of sixteen,[91] or, as Aristotle says, before eighteen,[92] the philosophers were standing out against a different practice, which imposed the role of motherhood on girls who were too young to sustain it. On this account alone, twelve was too young for a girl. But given that the problem of maternity obviously did not arise in the case of boys, why should twelve be considered too young?[93] This brings us to another problem: if the age for being loved was between twelve and seventeen, what was the age for being a lover?

It is usually said that the Greeks were not *erastai* all their lives, but only for the first few years of adulthood: more precisely, up to the age of marriage, the period during which their way of life became heterosexual. Relationships with *paides* were, at most, an occasional variant, offering the possibility of an alternative to a sexuality orientated predominantly, if not exclusively, towards relations with women (whether wives, concubines, courtesans or prostitutes).[94] But it seems highly questionable whether things really worked out like this in practice. One only has to look at some more or less famous examples, the first being Sophocles.

Already known in antiquity as 'a lover of pretty boys',[95] Sophocles continued to have pederastic relationships all his life. This was not – as was said of Plato[96] – because he did not like women: during his lifetime, in fact, Sophocles loved more than one woman. Married to Nicostrate, who gave him a son called Iophōn (also a tragic poet), he had another son named Ariston by a foreign woman, Theoris of Sicyon.[97] But despite this, he never lost his interest in boys. Ion of Chios (reported by Athenaeus)[98] recounts that Sophocles, recently nominated as military commander, found himself one day at Chios as a guest at a banquet given by Hermesilaus. Ion, a fellow-guest, witnessed an amusing episode. Attracted by the beauty of a boy who was pouring wine for the diners, the poet asked him: 'Do you want me to drink with pleasure?' Being answered in the affirmative, Sophocles commanded provocatively: 'Then don't be too rapid in handing me the cup and taking it away.' The boy blushed furiously, and Sophocles, after quoting to his friends a verse from Phrynicus, 'there shines upon his crimson cheeks the light of love', persevered in his process of seduction. The boy was trying to fish a tiny straw from the cup with his finger, but the poet suggested that instead of getting his finger wet, he should blow on the cup. While the boy was blowing, he moved the cup towards his own lips and kissed him. So how old was Sophocles when he engaged in this erotic game? Born in 496, he went to Chios in 441, so he was then fifty-five years of age. And he was certainly no stranger to this type of adventure. Plutarch tells how, one day in Athens, walking along with Pericles, his colleague in the generalship, the poet espied a fetching youth and could not contain himself. 'Lovely boy, Pericles!', he exclaimed, delighted. But Pericles gave him no support: 'My dear Sophocles,' he told him, 'a general must have not only chaste hands, but chaste eyes.'[99]

Lastly, another significant story about Sophocles is told by Hieronymus of Rhodes (again reproduced by Athenaeus): one day, the poet went outside the walls of Athens with a boy, for a very definite purpose. Far from prying eyes, he spread his cape out on the ground and lay down on it with the youth, wrapping himself up with him in the cape. Sadly, the boy, after the event, proved himself anything but a disinterested friend by making off with the poet's cape, and Sophocles was left in a very awkward situation, particularly because at that time he was already aged sixty-five.[100]

We now turn to a second, even more famous case: Euripides, who loved the handsome Agathon, as we know, all his life – or at least, it is said, until Agathon was forty years old and Euripides seventy-two.[101]

It may be objected that these are mere anecdotes. Maybe so. But they are anecdotes which fit well into the habits of the time, as confirmed by other direct testimony. In his oration *Against Timarchus*, Aeschines declares, as we saw, that he still has *erōmenoi*, and this oration was written at the age of forty-two. Lysias, already well into adulthood (being aged over fifty), writes in his oration *Against Simon* about his love for young Theodotus and his rivalry with Simon over the youth.[102]

Faced with such evidence, how can one avoid thinking that adult Greek males enjoyed almost untrammelled freedom, being allowed to devote time to pederastic relationships which were far more than an occasional variation, amounting to a normal, acceptable, natural alternative? How can we fail to conclude that these men (so long as they kept to an active role in their relationships, of course) were almost completely free to express their emotions and sexuality?

To sum up, the following were the rules of Greek sexual ethics in relation to age: between the ages of twelve and seventeen or eighteen, a male was a passive partner in a relationship which linked him to an adult. Once he reached the age of majority, having passed through the period of being a *neaniskos* (roughly, from the age of twenty-five onwards) he took on an active role, at first (up to the time of his marriage) with *paides*, and subsequently both with *paides* and with women.

All of this means that whereas the age of being loved had two very strict boundaries (the minimum age of twelve and maximum of seventeen or eighteen), the age for being a lover had only one unmovable limit: the lower one, meaning that the minimum acceptable age had been reached. The upward limit was really very fluid. It all depended, basically, on personal propensities, individual desires, and good taste. But what happened when the rules dealt with so far were infringed?

Breaking the Rules on Age: Custom and Law

Sexual relations with children

To make love to a child aged under twelve was an infamous deed.[103] But what punishment fell on the seducer? Was social opprobrium accompanied by some legal penalty? Albeit very cautiously, David Cohen puts forward the hypothesis that a relationship with a *pais* under a certain age (which is not, however, precisely stated) was considered, depending on the circumstances, a case of sexual violence or of *hybris*, and as such subject to criminal prosecution.[104] But this hypothesis, though interesting and plausible, does not appear to find confirmation in the sources.

The law on sexual violence, reported by Lysias,[105] provides for a financial penalty, as we have seen, if somebody outrages a free man, a *pais* or a woman by force. But nothing in a reading of this law allows us to assume that violence against the *pais* could be presumed. The law contains no reference to age. Thus, if we were to see it as designed to establish a presumption of violence in relations with *paides*, we would have to assume that relations with *paides* of any age were considered as constituting sexual violence. And given that boys were technically *paides* up to the age of eighteen, this assumption is clearly untenable.

Let us turn to the law on *hybris* reported by Aeschines in the oration *Against Timarchus*,[106] where there is mention of a penalty if an Athenian has committed *hybris* against a *pais*. This law is anything but easy to interpret, both on account of the multiple meanings of *hybris*, and on account of the difficulty of establishing the relationship between the crime defined by that name and the offence of sexual violence.

Hybris is a word which, although used very often in contexts referring to sexual behaviour, also appears in different contexts, covering a very wide range of aggravation, from verbal abuse to fisticuffs. When it is used to denote a crime (the one punished by means of a special law called *nomos hybreōs*) it seems to identify and punish, under this heading, a series of offences unified and characterised by a particular psychological attitude on the part of the perpetrator: a desire to damage the victim's honour and diminish the victim's social prestige through an offensive action, of whatever sort.[107]

This, then, is the context in which we should place the sexual *hybris* to which Aeschines alludes, and to which further reference is made by Demosthenes.[108] What seems to be involved is a form of outrageous behaviour which, while failing to reach the extremes of sexual violence, induces the victim to accept a dishonourable sexual relationship.

Moving beyond this immediate problem, one thing is certain: not even the law on *hybris* makes reference to the age of the *pais* who suffers it. Summing up what has been discussed, and bringing together what we have seen on the social rules of courtship and the laws on *paides* attributed to Solon, I believe there is some foundation for the following theory. Athenian society divided *paides* into three categories.

The first of these consisted of boys aged under twelve, with whom it was considered infamous to have any kind of relationship (even though, so far as we can discover, there were no legal penalties for anybody who did so). The second group comprised those *paides* aged between twelve and fourteen or fifteen, with whom it was permissible to entertain relationships, but only within the setting of a lasting emotional link, designed in particular to teach the beloved *pais* the virtues of a future citizen. Given the fact that, owing to their inexperience, *paides* of this age could easily fall prey to lovers who were incapable of educating them (because they were either too young or socially unsuited to the task), the law was concerned to prevent them (like their younger counterparts) from becoming involved in dangerous meetings or questionable company.

The third group was made up of those *paides* ranging from fourteen or fifteen up to eighteen years of age (already *neaniskoi*, in non-technical language) who in society's opinion were by now capable of choosing their own lovers deliberately. And yet society was concerned about them because, being now close to maturity, they might be tempted to assume a virile role prematurely.

These, I believe, were the social and legal norms which regulated love affairs between an adult and a boy, preventing them from degenerating into a merely sexual relationship. But what were the regulations governing love affairs between adults?

'Making oneself a woman' as an adult: social sanction and the vocabulary of infamy

As well as being broken at the lower end of the age band (that is, loving a *pais* aged under twelve), the rules of sexual morality could be infringed at the upper end. In the latter case, the rules could be broken in two different ways. The first was to continue having a *paidika* (meaning a youthful love object) after having reached a marriageable age. But in this case, as we have seen, transgression was tolerated. In practice, it happened very often that a man of marriageable age had a young lover, and public opinion accepted these relationships independently of whether or not he was married. To speculate, as is sometimes done, on whether pederastic relations were adulterous[109] is absolutely inappropriate. Given that only women were held to marital fidelity, a husband was quite free to have a relationship, and whether this was with a woman or with a boy was a matter of complete indifference.[110] In practice, then, the only infringement of the upper age limit was committed by a man who went on assuming a passive role although he had reached the age which made it compulsory for him to be the active partner. This was something which must have happened quite frequently, when the pederastic relationship went on beyond the accepted limits (need one cite again the case of Euripides and Agathon in this regard?). At other times it happened because two grown men fell in love at an age when both should theoretically have assumed an active sexual role. This was not unknown, as we can see, among other examples, from a passage in Aristophanes' *Frogs*.

Dionysus has confessed that he is in love. Heracles asks him who is the object of his love: a woman, perhaps? No, not a woman. A boy, then? Wrong again. In that case, it must be a man. Sadly, that's the truth, Dionysus replies; and, to make matters worse, the man in question is Cleisthenes, noted for his effeminacy.[111]

Heracles has listed in order the possible targets of love for a Greek man; and the order in which he lists them is no accident. After women (an almost obligatory option) came *paides*: a choice which, as we know, did not exclude the previous one, but was also added to it. And after *paides* came men, but on a different level. Love between two adult males posed some problems – at least for one member of the couple: the one who assumed the passive role of the beloved. He had to bear the heavy weight of social disapproval which is unequivocally attested, in fourth-century Athens, by the plays of Aristophanes.[112]

From these comic texts (which pitilessly held up for mockery a habit that was clearly very widespread) a picture emerges of a city where there were practically no adult males who resisted what Aristophanes considered one of the worst degenerations of behaviour, a collective vice which was not only shameful to those who practised it, but dangerous for the very survival of the city. All Athenian men, according to him, be they nobles or members of the populace, gave themselves to other men through habit or vice. And *paides* too (who need have feared no reproof if they had done it according to the rules) were now doing it without shame or respect for appearances.

In Aristophanes' *Clouds* the dispute between Right and Wrong is, perhaps, the poet's most explicit complaint, the point where we can most clearly see the bitterness sarcastically hidden in irony and paradox.

Right is defending old-fashioned education, the sort which long ago used to be given to reserved and modest youths, who exercised in the gymnasium so as to tone up their muscles and their minds together – and not, like the youth of today, to titillate their lovers. In the old days, says Right, nobody would have anointed himself with oil below the midriff, as young people nowadays do for obvious purposes. But, asks

Wrong, what use was all that shamefaced modesty? The final aim of everybody, *paides* and *erastai* alike, has always been precisely the same: *to binein* (the verb which most vulgarly indicates the sexual act).[113] Wrong is opposing crude reality to the praise and lamentation of Right (and Aristophanes himself) for the Platonic ideal of a reserved, noble kind of love. The nostalgia of Right, basically, is pure hypocrisy. Why not accept the truth and admit that all Athenians are nothing but *eurupróktoi* (another extremely vulgar term, to which we shall return, to indicate passive homosexuals)?[114]

Aristophanes' irony is bitter and despairing: his laughter exorcises the tragedy of Athens, the beloved city which he had seen, as a young man, at the height of its splendour, and which, after a few brief decades – corrupt, defenceless, governed by opportunists and incompetents – he now clearly perceives to be inexorably doomed to a tragic fate.

This is the framework in which we should interpret the critique which Aristophanes offers of the sexual mores of the Athenians. And in this framework one can understand why he directs his barbs exclusively at passive homosexuals. These were the men who, by abdicating their virile role, symbolised the extent to which Athens was no longer capable of ruling Greece. On closer examination, although he takes it to extremes, Aristophanes is merely reflecting the judgement of popular morality. Although there are some people who believe that the sources reveal a comprehensive condemnation of homosexual relations between adults,[115] my own view is that discredit and social opprobrium fell on only one member of the couple.

Unlike the situation which prevails today (at least as a rule) between two adult homosexuals, there was no interchangeability of roles between Greek couples. Following the model of the pederastic couple, couples consisting of two adults assumed that only one of them would take on the receptive role – and this gave rise to the social and moral problem that caused tensions, contradictions and quite a lot of hypocrisy. Only one of the pair was formally breaking the rules. Greek society responded to this situation by applying double standards. One of the two was the degenerate, a butt of ridicule: the one who was usually defined as the *katapygṓn*.

Underlying the Athenian's judgement of homosexuality between adults was the same principle, which, as we shall see in the case of prostitution, heaped condemnation exclusively on the prostitute. Only the one who had 'made a woman of himself' was guilty. This was true even when he had done it not for money, but for reasons of love and vice – except that in such cases (unlike when somebody had prostituted himself) the sanction was exclusively a social one. A consideration of the evidence shows that this situation did not only obtain in the works of Aristophanes.

From Aeschines, for example, we learn of a heavy-handed pun with which the Athenians used to taunt Demosthenes, who was accused of being a passive homosexual. Demosthenes had a nickname, Battalos, which according to the orator was due to a speech defect: he had been called Battalos, 'the stammerer' since childhood. But Aeschines and his political enemies did not call him Battalos; they called him *Batalos*, with one *t*; *batalos* means 'arse'.[116] This pun must have appealed greatly to the Athenians, whose linguistic imagination played around this topic with particular amusement.

There is a broad and colourful range of terms used to denote passive homosexuals in Aristophanes. One of the most frequent terms was *europrōktoi* – people whose hinder parts (*prōktoi*) had been enlarged through excessive use.[117] By way of contrast with the broad-arsed, we have the *stenoi*, meaning narrow or closed. Hence the term *stenoprōktos*[118] and the wordplay indulged in by the Sausage-seller, the demagogic protagonist of the *Knights*. When Paphlagon boasts that he is able to make the city 'now broad, now narrow', the Sausage-seller replies: 'my arse knows that same trick'.[119]

Also linked to the same root-word *prōktos* are the terms *chaunoprōktoi*[120] and *lakkoprōktoi*, 'tank-arses'.[121] As well as words deriving from *prōktos*, there are words from *pygē*, the hindquarters. First and foremost is *katapygōn*, which is very frequent and often used to contrast the homosexual with a respectable, reliable and proper person. In the Banquet, for example, two opposing characters are *ho katapygōn* and *ho sōphrōn* (the wise man).[122]

To add extra effectiveness to the reference, it was quite common practice to add a dash of colour. To have a pallid complexion was considered a sign of effeminacy. And so the homosexuals became *leukopygoi*, 'white-arses',[123] obviously in contrast with the *melanpygoi*, the 'black-arses' – or with the *dasuprōktoi*, 'rough-arses', who were real men, usually heterosexual, although now and again the *lasioi* ('hairy ones', meaning active homosexuals) could also be counted as real men.[124]

Aristophanes' satire is not lacking in references to the dimensions and proportions of those parts of the body which are, so to speak, implicated in sexual practices. The model of manly beauty included a small-sized phallus and buttocks moulded by sporting exercises.[125] A large phallus accompanied by small buttocks with unimpressive musculature therefore indicated soft living and a propensity to be the submissive partner in sexual activities.[126] The savage and ironic references to passive homosexuality were not only verbal; gestures on stage assisted in building up the comic effects and inflicting further shame on the poor *katapygones*. A gesture which is still well known, where the hand is rolled up into a fist, with the exception of the middle finger pointing upwards, was an unmistakable insult: in Photius the word *katapygōn* is glossed *ho mesos daktylos*, the middle finger.[127] And a specific verb (*skimalizein*) indicated the gesture involved[128] – that gesture which, when Strepsiades does it in the *Clouds*, causes Socrates to exclaim that anyone doing it is *skaios* and *agrios*, a rustic peasant dolt.[129]

Finally, the visualisation of the *katapygones* was aided by their appearance: they had long hair, often curly,[130] and their skin hair had been artificially removed.[131] But the most comic effect of all was achieved when the transvestites came on stage, presented for the amusement of the public, with great skill, in such a way that they appeared to be neither men nor women. For example, in the *Thesmophoriazusae*, Agathon makes his entry in women's clothing, wearing a brassière (*strophion*) and holding a mirror in his hand, but at the same time wielding a lyre and a sword.[132]

This, then, was the pitiless and savage irony with which the Athenians assailed passive homosexuals. The active ones, as we have seen, were granted immunity from satire and sometimes even considered examples of true manliness. This inevitably leads us to ask some more general questions on the problem of homosexuality, to which we shall return after examining the rules governing male prostitution.

Male Prostitution: The Oration of Aeschines Against Timarchus

Athenian public opinion had no doubt that a man should never prostitute himself to another man. Whatever his social class, whatever his financial position, whatever his education, the Athenian citizen (unless, of course, he happened himself to be a prostitute) took a very harsh view of those who sold themselves – the *pornoi*. And the social sanction was accompanied by quite heavy legal penalties. To assess the full implications of the legal penalties which fell on male prostitutes, we have to return to Aeschines' oration, *Against Timarchus*.

The long speech Aeschines delivers on pederasty during the course of this oration is merely a digression which the orator feels is necessary in order to reach his aim: proving that Timarchus was a *pornos*. This was a very important point to prove, not only for Aeschines, on account of its political consequences. To understand these consequences, one has to have some grasp of the background to the case.

A political ally of Demosthenes, and like him an opponent of Macedon, Timarchus had accused Aeschines of failing to follow instructions, and of signing a peace agreement with Philip of Macedon – the so-called Peace of Philocrates in 346 BC – which betrayed the interests of Athens. But Timarchus, Aeschines argued, did not have the right to speak in the courts. His private life debarred him. In an *antigraphē*, a preliminary issue raised before a hearing, Aeschines rebutted Timarchus' accusations not by defending himself but by accusing his accuser of having himself broken the law – more precisely, the law on *hetairēsis*.

The law on hetairēsis

If an Athenian has prostituted himself (*hetairēsē*), according to the law, 'he cannot serve as one of the nine archons, nor hold any priestly office, nor exercise the functions of a public advocate or magistrate, either inside or outside the city, whether chosen by election or by lot. He cannot be dispatched as a herald, or express his opinion, or be associated with public sacrifices, or publicly wear the crown, or enter within the purified boundaries of the *agora*. If he does any of these things after being found guilty of *hetairēsis*, then he shall be put to death.'[133]

The first problem posed by the text of this law is obviously how the term *hetairēsis* should be defined.

Undoubtedly, *hetairēsis* is prostitution. But what sort of prostitution? Like its female counterpart, male prostitution fell into two categories: *hetairēsis* and *porneia*. The latter variety (where one sold oneself for casual encounters of a purely sexual nature) was socially more unacceptable, and subject to different legal regulations, at least in part. The *pornos*, and only he, was registered in special lists, and had to pay a tax called the *pornikon telos*.[134] In a certain sense, therefore, the *pornos* was the only male prostitute whose professional status was officially recognised by the city. Similarly, among female prostitutes it gave official recognition only to the *pornē*, who was liable (unlike the *hetaira*) to pay a tax on her income.[135] Again, in the female field, the fact that only the *pornē* was officially a prostitute can be seen from Draco's law on adultery (*moicheia*),[136] which allowed a citizen to kill with impunity a man whom he surprised with his wife, concubine (*pallakē*), mother, sister or daughter, but ruled that the killing was unlawful when the woman surprised with the *moichos* was 'a woman who sold herself openly in the streets or in brothels'[137] – a *pornē*, then, not a courtesan.

But let us return to male prostitution. *Hetairēsis*, as we saw, was punished by the loss of civic rights. And *porneia*? Were there different, heavier penalties for the *pornos*? In the course of his oration, Aeschines explicitly states that Timarchus cannot be considered merely as a *hetairēkōs*: his behaviour has been such that he is a *pornos* (or *peporneumenos*).[138] Despite this, the law he is accused of violating is the law on *hetairēsis*. Obviously, therefore, for the purposes of punishment, there was no difference at all between *hetairēsis* and *porneia*. This is confirmed by the text of the oration, where Aeschines, listing those people forbidden to speak in public, mentions on the same level the *peporneumenos* and the *hetairēkōs*.[139]

The Athenian citizen, then, was punished if he prostituted himself, no matter what way he plied his trade. But what happened to his 'purchaser'? In other words, was the loss of civic rights confined purely to the seller of sexual favours, or were there penalties against his customer too? There are different opinions on this question, and some recent scholars have maintained that both contracting parties were punished.[140] K.J. Dover, however, does not agree. It is true, he says, that Aeschines affirms in the course of his oration that there were sanctions against the customer too; but Aeschines is lying.[141] I think that Dover is absolutely right here. Where are the references to sanctions against the client? In his oration Aeschines recalls the law which he says he has already quoted, according to which 'anyone who hires an Athenian' will be punished, exactly like the man who has hired himself out.[142] How much confidence should we have in these assertions? None. Aeschines is deceiving us, manipulating ambiguities with great skill: among the laws which have been cited during his oration there is in fact one which states that the father, uncle, brother or tutor of a *pais* who rents him out to third parties for sexual purposes will be punished like the client.[143] That case is clearly quite different from the one with which we are dealing: the person renting a *pais*, in particular, has not made an agreement with the person involved, but with a third party. But Aeschines, probably referring to this law, plays on the ambiguity and speaks of a (non-existent) provision which also punishes the male prostitute's client.

The historical and cultural foundation

At this point it is necessary to go into more detail on one problem: why should the prostitute lose his rights, while his customer did not? To understand this fully, one must return to an observation which has already been made several times, confirmed by Dover, maintained by Foucault in the volume on Greece in his *History of Sexuality* and extended by Veyne to the Roman sexual ethic: the fundamental dichotomy between different types of sexual behaviour, in antiquity, was not between heterosexuality and homosexuality, but between active and passive behaviour. Active behaviour properly belonged to adult males, while women and *paides* were supposed to practise passive behaviour.[144]

It is not hard to understand the reasons why this dichotomy prevailed over the heterosexual/homosexual distinction when one considers what we observed about the links with initiation in the origins of pederasty.

Love between men dates back to a time in Greek history when, although women were accessible (the segregation of women, as we saw, is linked to the birth of the *polis*), the man-woman relationship, for all its importance and its indispensable reproductive function, did not lie at the centre of social organisation. What occupied the central position was the relationship between men. In other words, heterosexual relations provided physical life, but the function of giving life within the adult male group, the function of creating a man as a social individual, belonged to the homosexual relationship, set up for this purpose, almost as an institution, between a grown man and a boy. But this relationship was supposed to last only for a well-defined period of time. Once maturity had been reached, as we also saw, the boy had to abandon the passive role (from both a cultural and a sexual point of view) and assume a doubly active role: heterosexually as husband, and homosexually as lover and educator of a 'beloved' boy.

I think that the social and legal rules which in the Classical age punished only the passive partner among two adult lovers can be seen, on mature reflection, as a further confirmation of the origins of homosexuality in initiation rites and the consequences of this (although in a very different cultural and political setting).[145]

Only one of the two, then, had broken the rules. Only one, therefore, was liable for punishment, which consisted of social sanctions in the case of non-mercenary loves, and legal sanctions in the case of mercenary loves.

The sanction

The rules of sexual morality, over the centuries, remained unchanged in at least one respect: passivity was felt to be unsuitable for adult males. The speech of Aeschines against Timarchus explicitly confirms this consideration, when the prosecutor retails a strange episode from Timarchus' life.

Under the archonship of Nicophemus, he alleges, Timarchus agreed with Hegesandrus, treasurer of the Parthenon goddess, to steal a thousand drachmas from the community. But a reputable citizen, Pamphilus of the deme Acherdous, denounced what was going on. He reported it in these terms in the assembly: 'A man and a woman are conspiring to steal one thousand drachmas of yours.' When he was asked who this woman might be, he replied: 'The woman, she is Timarchus yonder.'[146] Such was the infamy committed by a man who prostituted himself: he made himself into a woman.

That concept, which is crystal clear, is restated more than once in the course of the oration. Aeschines asks the Athenians how they could dare to 'let Timarchus go free, a man chargeable with the most shameful practices, a creature with the body of a man defiled with the sins of a woman'.[147] Anyone who turns 'woman' for money, then, is condemned. That is what Athenian law states.

Should this be taken to mean that male prostitution was forbidden by law? In order to reply, one thing needs to be specified: in the eyes of the civil law, the contract was valid. The fact that the activities of the *pornoi* were taxed obviously proves that their profession was permitted: anybody who wanted was free to prostitute himself, and receive the agreed reward for his endeavours. But this did not mean that he avoided all sanctions. Just like somebody who was maintained by a more or less steady lover, thereby coming into the category of the *hetairēkotes*,[148] the male prostitute lost the right that he enjoyed, as a citizen, to take part in the life of his city. Why should this be surprising, and why should we be surprised by the fact that *pornoi* and *hetairēkotes* received equal treatment? In both cases the prostitute had 'made a woman of himself', so he was entitled – like a real woman – to the status but not the functions of citizenship.

Before drawing this topic to a close, it seems useful to advance one final consideration: in some ways, the sanction established against male prostitutes recalls that against adulterous women (known as *memoicheumenai*). What sanction did the city take against women surprised with their lovers? They were excluded from participation in public religious ceremonies[149] – in other words, from the only form of participation in the life of the *polis* which was permitted to women.

The analogy does not stop here: for both adulteresses and *pornoi* the ban on participating in city life was simply a first-degree penalty, as it were. If that ban was not observed, a further second-degree punishment was added, but this was different in the two cases. An adulteress, if she was caught attending a public religious ceremony, could be punished by any citizen, who was entitled to do her any injury short of death.[150] A male prostitute, convicted on the basis of an indictment known as a *graphē hetairēseōs*, if he subsequently took part in political or judicial affairs, incurred the death penalty.[151] One could perhaps deduce from this that between the two parallel forms of infamy, the one committed by the male prostitute, in the eyes of the *polis*, was worse than that of the adulteress.

3

Homosexuality and Heterosexuality Compared in Philosophy and Literature

After trying to understand how homosexual relationships were experienced by individuals, and how they were considered from a social and legal point of view, it remains to be seen how they were assessed within the framework of theoretical considerations of Eros – in other words, what philosophers thought about them.

Placing the theme of Eros at the centre of their moral and political reflections, the philosophers – or at least some philosophers – found themselves faced with the need to reflect on the coexistence, among men, of impulses stimulated by love objects of different sexes. And so they set themselves the twofold objective of identifying the differences between homosexual and heterosexual love and (at least at a certain point) of establishing which of the two was superior. This concern revealed, behind the mass practice of homosexuality (without which the problem would not have arisen) a sort of unease – which was grounded, however, not on morality but on the question of social utility.

Socrates

On the evidence of his pupil Plato, the first theorist of love was Socrates. But given that Plato is the source of almost all our information on his master's attitude to Eros, it is necessary, from the outset, to attempt an understanding of how much the image of Socrates that Plato presents is 'Platonic', and whether this image may not have been to some extent distorted by the ideas and tendencies of the pupil.

According to an interpretation which is as authoritative as it is difficult to share, Plato was 'a sexual deviant'. Unlike other Greeks (happily homosexual in their youth, and then equally happily heterosexual), Plato is said to have been exclusively homosexual.[1] And the perception of the 'non-social' nature of his Eros is said to be one of the reasons why he advocates a spiritual type of love. By theorising about this love, he would be sheltered both from the criticisms of his fellow citizens and the nagging of his own conscience, anguished by an awareness of his abnormality. Hence, according to the supporters of this theory, Plato's desired effort to present a chaste Socrates, uninterested in sex and absolutely incorruptible in the face of male attempts at seduction: a sublimated image of the master, then, and at the same time a sort of self-defence against public opinion, to which, through the figure of Socrates, Plato could show that the love of boys, far from being a fault, could become a means to acquire wisdom.

However, when one looks more closely (and leaving aside the difficulty of accepting such an interpretation of Platonic Eros, a topic which will be further developed later), it is very difficult to believe that the refusal by Socrates of physical love is a forced interpretation by Plato.

In the first place, Socrates' wish to establish purely spiritual relationships with boys, while it emerges largely from the Platonic dialogues, is also reported by other sources. In Xenophon's *Memorabilia*, for example, Socrates speaks of 'this creature called "fair and young", more dangerous than the scorpion, seeing that it need not even come in contact, like the insect, but at any distance can inject a maddening poison into anyone who only looks at it'.[2] So in Socrates' view it is extremely dangerous to give in to the temptations of sex, and not only according to Plato's presentation of the master, but also according to the image which other witnesses had of him, including Xenophon, whose attitude to homosexuality (and we shall see how and why) was very different from Plato's.

Chastity, for Socrates, was an ideal which fitted in with a general aspiration towards self-control, having nothing to do with the gender of the love object. Sexual continence was just one aspect of that rigour which he believed indispensable, in every area of experience, if one was to reach the fullness of being, which consisted in the dominion of the mind (psyche) over the body.[3]

This does not mean that he did not love boys. On the contrary: described as naturally drawn to love and an expert in eroticism, Socrates declares, in Xenophon's *Symposium*, that he does not remember a moment of his life during which he was not in love.[4] In Plato's *Meno* he confesses that he cannot resist beauty.[5] And this beauty, it goes without saying, was the beauty of boys, as shown, without any possibility of doubt, by another celebrated passage from Plato. In the *Charmides*, while everybody praises the beauty of the young man, Socrates admits that Charmides would be irresistible if his physical beauty were matched by suitable moral qualities. To test his character, he engages in conversation with the boy, and is literally bowled over – not by Charmides' intellectual qualities, but by his hidden charms which at a certain point he happens to glimpse:

> But here, my friend, I began to feel perplexed, and my former confidence in looking forward to a quite easy time in talking with him had been knocked out of me. And when, on Critias telling him that it was I who knew the cure, he gave me such a look with his eyes as passes description, and was just about to plunge into a question, and when all the people in the wrestling-school surged round about us on every side – then, ah then, my noble friend . . . I saw inside his cloak and caught fire, and could possess myself no longer; and I thought none was so wise in love-matters as Cydias, who in speaking of a beautiful boy recommends someone to 'beware of coming as a fawn before the lion, and being seized as his portion of flesh'; for I too felt I had fallen a prey to some such creature.[6]

And what can be said of his love for Alcibiades? In Plato's narrative, Socrates resists the beautiful impudent youth who seeks to become his *erōmenos*.[7] But in the work of Aeschines of Spettos, he confesses in no uncertain terms the passion which this youth has aroused within him:

> From our part, the love I feel for Alcibiades has brought me to an experience which is exactly the same as that of the Bacchantes, who when they are inspired can draw milk and honey where others could not even draw water from a well. Similarly I myself, although I have not learned anything which I could transmit to somebody else in order to make him good, nevertheless feel that by virtue of my love, my company could have made him become better.[8]

'The irony is apparent,' writes W.K.C. Guthrie, 'The erotic delusion of Socrates, comparable to those of frenzied maenads, is that by his love he might be able to convert the dissolute Alcibiades to a better way of life.'[9] Socrates, in short, did not refuse masculine love. He rejected purely carnal loves: 'And if anyone is found to be a lover of Alcibiades' body, he has fallen in love, not with Alcibiades, but with something belonging to Alcibiades,' he suggests in *Alcibiades I*.[10] In Xenophon's *Symposium* he is even more trenchant: the union is servile when one's regard is for the body rather than the soul.[11] What conclusions can be drawn from all this on Socrates' opinions concerning love?

We already know that in rejecting physical relationships the problem of the gender of the love object did not have the slightest significance. If he resisted boys this was because they, and not women, were his true temptation, as was normal for a Greek. This does not mean, however, even in theory, that he was a misogynist. On the contrary: Socrates, unlike the majority of his fellow citizens, had a certain regard for women, and, in particular, did not believe them inferior by nature (as did both Plato and Aristotle, as we shall see).

In the *Symposium* of Xenophon, looking at the skill of a female juggler, Socrates observes that the woman is giving 'one of many proofs that woman's nature is really not a whit inferior to man's, except for its lack of judgment and physical strength'.[12] This latter proviso may seem misogynistic to us, but it was certainly not seen in that way within the framework of what Greeks at the time thought about the female sex. The important point is that for Socrates women were not 'naturally' inferior: what made them inferior, in his opinion, was predominantly lack of education. He explained that husbands had a duty to teach their wives how to be good companions, lest they become (in quite a perceptive phrase!) those people with whom they had the least conversation.[13] So it is no accident that when a woman was as well educated as Aspasia, Socrates was willing to recognise her superiority, at least in certain fields.[14] Socrates had great respect for the concubine of Pericles. In Xenophon's *Oeconomicus*, when asked about husbands who have good wives, 'did they train them themselves?', Socrates responds by suggesting that Aspasia should be questioned on this topic, as she has more knowledge than he possesses.[15]

But his theoretical respect for women, or at least some of them, did not prevent Socrates from loving boys, and considering women, in practice (when they were not, quite exceptionally, like Aspasia) people with whom, apart from statements of principle, one could not have even the slightest intellectual exchange: and with whom, consequently, it would be very difficult for him to fall in love. How else can we judge his attitude to his own wife, the well-known Xanthippe, who for some reason has become the prototype of the petulant scold? We know very little about the relationship between Socrates and Xanthippe. But I believe that one episode is highly significant.

After being condemned to death, while discussing the immortality of the soul with his friends in prison, Socrates receives a visit from the poor woman who, like all women, is incapable of behaving nobly. Seeing her husband who is about to meet his death, Xanthippe weeps and laments. Socrates, annoyed, without deigning to speak a single word to her, writes her off as follows: 'Crito, let somebody take her home.'[16]

To judge from this episode, we must conclude that Socrates had not put his theories into practice. Clearly Xanthippe had not received that instruction which, in the *Oeconomicus*, he said that husbands should impart to their wives. And so she had remained what in the view of Socrates a wife theoretically should not be: a person with whom her husband had no conversation.

The gender which attracted and tempted Socrates was the male sex: it was boys that he had to resist, in the name of his chosen morality. Resisting women was a problem that simply did not arise, either for Socrates or, for different reasons, for his pupil, Plato.

Plato

Unlike Socrates, Plato was profoundly convinced of the natural inferiority of women, which he explicitly stated several times in his theory of metempsychosis. In the *Timaeus*, on this topic, we read that anyone 'who lives well for his appointed time would return home to his native star and live an appropriately happy life; but anyone who failed to do so would be changed into a woman at his second birth. And if he still did not refrain from wrong, he would be changed into some animal suitable to his particular kind of wrongdoing.'[17]

According to Plato, at the time of creation each soul was directed to one star, and later they came down from this star into the world in the form of human beings of the male sex. The human race was originally composed exclusively of men, who were destined to return to the stars at the end of their mortal life if they lived well. And what about those who lived badly? 'At their second birth' they would be reborn as women. More precisely: 'The men of the first generation who lived cowardly lives were, it is reasonable to suppose, reborn in the second generation as women',[18] in execution of the design of 'those who framed us, who knew that later on women and other animals would be produced from men'.[19]

All of which shows that Plato's well-established reputation as a champion of female rights is decidedly odd. This reputation was already widespread during the Roman era, when emancipated women used to dangle their copies of Plato's *Republic* provocatively under the noses of thier menfolk.[20]

In the *Republic*, undoubtedly, Plato had envisaged an ideal state in which women, who were to be educated like men, could carry out the same tasks as them: being doctors, philosophers ('lovers of wisdom'), and even 'guardians', which is to say that they could belong to the power group to which control of the constitution was entrusted.[21] But does this mean that we can speak, as has recently been suggested, of a 'delightfully radical' programme proposing 'equal opportunities'?[22] In the *Laws*, the ideal city once again makes room for the family (which had been abolished in the *Republic*). And with the family, feminine subordination reappears: in marriage (which everyone is obliged to contract, and to dissolve after ten years in the case of childlessness) the woman has to submit not only to the control of her husband, but also to the control of the state.[23] As women are by nature 'more inclined to hidden ways and trickery', they 'can be the cause of ruin for the State, as happened in Sparta where, freed from family responsibilities and economically powerful, they undermined the stability of the city'.[24] As Wilamowitz-Möllendorff correctly observed, what Plato really wanted, as an alternative to female submission, was that having abolished all differences between the sexes, women should 'become men, and in his view imperfect men'.[25]

After this introduction, let us look at Plato's attitude to the more specific problem of sexual relations, and especially the different value judgements he made of them, according to whether they were heterosexual or homosexual. Again, it is not terribly important to know whether Plato himself had sexual relations with men. As well as being extremely probable and easy to imagine, it seems to emerge from some fragments of his poetry that he did in fact have such relations: 'Aster, you who look at the stars! Oh, if I were the heavens I could look on you with thousands of eyes', he writes to a young man who has fascinated him.[26] But this is not the point. The interesting thing, apart from the actual life of the philosopher, is the way in which he evaluated homosexuality in relation to heterosexuality. In this connection, a preliminary indication comes from his theory of the existence of two different types of love: the love inspired by the heavenly Aphrodite, and the love inspired by the common Aphrodite. As we have seen in connection with his ideas on pederastic courtship, Plato maintains that the first difference between the two types of love resides in the following: those inspired by the first Aphrodite love boys, whereas those inspired by the second Aphrodite love men and women, without distinction.[27] But the passage which expresses most clearly the conviction that love between men is superior is the celebrated myth of the origin of sexes, narrated by Aristophanes in the *Symposium*.

In the beginning, Aristophanes says, there were three sexes (not just one, as in the *Timaeus*): once upon a time, the human race was different. The form of a human being was 'a rounded whole, with double back and flanks forming a complete circle; it had four hands and an equal number of legs, and two identically similar faces upon a circular neck, with one head common to both the faces, which were turned in opposite directions. It had four ears and two organs of generation.' And depending on the two sexes with which each human being was equipped, humanity was divided into three species: men, who had two male organs; women, who had two female organs, and hermaphrodites, who had one male and one female organ. One day Zeus decided to punish these beings which had become insufferably arrogant, so he sliced them in two. Thus, Plato writes,

> each of us then is the mere broken tally of a man, the result of a bisection which has reduced us to a condition like that of a flat fish, and each of us is perpetually in search of his corresponding tally. Those men who are halves of a being of the common sex, which was called, as I told you, hermaphrodite, are lovers of women, and most adulterers come from this class, as also do women who are mad about men and sexually promiscuous. Women who are halves of a female whole direct their affections towards women and pay little attention to men; Lesbians belong to this category. But those who are halves of a male whole pursue males, and being slices, so to speak, of the male, love men throughout their boyhood, and take pleasure in physical contact with men. Such boys and lads are the best of their generation, because they are the most manly. Some people say that they are shameless, but they are wrong. It is not shamelessness which inspires their behaviour, but high spirit and manliness and virility, which lead them to welcome the society of their own kind. A striking proof of this is that such boys alone, when they reach maturity, engage in public life. When they grow to be men, they become lovers of boys, and it requires the compulsion of convention to overcome their natural disinclination to marriage and procreation; they are quite content to live with one another unwed.[28]

Men who love other men, therefore, are the best: descendants of an entirely manly being, and loving what resembles themselves, they are superior to those who, descended from a hermaphrodite, love people of the other sex. A word of warning, though – this argument does not hold good for all homosexuals, only for males. Dealing with women who love other women (and who, speaking impartially, should likewise be considered the best of their sex), Plato carefully refrains from giving a similar endorsement. But we shall return to this point. What is interesting for the moment is the rationalisation and theorisation, through myth, of the superiority of love between men over heterosexual love. This is the first attempt of its kind in Greek history, as far as we know, and certainly the most famous. Equally certainly, it is only one of many attempts which, over time, used a variety of arguments to bolster up a thesis which, far from being the fruit of Plato's misogyny, obviously reflected the deeply rooted convictions of many Greeks.

Before moving on to these later theories we must glance at some passages in Plato which have sometimes led people to argue that Plato, although himself homosexual (indeed, according to some scholars, precisely because he was exclusively homosexual), was still opposed to sexual relations between men.[29]

The first of these passages comes from *Phaedrus*. A man who loves a boy, says Lysias, constantly pesters his loved one, trying to stick close to him all the time and make physical contact; whereas the love object, faced with these manifestations of love, feels nothing but disgust.[30] However, as we know, when you take a passage out of its context you can make it say something very different from what it really says, and that is what has happened here. In the course of the dialogue, Lysias paradoxically has been trying to prove that a boy does much better to yield to somebody who does not love him, than to somebody who does. A man who is not in love, he argues, makes a better lover: he cannot reproach his beloved that he has neglected his business or family for him, and in particular he is not more attracted to his body than his spirit, as happens with those in the grip of Eros.[31] That is why, if the boy yields to somebody who is in love with him, the boy experiences disgust.

In this context (less paradoxical for Plato than for us: what emerges from the speech of Lysias, in the last analysis, is once again the need to control one's passions), the extract loses its negative connotations, and would be hard to interpret as a blanket condemnation of sex between men. Similarly, on mature consideration, no condemnation of homosexuality in itself emerges from the passages from the *Laws* and the *Republic* which are also cited in this connection.

In the first book of the *Laws*, Plato distinguishes relations between man and woman, defined as *kata physin* (according to nature) from homosexual relations, defined as *para physin* (against nature).[32] But a closer reading immediately reveals that, in Plato's opinion, 'according to nature' and 'against nature' meant something quite different from their modern meaning.

What Plato actually says is that 'when a man is united with a woman "for procreation", the pleasure which he feels is "according to nature"'. In other words, the pleasure experienced with people of the other sex is not always such; in Plato's opinion, any relationship (whether homosexual or heterosexual) is 'against nature' if it is not directed towards procreation.

As correctly observed by Paul Veyne, 'it is not enough simply to find the expression "against nature" in the texts. One has to understand what it meant to antiquity.' And if we make this effort, we can see that 'when an ancient says that something is not natural, he does not mean that it is disgraceful, but that it does not conform with the rules of society, or that it is perverted or artificial'.[33]

This is the background against which we should interpret Plato's statement that homosexuality is 'against nature'. For his ideal city, he wishes to prescribe those laws most likely to combat soft living and yielding to the impulses, against which he personally struggles. He condemns pederasty, banning it completely from a world which is not the world in which he himself lives, but the one to which he aspires, with all his personal contradictions. Plato's objective is not the direction of amorous passions to their correct nature – allowing only the love of women – but the suppression of all passion, with only reproductive sexuality being countenanced. In this perspective, his purpose now becomes clear, even where he writes that just as an unwritten law prohibits sex between parents and children, there should also be a law forbidding homosexuality, to avoid 'sowing seed on rocks and stones where it can never take root and have fruitful increase'.[34] As well as banning unions between males, Plato argues that the law should oblige men to keep away 'from every female field in which you would not desire the seed to spring up' (meaning relations with other men's women and with prostitutes).

Allowable sexual relations, then, can only mean heterosexual intercourse designed for procreation, already defined as 'according to nature': and the law which would impose this rule, Plato says, would have the advantage, among other things, of teaching husbands to love their wives more.[35] An advantage, by the way, which Plato would not at all have wished for himself, given that, as Veyne observes, 'it does not seem to have crossed his mind that one could be in love with a woman'.[36]

Lastly we may look at another law which Plato proposes for his ideal city, and which has also been quoted as proof of the philosopher's objection to sexual relations between men: the law by which anyone committing sexual violence should be put to death. Once again – leaving aside the consideration that it is one thing to condemn violence and quite another to condemn relations between consenting persons – one cannot avoid observing that even in this case Plato is not particularly concerned with homosexual relations. According to the text of his law, in fact, the only people to be punished are those committing violence to a free woman or a *pais*, without distinction.[37]

Plato's aim in dictating the laws for his utopian city is not specifically to outlaw homosexuality, but by banning homosexuality to establish control over all Eros, confining it purely to relations designed for reproduction. And I believe that this interpretation of authorial intentions (the encouragement of reproductive sexuality) is equally valid for other works dating from more or less the same period, starting with Xenophon's *Symposium*.

Xenophon

In the *Symposium* of Xenophon we read that a boy can only receive dishonour and shame from a sexual relationship with an adult, even in cases where he is not prostituting himself,[38] and that 'a youth does not share in the pleasure of the intercourse as a woman does, but looks on, sober, at another in love's intoxication. Consequently, it need not excite any surprise if contempt for the lover is engendered in him.'[39]

Unlike the similar speech by Lysias in the *Phaedrus*, the one we read in Xenophon does not form part of a paradox: the context in which it is delivered is an exaltation of marriage. But in order fully to understand Xenophon's beliefs it is necessary to remember why he wrote his work which, significantly, shares a title with Plato's most famous dialogue.

Dating from a few years after Plato's work of the same name, Xenophon's *Symposium* was written with the precise aim of opposing Plato's theories and offering the Athenians – in contrast with the exaltation of the love of boys – the advantages of union with women (just so long as that union was a marital one).[40] For Xenophon, marriage was a central concern to which he deliberately devoted a large part of another book which is indispensable in clarifying his viewpoint on sexuality. This work is the *Oeconomicus*, where Xenophon sets out to indicate the precepts for a well-run *oikos* or household, the institution which marriage was planned and organised to reproduce. Consequently, he explains what, in his view, should be the rules of a good marital relationship.

Replying to Socrates' questions, Ischomachus tells how he has organised his relationship with his wife, educating her so that, although she was a young bride of only fourteen, she could learn to be as he wished her to be, and as it was proper for her to be. 'How can I possibly help you? What power have I?', his wife had asked. And Ischomachus had replied: 'Why . . . of course you must try to do as well as possible what the gods made you capable of doing and the law sanctions.' There is quite a list: 'since both the indoor and the outdoor

63

tasks demand labour and attention, God from the first adapted the woman's nature, I think, to the indoor and man's to the outdoor tasks and cares.' In particular, women have to have babies, look after the running and the assets of the household, and nurse sick slaves.[41] As he was not at all misogynistic, and shared Socrates' idea that women shared some capabilities in common with men,[42] Xenophon assigned women a role which was anything but trivial for a Greek. Unlike others, he did not believe that they were useful only for reproduction: their contribution to the performance of domestic tasks was indispensable to good 'economics' (meaning the regulated life of the *oikos*).

But having said that, it should also be pointed out that he judged the female sex (albeit with a certain consideration) only within this perspective: the same perspective which inspires the *Symposium*, in which he explains his views on pederasty – views which must be evaluated within this perspective if we are to understand them correctly. I believe that this perspective provides a clearer idea of the terms in which the Athenians, when they began to think about it, posed the problem of comparing love for men and love for women. Even when they condemned it, like Xenophon, they did not draw a contrast between the pederastic relationship and the relationship with women, as such; the real contrast, for them, was between homosexuality and marriage. It was not a sudden and inexplicable discovery of the superior charms of women that induced the Athenians (or at least some of them) at a certain point to come out against pederasty. Rather, they were motivated by a social problem.

Robinson and Fluck correctly observe, in their study of love inscriptions (dealing with pederastic love) on Attic vases, that these writings disappear at the same time as the Peloponnesian war.[43] This was the same time in which Xenophon was writing, and Aristophanes, in the theatre, was aiming the shafts of his irony at homosexuals, pointing them out as the cause of the ills of Athens. And they had their reasons: these were the years when, as Thucydides says,[44] the morality of the city had undergone an absolute upheaval. The ancient discipline had been forgotten; pederasty had degenerated into vice, and the corrupt love of young men was exacerbated by the ever-increasing habit of protracting homosexual relations beyond the proper age limit, so much so that, according to Aristophanes, all Athenians were now *katapygones*. This factor – already more than enough in itself to induce a hostile reaction against a form of sexual behaviour which, detached from the ethical context in which it had formerly operated, caused a negative reaction among at least part of the population – was now joined by another factor, anything but negligible, which induced praise of the state of marriage. The Peloponnesian war had decimated the city's youth: it was vitally important for Athens that new families should be set up, and that they should produce many sons for the fatherland. Hence, perhaps, the newfound interest in women, also evident in painting and sculpture, which at this time present images of women which are more sensual and, in particular, less androgynous.[45] Hence, too, Plato's forward-looking blueprint of a city where sex (quite against the personal desires of the philosopher) would be limited exclusively to marital intercourse for reasons of social utility. This is the historical, social and cultural context in which we must interpret the attitudes and ideas of Aristotle.

Aristotle

As with Socrates and Plato, the fact that tradition also attributes male love affairs to Aristotle – who had not only a wife, Arimnestes, but also a mistress, Herphyllis (or Phyllis) – is not particularly significant. In fact, it would have been much more strange had there not been such a tradition. The stories tell in particular of his love for a male pupil whose name we do not know, coming from the Lycian city of Phaselis.[46] Once again, this is not the point. Even accepting – and I would say one must accept – that Aristotle, like all Greeks, fell in love with boys, what is interesting for our purposes is to note his moral, political and social evaluation of homosexuality. At least in the *Politics*, this is an attitude of condemnation. But to understand the meaning and scope of this condemnation one has to place it in the context of Aristotle's theory of marriage, and what he has to say about women.

Aristotle dealt with women, obviously, in relation to the question of reproduction. This was a problem which Greek thinkers before him had already tackled, placing it in highly significant terms: is a child born only from its father or also from its mother? The obvious fact that people are born from their mothers' bodies was completely ignored, at least by some writers. In the view of Hippias, and more generally for the Stoics, a child was born solely from its father. Anaxagoras, on the other hand, like Alcmeon, Parmenides, Empedocles, Democritus, Epicurus and the physician Hippocrates, held that the child was also born from its mother.[47]

But the theory which assigned a decisive role to mothers as well as fathers clearly did not meet with the approval of public opinion. In the *Oresteia*, presented in 458 BC, Aeschylus brings this topic before his audience, staging the story of Orestes, who has killed his mother to avenge his father, whom the mother has killed. Before the court which must judge him, Orestes is defended by Apollo. It is true, says the god, that Orestes killed his mother. But 'the mother of what is called her child is not its parent, but only the nurse of the newly implanted germ. The begetter is the parent, whereas she, as a stranger for a stranger, doth but preserve the sprout, except God shall blight its birth'.[48] This is the defence of Orestes, and after listening to it, the tribunal, with a casting vote from Athena, the goddess born from the head of Zeus, acquits the matricide, accepting Apollo's arguments. Aeschylus, and presumably his audience, did not believe that the mother's contribution to reproduction was decisive. This hypothesis was confirmed on a scientific level by Aristotle, who placed it in the context of a complex explanation of the reproductive process which, while recognising that the mother played a part, confined the woman in a subordinate position on both the biological and the social planes.

Aristotle explains that menstrual blood (*katamēnia*) works together with male sperm to form the embryo. However, the sperm (which also derives from blood) is a more fully processed type of blood than the female variety. Like all blood, it derives from food which, when it is not expelled, is transformed by body heat. But the woman is less hot than the man, and therefore is incapable of effecting the final transformation, which gives rise to sperm. It is the male seed, therefore, which, in the reproductive process, cooks the female blood and transforms it into a new being; which means that sperm plays an active part whereas the menstrual blood has a purely passive role. Although it is indispensable, the female contribution is that of matter, with which the woman is identified, whereas the male contribution, given that men are all form and spirit, is of an active type.[49] This biological construction inevitably led to the theory – destined to last throughout the centuries – of the inferiority and necessary subordination of women.

The *oikos*, the central element in Aristotle's political design, can only be commanded by a man: the male is 'by nature better fitted to command than the female (except in some cases where their union has been formed contrary to nature)'.[50] Only he, therefore, has the right to participate in running the *polis* and commanding children, wives and slaves. The slave, for his part, 'has not got the deliberative part at all, and the female has it, but without full authority, while the child has it, but in an undeveloped form'.[51]

In this framework, the conclusions on the family role of the woman are inevitable: it is part of household science for the man to rule like a statesman (*politikos*) over the woman, exercising a kind of 'republican government',[52] but with one special feature: whereas the authority of a statesman involves an alternation of authority between different citizens, in the power relationship between man and woman there can be no interchange: 'As between the sexes, the male is by nature superior and the female inferior, the male ruler and the female subject. And the same must also necessarily apply in the case of mankind as a whole.'[53] Nor is this all: the woman must be controlled not only by her husband but also by the state. Equipped with diminished and imperfect reasoning powers, incapable of controlling her lustful feelings, she is in fact highly dangerous if left to herself:

> Freedom in regard to women is detrimental both in regard to the purpose of the constitution and to the happiness of the state. For just as man and wife are part of a household, it is clear that the state also is divided nearly in half into its male and female population, so that in all constitutions in which the position of the woman is badly regulated one half of the state must be deemed to have been neglected in framing the law. And this has taken place in [Sparta], for the lawgiver wishing the whole city to be of strong character displays his intention clearly in relation to the men, but in the case of the women has entirely neglected the matter; for they live without restraint in respect of every sort of dissoluteness, and luxuriously.[54]

Here, then, is what Aristotle thought of women, and the role that he assigned to them. This adds a special irony (if I might be permitted a brief aside) to the venerable iconographic tradition which represents the great philosopher down on the ground, on all fours, being ridden by a woman. That image actually depicts a much later legend, which made its appearance during the first half of the thirteenth century, in a sermon by Jacques de Vitry.

Aristotle, we read in the sermon, one day reproached Alexander of Macedon, his pupil, with neglecting the affairs of state for his wife. Alexander's wife was determined to be avenged on Aristotle. After inveigling the philosopher to fall in love with her, she promised to grant him certain favours if he allowed her to ride upon his back first; and Aristotle agreed to this. As the lady had in the meantime informed her husband of what was about to happen, the pupil, unseen, witnessed the humiliation of his master.[55]

Taken up a few years later by Henri d'Andeli (in whose version Alexander found himself by chance witnessing the scene of Aristotle's mistress Phyllis riding on his back), the anecdote became a very popular iconographic theme; and poor Aristotle – such are the ironies of fate! – has been depicted through the centuries ridden by one of those creatures whose inferiority he had set out with such conviction to demonstrate.[56]

After this parenthesis, we may return to our problem: how to set Aristotle's opinions on homosexuality within his political design, where, as we saw, marriage occupied a central position. In this light, his infrequent stated positions on the problem of homosexuality take on an absolutely rigorous logic.

Not being conducive to the reproduction of *oikoi*, homosexuality in Aristotle's view was contrasted with matrimony as a form of waste which was not only useless but even dangerous.[57] That does not mean that it must necessarily be condemned always and everywhere. The philosopher's judgement on relations between men (given that these are his only focus of interest) derives from the circumstances in which they are practised. In Crete, for example, he observes, there was a serious problem of overpopulation, and homosexuality was therefore wide-spread, so that women would not have too many children.[58]

So in some circumstances Aristotle thought that relations between men were not only free from opprobrium but socially useful. If he takes a different line when referring to Athens, the reason should be sought in the different situation and the different needs of this city. His criticisms of relationships between men are a consequence of the political per-spective that informs some of his works. Where the perspective changes to a moral one judgement is suspended, and depends on considerations about why a homosexual choice is made.

Aristotle, in fact, believes that a distinction must be drawn between different types of people who have relations with persons of the same sex. In the *Nicomachean Ethics*, when he asks why people may be homosexual, he observes that 'some people devote themselves to this practice by nature, others by habit, such as for example those who have been sexually abused from their childhood years'.[59] In these two cases, the judgement is different.

As a habit, sexual relations between men should be avoided. In the *Historia animalium* we read that about the age of fourteen, when they reach puberty and begin to feel sexual impulses, young people need to be controlled: 'Girls who abandon themselves to pleasures when they are still very young become ever more lascivious, and the same is true of boys. . . . This happens because on the one hand the passages are dilated, facilitating bodily secretions along these paths, and on the other hand because the memory of pleasure experienced brings forth the desire to renew the connection which accompanied this pleasure.'[60]

The reference to 'passages being dilated' (which seems rather obscure to our eyes) becomes clear when one thinks about what Aristotle writes on the path followed by the seed within the male body. In the *Quaestiones* he asks why some men should feel pleasure in carrying out an active sexual role, while others do not.[61] And here is the answer: as a rule,

> the seed is deposited in the testicles and in the 'shameful parts' [*aidoia*], just as urine is deposited in the vescicle, food in the stomach, tears in the eyes, mucus in the nostrils, and blood in the veins. However, there are some men in whom the passages leading to the testicles are not in a natural condition, either because they are blocked (as happens with eunuchs and other impotent folk), or for some other reason. And then it happens that the seed runs in its place [*edra*], as shown by the contraction of this part of the body during the sexual act, and the liquid condition of the parts surrounding it. If a man engages excessively in intercourse, then, the seed is collected in that area, and when he feels desire, the part where seed has collected wishes to be stroked.[62]

The first observation to be made, with reference to this theory, is that it is not put forward to explain homosexuality in itself, but only passive homosexuality. What requires an explanation is not the fact that a man feels pleasure in having intercourse with other men, but only that he can experience this pleasure in a subordinate position. If he assumes the dominant role, obviously, his pleasure is completely normal. The second observation is that it is anomalous for a man to derive pleasure from passivity; but if it is congenital, then this anomaly is natural. Those who are homosexual by nature are judged differently from those who are homosexual by habit. Undoubtedly, homosexuality is in any case an unhealthy tendency: in the *Nicomachean Ethics*, where he speaks of 'bestial' and 'morbid' dispositions, Aristotle explains that an example of a bestial disposition of the mind is a female reputed to have 'ripped open the bellies of pregnant women and devoured their unborn children'. And then he adds that there are morbid dispositions, on the other hand, 'which derive from nature or from human customs: for example, tearing one's hair, biting one's nails, or nibbling charcoal or earth; another example is the practice of homosexual love between males.'[63]

Really, if it is comparable to tearing one's hair or biting one's nails, homosexuality does not appear to be a particularly worrying 'disposition'. And sometimes it is not even to be condemned: in the *Nicomachean Ethics*, again, we read that those who love other men 'by nature' (*physei*) are not immoral.

Plutarch

In Aristotle references to homosexuality are sporadic, incidental, placed like asides within discussions aimed at tackling and resolving other, different problems. This does not necessarily mean, of course, that Aristotle undervalued the topic: we know that he wrote a treatise, now lost, on love, where it is not unreasonable to suppose that he gave a fuller account of his views in this area. The theme of love continued to fascinate his pupils (Theophrastus, Ariston of Ceos, Hieronymus of Rhodes and Heraclides of Ponticus), the echo of whose opinions – their original treatises have been lost – has fortunately been preserved in a work which has come down to us almost in its entirety. This work, expressly dedicated to a discussion of the problem of homosexuality, is Plutarch's dialogue entitled *Amatorius*.

Written at an uncertain date, but certainly after AD 96 (during the course of the work Plutarch alludes to the end of the Flavian dynasty, which was extinguished in the year 96 with the death of Domitian),[64] the *Amatorius* is a dialogue which takes its pretext from a journey made by Plutarch and his wife to Thespiae, to sacrifice to Eros.

When Plutarch came to Thespiae, a group of friends was furiously arguing over an event which had split public opinion, giving rise to heated arguments: young Bacchon wanted to marry the widow Ismenodora. In itself, this would not have been too shocking, if there had not been a complication: Bacchon was the *erōmenos* of Pisias, who was obviously violently opposed to the marriage. And so the argument spread among their friends, moving beyond the concrete case in question to touch on the more general problem: is it better to love men or women?

'Why of course,' says Protogenes, speaking up for his friend Pisias, 'since [marital union] is necessary for producing children, there's no harm in legislators talking it up and singing its praises to the masses. But genuine Love has no connection whatsoever with the women's quarters. I deny that it is love that you have felt for women and girls – any more than flies feel love for milk or bees for honey or than caterers and cooks have tender emotions for the calves and fowls they fatten in the dark.'[65] No, that feeling for women is not love. Love 'attaches himself to a young and talented soul and through friendship [*philia*] brings it to a state of virtue; but the appetite for women we are speaking of, however well it turns out, has for net gain only an accrual of pleasure in the enjoyment of a ripe physical beauty. To this Aristippus bore witness when he replied to the man who denounced Laïs to him for not loving him: He didn't imagine, he said, that wine or fish loved him either, yet he partook of both with pleasure.'[66]

Daphnaeus intervenes in defence of the love of women:

If, then, Protogenes, we have regard for the truth, excitement about boys and women is one and the same thing: Love. But if, for the sake of argument, you choose to make distinctions, you will see that this boy-love of yours is not playing fair: like a late-born son, an aged man's bastard, a child of darkness, he tries to disinherit the Love that is his legitimate and elder brother. It was only yesterday, my friend, or the day before, in consequence of young men's stripping their bodies naked, that he crept furtively into the gymnasia. . . . He rails against and vilifies that great conjugal Love, which co-operates to win immortality for the human race. . . .[67]

The defence of the love of women takes place, as is immediately obvious, on a different terrain from the one where the supporters of homosexual love find arguments in favour of their choice. The fundamental point in favour of women is their biological utility. As previously in the writings of Xenophon, the love of women is taken into consideration only if it is within a marital context. Non-procreative heterosexual love, the love for a woman as a woman, in short, is not even envisaged – which is extremely informative, once more, about the notion that the Greeks had of man-woman relationships, even when, like Xenophon or Daphnaeus, they belonged to the party which maintained the superiority of heterosexual love. But something different appears when Plutarch himself speaks at the end of the dialogue.

During the course of the dialogue Plutarch had already made some contributions, relating, among other things, a series of episodes which proved that love between men inspired warlike virtues. 'You know, of course, the story of Cleomachus of Pharsalia?', he asked. Receiving a negative response from his friends, he told the story. Cleomachus was fighting beside the Chalcidians against the Eretrians, and was asked by the Chalcidians to lead the attack on the enemy's horsemen. Cleomachus then asked his young boyfriend if he was going to watch the battle, and having heard that he would, he launched himself into the attack, scattering the enemy cavalry before being killed. The Chalcidians, who up to that moment had reproved pederasty, now decided to practise it and honour it more than any other people. And they composed a song: 'Ye lads of grace and sprung from worthy stock, Grudge not to brave men converse with your beauty: In cities of Chalcis, Love, looser of limbs, Thrives side by side with courage.'[68]

So far there is nothing new in Plutarch's words. The novelty arises at the end of the dialogue, when he begins to speak of the love of women. Unlike Daphnaeus, he introduces a distinction between one woman and another. Just as the most virtuous among boys love each other, he says, thus one falls in love with the best of women. In his opinion, heterosexuality is not just a choice of gender attributable to functional reasons, but an individual choice, the expression of a feeling inspired by a particular person, quite independently of the gender to which that person belongs. Nor is this all: living together, he observes, over time introduces reciprocal affection in the constriction (*ananke*) of the marital link, leading to virtue: fidelity, at this point, is no longer attributable to fear of legal sanctions, but to self-control which, inspired by love, induces the spouse to eschew other lovers.[69]

These are the undeniable elements of innovation in Plutarch's speech. Beyond these, however, one point seems fundamental: his thesis of the superiority of love for women (always, of course, within marriage) does not imply any condemnation of homosexuality. After having Daphnaeus say that love for women and for men proceed from one and the same principle (which amounts to saying that neither choice is 'against nature') Plutarch explains how we happen to fall in love:

> The causes that they give for the generation of love are peculiar to neither sex and common to both. For is it really the case that visual shapes emanating from boys can, but the same from women cannot, enter the body of the lover where, coursing through him, they stimulate and tickle the whole mass and, by gliding along with the other configurations of atoms, produce seed?[70]

Leaving aside the observation, by no means unimportant, that the love of which Plutarch identifies the causes is exclusively that felt by men (as they are the ones who produce sperm), how can we avoid seeing in his words, beyond the explicit declaration of the naturalness of love for boys, the need to convince his hearers – and perhaps himself – that women *too*, as well as men, can cause one to fall in love?

It is no surprise, then, that in his life of Pelopidas, he praises the virtue of the sacred battalion of Thebans, made up of 150 couples of lovers. These remained undefeated until the battle of Chaeroneia, where they died heroically, each beside his lover, to prove to the lover that he had deserved his love.[71] Exactly as in the *Amatorius*, where he speaks of Cleomachus, he reveals here – apart from his novel ideas about relations with women, and his conviction that getting married was not only convenient, but morally formative – that the noblest love, for him, was love between men. This was the love which had always been considered the only sentiment capable of spurring man on to valour and the practice of those virtues which, for the Greeks, held the highest place in the hierarchy of values: the public virtues. By comparison with these, the private virtues induced by marriage were pretty negligible.

The *Greek Anthology*, Achilles Tatius and Pseudo-Lucian

The comparison of the merits of *paides* and women became something of a fashionable literary topic – and what is more, the comparison gave the advantage to the *paides*. In the *Greek Anthology*, where the topic appears several times, here is the position taken up by Strato – not really a very romantic one:

> In a maid there is no question of a real sphincter nor a simple kiss, no natural nice smell of the skin, nor of that sweet sexy talk or limpid look. Besides, when she's being taught she's worse. And they're all cold behind; but a greater nuisance is this – there's no place where you can put your wandering hand.[72]

It must be said, to be fair, that there are comparisons, albeit less frequent, where the female sex comes out best. Again in the *Greek Anthology*, Eratosthenes Scholasticus is a convinced supporter of the superiority of loving women:

> Let males be for others. I can love but women, whose charms are more enduring. There is no beauty in youths at the age of puberty; I hate the unkind hair that begins to grow too soon.

Eratosthenes[73] praises the longer duration of relationships with women, an argument which we have already seen developed in Plutarch's *Amatorius* although in a completely different perspective. For Plutarch, this has a moral character: shared life with a woman leads to affection and thus to virtue. In Eratosthenes, the same advantage is an erotic one: *paides* as love objects are perishable; their beauty disappears with the emergence of those horrifying hairs. Eratosthenes's opinion is shared (although no reason is given) by Agathias Scholasticus:

> May Aphrodite herself and the darling Loves melt my empty heart for hate of me, if I ever am inclined to love males. May I never make such conquests or fall into the graver sin. It is enough to sin with women. This I will indulge in, but leave young men to foolish Pittalacus.[74]

In another literary work the topic reappears incidentally. This is a romance of uncertain date, but definitely from the second century: *Leucippe and Clitophon* by Achilles Tatius.[75] Here there is no victory, either for the *paides* or for the women. The arguments in favour of both sides are balanced, and the discussion, conducted in what might be called a worldly-wise spirit and tone, ends without winners or losers. But the *paides* score a victory, once again (against the minority opinion represented by Xenophon and Plutarch) in a comparison carried out in another work explicitly dedicated, like Plutarch's *Amatorius*, to this question: the dialogue entitled *Amores* by pseudo-Lucian of Samosata, written not before the last quarter of the third century AD.[76] The protagonists in this dialogue are Licinus and Theomnestus, a young man noted for his passionate character and for his many bisexual adventures. Asked by Licinus to tell of his loves, Theomnestus replies by asking a question of his own to his friend: given that I, who love both women and *paides*, am not a good judge, could you tell me, as an impartial referee, which of the two types of love is better?

Licinus' reply comes at the end of a long narrative. He starts by saying how one day, during a journey, he met two people who had a very different attitude to that of Theomnestus. Each of them loved only one sex, and kept away from affairs with the other. Caricles of Corinth loved women; Callicratidas of Athens loved only *paides*, and detested women. Having witnessed a clash between the two on this subject, Licinus believes it would be helpful, before giving his own opinion, to report their arguments. And he does so, starting with those of Caricles.[77]

To support the superiority of love for women, Caricles starts out from the creation of the universe. What had been created, he says, was intended to survive the death of individuals, who were divided for this purpose into two sexes (the men who carried the seed, and the women who received it) reciprocally attracted by nature. It is against nature that women (*thēlu*) should become masculine and that men should become 'soft' (*malakizesthai*). However, with the passage of time, this is exactly what happened: the same sex entered the same bed.[78] And by scattering their seed on the rocks, men have paid a very high price for a little pleasure: they risk extinction on account of their degeneracy. Animals, on the other hand, have respect for the laws of nature: lions couple with lionesses, bulls with cows, male wolves with female wolves.

This is the first argument put up by Caricles, and it is supplemented by a second argument of a moral kind: men who love other men do so because they are attracted, in the first place, by physical beauty. Alcibiades is irrefutable proof of this. After being loved by everybody in his youth, on account of his beauty, he was hated by all as an old man. And then one has to consider the advantages offered by women. The love they inspire in the first place is longer lasting. A woman is beautiful even after the first flower of her youth, up to middle age (*mesē hēlikia*) and only ceases to be desirable when, in old age, she is devastated by wrinkles. Does not the poet say that the voice of experience is sweeter than the babblings of youth?[79]

Things are different with men. After the age of twenty they become ugly: they develop large masculine flanks, rough cheeks and thighs covered in hair.[80] This being so, why not look for reciprocal pleasure, which can only be offered by women, as they are capable of deriving from sexual relations a pleasure equal to that felt by men (if not indeed greater, as Tiresias says)?[81] The *paides*, on the other hand, experience no pleasure: indeed, in the beginning, all they receive from intercourse with a man is pain and tears. Later, when they have got used to it, they manage to suffer less. But *paides* never feel true pleasure. Finally, women present a further advantage: they can be used like a man, whereas men, obviously, cannot provide what women have to offer.[82]

So far, these are arguments which we already know, having found them in Xenophon, Plutarch or the poets of the *Greek Anthology*. Basically, Caricles is merely repeating what were obviously the regular arguments in any discussion of this topic, with a single exception. At the end of his defence of heterosexual love he introduces a completely new point. If men find it acceptable to make love to each other, why should women not be allowed to do the same thing?[83] This innovation is by no means trifling: although Caricles considers love between women a monstrous thing (in keeping with his idea that all relations between people of the same sex are unnatural), nevertheless his speech presents, for the first time, the idea that female homosexuality is not terribly different from the male variety: and that, for a Greek, is absolutely revolutionary.

But it would be quite inappropriate to imagine that Caricles supports a policy of equality for the sexes: on closer inspection, he too believes that women are nothing but instruments of pleasure. How could one otherwise explain the strange contradiction into which he falls when, after having condemned male homosexuality because it denies the passive partner's right to pleasure, he affirms that women have the advantage of being able to be used like men? The altruism and respect for the beloved which inspired his ethics when he spoke about boys suddenly disappears when he moves on to speak of women. What was an outrage (*hybris*) against a boy becomes merely an extra option with a woman, something which makes her more desirable.

When Caricles' speech comes to an end, Callicratidas gets a chance to defend his cause.[84] Love for men, says the Athenian, is the only one which allows pleasure and virtue to be brought together. Not a terribly original line, to tell the truth. His next argument, however, is indeed quite original: marriage, he says, is a remedy (*pharmaka*) invented to ensure the continuity of the species. But something which is done out of pure necessity is inferior to something which has an aesthetic value – such as, to take an example, making love to boys. At the beginning of history, man was constrained by necessity to obtain food in order to live. He therefore fed on roots and berries. But as time went on he discovered how to sow oats and barley, and only animals went on feeding on roots and berries. Would anyone be crazy enough to believe that animals are superior to men because of this?[85] So why do we not apply the same standard in judging love? Loving women was a primitive necessity. Loving men was a conquest of divine philosophy.[86]

It must be said that Callicratidas has brilliantly overcome the usual argument about naturalness. Not being able to deny it, he turns it to his own advantage, in the context of a speech aimed at proving the superiority of culture over nature. He therefore dismisses the argument that animals are heterosexual. It stands to reason, he says, that if Prometheus or somebody else had given animals a mind (*noun*), they would not live up in the mountains, eating each other, but instead would have built temples to the gods, and learned to be homosexual. Loving women, basically, is primitive and violent, like everything else that is linked to the necessities of life. Loving boys, on the other hand, marked the beginning of the prehistoric Ogygian age and inspired a temperate form of love (*dianoia*) which made it possible to combine pleasure and virtue.[87] This does not mean, however, that the love of women ought to be outlawed; as it is necessary, it cannot be eliminated. But women must serve only to produce children. Anyway, do they deserve anything else?[88]

At this point, Callicratidas launches into a ferocious invective against the female sex. If you see a woman who has just woken up, he says, you would think that she is uglier than one of those animals which it is bad luck to name during the morning time.[89] That is why they stay shut up in their houses, do not allow men to see them, and spend their time putting on make-up, perfume, and expensive clothes and jewellery. In contrast, boys are truly beautiful and spend their time in noble pursuits, cultivating their bodies and their minds. Consequently, the love which they inspire conforms to divine laws (*theiois nomois*).[90] Thus ends the discourse of Callicratidas the Athenian: with an invective of such virulent misogyny that it is striking even in the context of a literature like that of Greece, in which contempt for women is an absolute leitmotiv.[91] Licinus then draws the threads together. Having considered all the arguments that I have heard being put forward, he says, I incline to the view that marriage is in fact necessary, and that all men must get married. But at the same time, I think they must be allowed to make love to boys, thus cultivating the better part of themselves.[92]

This is the end of the dialogue, the final passage being devoted to the concluding comments of Theomnestus. He is happy with the solution, but worried by one detail. What has been said wins my agreement, he says, but on one condition: loving boys should not become some sort of Tantalus torture. Boys must not be simply admired and loved from afar, spiritually, without thinking of physical pleasure (which, in any case, they share). Nobody has ever loved boys in this ascetic way. Do you really believe that Alcibiades, after spending the night under Socrates' mantle, got up in the morning without having undergone any assault (*aplēx*)?[93] Or do you perhaps believe that Achilles and Patroclus confined themselves to loving each other, 'sitting opposite each other'? No: pleasure (*hēdonē*) was the mediator of their love (*philia*).

What conclusions may we draw when faced with the detailed and complex picture of the feelings, the social and legal rules, and finally the political and theoretical reflections of the Greeks on the subject of homosexuality? Despite the quantity of sources examined and information gathered, I believe it would be hazardous to attempt a final assessment without having analysed, as far as we can, another by no means unimportant aspect of the problem – the extent and role of homosexuality in the life of women.

4

Women and Homosexuality

Love Between Women

Love in the thiasoi: Sappho, Alcman's Partheneion and fer·nle initiation

Although the present discussion of homosexuality set out from evidence of love between women, we then shifted our attention to the long-drawn-out and much more visible history of love between men. There was good reason for this. Unlike pederasty (the most important manifestation of Greek homosexuality), love between women, as it did not serve as an instrument to form the citizen, was of no interest to the city. Consequently it found no space in the reflections of philosophers and even less in the laws which, as we saw, intervened in this area of sexual life only to prevent a culturally important feature such as pederasty from degenerating into trivial love affairs, and to punish those adult males who, in breaking the rules, not only continued to behave 'like women', but did so in pursuit of easy money. And love between women, which in this perspective was perfectly irrelevant, remained something of which only women continued to speak. Thus, sadly, we know little or nothing of how they experienced it, what space it occupied in their lives, what effects it had on their emotional life and its consequences on their attitude to men. Everything we know about female homosexuality (apart from what men say about it) comes, in fact, from Sappho.

Daughter of Scamandronymus and Cleis, Sappho was born in Mytilene, in the island of Lesbos, about 612 BC.[1] From an aristocratic family (we know that her brother was a cup-bearer in the town hall of Mytilene), Sappho was married to a man called Cercylas, to whom she bore a daughter named Cleis. In Mytilene, where she spent a great part of her life (between 604 and 595 she lived in Sicily), Sappho was at the head of one of those associations of young women called *thiasoi*, on the nature and function of which we must dwell in order to understand the conditions under which the loves of Sappho were born and, as we shall see, were inevitably destined to end.

The *thiasoi* were communities of women, the existence of which is documented not only in Lesbos where, as well as Sappho's *thiasos* there were also the *thiasoi* of her rivals Gorgo and Andromeda, but also in other areas of Greece, especially in Sparta.[2] What sort of communities were these? They were not simply 'finishing-schools for young ladies', as some definitions have suggested, where purely spiritual loves flourished between the girls.[3] The *thiasoi* were something different and more complex.[4] They were groups with their own divinities and ceremonies, where girls, before marriage, went through a global experience of life which – leaving aside the differences attributable to differences of gender – was in some way analogous to the experience of life that men had in corresponding masculine groups.[5] And the girls received an education within this community life. With reference to Lesbos, in particular, the *Suda* names three *mathētriai*, meaning three 'pupils' of Sappho, who was called *didaskalos*, or 'schoolmistress'.[6]

What did Sappho teach her pupils? First of all music, singing and dancing: the instruments which transformed them from uncultivated little girls, which is what they were when they came to her, into women whose memory might live:

> But when you die you will lie there, and afterwards there will never be any recollection of you or any longing for you since you have no share in the roses of Pieria; unseen in the house of Hades also, flown from our midst, you will go to and fro among the shadowy corpses.[7]

Sappho writes this to a rival, who has not learned from her those things which would have allowed her to escape from ignorance, and thus from oblivion. But Sappho was not only a mistress of the intellect: her girls also learned from her the weapons of beauty, seduction and fascination: they learned the grace (*charis*) which made them into desirable women. From this point of view, the definition of Sappho's circle as 'a finishing-school for young ladies' is not mistaken. But the description is certainly inadequate: in these 'ladies' clubs' the girls of Lesbos (and of other cities, given that Sappho's pupils included Atthis of Miletus, Gongyla of Colophon, Eunica of Salamina) went through an experience which, in our eyes, was quite unsuitable for 'respectable young ladies' – they loved other women. And they loved them with a passionate love, experienced with exceptional sensibility and ecstasy, as we can see without the slightest hint of doubt in the poems which Sappho, over the years, dedicated to her girlfriends at different times: 'I bid you, Abanthis, take (your lyre?) and sing of Gongyla, while desire once again flies around you, the lovely one – for her dress excited you when you saw it; and I rejoice . . .'. That is her request to one friend.[8]

'The moon has set and the Pleiades; it is midnight, and time goes by, and I lie alone.' Here, on the other hand, is the fruitless wait for love.[9] That love, sadly and inevitably, was destined to end when the beloved girl had to leave the *thiasos*, to be married:

> . . . and honestly I wish I were dead. She was leaving me with many tears and said this: 'Oh what bad luck has been ours, Sappho; truly I leave you against my will.' I replied to her thus: 'Go and fare well and remember me, for you know how we cared for you. If not, why then I want to remind you . . . and the good times we had. You put on many wreaths of violets and roses and [crocuses] together by my side, and round your tender neck you put many woven garlands made from flowers and . . . with much flowery perfume, fit for a queen, you anointed yourself. . . .'[10]

Then, once again, another love affair: 'Love shook my heart like a wind falling on oaks on a mountain.'[11] And another, painful and invincible: 'Once again limb-loosening Love makes me tremble, the bitter-sweet, irresistible creature. . . .'[12]

Love remains her theme in the very celebrated ode cited by the anonymous author of *On the Sublime*, and imitated countless times (among others, by Catullus). It is certainly the most famous poem not only by Sappho but in the whole of Greek lyric poetry: the ode for a friend whom Sappho contemplates while, forgetting her, she speaks with a man, perhaps the one who is to become her husband:

> He seems as fortunate as the gods to me, the man who sits opposite you and listens nearby to your sweet voice and lovely laughter. Truly that sets my heart trembling in my breast. For when I look at you for a moment, then it is no longer possible for me to speak; my tongue has snapped, at once a subtle fire has stolen beneath my flesh, I see nothing with my eyes, my ears hum, sweat pours from me, a trembling seizes me all over, I am greener than grass, and it seems to me that I am little short of dying . . .[13]

Such are the accents of love in Sappho's poetry. If one puts aside all preconceived notions, it is difficult to deny that what we have here is true love, in the fullest sense of the term. The fact that this is true love has recently been highlighted in a very strange perspective by George Devereux, who examines Sappho's attitudes and expressions in a medical and psychoanalytical vein; in fragment 31 Devereux reads the unmistakable symptoms of an 'anxiety attack'.[14]

Sappho, he observes, reveals among other things the following symptoms: abnormal heartbeat and a psycho-physiological inhibition of speech ('For when I look at you for a moment, then it is no longer possible for me to speak; my tongue has snapped'); a sight disturbance, probably of vascular origin, and a roaring in the ears ('I see nothing with my eyes, my ears hum'); trembling and pallor caused by the constriction of the surface capillaries and by a streaming of blood toward the inner organs ('a trembling seizes me all over, I am greener than grass'). In clinical terms, these are the symptoms of an anxiety attack. And having explained all this, his conclusion is as follows: what Sappho felt was true love, but of a rather special kind. It is true, Devereux concedes, that anxiety manifestations can occur in any love-crisis, but he observes that in the Greek sources the crises that provoke anxiety attacks arise from pederastic, and not heterosexual, love. This observation is correct for a simple reason: for the Greeks true love, passion, the cause of anguish and torment, meant homosexual love. But Devereux sees things differently. In his view, what makes the manifestations of homosexual love anxious is the perceived 'abnormality' of the feeling. An abnormality, he adds, which by no means contradicts the hypothesis that Sappho was also a schoolmistress or a cult-leader: one frequently finds cases of women who, precisely because they were homosexual, 'tended to gravitate into professions which brought them in close contact with young girls, whose partial segregation and considerable psycho-sexual immaturity – and therefore incomplete differentiatedness – made them willing participants in lesbian experimentation.'[15] These are the words of Professor Devereux, whose interpretation of Greek female homosexuality does seem to me to reveal certain symptoms: symptoms of the distortions which can result from a refusal to accept in practice (whatever about general statements of principle) the reality of cultural differences, and the consequent evaluation of one aspect of a people's way of life in a framework which alters its meaning and renders its value incomprehensible.

Greek culture in the seventh and sixth centuries BC (the period with which we are concerned) not only accepted as normal the existence of love relationships between women in the life of the *thiasoi*, but formalised these, through the celebration of an initiation-type ceremony, which brought two girls together in an exclusive paired bonding of a marital type.

To clarify the meaning of initiation marriages within the *thiasoi*, and to provide proof of their existence, we have the celebrated parthenion (a song for a chorus of virgins) by Alcman, the 'Louvre parthenion'.[16] Composed in Sparta on commission, this celebrated the recognition by

81

the *thiasos* of a love affair which had now become exclusive between two girls, Agido and Hagesichora; an official union, one might say, which was solemnised by the recitation of a choral song.

Significantly, given that not all directors of *thiasoi* were capable, like Sappho, of composing songs personally, this one was written on commission by Alcman. But what exactly did the song proclaim?

Agido and Hagesichora (who seems to be the leader of the choir) appear in the song unambiguously in the role of a couple whose bond, now an exclusive one, takes away all hope from the girls in the choir, who are aware of the fact that nothing, no present and no temptation, will ever be able to detach Agido from Hagesichora, and persuade her to love another:

> For abundance of purple is not sufficient for protection, nor intricate snake of solid gold, no, nor Lydian headband, pride of dark-eyed girls, nor the hair of Nanno, nor again godlike Areta nor Thylacis and Cleësithera[17]

they sing. And then, turning directly to Agido,

> nor will you go to Aenesimbrota's and say, If only Astaphis were mine, if only Philylla were to look my way and Damareta and lovely Ianthemis; no, Hagesichora guards me.[18]

Agido, therefore, will no longer confide her love affairs to Aenesimbrota (evidently the director of the *thiasos*), and will no longer seek her intervention to obtain the love of one among her many companions: she now loves only Hagesichora, for ever.

Alcman's verses, identified by A. Griffiths as a nuptial song,[19] do in fact celebrate a marriage: but not a heterosexual marriage, as Griffiths thought. As already stated, they are the consecration within the *thiasos* of an initiation ceremony of the type which, as attested by Himerius,[20] were also celebrated in the *thiasos* of Sappho, to which Aristaenetus also refers.[21]

At this point, after noting that love affairs between women emerged in a context of initiation (which is what these 'ladies' clubs' were concerned with), is it reasonable to establish a parallel with male homosexuality?

Recently, Bernard Sergent has highlighted a set of features which are shared by female and male initiation procedures. Just as boys spent a period of segregation far from the inhabited community, learning the arts of hunting and war, so also the girls congregated at the edges of cities, in border zones: at Karyai, between Laconia and Arcadia, or at Limnai, between Laconia and Messenia, if they were Spartan; at

Brauron, one of the areas of Attica furthest from the city, if they were Athenian. In these places, where special sanctuaries were established, they spent a period of segregation, exactly like their male counterparts, and in this context amorous relations grew up between the mistress and some of her pupils. But even after listing and noting these points, I cannot agree with the consequences drawn by Sergent: that the most ancient testimony on homosexuality (that of Sappho) makes an institutional link between love between women and that fundamental rite of passage in female life – marriage.

Undoubtedly, as already noted, love affairs between women (at least the ones we know about) arose during the period of female life institutionally designed to mark the passage of a girl from the class of virgins to the class of married women. But a fundamental difference springs to mind when one thinks of female and male love affairs. Sex during initiation, for boys, was with an adult. For girls, on the other hand, it was sometimes with their mistresses, and sometimes (as shown by Alcman's parthenion) with another young girl of the same age. The educational function, which in the male initiation process was directly linked to the sexual relationship, in female initiations seems to be fulfilled in the first place by the whole experience of community life. Within this life the homosexual bond, even if institutionalised through a ritual marriage (as in the case of Agido and Hagesichora), appears less like an educational relationship and more like the free expression of reciprocal feeling, giving rise to an equal relationship between two people who have chosen each other, neither having authority over the other nor accumulated experience to pass on.[22]

The homosexual relationship can be explained in the context of male initiations – in different ways, admittedly, but at least it is capable of explanation. According to Bethe, as we saw, the lover, by subordinating the beloved, 'inspired' him with virile power by transmitting his sperm to him. Other scholars maintain that sodomy was an act of submission by a young male to an adult, a form of necessary humiliation before being admitted to the dominant group which held power. But what symbolic and social significance could be attached to love between women? Sex between women takes place on an equal basis, it does not involve submission, it cannot symbolise the transmission of power (not even the power of generation, the only power held by women).

There is no possible symbolic meaning, then, and no possible social meaning, when one thinks about it: a woman, when she gets married, does not join a group of older people with power over younger people of the same sex. She enters the family of her husband, where she is subject to him and to the other men who form part of the *oikos*. In this context, if any sexual relationship can have a meaning as an act of initiation, it would have to be heterosexual intercourse, possibly symbolised in ritual form.[23] It certainly could not be a relationship with another woman.

Clearly, I do not wish to deny the initiation value of female societies. What I do wonder, however, is whether in the light of what we have seen so far we are entitled to think about the homosexual relationship as a stage in the initiation of women to marriage. And I believe that the response must be negative. The homosexual relationship, although linked by context and culture to the period of a woman's life when girls changed from the status of virgins to the status of married women, seems to me devoid of the institutional educational value which was attached, in male initiations, to intercourse with another man.

Female homosexual relationships were very different from those which linked the male subject of initiation to his adult lover. On the male side, this was inevitably shaped by assymetrical roles within which the physical and intellectual inferiority of the boy was a necessary condition for the realisation of the indispensable pedagogical function. My feeling, in short, is that female homosexuality, which in the *thiasoi* found the widest possibilities for expression as a free bond of affection, was constructed from outside – which is to say, by men – on the model of pederasty.

It is no coincidence, I believe, if the emphasis on the pedagogical aspect of relations between women is placed by a man such as Plutarch. In Sparta, he writes, the best women loved girls, and when it happened that two of them were in love with the same girl, they tried (although they were rivals) to co-operate in the improvement of their beloved.[24]

It is no coincidence that it is men who make female homosexuality into a perfect mirror of the male variety, forgetting the fundamental differences which I have tried to bring out. Nor is it a coincidence that the term used to indicate the young love object, *aitis*, is taken from the male sphere.[25]

The idea that female homosexuality had a function of initiation does not emerge from a reading of Sappho. Undoubtedly, Sappho is well aware of the importance of education in the life of the *thiasos*. She is proud of the role of 'teacher' which she performs there. She speaks with evident and clear-cut contempt of those girls who have not learned grace, poetry and culture from her. But the tone of her love poetry leaves all this aside. Homosexuality, in the female sodalities, is not pedagogical: it is an elevated, 'cultured' relationship. It is something which ennobles, as the love relationship always does (or at least, so they say). But that is all it is: simply love.

It is now necessary to set the evidence on female homosexuality within its social and historical context. The seventh and sixth centuries BC were a time of transition in Greece, which was moving away from the pre-literacy of Homeric times, and towards a literate society.[26] Formerly, communities regulated their lives around institutions with powers that were still fluid (such as the assembly and the council of elders in Homer). Now Greece was developing into a fully and completely political society. This was a far-reaching transformation, with inevitable consequences for women's lives. In Homeric society, marriage was an instrument for establishing relations of friendship and power through an exchange of women. In the *polis* it became the institution designed to perpetuate the *oikoi*, and with them, the city itself.[27] As we know, in tandem with this transformation, women were relegated to a reproductive role and definitively segregated within the confines of the domestic walls, or within the still more limited boundaries of the women's quarters.

But Sappho lived before all this happened. She lived, in fact, during the turbulent period of transition, when women still had some possibility of living not simply as potential or actual instruments of reproduction, but as individuals who, at least during one phase of their lives, were socialised and instructed. It was understandable, then, that some of them, including Sappho, were capable of writing about themselves and their own feelings.[28]

Things changed quickly. The *thiasoi* disappeared, and with them the possibility for women to be cultivated, and perhaps also to experience true love. Now destined for marriage from the youngest age, and prepared for this and nothing else, women learned to know only one type of love: the one they were supposed to feel for a husband whom they would not be allowed to choose for themselves. This does not mean that they did not love this husband: on the contrary, it is most probable that they loved him sincerely. Having no other choice, and not being able even to conceive of a different destiny (if they were not wives, they were courtesans or prostitutes), marriage was truly the locus of love for them, but a love made up, first and foremost, of devotion, obedience and respect. This was the love which the Greeks taught their women. What about passion? What about freedom to choose the object of one's love, freedom to leave him, abandonment and repentance, hope and despair, all of those things which, along with affection, are fundamental parts of love?

It seems very unlikely that Greek women experienced all of this within marriage (apart from some exceptional cases). Perhaps – in addition to adultery, where they presumably tried to find it – they continued to experience this type of passionate love in homosexual relationships. And perhaps it is true that at this point, as Dover suggests,[29] homosexuality for them was a type of 'counter-culture', in which they received from their own sex what segregation and monogamy denied them from men. But on all of this, after Sappho, silence has fallen.

Love at banquets

Together with the *thiasoi*, and extending beyond the time when these disappeared, ancient Greece had other places where it is not only possible but even probable that women loved freely among themselves. This seems to be documented to a certain extent. But in these cases the love involved was very different from that concerned with initiation. These other places were banquets, on whose social and cultural function we have already dwelt in speaking of male homosexuality.

The banquets were meeting places reserved for men. The only women admitted were flute players, dancers, acrobats and courtesans: Leucippe, for example,[30] or the blonde Euripile,[31] or again the noisy Gastrodora[32] and Callicrite.[33] These women hired by men had different roles but a single function: making the banquet more enjoyable for those who paid them. And it seems plausible that in the course of these banquets, either as a spontaneous consequence of participation in a feast where eroticism played a major role, or perhaps (although this is only conjecture) at the request of the males present, there were more or less casual amorous encounters between courtesans, flautists, acrobats and dancers.

Apart from reasonable speculation, this possibility is attested by a lyric poem, as celebrated as it is controversial, dedicated by Anacreon to a girl from Lesbos:

> Once again golden-haired Love strikes me with his purple ball and summons me to play with the girl in the fancy sandals; but she – she comes from Lesbos with its fine cities – finds fault with my hair because it is white, and gapes after another.[34]

The last two lines are ambiguous in the original Greek, and have given rise to a problem which is still debated by the critics. Is the 'other', towards whom the girl from Lesbos turns, scorning the white hair of the poet, another girl, or another shock of hair, younger but also male?

The correct response can be sought, in the first place, through Anacreon's use of the verb *chaskei* ('gapes'). This verb indicates an attitude of ecstatic stupor, which the critics (when they do not extract themselves from embarrassment by reading 'another' as male rather than female, arguing that the correct reading of the Greek word is *allon*, masculine, and not *allēn*, feminine)[35] have usually considered as referring to another woman, partly basing this assertion on the well-established homosexual reputation of the girls of Lesbos.[36] If true, this would confirm my hypothesis on the identification of banquets as a place where love affairs between women flourished. But the correctness of this interpretation has been hotly debated in recent years. In fact, according to Bruno Gentili,[37] the erotic renown of the girls of Lesbos in antiquity was attributable to another 'speciality': oral sex which, according to the ancients, was actually invented on this island,[38] and which the Greeks indicated with the verb *lesbiazein*.[39]

The word *lesbia* would thus have nothing to do with the current meaning of the term. A homosexual woman in antiquity was called a *tribas*; the use of *lesbia* in this sense does not go back earlier than the ninth or tenth century.[40] Similar considerations apply to the verb *lesbiazein* which, as already pointed out by Wilamowitz-Möllendorff, has no connections with Sappho.[41]

In conclusion, the girl from Lesbos, according to this view, is not being described by Anacreon while she is looking at another woman in an ecstasy of love. The 'other' towards which the girl from Lesbos turns with open mouth, scorning the white hair of the poet, Gentili argues, 'is probably another shock of different (pubic) hair, obviously black, belonging to another of the male guests at the banquet'.[42] This hypothesis deserves careful consideration on account of the well-deserved authority of its proponent. But I believe that the translation of *allēn* as 'another girl' remains possible, and leads to some reflections on female homosexuality which it would be a mistake to leave out, and which do not necessarily derive from an anachronistic interpretation of the term 'lesbian'. The idea of a young courtesan being attracted by another woman is quite plausible, whether or not she comes from Sappho's island. Banquets, for courtesans, were a place of work. They were paid to entertain the guests during a feast where, in all probability, mainly masculine loves arose. In this erotic atmosphere, it is not difficult to imagine that they too might feel homosexual desires. Deep down, other women were the only ones that they were not obliged to love 'under contract'. Might one not imagine that sometimes – perhaps even frequently – banquets allowed them to escape their professional destiny, and feel some non-mercenary emotions? One can hardly avoid speculating that elements of homosexuality formed part of the relationship between courtesans. And this is confirmed by the evidence of Alciphron, an author from much the same period as Lucian (perhaps a younger contemporary). Four books of his 'letters' have survived: from fisher-men, farmers, parasites, and courtesans.

These elegant, linguistically refined prose epistles (Alciphron is defined *attikistēs* by Eustathius)[43] describe in particular with great psychological subtlety the world of the courtesans, their customs, their problems, their relations with their lovers and with other courtesans, sometimes rivals, sometimes friends. And the letters also describe their moments of rest, the days in which, far from men, they carry on together riotously, free at last. 'Songs, gibes, toasts until cockcrow, perfumes, crowns, little cakes.' Thus Megara describes a feast to Bacchis, who has not taken part in it:

> But the thing that gave us the greatest pleasure, anyhow, was a serious rivalry that arose between Thryallis and Myrrhina in the matter of buttocks – as to which could display the lovelier, softer pair. And first Myrrhina unfastened her girdle (her shift was silk), and began to shake her loins (visible through her shift), which quivered like junkets, the while she cocked her eye back at the wagglings of her buttocks. And so gently, as if she were in the act, she sighed a bit, that, by Aphrodite, I was thunderstruck.[44]

A homosexual turn-on? Barely hinted at, the hypothesis cannot be ruled out, especially in view of the fact that an explicit reference to a rela-tionship between women appears in the same author's 'Letters from Farmers'.

Women and Male Homosexuality

The fundamental importance of love between men, combined with the widespread prevalence of these relationships throughout the course of Greek history, inevitably had a profound impact on heterosexual re-lationships, both by determining male attitudes to the female sex and by forcing women to reckon with a sector of their men's emotional lives from which they were totally excluded. But what exactly did Greek women think of male sexual habits?

Unfortunately, we are not in a position to know whether they saw the *erōmenoi* as dangerous rivals. Posing this question, Dover writes: 'in general the pursuit of eromenoi was characteristic of the years before marriage . . . so that wives will comparatively seldom have had grounds for fearing that their husbands were forming enduring homosexual attachments.'[45] But while this was true in many cases, in many others these 'competitive' attachments remained in being, as Dover himself admits when he recalls what the heroine says in Euripides' *Medea*. In her celebrated lament on the unhappy fate of womankind, she points out that a woman must first submit to the will of her father, who gives her a husband that she has not chosen. She is then forced to stay with this man, whether she wants to or not. Otherwise, she would be open to blame. Meanwhile, the husband can leave her whenever he feels like it, without suffering any consequences. Nor is this all. Whenever a husband feels that he has enough of his home he can go out and recover his spirits with somebody who is *philos* – obviously meaning an *erōmenos*.[46]

In Xenophon's *Symposium*, furthermore, Critobulus, just married, speaks such a passionate paean of praise about his friend Cleinias that we are left in no doubt as to their relationship. At night, he says, I can't sleep because I can't see him. By day, the best thing that can happen to me is to see him. I would give him everything I own, willingly and with no sense of sacrifice. If he wanted me to, I would be his slave; for him, I would even go into the fire.[47]

Xenophon again, this time in the *Hellenica*,[48] tells how Alexander, tyrant of Pherai (respectably married) had a young *erōmenos*. One day, being angered with him, he imprisoned him as a punishment. Alexander's wife then interceded on behalf of the youth, but this led to disastrous results. Alexander put his young friend to death, and the woman, overcome by grief, killed herself.

An unusual tale, as Dover observes. Reading it, the thought strikes him that Alexander may have suspected a love affair between his *paidika* and his wife. Indeed, the suspicion is almost inescapable. But does it make sense to generalise the implications of this suspicion, and imagine that wives, far from being jealous, took advantage of the possibilities which their husbands' homosexual attachments offered them? If this were the case, the foremost topic of interest would not be female jealousy, but male jealousy. Take a husband betrayed by both his wife and his *pais*: of whom was he more jealous, the wife or the boy? On mature reflection, the problem does not merely affect married men: women were very dangerous rivals for all pederasts. When they reached a certain age, their beloved boys inevitably began to be attracted by the female sex, or at least to think of getting married. The lovers were equally certain to be stricken by frightful jealousy.

In Plutarch's *Amatorius* we have already had an opportunity to see the torment and rage felt by Pisias when Bacchion, his *erōmenos*, decides to marry Ismenidora. And one of Theocritus' *Idylls* shows that the case of Pisias is anything but exceptional.

Theocritus, in his thirteenth *Idyll*, tells of the capture of the young

Ilas by three nymphs, and the despair of his lover Heracles. A myth, of course, but the idyll is addressed to Nicias, whom Theocritus wishes to console for the loss of his *erōmenos,* by persuading him that it is natural for boys, at a certain age, to start to appreciate women. What has happened to Nicias, he points out, previously happened to Heracles. And Heracles, in the end, resigned himself in the face of the inevitable; so Nicias must do the same.[49]

After this aside, we may return to the problem of how women experienced male homosexuality. On reflection, I believe that the women with most to fear from male rivals were not wives, but courtesans.

In the long run, what did wives have to lose? The loves which a Greek man felt for his wife and his *pais* were so different that in all probability, unless he was really going too far, the husband's male attachment did not take anything away from his wife. Wives and *paides* lived, so to speak, in different territories, not only materially (the wives in the house and family life, the *paides* in banquets and social life) but also emotionally. Conjugal love, with some rare exceptions, was really a form of affection, as we know, with marital sex orientated prevalently not to say exclusively towards procreation. The love for *paides,* on the other hand, contained a major intellectual component, and sex with them, judging from descriptions, was erotically exhilarating.[50]

The real rivals of wives were not the *paides,* but other 'respectable' women who could induce their husbands to divorce them, thereby depriving them of what marriage had brought: their married status. This is the meaning of the expression *lechos* (the bed) for which Greek women became each other's rivals, sometimes, like Medea, even being prepared to kill for it. 'Woman', says Medea, 'quails at every peril, / Faint-heart to face the fray and look on steel; / But when in wedlock-rights she suffers wrong, / No spirit more bloodthirsty shall be found.'[51]

The 'bed', then, is the only force capable of provoking rebellion among women. And in Greek tragedy, 'bed' is a key word in understanding how relationships within marriage or comparable situations were experienced. Given the impossibility of devoting much space to this topic, it will be enough to consider the meaning of the 'bed' in a tragedy which has two women as its protagonists: Euripides' *Andromache.*

Andromache, after Hector's death, has been assigned as part of the spoils of war to Neoptolemus, who keeps her as a concubine. Hermione, wife of Neoptolemus, daughter of Helen and Menelaus, accuses her of having caused her sterility with her evil arts, and taking advantage of her husband's absence, becomes involved in a plot to kill her rival and the son whom the rival has given to Neoptolemus. But the plan fails and Hermione, to escape her husband's wrath, runs away with Orestes, to whom she had been betrothed before marrying Neoptolemus.

This is the plot of the tragedy, but what is of great interest to us is the attitude of the two women. Andromache does not love Neoptolemus, and continues to think of Hector as her true 'husband'. But she defends her status as a concubine. Hermione, whose jealousy has left her prepared to commit two murders, displays no sorrow when Orestes tells her that he has hatched a plot to slay Neoptolemus. The only object of competition is the 'bed', a key word which occurs no fewer than twenty times in the tragedy. And what the bed means, first and foremost, is social security, both for wives and for concubines.[52] This security could never be taken away by a husband's or a lover's *erōmenos*. *Paides* were not real rivals for wives. They were real and dangerous rivals only for courtesans, the companions of social life for Greek men. The *paides* could not only take away the attention of a courtesan's more or less occasional clients, but thereby also remove her earning power, and thus her livelihood. A hint of the rivalry between this category of women and the young men in question can easily be seen in one of Theocritus' *Idylls*, where Simichidas is hoping that one day the lovely Philinus, who is causing pain to Aratus, who is in love with him, may one day learn the pains of love himself. 'Can't you see? He's riper than a pear,' says Simichidas, 'and the women say, "oh dear, Philinus, your pretty flowers are dropping!"'[53]

'The women,' says Theocritus: but would 'respectable' women in Greece ever have used such language? Locked away in their women's quarters, how could they have known at what stage of ripeness were Philinus' 'flowers'? What occasion would they have had to meet him and make him the butt of their gibes? Despite the greater freedom of the Hellenistic era in which Theocritus writes, it would be truly unlikely that the women in question could be anything other than courtesans.

Female Homosexuality Seen By Men

As we have seen, once the period of 'initiation' homosexuality is passed, it is very difficult to imagine what women really felt about loving other women, and to identify the space and function that it had in their lives. It is anything but difficult, on the other hand, to determine what men thought about women who loved each other.

Although rare, the references are crystal clear. We start again with

Plato's well-known myth on the origin of the sexes, in the *Symposium*: as men and women were two halves of an original being (which was, as we saw, either a double man, or a double woman, or a hermaphrodite), and given that each of the halved creatures searches for its other half, those who derive from the hermaphrodite are heterosexual, while those who are descendants of those beings which were originally equipped with two sets of male organs or two sets of female organs are homosexual, and they search for another man or another woman respectively. There is one difference, however: men attracted to other men are the best, the only ones capable of dealing with public affairs, the only ones who, precisely because they love what is similar to themselves, attain fullness of being. Women attracted by other women, on the other hand, are *tribades*. This word is full of disturbing significance: *tribades* were savage, uncontrollable, dangerous females.

What remains to be decided is whether the image of homosexual women remained constant over time, or whether it changed in some way, and if so, in what direction. But here we are faced again with a lack of sources: after Plato, silence descends on this subject, and the only chink in the darkness allowing some information to seep out opens up after several centuries, with Lucian of Samosata. In a work of undoubted authenticity (unlike the *Amores*, which was attributed to him but is not his work) Lucian directly tackles the question of female homosexuality.

In the fifth of his *Dialogues of Courtesans*, Clonarium and Leaena, two courtesans, are exchanging confidences. Clonarium has heard that Leaena is the lover of a rich lady from Lesbos, Megilla, who loves her *hōsper andra*, like a man. Leaena admits this, saying however that she is ashamed of it, because it is unnatural (*allokoton*). But this confession is not enough for Clonarium: she wants to know what sort of woman Megilla is. Leaena replies: *hē deinōs andrikē* – she is frightfully masculine.[54] Then, giving in to the insistence of her friend, Leaena relates how the story began. Megilla had organised a feast, together with her friend Demonassa of Corinth, and had hired Leaena as a harpist. But the party ended late, and Leaena was invited to spend the night with Megilla and Demonassa. Remaining alone with her, they began to kiss her and try increasingly daring approaches, until Megilla, now very excited, took off her wig, revealing a completely shaven head, like an athlete's. She claimed she was really a man, living with Demonassa as with a wife. But Megilla was not a man in the physical sense of the term. In response to Leaena's question, she said that she did not have *to andreion* ('the men's thing'). She had no need of this male 'thing': she had her own way, much more pleasant, of playing the husband. I was born a woman like all of you, she says, but my mind (*gnōmē*), my desires (*epithumia*) and all the rest (*talla panta*) are those of a man. Then, she asked Leaena to allow her to demonstrate that she was no less able than a man (*ouden endeousan mē tōn andrōn*): and Leaena permitted her this privilege. But despite the insistence of her friend Clonarium, Leaena does not wish to relate the details of what happened. These details, she protests, are *aischra* (shameful).[55]

This dialogue is very significant, firstly, I believe, on account of the characterisation of Megilla, a woman who shaves her hair to appear like a man, and who, on Leaena's explicit declaration, is 'frightfully masculine'. In fact, the description of Megilla shows us not so much a homosexual as a 'transvestite'. Unlike pederasts, the most virile-looking of all men, homosexual women lose the natural characteristics of their sex, becoming a sort of caricature of maleness and appearing as a phenomenon in nature which reveals its monstrosity at first sight. So much for Megilla, the man-woman. And what about Leaena, who gets seduced? Not for nothing is she a courtesan. It is no mistake that she has not become the mistress of Megilla either for love or because she is carried away. As she explicitly states, she was attracted by the woman's rich gifts.[56] Prostitutes, then, give themselves to homosexual love affairs. And even women with as little sense of decorum as prostitutes know that to love another woman is an unforgivable act. As well as saying this explicitly, Leaena blushes in recounting her adventure.[57]

After many centuries, the negative connotations of female homosexuality, and its condemnation, emerge even in a dialogue like this, which is anything but a moral tract, with the same clarity as from Plato's few inexorable words.

PART TWO

Rome

5

The Archaic Period and the Republic

The Indigenous Features of Roman Homosexuality

For the Romans, pederasty was 'the Greek vice'. The sexual customs of
their ancestors, they maintained, were untouched by this aspect of love,
introduced and disseminated by contact with a culture which, by
making the joys of loving boys known and appreciated, had sapped the
ancient sternness, making Romans forget the purity of the *mores
maiorum*, and weakening the manliness of a people destined for
command and conquest.

Graecia capta ferum victorem cepit, writes Horace:[1] vanquished
Greece vanquished its savage victor. Obviously Greece conquered Rome
with its culture: and an integral part of this culture was the sweetness
(or the softness, as the Romans would say) of the love for young boys.
The wide acceptance of this sort of love caused quite a lot of anxiety to
moralists.

'For my part I think this practice had its origins in the Greek
gymnasia, where that kind of loving was free and permitted,'[2] writes
Cicero – who in his own private life was no stranger to homosexual
love. In a letter to his friend Pontius, Pliny the Younger speaks of an
epigram dedicated by Cicero to his Tiro, the young slave whom Cicero
went on loving even after freeing him from slavery. And Pliny, it may be
remarked in passing, confesses to his friend that this example has been
an encouragement to himself to enjoy the good things of life. If even a
man like Cicero allows himself to speak of kisses stolen in the night-
time from his young boyfriend, Pliny writes, why should he himself hide
his loves?[3]

But enough of Pliny's personal life. What should one say of Cicero?
Private vices, public virtues? Not at all. Cicero, in his moralistic invec-
tives, does not condemn homosexuality as such: he condemns only one
particular form: pederasty, in the Greek sense of the term – making love
to freeborn boys. And it is this misunderstanding – the absolutely

mistaken idea that the Romans lumped homosexuality together with pederasty and condemned both – that has given rise to the myth that Roman manliness meant strict heterosexuality. Let us try to clarify the terms of the problem.

Undoubtedly, for a Roman, virility was the greatest of virtues: a political virtue. From earliest childhood, a Roman was raised to be a dominator. As a *civis romanus*, he was destined for a single task, to rule the world. *Parcere subiectis et debellare superbos*, writes Virgil:[4] spare those who surrender and overcome those who dare to oppose us. Complete dominance lay at the root of Roman ethics. Always and everywhere, he had to impose himself: on fellow citizens, through the political use of language; and on all others – those who were not Romans – with the force of his arms and the superiority of his laws.

In order to become a *civis romanus* worthy of the name, he had to learn from the earliest age never to submit, and to impose his will on everybody – including his sexual will. Hence, in this field, the myth of a virility which has correctly been defined as 'based on rape'.[5] In this myth, and the need to defend it, lies the explanation of the absolute need for the Romans to insist that pederasty was a Greek vice. Pederasty required that the lover should engage in an intellectual, psychological and sexual game which lay completely outside the mentality of a Roman. In Greece, as we know, anyone who loved a boy had to court him, flatter him, prove his love for him, persuade him of the seriousness of his intentions. For a Roman, all of this would show a lack of virility. As his psychology was that of a conqueror (and in the sexual field, that of a rapist), pederasty for him, with all that it involved, was in effect something quite inconceivable.

But it would be completely wrong to assume, on this account, that the Romans were rigorously heterosexual. For a Roman, the highest expression of virility consisted in putting other men down. It was all too easy, and too paltry, for a real man merely to subject women to his desires. For the powerful and inexhaustible Roman male, women could not suffice. His exuberant and irrepressible sexuality had to be expressed without limitations: he had to possess all the possible objects of his desire, independently of their sex.

These, then, were the cultural and psychological roots of Roman homosexuality, which was widespread in Rome with these characteristics, long before coming into contact with Greek culture. This is proved, in the first place, by an absolutely fundamental consideration: the Romans, at least during the first centuries of their history, before the undeniable influence of Hellenic culture contributed to changing the ethics of their sexual relations (and we will see later what form this took), did not make love to freeborn boys, as the Greeks did. They loved young slaves. This fact by itself is enough to show very clearly that homosexuality was not imported from Greece. For a Greek, loving a slave would be meaningless. The educational and cultural function of pederasty required, by definition, that the beloved boy should be free: the lover had to make a good citizen of him, and the slave, as a lesser being, did not belong to the world of the city. What could it have meant to love him? If the Romans made love to slaves even in the first centuries of their history, how can we assume that their homosexuality derived from its Greek counterpart?

Relationships between men in Rome were simply an aspect and manifestation of the ethics of the city. In personal and family life, the Roman *paterfamilias* was an absolute master, with unlimited power over everything belonging to him, whether persons or things. And among the things belonging to him were his slaves, over whom – at least during the first centuries of the city's history – he exercised a power outside any control of society and the state. In this situation, why on earth should he refrain from sodomising his houseboys, whose domestic duties included the obligation to let him have his way with them?

This was not true only during the first centuries. Seneca, in his *Controversies*, writes of a freedman (an ex-slave), criticised for having a relationship with his former master, being defended by his lawyer in the following terms: 'Losing one's virtue [sexual passivity, *impudicitia*] is a crime for the free-born, a necessity in a slave, a duty for the freedman.'[6] Not even if he had been liberated, then, could the freedman escape his 'sexual service'. Although no longer compelled, he was still morally bound to submit to his former master. And it transpires clearly from the literature that masters used to take advantage of this right, and public opinion accepted this without any difficulty.

Paul Veyne correctly observes in this connection that

> Rome did not have to wait for hellenisation to allow various forms of love between males. One of the earliest relics of Latin literature, the plays of Plautus, which pre-date the craze for things Greek, are full of homosexual allusions of a very native character. A much repeated way of teasing a slave is to remind him of what his master expects of him, i.e. to get down on all fours.[7]

Although a great deal could be said about the relationship between Plautus and Greek culture (as his comedies are very probably modelled on Greek originals, more precisely the comedies of Menander),[8] the fact still remains that his references to homosexual love were without question typically Roman, and that the representation of these domestic loves on stage filled the audience with mirth. Not only did they recognise an aspect of everyday reality, but – far from being indignant – they showed particular appreciation for an irony which was full of self-satisfaction and, deep down, self-glorification.

Homosexuality, then, was at the same time a social manifestation of the personal power of a citizen over slaves, and a personal reconfirmation of his virile potency. Only one limit was placed on the expression of this potency, for the good of the city. Men and women without distinction – that was all right. But not free men. What sort of citizen would a boy become if, during the years of his education, he had had to submit to another man? How could he, as an adult, become the supermale which he was supposed to be, in all fields, if instead of learning how to impose himself, he had been compelled to comply with the desires of others?

And indeed the Romans protected their sons from such a risk. Plutarch, for example, relates that they used to put a golden *bulla* around their necks, so that when they were playing in the nude, they would not be mistaken for slaves, and subjected to attempts at seduction.[9] It is possible to dispute the credibility of this fact. The *bulla*, without doubt, was a status symbol. It is very improbable that it would have been designed as a sexual safe-conduct for freeborn youths. But despite this, the explanation given by Plutarch of its function is highly significant: obviously, in Rome, attempts to seduce boys were by no means unusual. In confirmation of this, for the Republican era, we have a regulation issued by the urban praetor for the protection of the *pudicitia* (modesty or honour) not only of women but also of *praetextati*, meaning those boys who had not yet reached puberty, and were still wearing the *praetexta* tunic.

'Si quis matremfamilias aut praetextatum adsectatus fuerit', the praetor proclaimed, in the second century BC, he will be punished.[10] What does *adsectari* mean? It means 'following on the street', paying court for purposes of seduction. If the praetor was obliged, for the protection cf *pudicitia*, to lay down a penalty not only for those making attempts on the virtue and innocence of *matresfamilias* – meaning respectable women[11] – but also against those pestering a boy on the street, this obviously means that attempts to seduce *praetextati* were commonplace, and that boys were the object of sexual attention exactly like women.

Having considered all of this, let us return to the problem of the 'origins' of homosexuality in Rome. Is it a Greek vice, as the defenders of the purity (at least the original purity) of the Romans so anxiously reiterate, starting with historians as well known as Gibbon?[12]

After what we have seen on the profound, irreconcilable difference between the concepts underlying homosexual ethics in Greece and in Rome, it becomes very difficult to accept such a theory.

Legitimate Forms of Love: Subjecting One's Own Slave, Paying a Prostitute

Let us now look more closely, trying to identify them with greater precision, at exactly what were the rules of Roman sexual ethics, and especially, what happened when these rules were broken.

A Roman could freely engage in sexual relations with a slave. Confirmation of what we have already seen, alongside the references from Plautus, can be found in some evidence which is historically more or less reliable, but which in any event provides a clear and definite glimpse of a social custom that is anything but exceptional.

Valerius Maximus relates, in the first place, that a Roman man one day led into the countryside the young slave with whom he was sexually involved. In order to please the youth, who had expressed a desire to eat tripe – there was nowhere in the vicinity where beef products could be bought – he had a domestic ox killed. For this he was tried and found guilty, but not for his relationship with the slave. Nobody had anything to say about that. His offence consisted purely in violating the rule which banned the slaughter of work animals.[13]

In ancient times, such as the period of this episode, the rules of an economy which was still very poor and predominantly agricultural made the killing of a work animal such a serious act as to call for punishment, yet even then homosexuality was not legally forbidden as such. Confirmation of this comes from a story in Livy. In 184 BC the former consul Lucius Flaminius was expelled from the Senate by the censors, and particularly by Cato, who pronounced one of his most violent speeches against him. Lucius Flaminius had fallen in love with a young Carthaginian named Philip, and had brought him to Gaul. But the boy complained that by leaving Rome he had missed a gladiatorial show which he had wanted to attend. And Lucius Flaminius, by way of compensation, had provided a private spectacle for him: one evening, during a banquet, he had organised an execution for his delectation.[14] But even in this case, Lucius Flaminius was not punished for his homosexuality: his crime was killing a man without respecting the rules governing capital punishment. His relationship with Philip, in itself, gave rise to no scandal. The boy was a prostitute (*scortum*), and as such belonged to the second category of men with whom Romans considered it not only legitimate but absolutely normal to have sexual relations.

Incidentally, according to Livy's account, Lucius Flaminius was later pardoned by the people. One day, during a public spectacle, he was seen sitting among the plebs, far from the senators, for whom the first rows were normally reserved. The crowd, moved by this, acclaimed Lucius until they saw him sitting among his peers in the position which they felt he still deserved to occupy.[15]

How could one explain, unless there was total acceptance of relationships with prostitutes, the fact that the Roman calendar contained not only a feast day for female prostitutes (26 April) but also, on the 25th of the same month, a day dedicated to male prostitutes?[16]

But the interesting thing to note about male prostitution is not merely the fact that it was widespread. It had also become, as one might say, a luxury item. And Cato, if one can believe what Polybius says, was profoundly angry about this. His fellow-citizens were willing to pay 300 drachmas for a jar of Black Sea caviare, and to pay a pretty boy more than the value of a farm for his services. In Cato's view, these were two equally shameful extravagances. What he reproved, though, was not the fact that his citizens abandoned themselves to homosexual loves. It was that they were ready to waste their substance in order to enjoy it.[17]

Young male prostitutes, unlike their female counterparts, were not normally social outcasts who scraped together a meagre living. Flattered and spoiled, as we can see from the case of Lucius Flaminius and young Philip, they seem rather to belong to a category of high-class courtesans, used to a life of luxury and refinement, to the extent that they can decide to ask not merely for money, but for costly and sophisticated consumer goods in exchange for their services.[18]

There is no condemnation and no punishment, then, in Republican Rome, for homosexuality in itself. In the case of relations between men, the only thing that attracts criticism (unless a freeborn youth is involved) is the excesses to which such love affairs led, and the fact that they could lead a citizen to adopt a lifestyle not consonant with the austere and rigorous model that the Romans continued to praise and propagate, even after the increased wealth of the city had brought in new luxuries and new forms of soft living.

Despite this, sexual relations with a slave could sometimes be problematical. What happened, for example, when a Roman citizen became involved with a slave who did not belong to him? Apart from being easily imagined, the fact that such attachments grew up can be clearly seen from the sources. Valerius Maximus tells that one day a man called Calidius Bomboniensis, surprised in the bedchamber of a married lady, defended himself by claiming to have got into the house because he was in love with a young slave (obviously, therefore, not a slave belonging to himself). His confession of intemperance, Valerius Maximus comments, saved him from the charge of 'lechery'.[19] At first sight, this would make it appear that the affair was absolutely legitimate. But I do not believe that this is so at all.

The sources clearly indicate that having a relationship with another person's slave was frowned on. Cicero, for example, although he did not condemn homosexuality in itself (how could he have done so, given his relationship with Tiro?), strongly condemned those who, indulging in excessive luxury, took on too many *pueri* for their personal service (including sexual services). All the more so if, as sometimes happened, these were slaves wrongfully taken away from other people.[20] Why should this be so? The reason is obvious. The slave was part of a workforce in whose productivity the owner had a very considerable interest. His possible sexual relations (heterosexual or homosexual) could interfere with this output. Making one's own slave into one's lover, whether on a casual or a permanent basis, was a choice which the master could make. He derived other advantages to compensate for any possible shortfall in the work output of his favourite. But allowing other people to do this was something quite different. Masters consequently paid great attention to the sex lives of their male slaves, only allowing them to have relationships with female slaves in their own households. Any children born from these liaisons contributed to increase their patrimony and available workforce.[21]

But, beyond all this, slaves were not supposed to dissipate their energies. This is demonstrated, without any possible ambiguity, by the rule passed by the Claudian session of the senate in AD 52, whereby a free woman forming a relationship with another person's slave, if she did not break it off after three successive warnings by his master, became a slave herself (obviously belonging to the slave's owner).[22] The protection of property rights over *servi* was so strong, then, that it could even overcome the reluctance of the Romans to permit 'Roman blood' to be reduced to a state of slavery.

Given this state of affairs, why should a master allow his slave to become the lover of another man? The defence put up by Calidius Bomboniensis was probably just the choice of the lesser evil. To have sex with another man's wife was very dangerous in Rome: the betrayed husband could subject his wife's lover to shameful practices such as the celebrated punishment of the radish and the mullet, which consisted in subjecting the unfortunate victim to sexual violence inflicted with this particularly pungent root or by means of a fish famed for its barbs.[23] Alternatively, the injured husband could hand the man over to his slaves to be sodomised, or he could do it personally.[24] He could cut off his nose and his ears,[25] he could force him to perform fellatio, the most odious act for a Roman,[26] he could deprive him of his manhood,[27] and finally, if he wished, he could kill him without incurring the sanctions applicable to homicide.[28] This last was an ancient rule which remained in force, although it was subject to some limitations, even after Augustus' *Lex Iulia de adulteriis*, which removed adultery from the sphere of family justice (according to whose customs it had been punished up to that time), and made it into a crime, subject to prosecution on the initiative of any citizen. But it still left a wronged husband, in some cases, free to kill the adulterer.

Given the risks he would have faced if he confessed to adultery, it made a lot of sense for Calidius Bomboniensis to say, as he did, that he was carrying on a relationship with a male slave. Even though (as the slave was somebody else's property) the affair attracted some punishment, this was certainly going to be less serious than the penalty for adultery.[29]

To sum up, homosexuality in itself was neither a crime nor a socially reproved form of behaviour. Carrying on with a slave (so long as he did not belong to somebody else) was accepted as normal behaviour, as was paying a male prostitute. The only thing that was not acceptable was to make love to a young free Roman citizen.

Prohibited Loves: Subjecting a Roman

Valerius Maximus says that during the Samnite Wars around 330 BC Titus Veturius, the son of a magistrate who had lost all his money, in order to pay his debt was forced to sell himself as a slave to Publius Plotius, who tried to abuse him.[30] This did not necessarily mean that he tried to rape him. The word used was *stuprare*, a fairly general term meaning carrying on illicit, meaning extra-marital, sexual relations with somebody. As the jurist Modestinus writes, 'stuprum committit qui liberam mulierem consuetudinis causa, non matrimonii continet, excepta videlicet concubina' (*stuprum* is committed by anyone who has sexual relations with a free woman who is not his wife, with the exception of a concubine). And it goes on to specify: 'Stuprum in vidua vel virgine vel puero committitur' (*stuprum* is committed if one has sexual relations with a widow, a virgin or a boy).[31] *Stuprum* did not consist in imposing sex by force: it simply consisted in having an illicit relationship even with a consenting person.

After this aside, we may return to the story of Titus Veturius. Although he was whipped by Plotius, Titus Veturius did not yield to his desires. He denounced his owner to the consuls, who reported his behaviour to the Senate. Plotius was put in jail.

At first sight, the story may seem surprising, given its apparent contradiction with the numerous sources from which, as we know, it clearly emerges that nothing and nobody could prevent an owner from subjecting a slave to his desires. But the case of Titus Veturius is a very special one. Although *de facto* he was a slave, nevertheless he had been born a Roman. Consequently, although for all other purposes he was completely under the command of the man who had bought him, he still had to be protected from the risk of suffering the treatment that Plotius wished to inflict on him. As Valerius Maximus explicitly says, the Senate, by jailing Plotius, willed that in whatever condition it might find itself, Roman blood might have its *pudicitia* protected.

Confirmation of this rule comes from a story in Livy. A young man, who had also sold himself as a slave to pay his debts, had killed his master, who wished to force sex on him. The Romans abolished slavery for debt, to prevent the occurrence of similar episodes.[32]

The close analogy with the case narrated by Valerius Maximus is clear. Names change, details differ, but the moral remains the same. Although in all probability the facts reported are false in both cases,[33] the two episodes are highly significant. In the fourth century BC (326 to be precise), a series of complex reasons had induced the Romans to pass a law, the *Lex Poetelia Papiria*, abolishing slavery for debt. Tradition traced this decision back to the case of Veturius. Although in all probability this had nothing to do with the passing of the law, the Romans were so convinced of its importance that they identified it as the cause of one of the legislative initiatives which had the most profound impact on the economic and social history of Rome in the early centuries.

And there are further moral tales which highlight the infamy of anyone who so much as attempted to have sex with a Roman man. Letorius Mergus, for example, was accused in 317 BC of having seduced a young standard-bearer. He was put on trial, and killed himself before sentence was passed.[34] A few years later (about 280 BC), Caius Cornelius, accused of having a liaison with a young man of free status, was put in jail, and after trying in vain to defend himself on the grounds that the youth was a prostitute, was forced to die there.[35]

Another significant episode, which crops up several times in the sources, concerned Caius Lusius, nephew of Marius and an officer in the army commanded by his uncle. The year was 102 BC. Caius Lusius fell in love with a soldier named Trebonius, and after courting him for a long time he invited him into his tent one evening and tried to put his desires into effect. But Trebonius killed him rather than submit. Panic spread throughout the camp: how were they going to tell the general what had happened, when he came back? Nobody dared to come forward as a spontaneous witness on behalf of Trebonius. Keeping a brave face, Trebonius gave Marius the names of those who had witnessed the repeated attempts at seduction to which he had been subjected. Having thus found out the true facts, Marius showed his impartiality. Not only did he acquit Trebonius of the charge of homicide, he honoured him with a crown so that his virtue might serve as an example to all.[36] This is a celebrated case, referred to by Cicero, Valerius Maximus, Quintilian and Dionysius of Halicarnassus as well as Plutarch.[37]

Condemnation and punishment, in short, were not confined to *stuprum* and *stupri commercium* (meaning, respectively, occasional and continuous sexual relations). They also extended to any attempt at seducing a young Roman, regardless of the outcome of this attempt. Having said that, a problem still remains: what penalty was prescribed for the guilty party?

Cases reporting punishments meted out during military campaigns are not very helpful. In the first place, the references to penalties are extremely vague. The case of Caius Cornelius, for example, might cause the reader to assume that the death penalty was imposed. As we saw, Valerius Maximus recorded that Caius was 'forced to die in prison'. But how? Of malnutrition, perhaps, as hinted by the text? If so, it was a very strange execution. The rich repertoire of capital punishment in Rome reserved death by starvation for women, especially Vestal Virgins who had broken their vow of chastity.[38] Moreover, one cannot generalise from what happened to Cornelius: his case came under the laws of war, which were exceptional in Rome as in other places.[39] If we want to solve the puzzle we must look elsewhere: at everyday life, far from the stories of more or less exemplary cases. This means that we must try to see whether the common law (as opposed to the special laws regulating soldiers' conduct) protected young *ingenui* (meaning free-born youths), penalising all those who made attempts on their *pudicitia*.

The *Lex Scatinia*

Although notably short on detailed facts, the sources tell of a *Lex Scatinia* dating from the Republican era, designed to regulate the sexual

behaviour of the Romans, and in particular their homosexual behaviour.[40] Explicit references to this law are contained in the writings
of Cicero, Suetonius, Juvenal, Ausonius, Tertullian and Prudentius.

From Cicero's correspondence we learn of a political case where the
Lex Scatinia was used by both contending parties. Celius' adversaries
charged him with violating this law, and Celius, in reply, reproached
the censor with offences under the same legislation.[41] Obviously,
whether true or false in the individual case, the accusation of having
broken the *Lex Scatinia* was a scandalous one. Equally obviously, few
people were completely free of suspicion in this area – as we can see,
among other things, from the amusement which Celius displays when
he reveals that the judge in these matters was a certain Drusus, unknown to us but clearly well known to his fellow citizens for his not
entirely praiseworthy sexual proclivities.[42]

Having said all that, it should be pointed out that Cicero's evidence is
very generic, and does not allow us to determine exactly which types of
behaviour were penalised under the *Lex Scatinia*. Nothing is added to
our knowledge by Suetonius' brief report that the emperor Domitian
punished some people on the basis of its provisions.[43] We can, however,
link the *Lex Scatinia* more definitely to male homosexuality from
evidence provided by Juvenal (subsequently confirmed by Ausonius,
Tertullian and Prudentius).[44]

In the course of an invective against female dissoluteness, a severe
censor was calling for the application of the *Lex Iulia de adulteriis*,
which was supposed to punish the corruption of women, but was not
being applied (*ubi nunc lex Iulia, dormis?* – where are you, Julian Law,
have you perhaps fallen asleep?). A woman called Laronia responds in
no uncertain terms that if men were anxious for the *Lex Iulia* to be
applied, they ought to remember the *Lex Scatinia*:

> Laronia could not contain herself when one of these sour-faced
> worthies cried out, 'What of you, Julian Law? What, gone to sleep?'
> To which she answered smilingly, 'O happy times to have you for a
> censor of our morals! Once more may Rome regain her modesty; a
> third Cato has come down to us from the skies! But tell me, where
> did you buy that balsam juice that exhales from your hairy neck?
> Don't be ashamed to point out to me the shopman! If laws and
> statutes[45] are to be raked up, you should cite first of all the Scatinian:
> inquire first into the things that are done by men; men do more
> wicked things than we do, but they are protected by their numbers,
> and the tight-locked shields of their phalanx. Male effeminates agree
> wondrously well among themselves; never in our sex will you find
> such loathsome examples of evil . . .'[46]

Quick to bring accusations against women, men did not lag behind them in violating the laws. And the law that they broke *en masse*, giving themselves up to homosexual involvements (as revealed by their being called *molles*, meaning effeminates, softies), was in fact the *Lex Scatinia*.

Can we then conclude from this reference that the *Lex Scatinia* penalised all sexual relations between men?

Gibbon declares explicitly that he would be very glad to think that in Rome, as in Greece, '. . . the voluntary and effeminate deserter of his sex was degraded from the honours and the rights of a citizen' (which actually was not the case in Greece, since only male prostitutes were punished in this way, as we saw). Yet even he is forced to admit that the *Lex Scatinia*, unfortunately, confined itself to repressing some particularly grave manifestations of homosexuality: violence, he says, and perhaps seduction.[47] This conclusion is incorrect in one sense (the *Lex Scatinia* did not penalise homosexual violence), but correct in another way: the law did not provide for the punishment of homosexuality as such, but only some precise and clearly defined cases. This emerges with absolute certainty from the sources.

To begin with, Cicero, in his oration on behalf of Gnaeus Plancius, defends his client from the charge of taking his boyfriend out into the countryside, by stating that this, at all events, is no crime.[48] Given that he was aware of the *Lex Scatinia*, as we know, the inescapable conclusion is that this law did not penalise every homosexual relationship, of whatever kind. That conclusion is confirmed, moreover, by the attitude taken by Cicero in relation to Catilina.

Catilina, says Cicero, lives in the midst of vice. He surrounds himself with women of loose morals and dissolute men who corrupt young lads;[49] men who, languid after wine, splash perfumes all over their bodies,[50] and love to dance and sing in the nude;[51] men dedicated to *stuprum*,[52] addicted to every form of lasciviousness. Nor is this all: Catilina has a boyfriend who has even dared to intercede on his behalf in the Senate:[53] a boyfriend-wife, Gabinius,[54] who dances for him, who is his delight, his lantern-bearer.[55] Now, if homosexuality in itself were a criminal offence, could Cicero possibly have refrained from entering a formal charge (not just in the moral sense) against his enemy?

Obviously, then, the *Lex Scatinia* only concerned itself with certain cases of homosexuality. Which cases, precisely? To try to answer this we must start out from a celebrated case involving a certain Caius Scatinius Capitolinus (whose name, it is widely thought, is recorded in the name of the law). Plutarch relates that Caius Scatinius Capitolinus tried to seduce the son of Marcus Claudius Marcellus. Marcellus denounced him to the Senate and had him condemned.[56]

This episode, which took place in 227 BC, also appears in Valerius Maximus, although his account contains some variants. This time Scatinius (whom Plutarch describes as an aedile) is a tribune of the plebs, and Marcellus accuses him in front of the people, not the Senate.[57] But apart from these variants, the tradition is in agreement on the fact that Scatinius was found guilty of attempted seduction and was sentenced to a fine, as Plutarch specifically states. This does not mean that the episode poses no problems. The first problem is the following: what is the relationship between the case of Scatinius Capitolinus and the *Lex Scatinia*?

It is often stated that the law took its name from Scatinius, as he was the first person sentenced under its provisions. But this is clearly an unsustainable hypothesis. Apart from breaking the rule whereby laws took their names from their proposers rather than their targets, it is contradicted by Cicero. Writing about the *municipium aricinum*, home of the Scatinii, he states in its honour that from here (i.e. in Aricia) came many *sellae curules*, the *Lex Voconia* and the *Lex Scatinia*.[58] Obviously, if the law had taken its name from the Scatinius who was found guilty, it would not have been much of a proud boast for his home town.

To resolve this problem, Christius (who published, in 1727, the only study expressly dedicated to this law) speculates whether Scatinius might not perhaps have been sentenced on the basis of a provision which he himself had proposed, before getting involved in the unfortunate incident mentioned above. He rightly rejects this hypothesis.[59] Why on earth, if he was so fond of *pueri* that he tried to seduce one who was not only free-born, but actually the son of a prominent personage like Marcellus, would Scatinius be the one to propose a law which, for the first time in the history of the city, penalised his own proclivities? On the other hand, if the *Lex Scatinia* did not exist in 227 BC, how and why was Scatinius condemned?

Mommsen rightly observes, in this connection, that before the *Lex Scatinia* was passed, pederasty was repressed through non-judicial sanctions (obviously we are talking about the kind of pederasty which was outlawed on the grounds that a free-born boy was involved).[60] Such a conclusion would be prompted, for example, by the case of that Cornelius already recalled, who in 289 BC was arrested for committing a sexual outrage against a lower magistrate (one of those people entitled to take administrative sanctions), and was allowed to die in prison by the tribunes of the plebs.[61] The same inference could be drawn from the case of C. Scatinius Capitolinus. The fine imposed on him was probably a *multa rogata*, meaning one proposed to the people by a magistrate

109

who, on each occasion, could decide whether or not to recommend it, and the amount involved.[62] We shall return to this topic later on, after trying to establish when the vote was taken (obviously after 227 BC) to change *stuprum cum puero* from an administrative misdemeanour into a criminal offence.

The problem of the date

According to the opinion which currently holds the field, the *Lex Scatinia* was passed in 149 BC.[63]

This hypothesis is based on a few legible words in lines 115–16 of column V in the new Livy text from the papyri found at Oxyrhynchus, where we find the name *Scantius* followed, after a gap of nine letters, by the following: ... *am tulit in stupro deprehensi.*[64] The text has been conjecturally completed and corı cted to read *Scatinius plebiscitum tulit de in stupro deprehensis* (Scatinius proposed a plebiscite on those caught engaging in sexual outrages). Thus amended, it has been taken as proof that in 149 BC – the year to which the fragment refers – a certain Scatinius proposed the item of legislation which bears his name. But Kornemann does not accept the emendation of *Scatinius* for *Scantius.*[65] As *Scantius* is a name attested in the sources, it is hard to see why it should be replaced by another name. The reading *Scantius* is predominant today, and is accepted by, among others, Rossbach in the Teubner edition of Livy.

Line 116, furthermore, has been completed in other ways, none of which allows us to see *Scantius* – or *Scatinius*, for those who prefer that reading – as the proposer of a law or a plebiscite.

Luterbacher, for example, proposes the reading *turpem famam tulit in stupro deprehensus*: 'Scantius gained a foul reputation because he was caught committing *stuprum*'. Müller suggests a variant: *gravem poenam tulit in stupro deprehensus*: 'he was condemned to a heavy punishment because he was caught committing *stuprum*'; or alternatively *censoris notam tulit in stupro deprehensus*: 'he received a censor's note because he was caught committing *stuprum*'.[66] In the light of these readings (leaving aside the question of the variants), 149 BC is not necessarily the year in which the law was proposed; it could equally well be the year when a man called Scantius committed an act of *stuprum*.

The proposal that the *Lex Scatinia* should be dated to 149 BC, therefore, finds no support in the sources. What other dates are possible, then?

Faced with the obscurity of the sources, some scholars confine themselves to observing that the law was in force at the end of the Republican era.[67] Others propose a different perspective: the law was passed at the time of Second Punic War. Christius, the first to advance this hypothesis,[68] observed that at the time of the Second Punic War there was a prominent plebeian family in Rome called the *Scatinii*. A celebrated figure in this family was the pontifex P. Scatinius, who died in 216 BC.[69] Clearly, then, the law dates from this period. Could we not surmise that it was proposed to bury the memory of the infamy which had fallen on the family owing to the reprehensible behaviour of Scatinius Capitolinus in 227? One member of the *gens* had sullied the good name of the Scatinii. Another Scatinius, shortly afterwards, took care to rescue the family reputation, by proposing this law. The *Lex Scatinia* (as Voigt also maintains)[70] can therefore be taken as coming a few years after that date.

The content and the penalty

We now turn to the second problem raised by this law: its content. I have said several times that the *Lex Scatinia* did not state that all homosexual relationships should be punished, but merely identified some of these relationships as reprehensible, and specified legal penalties only against these. Which sorts, precisely?

Based as it is on very vague evidence, the attempt to establish precisely the content of the *Lex Scatinia* is anything but easy. Consequently, there need be no surprise that the hypotheses vary. Some authorities state that it only punished *stuprum cum puero* (a free-born boy, of course).[71] Others, however, argue that it also penalised sex between adults,[72] one school of thought maintaining that the law only punished the passive partner, while others conjecture that the active partner was also subject to penalties.[73] To resolve this problem, we might speculate that the *Lex Scatinia* may not simply have contained a single provision, but two (one concerned with relationships with *pueri*, the other with relationships between adults). On this hypothesis, the two provisions would each have punished only one partner: in the case of relationships with *pueri*, only the adult would be punished, while in the case of relationships between adults, only the passive partner would be punished.

Let us start with the first of these provisions. What would allow us to assert that this law punished *stuprum cum puero*?

The story of Caius Scatinius Capitolinus shows that in 227 BC sexual relationships with free-born boys were punished through a *multa rogata*. It is more than reasonable to suppose – I would almost say, one

111

is forced to conclude – that when a law like the *Lex Scatinia* was introduced, punishing certain homosexual liaisons, the first concern of that law would be to set out legal penalties against this type of behaviour, removing the magistrate's former discretion as to whether or not the transgressor should be penalised, and in what amount.

To this we may add, on the one hand, that the sources from a later date explicitly state that *stuprum cum puero* is a crime,[74] and on the other hand that the *Lex Scatinia* was the only provision to deal with homosexuality before an Imperial Constitution dated AD 342, to which we shall return. The specification of *stuprum cum puero* as a crime, therefore, can only have derived from this law.

Now let us turn to the problem of relationships between adults. In Juvenal's second *Satire*, we saw Laronia scoffing at the man who, reeking of perfume, dares to accuse women of breaking the *Lex Iulia* while himself indulging in illicit loves. 'Where did you buy that balsam juice that exhales from your hairy neck?', she demands at the same time that she accuses him of breaking the *Lex Scatinia*.[75]

Obviously, the man in question was not a beardless adolescent, but a bearded adult male. Similarly, the other men whom Laronia charges with the same offence were not adolescents: she defines them as the phalanx of *molles*, soft boys. 'Soft boys', for the Romans, certainly did not mean homosexuals who assumed an active role, but only their passive brethren. *Molles* is a precise, unequivocal, almost technical term.[76] The *molles*, then, were those men who broke the *Lex Scatinia*. This meant that in the cases of homosexual attachments between adults, the penalty laid down by the law (unlike what happened in cases of *stuprum cum puero*) fell on the passive partner. Support for Juvenal's testimony appears to come from Seneca. In a speech, as we saw, for a freedman accused of having an affair with his former owner, Seneca's argument stated that 'inpudicitia in ingenuo crimen est, in servo necessitas, in liberto officium'. Defending the freedman from the charge of *inpudicitia* (a word which, when referring to a man, means sexual passivity), Seneca thus affirms without hesitation that the same behaviour, in a free citizen, would be a crime.[77]

Additional evidence comes from an epigram by Ausonius, mocking a man accused of being a passive homosexual:

> Iurisconsulto, cui vivit adultera coniunx
> Papia placuit, Iulia displacuit.
> Queritur, unde haec sit distantia? Semivir ipse
> Scatiniam metuens non timuit Titiam.[78]

To paraphrase: A prominent lawyer, who had an adulterous wife, was all in favour of the *Lex Papia*, the law which rewarded those who engaged in procreation – obviously something which his adulterous wife did – but had no time for the *Lex Iulia*, an Augustan law which we shall discuss further on, punishing adultery. Why such a disparity of judgement? For the same reason that, being only half a man, he had no fear of the *Lex Titia*[79] but quaked at the very mention of the *Lex Scatinia*.

At this point, the hypothesis that the *Lex Scatinia* also punished passive homosexuals is anything but implausible. These *molles* were the sort of men who, by taking a subordinate position like a woman, revealed their basic unsuitability to be Roman citizens; they were incapable of playing a dominant role, and thus exposed themselves to the ridicule and jokes of real men.

Already socially pilloried, passivity was now stigmatised also on a legal level, albeit in a very bland fashion, with a simple financial penalty which does not appear to have been applied. If our hypothesis is true, the *Lex Scatinia* ushered in a set of provisions designed to enforce a double standard of morality which remained unchanged for more than seven centuries: a Roman male, if he engaged in homosexual relations (so long as he did not violate a *puer*), incurred punishment only if he took a passive role. But what exactly was this punishment?

Previously, the only punishable homosexual behaviour had been *stuprum cum puero*, with the *multa rogata* as the regular penalty. The first innovation introduced by the *Lex Scatinia*, as we saw, was to fix the fine at a set tariff, removing the amount from the magistrate's discretion. The set amount appears to have been 10,000 sestertii.

In his *Institutio Oratoria*, Quintilian puts forward the case of a person having committed gross indecency on an *ingenuus* who had subsequently hanged himself on account of the outrage he had suffered. And Quintilian notes: the man was not punished for the death as though responsible for the hanging. He was sentenced to pay 10,000 sestertii, the set penalty for sexual abusers.[80]

This passage raises a problem. Could Quintilian be referring to gross indecency involving the use of violence? If the indecency had taken place between consenting parties, why should the person who had accepted this type of liaison subsequently hang himself? The problem is not negligible: if the case in question involved violence, the reference to the *Lex Scatinia* would obviously no longer apply. To work out what crime Quintilian has in mind, it is necessary to digress briefly on the laws against sexual violence.

By the time of Ulpian, gross indecency involving the use of violence was punishable under the *Lex Iulia de vi publica*.[81] That much can be stated with certainty, as it appears more than once in the sources.[82] And the penalty prescribed by law for public violence was capital punishment. In the *Pauli Sententiae*, for example, we read: 'He who violates a free-born male against his will is to be put to death.'[83]

But back in Quintilian's time, things had not yet reached this stage. Violent rape had not yet been brought under the terms of the Augustan law (the *Lex Iulia de vi publica* was passed by Augustus). It was still being punished by a simple *multa rogata*,[84] just like *stuprum cum puero* before the passing of the *Lex Scatinia*. In the light of these observations, Quintilian may be alluding to a violent outrage, and 10,000 sestertii may be the set penalty for this type of offence. The hypothesis is not implausible – which does not mean that it is necessarily correct.

Quintilian speaks of the 10,000 sestertii as a *poena constituta*, meaning that it was fixed *ex lege*, always the same. And in fact a *multa ex lege* was never laid down for gross indecency involving the use of violence. There was an immediate shift from the *multa rogata* to the death penalty. What Quintilian is referring to, then, is the penalty laid down for *stuprum cum puero* under the *Lex Scatinia*. Something that the sources never tell us is what penalty was prescribed for passive homosexuals, who also came to be punished under this law (which was the second major innovation introduced by the *Lex Scatinia*). Given the silence of the sources, it seems reasonable to infer that the penalty was, once again, 10,000 sestertii.

We have now reached the end of this long but unavoidable aside on the *Lex Scatinia*, and must face a further problem. In the section of the law covering relationships with *pueri*, was there a penalty not only for successful, but also for attempted indecency?

Christius, for example, maintains that this law struck at anybody who 'outraged a puer, tried to seduce him, or bribed his minders for that purpose'.[85] But Christius' reconstruction of the text of the law is based on a misreading. He confuses the provisions of the *Lex Scatinia* with the very different measures contained in the urban praetor's edict which, as already mentioned, protected free-born youths from people who followed them along the street, just as they followed women, subjecting them to insufferable and unrelenting harassment. A most intriguing edict, on which we must concentrate for a moment if we are to understand the sexual behaviour of the Romans. We must try to identify the reasons which led the praetor to issue the edict, and the specific types of behaviour which he wanted to outlaw.

The Edict *De adtemptata pudicitia*

The *Lex Scatinia* had punished pederasty. But clearly its provisions had
not scared off the Roman public. Perhaps the threatened punishment,
being only a simple financial penalty, was not such as to worry them
unduly. Roman youths went on being objects of desire, exactly as they
had been in the preceding centuries. Heedless of the law, adult males
did not scruple to show their intentions openly, and used all their wiles
to win the youngest and most fetching boys. In a city where increased
economic well-being had introduced a new lifestyle, and where respect
both formal and substantial for ancient rules had been lost, the situation had become disquieting. Boys were actually being pestered in the
streets, openly and brazenly: precisely those free-born lads who should
have been untouchable, if the *Lex Scatinia* were respected. At this point
it was necessary to take remedial action, and it fell to the urban praetor
to try to put things right.

It was customary for a new praetor, at the beginning of his year of
office, to issue an edict informing the citizens of the criteria which
would govern his administration of justice. One man, whose name is
unknown, established a penalty (also unknown) against anybody who
disturbed, on the public highway, not only respectable women, but also
praetextati.

Who exactly were these *praetextati*? They were the boys who wore a
praetexta tunic, meaning a white tunic, hemmed with purple, different
from the single-coloured tunic worn by full citizens. As they had not yet
attained political capabilities, the boys were not entitled to wear the
single-coloured tunic, so they wore the *praetexta*: the same toga which
was worn by priests and magistrates. This seems surprising at first sight,
but it should not. The boys, in fact, had a certain religious capacity, and
could take part in some religious ceremonies both private and public.[86]
The *praetextati*, then, were simply free-born youths: and the praetor
was protecting them, through his edict, from the attentions of cruising
lechers. More precisely, they were protected by those who followed
them 'silently and insistently' along the street – and it was obvious that
this happened very often. This was the meaning of the term *adsectari*:
following somebody along the street *tacite ac frequenter*, as explained
by the jurist Ulpian in his commentary on the praetor's edict. Ulpian
specifies that not everybody who behaved in this way was punished on
the basis of the edict, but only those who did it *contra bonos mores*[87] –
against the dictates of propriety – which fitted in perfectly with the title
of the edict: *de adtemptata pudicitia*.[88]

More than one type of behaviour was punished on the basis of this

115

edict, if we can believe what Ulpian tells us. More precisely, three acts were condemned. There were penalties for those who followed a *praetextatus* or a *materfamilias* along the street, but also for anybody who deprived them of their escort. Like respectable women, respectable boys in Rome were not allowed to go out on their own: they had to be accompanied by their *comites* (including teachers for the boys, writes Ulpian). The edict, therefore, punished anyone who *comites abduxit*, meaning anyone who had removed the people accompanying a woman or a boy.[89] Nor were these the only ones. Ulpian writes: 'tenetur hoc edicto non solum qui comitem abduxit, vel etiam si quis eorum quem appellavisset...'. ('The edict applies not only to one who abducts an attendant but also to one who accosts...one of them.')'[90] *Appellare*: this is the third case for punishment. The word *appellare*, according to Ulpian, meant addressing the woman or the boy *blanda oratione* – with coaxing words.[91]

This is the content of the edict according to Ulpian's commentary. It is much more extensive than would appear from a reading of Gaius who, towards the middle of the second century, refers only to cases of *adsectatio*. Should we conclude that, with the passage of time, the types of behaviour punished on the basis of the edict were increased? The hypothesis should not be ruled out. By the time of Ulpian *adtemptata pudicitia*, which had started out as a free-standing offence, had come to form part of the concept of *iniuria*. And *iniuria* (which originally meant personal injury) by now had come to include attempts on personal honour.[92] Together with *adsectatio*, and together with the behaviour of those who addressed the object of their desires with persuasive words (a type of behaviour very close to *adsectatio*, and which had probably been quickly perceived as equivalent to it) it was therefore more than logical to punish the behaviour of *comites abducere*. Anyone removing the escort of a *materfamilias* or a *praetextatus* was placing that person's public image in peril: without their retinue, they appeared to those who met them in the street as persons of low moral standing.

The problem of *pudicitia*, then, arose on two different levels: one of substance and one of form. On the level of substance, *pudicitia* meant virginity. This applied both to men and to women. As we know, a man too had his *pudicitia*, which he lost (becoming *inpudicus*) if he became the passive partner in homosexual intercourse (while the active partner in the same duo did not become *inpudicus*). Protecting the *pudicitia* of a *praetextatus* therefore meant, in the first place, preventing him from becoming involved in a homosexual relationship which, given his age, would certainly have placed him in the position of the *inpudicus*.[93] The *Lex Scatinia* was designed to ensure that this did not happen.

On the formal level, on the other hand, *pudicitia* was a problem of image. If one met a *materfamilias* or a boy on the street, one had to be able to classify them immediately, at first sight, as respectable people. Hence the laws against unwanted admirers.[94] These laws were not a repressive measure against homosexuality as such. By protecting the honour of women and boys at the same time and in the same way, this legislation shows, if anything, that the dichotomy between heterosexual and homosexual behaviour was beside the point – the *inpudicitia* of *pueri* was neither more nor less serious than that of women. *Matres-familias* and *pueri* were to be protected, without distinction, from persistent and troublesome suitors in public places. These two supposedly respectable categories of people were defended in exactly the same way from a type of behaviour which is familiar to anyone who lives in a Mediterranean country. Actually, this behaviour is not exclusively motivated by a real desire to seduce the victim; it also stems from a need felt by the male of the species to give a theatrical display and proof of virility. A ritual game, in short, where each player performs a time-honoured part: the male plays the hunter, while the woman (or in Rome the boy) plays the prey.

Let us return to the problem of the relationship between the edict and the *Lex Scatinia*.

Given what we have noted about the respective content of the two provisions, there seems little room for doubt. The praetor's edict is obviously later, and the type of behaviour that it punishes is less serious than that punished by the law, presupposing, therefore, that the more serious behaviour was already outlawed. What would be the point of penalising somebody who importuned a boy on the street, in a situation where somebody seducing the same boy would remain unpunished? Confirmation of this point comes from a passage in Plautus, which I believe allows us to date the edict with remarkable precision.

In the *Curculio* the slave Palinurus meets Phaedromus at night, in the street. Phaedromus is hoping to catch a glimpse of Planesium, the girl whom he loves, and whom Cappadox the pimp is preventing him from meeting. Palinurus advises him in the following terms:

> nemo ire quemquam publica prohibet via
> dum ne per fundum saeptum facias semitam
> dum te abstineas nupta vidua virgine
> iuventute ac pueris liberis ama quidlubet.[95]

Nobody stops anyone from walking along the public highway. Provided you don't make inroads on fenced-in preserves, provided you keep away from married women, widows, virgins, young innocents, and children of respectable families, love anyone you want.

Plautus is usually thought to be referring to the *Lex Scatinia* here.[96] But this assumption is really quite unlikely. The *Lex Scatinia* dealt only with homosexual relationships. Plautus, on the other hand, is alluding to a provision which offered protection, at the same time and in the same way, to women and boys. Obviously, he was thinking of something different from the law – to be precise, the praetor's edict.

It may be noted, additionally, that the edict was directed towards those who made a nuisance of themselves in the street, and that Plautus explicitly states that nobody can forbid anyone (if he refrains from pestering women and boys) from parading along the public highway. If he had been thinking about the ban on committing *stuprum*, what would have been the meaning of this reference?

Lastly, one might note the absolutely identical categories of people protected in the edict and people whom Plautus says are not be annoyed on the public highway. Who were Plautus' *nuptae, viduae* and *virgines*, if not the *matresfamilias* of the edict? And what were Plautus' *pueri* if not *praetextati*?

The term *puer*, writes the jurist Paulus, has three meanings: the first is 'slave', the second indicates the male (as opposed to the female) sex, and the third refers to the *aetas puerilis*, the boyhood years.[97] But what exactly is the *aetas puerilis*? According to a rather dubious etymology supplied by Isidore of Seville, the word *puer* derives *a puritate*: it indicates the purity of those who bear this title.[98] And Censorinus adds that *pueri* are so called because they are *puri*, meaning pre-pubescent.[99] Once again, an extremely questionable assertion on the etymological level, but highly significant for our purposes: on this account, boys stopped being *pueri* when they reached puberty. Now, the Romans had decreed that a boy reached puberty at the age of fourteen (we may disregard the theory that an *inspectio corporis* was necessary to establish when a boy had reached puberty), so *pueri* were boys under that age.[100] In other words, they were the *praetextati*, the boys who had not yet reached the age of political capacity (which was conferred on reaching puberty), and so wore the *praetexta*.

At this point, the circle closes: Plautus can only be alluding to the edict *De adtemptata pudicitia*: and given that his comedy dates from 193 BC,[101] the edict must be earlier than that date. But not much earlier: the words of Palinurus, paraphrasing the edict, clearly refer to a recent event, a gag designed to raise a laugh from the audience, an allusion to an item of current affairs, which was a subject of discussion and probably the target for some cynical humour.

The edict, then, was promulgated about thirty years after the *Lex Scatinia* was passed. Obviously the Romans had been not in the least perturbed by the threat of financial penalties. Boys continued to be pestered, just like women. The law punished those who carried on sexual liaisons with them; the edict punished those who harassed them on the streets: but the Romans went on courting them just the same.

6

The Late Republic and the Principate

The Poets

By the second century BC, the Romans had got into the habit of openly
and brazenly courting free-born boys. Homosexuality was undergoing a
sea-change. Formerly, in the early centuries, it had been an expression
of total and irrepressible masculinity, imposed on slaves in a frenzy of
aggressive virility. Now it had turned into a desire to be seductive, not
only in the sexual sense. And that desire was sometimes – indeed,
increasingly – triggered by free-born boys.

A new situation, then, which the law disallowed and the city authorities had tried to control, but without success. One important factor
undermining the attempt to contain homosexual relationships within
the boundaries allowed by former *mores* was the gradual Hellenisation
of Roman culture. And loving boys soon became, as in Greece, a
fashionable literary theme:

> My soul has left me; it has fled, methinks,
> To Theotimus; he its refuge is.
> But what if I should beg that he refuse
> The truant to admit, but cast it out?
> I'll go to him; but what if I be caught?
> What shall I do? Queen Venus, lend me aid.

These lines were written by Quintus Lutatius Catulus, consul in 102 BC
and victor over the Cimbri in 101 at the Campi Raudii, a highly refined
man of letters, and such a connoisseur of Greek that the Greeks themselves accepted him as an authority.[1] And in fact his verses echo the
forty-first epigram of Callimachus. As well as providing evidence of a
literary fashion, they are clear proof of the fact that by now, in Rome,
the love of *pueri* was experienced 'in the Greek style'. How could the
fashion of celebrating pederastic relationships in verse have spread in a

society where a social interdict weighed down on this kind of relationship? Quintus Lutatius Catulus was not its only literary exponent.

> O Phileros, why a torch, that we need not?
> Just as we are we'll go, our hearts aflame.
> That flame no wild wind's blast can ever quench,
> Or rain that falls torrential from the skies;
> Venus herself alone can quell her fire,
> No other force there is that has such power.

Thus writes Valerius Aedituus in a poem inspired by a boy, reproduced (like the one by Lutatius) by Aulus Gellius. In a highly significant
passage from his *Attic Nights*, we read of a discussion about Greek and
Latin culture. One speaker alleges that nobody in Rome had written
verses as lovely as the Greek poets, whereupon a defender of Latin
literature replies by quoting some Roman erotic poetry. These examples
include the two poems for Theotimus and Phileros, side by side with
ones on heterosexual love. No distinction is drawn.[2]

Clearly, the romantic love of *pueri* was now fully accepted. And
before long it was to be sung by poets far more famous (or at least
better known to us) than Lutatius and Aedituus: for example, Catullus.

Catullus

Even those who know nothing of Catullus apart from his name (which
is uncertain, by the way: Gaius Catullus, as Apuleius and Jerome have
it, or Quintus Catullus, as we read in some minor manuscripts of Pliny
the Elder?) know that this poet from Verona loved a woman whom he
celebrated under the name of Lesbia.[3]

Less well known is the fact that, as well as the kisses of Lesbia (those
thousands of kisses which he begs in the famous fifth poem), Catullus
desired other kisses, no less sweet than those of the lady who threw his
life into disarray – the kisses of Juventius:

> Your honeyed eyes, Juventius,
> If someone let me go on kissing,
> I'd kiss three hundred thousand times
> Nor never think I'd had enough,
> Not if our osculation's crop
> Were closer-packed than dried corn-ears.[4]

But who was this honey-eyed Juventius that Catullus wanted to kiss
endlessly? An actual person with whom the poet had an affair, or
merely a literary fiction?

The parallel with the more famous poem number 5, dedicated to Lesbia, and the appearance in both poems of the same theme of thousands of kisses, with other infinite numbers to follow, have caused (and still cause) some scholars to believe that Catullus' eight poems for Juventius are nothing but a literary fiction.

The influence of Alexandrian poetry, according to the supporters of this theory, had introduced the theme of love affairs with men in the Rome of Catullus' time – meaning the first century BC. But for the Romans, this was purely a literary theme, a poetic fiction, a stylistic exercise: it did not tell of a real life experience.[5] In the case of Catullus, in particular, the comparison between the poems dedicated to Lesbia and those for Juventius is put forward as proof of this. The ones for Lesbia are sincere, passionate, inspired by deep and irresistible feeling, while those for Juventius reveal, by comparison, their weakness, artificial style, lack of sincerity and inspiration – in other words the absence of that transport of ecstasy which makes the poems for Lesbia, and only those, into true love poems. The same judgement is offered of the entire canon of Augustan poetry. But on closer examination, this interpretation of Latin verse as a literary product totally detached from individual experience of life, and especially from the everyday reality experienced by the poets, is very hard to accept.[6]

This is not to say, of course, that one can deny the influence of Alexandrian poetry on the Roman love elegy. Nor does it mean that we can treat poets like Catullus, in whom the sincerity of poetic inspiration shines forth, on the same basis as poets like Tibullus and Propertius, of whom it is true to say that the element of literary exercise not infrequently gains the upper hand over spontaneity, to such an extent that one seriously doubts the relationship between the facts narrated and any real experience of life.[7]

But that is a different matter, relating to the entire output of the poets in the generation following Catullus: their entire production, be it noted, not just a single component, their homosexual love poetry. With Tibullus, for example, we may reasonably enquire not only whether his love for Marathus is genuine, but also whether the story of his love affair with Delia is true.[8] This problem is quite independent of whether the love being celebrated is heterosexual or homosexual. And it is a very different problem from the one which is sometimes raised in the case of Catullus. There seems to be no problem about the reality of Catullus' love for Lesbia. The critics only question his love for Juventius, which they see as a literary concession to the Alexandrian fashion. But the arguments in support of this hypothesis are really very weak.

Homosexual liaisons with free-born boys, it is argued, were prohibited by the *Lex Scatinia*, and Juventius was a boy not only of a free, but probably of a noble family.[9] True enough. But it is equally true that the *Lex Scatinia*, as we have seen, was not always obeyed. Besides, sexual relationships with women other than one's own wife were prohibited far more severely – and yet the heterosexual love affairs celebrated by the elegiac poets were all extramarital, starting with the one between Catullus and Lesbia. Would legal impediments be enough to rule out the reality of a genuinely consummated relationship?

After these introductory remarks, we may now attempt to reconstruct the story of Catullus and Juventius, starting with one of the loveliest poems dedicated to the boy, number 99:

> Honeyed Juventius, while you were playing I stole from you
> A sweeter kiss than sweet ambrosia.
> Yes, but I didn't get it scot-free, for I remember
> Being stuck for more than an hour on a cross
> While I made my excuses to you but could not move
> Your cruelty one bit with all my tears.
> For hardly was it done before you drenched your lips
> With water-drops and wiped them with soft knuckles,
> Lest anything infectious from my mouth remain,
> As though it were some pissed-on whore's foul spittle.
> Besides you were not slow to hand wretched me over
> To angry Love and crucify me every way,
> So that for me that kiss was now turned from ambrosia
> To something sourer than sour hellebore.
> Since you propose this penalty for a wretched lover,
> Henceforth I'll never steal a kiss again.[10]

Here again we find the theme of the kisses. This time they are not only dreamed about; this time, there is a stolen kiss.[11] And Juventius, as sweet as he is capricious, pretends to be disgusted: in short, he plays hard to get, forcing Catullus to beg pardon, to cry, to promise that he will never again try such an approach. He forces the poet, then, to conform to a model of behaviour which is very different from the one which his virility would enjoin, and which perfectly matches the Greek style of pederastic love.

But Catullus, although he accepts the rules of the game, is a man worthy of the name, proud of his image as a 'ravisher' and intolerant of insinuations against his manliness. When Furius and Aurelius, formerly his friends, dare to snigger about his feelings for Juventius and to defame him, saying that he is effeminate like his verses, Catullus reacts like a true Roman male:

I'll bugger you and stuff your gobs,
Aurelius Kink and Poofter Furius,
For thinking me, because my verses
Are rather sissy, not quite decent.
For the true poet should be chaste
Himself, his verses need not be.
Indeed they've salt and charm then only
When rather sissy and not quite decent
And when they can excite an itch
I don't say in boys but in those hairy
Victims of lumbar sclerosis.
Because you've read of my x thousand
Kisses you doubt my virility?
I'll bugger you and stuff your gobs.[12]

Aurelius and Furius call him effeminate, but the real sissies are themselves. The first is *pathicus*, the second *cinaedus*. *Pathicus* (from the Greek) means passive. *Cinaedus* (also from the Greek *kinaidos*) is a term which indicates homosexuality as far back as Lucilius.[13] Aurelius and Furius, men who are unworthy of the name, will get what they deserve. As well as buggering them (*pedicabo vos*), Catullus will force them to perform fellatio (*irrumabo*). In the sexual ethics of Rome, this is the act which more than any other offends the dignity of the person forced to perform it, and proves the infamous character of anyone who performs it spontaneously.[14]

Fellare meant doing something which was exactly the opposite of what a Roman male ought to do. Instead of taking his own pleasure, a man performing fellatio placed himself at the service of another man's enjoyment. This is how Catullus reaffirms his virility. It is a threat which often recurs in his poetry, and which he utters once more against Aurelius, who as well as mocking him has tried to steal Juventius from him:

Aurelius, father of the hungers,
Not just of these but of all that were
Ere this or will be in other years,
You long to bugger my love, and not
In secret. You're with him, sharing jokes,
Close at his side, trying everything.
It's no good. If you plot against me
I'll get in first and stuff your gob.
I'd keep quiet if you did it well fed;
But it annoys me that the boy

Will learn from you to hunger and thirst.
So stop it while you decently may,
In case you make your end – gob-stuffed.[15]

Catullus' sexuality is undoubtedly different from that of the Romans in the early centuries. On the one hand, he does conform to the old model of the roué, whose virility is entrusted to his ability to have his way with men and women without distinction. On the other hand, unlike his predecessors, he uses his role as violator of men only as a punishment, against his enemies, against all those whom he despises or who have done him wrong. His beloved Juventius, however, receives only favours, caresses and kisses: all the rewards of romantic love.

In Catullus we see the coexistence of two different cultural models: the Roman and the Greek. This is no accident. The Greek example, while it was certainly not the cause of the spread of homosexuality in Rome, was equally certainly an element which, by profoundly influencing Roman culture, transformed the characteristics of indigenous homosexuality, introducing a new type of relationship between men.

There was a real love affair between the lover and the beloved youth, exactly as in Greece (with the exception that in Rome the relationship did not involve the educational aspect, which as we saw was fundamentally important in Greece). This affair was destined to come to an end (at least theoretically, exactly as in Greece) at the moment when the boy entered a bond which for the Romans was normally nothing but a social duty, marking the beginning of a new era in his life: the bond of matrimony. This can be seen in another celebrated poem by Catullus, number 61, written on the occasion of the marriage of Manlius Torquatus.

Manlius Torquatus has decided to get married, and as always the nuptial ceremony is celebrated with great solemnity. As the bride arrives, covered by the traditional purple veil (the *flammeum*) a boy distributes nuts to the wedding guests – a ritual action, wishing fertility for the marriage.[16] But the little boy who performs this ritual is doing so with an ill grace, and for a good reason. He is the bridegroom's *concubinus*, that is to say, the young slave with whom (according to a typically Roman custom in this case) the master has a stable sexual relationship, not exclusive but privileged. Catullus turns to this *concubinus*, urging him to carry out his duties more graciously. While it is undeniable that by handing out the nuts he is marking not only the marriage of his owner but also the end of his own love affair with him, it is nevertheless also true that this progress is natural and inevitable. Their love was doomed to end: the bridegroom must henceforth serve Talassius, the

125

god of matrimony. For him, poor concubine, the 'time of nuts' is over:

> Let the ribald Fescennine
> Jesting not be silent longer
> Nor boy concubine refuse
> Nuts to the children when he hears
> Of master's love abandoned.
>
> Give the children nuts, you idle
> Concubine. For long enough
> You have played with nuts, but now
> It's time to serve Talassius.
> Concubine, give nuts.[17]

Talassius is the god of matrimony, the god who must henceforth be served. A new season of life begins, not only for the boy concubine, but also for the bridegroom:

> You are said to find it hard,
> Perfumed bridegroom, to give up
> Smooth-skinned boys, but give them up,
> O Hymen Hymeneal O,
> O Hymen Hymeneal.
>
> We realize you've only known
> Permitted pleasures; husbands, though,
> Have no right to the same pleasures.
> O Hymen Hymeneal O,
> O Hymen Hymeneal.[18]

It would be hard to ask for a more explicit enunciation of what the Romans thought permissible in the line of homosexuality. Before getting married, a man was allowed to have relationships with slaves; after marriage, this could no longer be countenanced.

Celebrating a wedding, Catullus cleaves to the canons of traditional sexual morality: the homosexual loves to which he refers are indulged in with the household staff. But something very significant emerges from his words. Clearly, by this time premarital homosexual love affairs were often carried on by free-born boys. If this had not been the case, what would have been the point of the phrase with which Catullus reassures the bridegroom when he says to him (not without a certain tinge of irony, almost as if to suggest that this was not in fact the case) that everybody knows that his loves were always exclusively permissible?

But let us leave Manlius Torquatus, and return to the story of Catullus. His love for Juventius, certainly outside the ambit of the most authentic Roman traditions, is carried on according to a paradigm which, while theoretically inadmissible, is now widespread in Rome, and as we shall see, will continue to spread in the years that follow. This is a passionate and romantic love, not at all different in style from his love for Lesbia (although it reaches a different degree of intensity). And that certainly represents a remarkable innovation in Roman culture. To understand why, we must digress for a moment on the new attitudes to feelings expressed by the elegiac poets.

As already noted, Lesbia is not Catullus' wife, just as none of the women loved by the poets in the succeeding generation is the wife of her celebrator. Delia is not Tibullus' wife, Cynthia is not Propertius' wife, Corinna is not Ovid's wife. But why should we be surprised? Marriage, as we know, is not the place for love. Love, taken as a romantic passion (whether genuine or literary: even admitting that in some cases we are dealing with literary fictions, what is important for present purposes is to identify the social model of love), is experienced outside of marriage, with women (like Lesbia, Delia, Cynthia or Corinna) belonging to a *demi-monde* in which it is possible to move from one lover to the next, and live in luxury thanks to the gifts which lovers are obliged to bestow, and which their beloved ladies benignly accept.[19]

However, alongside these women there is now another object of romantic love, and this new object is provided by free-born boys like Juventius, praised by their lovers exactly as the women are praised. 'O you, the delicious flower of all the Juventiuses that are, and were and will be . . .', Catullus writes.[20]

Juventius, the most adorable of all boys in the world, as is obvious and, one might almost say, inevitable for anyone who is the object of such a love, is capricious and unfaithful – like Lesbia, and like all women. Not satisfied with tormenting poor Catullus over a small stolen kiss, he betrays his love exactly like Lesbia. On one occasion, the man involved is a foreigner from Pesaro:

> Among so many people was there really no 'nice man',
> Juventius, for you to fall in love with
> Except that guest of yours from moribund Pisaurum
> More jaundiced than a gilded statue,
> Who tickles your present fancy, whom you dare prefer to us
> Not knowing what a shocker you are making?[21]

On another occasion the man involved was an unknown *homo bellus*. Or rather, a man whom Juventius sees as a respectable citizen, but Catullus points out that he does not own 'a single slave or strong-box'. He is anything but comfortably off: once again, as in the case of Aurelius, Catullus lashes out at his rivals by declaring that they are quite destitute. In his elegant and refined world, poverty (whether genuine or supposed) is a sign of unworthiness.[22] On yet another occasion the man involved was called Ravidus, and Catullus shames him in front of everybody with his savage iambics.[23] To say nothing of Furius, the accomplice of Aurelius (who has now seduced Juventius) and guilty, with him, of having corrupted him. Catullus, as we saw, threatens Furius, as well as Aurelius, that he will inflict on him the penalty which husbands inflicted on their wives' lovers.[24]

Catullus, in short, lives out his heterosexual and homosexual love affairs in an absolutely identical way. The love for Lesbia is undoubtedly the love of his life, but the love for Juventius is positioned on the same emotional register, albeit at a lower level. It is simply another love affair, and if it happens to be less elevated than the love for Lesbia, this is certainly not because Juventius is a man. From an emotional and sexual point of view, Catullus is bisexual. It is really very difficult to accept the hypothesis that his feelings for Juventius were in many ways paternal, as E.A. Havelock, for example, maintains.[25]

For Catullus, men and women are interchangeable love objects – always remembering that he adopted a sexually active role with men. The old convention of virility, seen as the assumption of the male role, is still very much alive in Catullus. The one new element in his poetry is his romantic psychological attitude, and his infringement of the rule whereby the beloved boy was supposed to be a slave. What we are looking at, in short, is the emergence of a new model of homosexual relationships, taking over part of the Roman and part of the Greek tradition. And we will find this new model substantially unchanged in the poets of the following generation.

Tibullus

One generation younger than Catullus, Albius Tibullus, probably born in 54 BC, was a handsome man from a well-to-do family. That is how Horace describes him in the fourth Epistle of his first book: *di tibi formam, di tibi divitias dederunt.* ('The gods gave you beauty and riches.')[26] A fortunate man, then. His references (in the first Elegy of the first book) to the *paupertas* in which he had lived have often caused his readers to imagine some drastic change in his financial situation, due to the confiscation of his family's goods, which were distributed to veterans after the battle of Philippi. But in all probability these complaints should not be taken too literally: Tibullus loved to grouse. As Horace said, he was prey to unease, and magnified his problems out of proportion. A difficult and tormented man, in short. In keeping with his character, his love affairs were also tormented. The ones which are of interest in the present context are not the affair with Delia or that with Nemesis, but the one with Marathus, the beautiful lad to whom Elegies 8 and 9 are dedicated.

A literary exercise, perhaps? A concession to fashionable subject matter, as is often alleged?[27] Here again we may refer to the remarks made about the love between Catullus and Juventius, leaving aside the observation that in fact, in Tibullus' case, the artificial nature of the verses makes it anything but improbable that he was telling imaginary tales, whether heterosexual or homosexual. The poems for Marathus are no more artificial than the ones for Delia.[28] Once again, in relation to Tibullus, we must reiterate the point that while it is a mistake to imagine a total split between the more or less genuine inspiration of a poet and his style of life, it is equally mistaken to believe everything he says about himself and his love affairs as the literal truth. References to episodes, facts, details of an affair may be imaginary: but the poetic themes chosen must correspond to a mental attitude, individual habits and genuine inclinations. The feelings described (leaving aside the person giving rise to the feelings and the truthfulness of individual episodes) must have been experienced in some shape or form; they must have been part of the poet's life experience. This means that Tibullus, whether his affair with Marathus was genuine or fictional, had a very good understanding of the love of boys. The elegies for Marathus, in other words, inevitably reveal an aspect (which is anything but negligible, as we shall see) of his sentimental and sexual life: that part of it which was taken up by loves for other men which, given his temperament, caused him continual torment.

Marathus was unfaithful to Tibullus. Unlike Juventius, who betrayed Catullus with other men, Marathus betrays Tibullus with a woman, or rather, he has fallen in love with a woman, who resists him, has other lovers and makes him suffer. And how does Tibullus react to this? At first he takes the attitude of an altruistic and generous lover, whose only desire is the happiness of his beloved. Believing, perhaps, that Marathus will continue to love him in any case, he even goes so far as to urge his fair rival not to keept the boy on tenterhooks:

> Do not be hard for your young man to win;
> Venus will punish such a heinous sin.
> Don't ask for gifts — they're for grey heads to give,

129

That their cold limbs may in soft arms revive.
Dearer than gold a boy of smooth white face,
And no rough beard to chafe your long embrace.
Give him your gleaming arms for his support,
And kings' great riches may be set at nought. . . .
Don't torture him; what glory can it hold
To rout a boy? Be hard but to the old.
Spare the green youth; he knows no taint of blame,
But too much love has sallowed his whole frame.
This boy once laughed at wretched lovers' kind,
Not seeing the god of vengeance close behind.
He often mocked at tears of pain, they say,
And checked an eager love with feigned delay.
Now he can't bear to be held at a distance,
And hates to meet the barred door's stern resistance.
But punishment, my girl, awaits disdain;
How much you'll long to live this day again![29]

But this attitude soon changes. The poet realises that he has lost Marathus. The boy is not content with loving the woman whom the poet himself has often, in his innocence, helped him to meet. He has done much worse: he has been corrupted by gifts from a man. And as well as being the lover of that man he is also the lover of his wife. For Tibullus, this is the end:

Why, being then set to wrong my helpless love,
Swear, but to break them, oaths by heaven above? . . .
My boy has been ensnared by gifts – gods turn
All gifts to water which they do not burn.
But soon he'll pay the price; dust will not spare
His glamour, winds will make coarse his sleek hair,
His face be tanned, bleached by the sun his head,
His tender feet with long roads chafed and red.
How often have I urged 'Don't smirch that grace
With gold; harm hides behind gold's glinting face.
If some, ensnared by wealth, have outraged love,
Venus is harsh to such, and hard to move. . . .
Then would you swear that for no weight of gold
Or gems would your true faith ever be sold.
Not if Campania could thus be got,
Or the Falernian field, the wine-god's plot.
You'd make me think, with such deceiving skill,
That stars don't shine and rivers run uphill.

You even wept: unschooled like you to lie
I'd fondly wipe your cheeks' moist channels dry.
What could I do – but that you suffered too?
May your girl's heart prove light, so taught by you.
To keep eavesdroppers from your talk at night,
I've often stood outside holding a light.
Often she's come, when I took up your cause,
Unhoped for, hiding veiled behind closed doors.
I wrecked my hopes, so trusting, so obtuse;
I might have been more wary of your noose. . . .
Curse you, whose aim is but to sell your charms
And win fat recompense in brimful palms,
And you who dared corrupt the boy with gifts –
May your wife ever mock you with her shifts,
And when she's tired her lover out unseen,
Lie with you spent – a blanket in between; . . .
Do you suppose she draws the toothed comb through
Those locks, and prinks them up, for you?
Does she walk out because of your fair charms
In Tyrian drapes, with gold bands on her arms?
No – but she wants to attract a young man's eye . . .
And yet with him my boy has passed the night –
He'd even act a wild beast's catamite.
You dared to sell caresses owed to me,
And pass my kisses round promiscuously.
You'll weep when I'm held in another's chains,
Wielding his proud rod over your domains;
And I'll be glad; a golden palm set up
For Venus shall attest my flowing cup:
Freed from false love Tibullus offers this,
And begs you think of him with gratefulness.[30]

This, then, is the affair with Marathus, as Tibullus tells it. Even were
we to conclude that this is not a true story, such a conclusion would be
quite irrelevant. If Tibullus was able to imagine a story of this kind
(always supposing that we are dealing with an imaginative account) it
still proves that relationships with boys were seen in social and sentimental terms. They served as an open and explicit alternative to
relationships with women, as the expression of a feeling which was
sometimes stronger, sometimes weaker than the heterosexual feeling;
but in any event both types of love held their place by right in the world
of love. Confirmation of this comes from another elegy by Tibullus,

which gives an explicit programmatic account of the rules for the new sentimental education.

In the fourth elegy of the first book Tibullus turns to Priapus, asking him to reveal the secret of his success in this field. The god replies, giving the poet (and through him his readership) a lengthy recital of advice, warnings and precepts which will help lovers to gain the favours they seek:

'Avoid them; don't let yourself near a gang of blooming boys;
In every one of them there'll be some ground for passion.
One boy is delightful for his tight rein on a horse,
Another parts still water with a chest as white as snow;
One captivates you with his bold effrontery; another boy's
Soft cheeks have virgin modesty standing guard.
Even if at first he does refuse, don't you give in
Through lack of perseverance; he'll soon accept the yoke. . . .
Don't hesitate to swear; the winds sweep off false oaths of love
Across the land and wavetops into nothingness.
Praise be to Jupiter – the Father decreed they had no force,
If sworn in desire by misplaced love.
Dictynna overlooks the protestations you make by her arrows;
Likewise Minerva with her locks.[31]

You now, give in to your young man's every whim;
Love wins a million victories by pandering.
Agree to go with him, however long a road he contemplates,
Even when the dog-star grills the fields with baking thirst;
Even if the rainbow stripes the dark sky with iridescent streaks,
Threatening the coming downpour;
Or if he intends to pass on shipboard through the inky waves,
Seize oars and urge the boat through the sea yourself;
Have no regret for unremitting toil endured,
Or hands worn down with unaccustomed tasks;
If his desire is to hem high valleys with his snares,
And you can please him by it, shoulder cheerfully the nets.
If fencing's what he wants, then limber up your arm and take him on;
Occasionally presenting him your open flank, so he can win.
Then he'll be kind, then you can grasp
The precious kiss; he will resist, but snatch and you'll have it.
At first you'll have to snatch; later you'll only have to ask;
And finally he'll embrace you at his own desire.
Unfortunately our age has grown used to some miserable practices –
Nowadays a tender young boy will expect a present.

132

A malevolent stone lie heavy on your bones,
You, who first introduced to men the sale of love.
Give your heart where the Muses are, boys; love learned poets;
Golden gifts should not outshine the damsels of Pierus.[32]

... Venus indeed wills that we should woo our loves,
Ant takes the part of doleful entreaties and lovelorn tears.'

So pronounced the god – for me to recite to Titius;[33]
But Titius' wife won't let him recall my words for an instant.
In his case he can obey her, if he must; but you, maltreated of some sly,
   sophisticated boy,
You must make of me your well-attended schoolmaster.
Each man has his point of pride – I stand to be consultant
To scorned lovers; my door is open to you all.
I'll see the day, when, as I bear the torch of Venus' precepts,
Old as I am, my young supporters shall chair me home.
But oh, how lingering the tortures Marathus inflicts;
My techniques, my subterfuges are not quite enough.
Spare me I beg you, boy, lest I become a cautionary tale,
And people titter at my useless pedantry.[34]

The identical nature of the rules which Tibullus recommends for
lovers, and the rules of pederastic courtship in Athens, is so obvious as
to require no comment. In Rome too, the *pueri* played hard to get,
requiring to be flattered and courted. In Rome too, their lovers had
to put up with this behaviour, satisfying their desires, proving their
dedication, swearing eternal love. The impression that the Roman
model is now a perfect copy of its Greek original is strengthened still
further by one particularly significant detail. Lovers, says Tibullus, are
permitted to swear false: the gods make an exception and permit this.
This statement has already been found in Plato. A perfect match, then.
If there is a difference, it may consist in the increased emphasis on the
rules of the game, which in Rome (at least in Tibullus' description) seem
to have been taken to excess, forcing the lover to become almost the
slave of a beloved who, for his part, goes to extremes in promoting
himself as an object of desire. Instead of playing modest and reserved,
as the Athenian rules demanded of a *pais*, his Roman counterpart was a
capricious, spoiled, pretentious brat.

But perhaps, on further reflection, it is not so strange that this was
the case in Rome. Removed from the historical and cultural context in
which they had first developed, transferred into an environment where
pederasty lacked the well-established roots which it had had in Greece,

applied in a world where they were no longer useful – as they had been in Greece – for guaranteeing the moral, cultural and political formation of boys, the rules of the game for pederasty in Rome were essentially an empty code. They reproduced the style, but not the substance, of the relationship with the *paides*. Consequently, the rules were interpreted and played in a formal, extreme and fatuous manner. One thing, however, is certain: by the Augustan age, homosexual relationships in Rome had changed to such a degree that Tibullus feels the need to set forth the rules of a new code of love. And this is clearly not done for the sake of his own personal preference for pederastic loves.

It is undeniable that Tibullus preferred *pueri* to women. The tone of the fourth elegy in the first book is unequivocal. Reading about the beauty of the *pueri*, all equally seductive in so many different ways, it is hard to avoid the impression that the poet is declaring his weakness in the face of their fascination. His exaltation of the love of boys is redolent of a special personal commitment and involvement, contrasting with the pity and scorn expressed in the last lines of the elegy for that unknown Titius who, dominated by his wife, is unable to take advantage of the poet's advice.

But moving beyond these personal observations about Tibullus, the fact that emerges clearly from a reading of his verses is that the 'Greek model' has now invaded Rome. If it were otherwise, what would be the point of Tibullus' aspiration to be considered the teacher of all those who loved a *puer* and suffered in their attempts to win him? Romantic love for a boy was now part of the sentimental experience of Romans. Confirmation of this point comes from the evidence of Propertius.

Propertius

Less personally given to the love of young men than Tibullus,[35] Propertius is nonetheless an author whose work presents many highly informative sidelights on the way in which Roman men experienced their affairs with boys. His elegies, collected in four books (the first of which was published in 28–27 and the fourth in 14 BC, perhaps posthumously), are dominated, it must be said, by his love for a woman called Hostia,[36] celebrated under the name of Cynthia. But despite this, Propertius too – albeit in a non-autobiographical manner – presents the theme of love for boys, seen as a very live issue. Not for the poet himself, of course, but for his friend Gallus, who in the fifth elegy of the first book is identified as a rival of Propertius in his love for Cynthia,[37] but who is later found (in the twentieth elegy of the same book) to have fallen in love with a boy. And Propertius (who in the fifth elegy exhorted him to leave Cynthia alone) in this case urges him to fight for his love.

The boy whom Gallus loves is beautiful: according to Propertius, no less lovely than Hylas. This Hylas is a character whom we have already met. Theocritus, in his thirteenth *Idyll*, tells how one day Hylas was snatched away by three nymphs, who stole him from his lover Hercules, and Hercules suffered terribly, weeping for his beloved, until he finally bowed to the inevitable. The myth of Hylas is also reproduced by Propertius, but he however, draws a different moral from Theocritus. Theocritus had addressed his *Idyll* to his friend Nicias, abandoned by his beloved for a woman, so as to persuade him that this is a natural fate. When the beloved boy grows up and reaches marriageable age, women gain the upper hand. If this has happened even to Hercules, and if even Hercules has resigned himself to this, why should Nicias not also have to yield?

But Propertius makes different use of this myth: it should serve Gallus as a preventive warning. Gallus must understand, before it is too late, that women can take away his boy. And once he knows this, he can prevent it from happening: 'Warned by this tale, my Gallus, thou shalt keep thy love secure, thou that aforetime didst seem to entrust thy Hylas to the nymphs.' Thus the poet addresses his friend in the last lines of the elegy, at the end of his mythical story. A few words, but very significant ones. There is a clear impression that according to Propertius, his friend Gallus is blissfully unaware of the hazard represented by a rival of the female sex. He appears to be 'entrusting' his beloved to the nymphs. At this point one naturally thinks of the affair of Tibullus and Marathus. Tibullus, too, found himself vying with a woman. And, at least in the beginning, he took this rather lightly. If he went so far as to assist the clandestine meetings between the boy and his new mistress, he obviously had no idea that this love could threaten his own. But he was forced to think again.

Could women, then, make dangerous rivals? Certainly, but only when they were not merely housekeepers and mothers – not merely wives, in short. The conjugal relationship was essentially a social duty, often a distasteful one. Lucilius writes in this connection:

> Homines isti sibi molestiam ultro atque aerumnam offerunt
> ducunt uxores, producunt, quibus haec faciant, liberos.[38]

Men bring this curse on their own heads: they get married and procreate, thereby producing their own ills. Given this state of affairs, it is obvious that the Romans went to all possible lengths to avoid matrimony. They showed such reluctance in taking wives that the

authorities were several times forced to urge them to take this un-
pleasant but necessary step.

In the year 131 BC the censor Metellus Numidicus had issued the
following statement: 'If we could get on without a wife, Romans, we
would all avoid that annoyance; but since nature has ordained that we
can neither live very comfortably with them nor at all without them,
we must take thought for our lasting well-being rather than for the
pleasure of the moment.'[39] And things had not changed over time.
More than a century later, Augustus reiterated this same point in the
Senate, in the context of his demographic policy, and had it publicly
posted so that everyone would be aware of it. Two hundred years later,
the rhetorician Titus Castricius wondered whether Metellus might not
perhaps have made a mistake when he appealed to the necessities of
nature, instead of exalting the joys of marriage. But he concluded that
Metellus had not made a mistake. Orators, he says, are entitled to make
false, tendentious, captious and deceptive statements so as to convince
their hearers, but only if these statements are credible. The drawbacks
of marriage are well known to all, so Metellus did well not to try and
conceal them. The needs of the state are really the only argument which
could induce men to marry.[40]

This, then, was what the Romans thought of matrimony; so why
should we be surprised that men did not consider wives as dangerous
rivals? The relationship with them took place on a level other than the
one on which homosexual liaisons were made.

Wives, however, were not the only category in the female universe.
There were also mistresses – sometimes other men's wives, sometimes
unattached. There were plenty of women of easy virtue, more or less
venal, more or less in love, but essentially available. With these women,
relationships were completely different. These were the Lesbias, the
Cynthias, the Corinnas; with them one experienced *l'amour passion*,
just like with *pueri*. These ladies were real rivals for the (male) lover of
a Roman. And the presence of these women simply made homosexual
love affairs more violent, more passionate, and more fraught with
suffering. True love, according to a tradition now well established, was
torment, and the existence of rivals of the female as well as the male sex
guaranteed, as one might say, one extra torment, one extra pretext for
suffering, hating, lacerating oneself with doubt. In short, it guaranteed
the existence of real love stories.

Lucretius, Virgil, Horace and Ovid

Evidence both of the total acceptance of love between men and of the
far-reaching transformation which had taken place, in the first century

136

BC, within Roman homosexual culture, comes not only from the elegiac poets. In a different, but no less significant way, poets like Lucretius, Virgil, Horace and Ovid help to fill out the picture of our knowledge, and clarify the main lines of 'sentimental education' during that period. This education was the consequence (in some ways strange, in others absolutely predictable) of the overlap and merging of two profoundly different cultures of homosexuality, the Roman and the Greek. In some ways it was new, in others very old indeed.

The basic rule of sex – on which are grafted the new elements introduced by contact with Greece, favoured by the new economic potential of Rome and the ethic which found legitimacy and confirmation in that wealth – remains the ancient indigenous rule, by which a man may satisfy his sexual desires by subjugating women and boys without distinction. A rule as old as Rome herself, which in the first half of the first century BC is not only confirmed but presented by Lucretius as a rule of nature. We read in *De rerum natura*, in fact, that pleasure is nothing other than the satisfaction of the desire to transfer one's own seed into the body of another, whose fascination and charm has caused the formation and accumulation of this same seed.[41] And this person, writes Lucretius, can be either a boy (listed in pride of place as the first possible sexual stimulus), or a woman:

> Thus, anyone who is struck by the darts of love, whether thrown by a lad with feminine limbs, or by a woman who breathes love from her whole body, is attracted by the one who has struck him, and wishes to be united with him, and throw into his body the humour drawn from his own body.[42]

This clear concept is formulated as an elementary rule and repeated without hesitation, and with some autobiographical references, by Horace.

When it comes to satisfying one's own requirements, writes the poet, there is no point in being over-subtle and complicating life. If one has a sudden irrepressible desire, and there is a handy household slave, male or female, standing by to satisfy his desire, why should one bother to look for more difficult solutions? If other people want to undergo this suffering, that's their funeral. I do not belong to this category of persons: *parabilem amo Venerem facilemque* ('the pleasures I love are those easy to attain').[43] The best loves, then, are the simple ones, within easy reach: household loves, quite independently of whether they are hetero or homosexual.

Ovid is the only one who does not share this attitude of complete indifference. Like everyone else, he belongs to a world where boys are considered as desirable as women. And he himself is not indifferent to

137

the fascination of *pueri*. In the first book of the *Amores*, to confine ourselves to one example, he declares that inspiration for his verses can come either from a *puer* or a *puella* with long and well-kept hair.[44] But having said that, he prefers women:

> I hate a union that exhausts not both:
> To fondle boys it's this that makes me loth.

Thus writes Ovid in the *Ars amatoria*, revealing the criteria underlying his preferences in the matter of love.[45] But it would be completely wrong to infer, from these verses, that he hated homosexual attachments. His affirmation of preference for *puellae* (for we are dealing only with a preference, not an exclusive choice) falls into the context of a wider discourse on pleasure, which the poet believes cannot and must not be a unilateral satisfaction of desire. Pleasure, to be genuine, must be reciprocal. An act of love performed out of complaisance or calculation or without real involvement is never satisfying, whether or not it is heterosexual:

> I like not joy bestowed in duty's fee,
> I'll have no woman dutiful to me.[46]

The reason why Ovid preferred *puellae*, therefore, is not linked to an ethical rejection of homosexuality: it stems from his conviction that women derive more pleasure than men from love. This belief is confirmed in the myth of Tiresias, the Theban soothsayer who, as we know, had lived both as a man and a woman, and declared on good authority that women got nine times as much pleasure from sexual intercourse as men.[47] This ancient idea had already preoccupied the Greeks quite a lot. They had seen it as a proof of the animal nature of women, and their lack of self-control, hence the necessity for men to control them.[48] But Ovid does not worry about this at all. He draws completely different inferences from this myth: if women experience more pleasure than men, given the fact that pleasure is greater when it is reciprocal, men have a considerable vested interest in going along with their mistresses' desires:

> The parts a woman loves to have caressed
> Once found, caress, though modesty protest.
> You'll see her eyes lit up with trembling gleams,
> As sunlight glitters in pellucid streams;
> Then plaintive tones and loving murmurs rise
> And playful words and softly sounding sighs.

But ne'er must you with fuller sail outpace
Your consort, nor she beat you in the race:
Together reach the goal: it's rapture's height
When man and woman in collapse unite.[49]

The conclusion is this: as the pleasure one feels with women is greater, being reciprocal, it is better to make love to women. But one can hardly overlook the fact that in the *Ars amatoria*, where Ovid translates this notion into a statement of personal preference, he feels obliged to justify it, almost as though it was an unusual, surprising choice (as indeed it was), which his fellow citizens would otherwise not have understood. In their opinion boys were, if not preferable to women, at the very least just as desirable.

The fundamental rule for the Romans' sexual code, at the end of the Republic and the beginning of the Augustan age, continued to decree that women and *pueri* could equally well be objects of desire. There is one innovation, however, by comparison with the earlier centuries, and this has already been pointed out: by now the *pueri* were no longer merely supposed to satisfy requirements of a purely physical sort. They had become love objects. Of the tender Lycidas, Horace writes that 'this year his beauty kindles the young men: soon the girls will catch fire also.'[50] For Horace, exactly like Lucretius, it was a law of nature that men should inspire male desire: before becoming an adult, and being desired by women, a man is desired by other men[51] – but only until that fateful moment when his beard begins to grow:

Ah Ligurinus,
Still cruel and swaggering with the gifts of Venus,
The day's not far
When stealing unawares, a beard will mar
That debonair
Insouciance; that shoulder-rippling hair
Fall; and the skin
Now pinker than the pinkest petal in
A bed of roses
Suffer a rude and bristling metamorphosis.
You'll say, 'Alas'
(Seeing the changed face in the looking-glass),
'Why as a boy
Did I spurn the wisdom that I now enjoy?
How now graft back
To wiser cheeks the rosiness they lack?'[52]

This is Horace's threat to Ligurinus, who keeps him on tenterhooks. The ploy, as we have seen, is a commonplace of Hellenistic literature. When boys hold out and play hard to ̧et, their suitors summon up the scarecrow of advancing age. Once they are less sweet, less lovely, once they have inexorably taken on a manly aspect, they will no longer be courted. It will be their turn to play the role of the lover who begs, who dogs the footsteps, who suffers. And they will suffer, then, both on account of women, and on account of *pueri*, who have now turned into objects of disturbing passion. The Romans, by now, were consuming themselves in torments over *pueri*. This happens to Horace, and not only over Ligurinus:

> O Pettius, no more do I delight as formerly to write my verses, for I am stricken with the heavy dart of Love, yea of Love who seeks to kindle me beyond all others with passion for tender boys and maids,

he confesses.[53] We are faced here with a recurrent theme in the output of this poet, who likes to present himself as easy meat for *mille puellarum mille puerorum furores*: a thousand tormented loves both for young girls and for young boys.[54] And the passion which, this time around (as he confides to Pettius), is even preventing him from writing, has been provoked by a boy:

> Affection for Lyciscus now enthrals me, for Lyciscus, who claims in tenderness to outdo any woman, and from whom no friends' frank counsels or stern reproaches have power to set me free, but only another flame, either for some fair maid or slender youth, with long hair gathered in a knot.[55]

The poet's love for Lyciscus is no less tormented than his feelings for Inachia, the woman with whom he had been in love before being bewitched by Lyciscus.[56] With Lyciscus he is an impotent, subjugated, humiliated victim. He can only be saved by a new love, quite independently of who causes it, a woman or a long-haired *puer*.

For Horace, deep down, the passion of love knows no barriers of sex. When he wants to describe to Maecenas how far he is disturbed by his love for a woman named Phryne, when he wants to compare his love to a famous, equally disturbing love, the comparison he draws is with a homosexual love affair:

> Not otherwise enamoured of Samian Bathyllus, do they say, was Teian Anacreon, who on his hollow shell sang full oft his plaintive strains of love in simple measure.... I am consumed with love for Phryne, a freed-woman, with a single lover not content.[57]

There is no difference, for Horace, in loving women and men. A special case, an exception to the rule? Not in the least. Further evidence that bisexuality is now expressed on the level of finer feelings comes from Virgil.

In the *Aeneid* Virgil tells the famous tale of Euryalus and Nisus, two young men whose reciprocal love gave them the courage to fight and die like heroes.[58] This is a theme which obviously picks up a Greek model – the model of lovers prepared to face death to prove their virtue to each other. This was the model, for example, of the Theban battalion whose exploits have already been mentioned. But far more significant than the episode of Euryalus and Nisus is the story of the love between Corydon and Alexis in the second *Eclogue*.

The shepherd Corydon is suffering so much over the lovely Alexis that he fears death. His sufferings are greater than those caused by any other love. Would it not have been better to love Menalcas, 'though he was swart and you are fair?'[59] Here we have a romantic love affair with all the trimmings, which the critics have sometimes interpreted as an account of a personal experience of the poet.[60] But the question of whether or not Virgil is describing his personal torments and attributing them to the shepherd is of no interest to us. Even if this story were not autobiographical, it would still offer confirmation of the fact that the sexual versatility of the Roman male had changed from a simple manifestation of physical needs into an ethics of love which allowed total freedom in the selection of a love object.

All types of choice were now available: if a man wanted secure affection, tranquil feeling, somebody to respect him and be faithful to him, all he had to do was choose a wife (the fact that this lady might not always match the ideal is another matter). But if he wanted to love passionately, and venture into an affair which was more problematical but also closer to the idea of love as passion and torment, he could make an alternative choice: either one of the many women belonging to the Roman *demi-monde*, free, broadminded and available, or else one of the many sweet capricious *pueri*, no less numerous and no less available than the women. Either way, nobody would say a word against him. The *Lex Scatinia* had been forgotten, and the crime it had defined as *stuprum cum puero* had now become in practice an absolutely normal relationship, socially accepted, engaged in with total freedom, and celebrated by the poets.

The *Lex Iulia de adulteriis coercendis*

In the year 18 BC, on a proposal from Augustus, the *Lex Iulia de adulteriis coercendis* was passed. This basic law marked a very important event in the history of Roman law – far more so than its name might suggest.

The new law did not confine itself to creating regulations governing the violation of marital fidelity. As part of the general demographic and moralising policies of Augustus,[61] it went much further and established that any sexual relationship outside matrimony or concubinal relations should be punished as a *crimen* (meaning a public offence, which could be prosecuted on the initiative of any citizen). Exceptions could be made for liaisons with prostitutes or women who were equivalent to them, either on account of their profession or because these women had previous convictions for immora. conduct.[62]

The term adultery is used by Augustus in a broad sense, to include *stuprum* (illicit sexual relations).[63] The sphere of sexual morality is essentially being removed from the competence of family legislation, and is becoming an affair of state. This, then, is a fundamental shift in the history of Roman law and in the interaction of ethics and law.

The *Lex Iulia* punishes *stuprum*, among other things, as a crime. But *stuprum*, as we know, can be committed not ony with virgins and widows, but also *cum puero*.[64] Should we infer that this law also set up new regulations for homosexual relationships? Some authors, such as Christius and Mommsen, believe that this can be ruled out.[65] Others, such as Gonfroy, Csillag, Richlin and Dalla, maintain that the law set out to regulate the entire field of sexuality, including male homosexuality.[66] The supporters of the first position point out that homosexuality forms no part of Augustus' legislative interests, which were aimed at restoring family morality. Those who take the contrary view can cite evidence from several sources in support of their hypothesis.

Alongside the passage from Modestinus (cited several times) who wrote in the *Regulae* that *stuprum* can also be committed *cum puero*, there are two passages which seem to include homosexual *stuprum* within the field of application of the *Lex Iulia*. The first of these comes from the *Pauli receptae Sententiae*, according to which anyone violating a free-born male is to be punished with death, while a person voluntarily undergoing homosexual *stuprum* is punished by confiscation of half his property, and is deprived of the capacity to make a will covering a larger part of it.[67] The second passage comes from Justinian's *Institutes*, where we read that the *Lex Iulia* did not confine itself to punishing those endangering other people's marriages, but also 'eos qui cum masculo infandam libidinem exercere audent': those who dared to exercise their shameful lusts with a man.[68]

On closer examination, however, these two pieces of evidence prove highly unreliable. For a start, the *Pauli receptae Sententiae* are not authentic, but were reconstructed by modern scholars on the basis of passages attributed to Paulus in post-classical works.[69] And they attribute to the *Lex Iulia de adulteriis coercendis* provisions which this law did not contain, such as the punishment of violent *stuprum*.[70] This observation in itself is enough to give rise to quite a few doubts about their reliability. The doubts grow when we read in Justinian's *Institutes* that the penalty laid down by the *Lex Iulia* for homosexuality was not a financial one – as stated in the *Pauli Sententiae* – but the death penalty.

As well as being mutually contradictory when they speak of punishments, the *Sententiae* and the *Institutes* also disagree when they refer to the types of homosexual behaviour punished by the *Lex Iulia*. The *Sententiae* speak of a penalty directed solely against passive homosexuals, while the *Institutes* also prescribe a penalty for their active counterparts. Lastly, it is worth pointing out that the *Institutes* claim that this penalty was prescribed by the *Lex Iulia* for both homosexuals and adulterers. This is absolutely false. The penalty prescribed by the *Lex Iulia* for adultery was not death, but *relegatio in insulam* accompanied by a financial penalty.[71] The rule established under the second paragraph of the law, granting immunity to the husband and father of the adulteress if they killed her accomplice (and in the case of the father, if he killed his daughter too), was a special concession exclusively available to the father and husband, subject to the existence of a whole set of circumstances (for example the adulterers had to be caught *in flagrante*), specifically listed by the law.[72] But generally speaking, the penalty for adultery was not death.

How can this problem be resolved? What conclusions can be drawn from all of this? Obviously, we should consider that neither the *Sententiae* of Paulus nor Justinian's *Institutes* reproduce the regulations from the *Lex Iulia*: what they actually give are the rules in force at a later time, the post-classical age and the age of Justinian – the rules that had grown up during the centuries when, as we shall see, the repression of homosexuality grew progressively harsher, and extended to cover, in effect, each and every manifestation of homosexuality, without distinction of roles.

Only one text remains which would suggest that the *Lex Iulia* subjected all homosexuality to regulation. This is a passage from Papinianus, where we read that any person lending his house so that an adultery or *stuprum* can be carried on there (including homosexual *stuprum*) is to be punished as an adulterer.[73]

But on closer examination, this too turns out to be a highly suspect passage. Homosexual *stuprum* is defined – rather singularly – as *stuprum cum masculo*. This expression is foreign to the classical sources, which speak of *stuprum cum puero*. The passage was therefore clearly reworked in the post-classical era, when imperial legislation set out to broaden the field of forbidden homosexual relations, and the word 'boy' was replaced by the word 'man'.[74] Even if one wanted to rule out the possibility of rewriting, that would still not prove Mommsen's contention that Papinianus was referring to the only case in which, quite exceptionally, Augustan legislation took account of this area of sexuality.[75] And finally, we receive unequivocal confirmation that the *Lex Iulia* was concerned exclusively with heterosexual behaviour when we look at a series of positive proofs, represented in passages from numerous authors who, at a later period than the passing of the *Lex Iulia*, trace the punishment of homosexuality solely to the *Lex Scatinia*.

Suetonius, as we know, says that Domitian condemned certain people on the basis of the *Lex Scatinia*.[76] If the *Lex Iulia* had superseded the *Lex Scatinia*, how could he have done this? In Juvenal's second *Satire* (as we have already seen) Laronia observed that while it is true that women who commit adultery are no longer punished, because the *Lex Iulia* has been forgotten, it is equally true that not even the *molles* are punished, because the *Lex Scatinia* has also been forgotten.[77]

Clearly, then, the two laws ran side by side, neither interfering with the other, each regulating a different sector of sexual life.

Nor is this all: during the first decades of the third century, Tertullian alludes to the *Lex Scatinia* as a law still in force.[78] In the fourth century, Ausonius confirms the accuracy of this reference.[79] At the end of the same century, Prudentius wonders why on earth he should honour Jove:

> Qui si citetur legibus vestris reus,
> laqueis minacis implicatus Iuliae
> luat severam victus et Scatiniam.[80]

If Jove were to be judged according to the laws of Rome, he says, as well as being caught in the toils of the *Lex Iulia*, he would be condemned and severely punished on the basis of the *Lex Scatinia*. Jove, well known for his extramarital adventures, was not averse to homosexual affairs, as shown by his famous escapade with Ganymede. These loves would have earned him condemnation on the basis of the *Lex Scatinia*.

We have enough evidence here to conclude, without much hesitation, that Augustus took absolutely no interest in the problem, and that the legislation of Republican Rome remained unaltered up to the point when, from the fourth century onwards, the emperors decided to launch a new policy in this area: an ever more severe policy of repression, aimed at first at stemming the spread of homosexuality between adults, going so far as to established the death penalty for passive homosexuality, and later extending the field of forbidden behaviour, prescribing punishment also for active homosexuality.

We shall return to all this in due course, to examine the new rules in detail, and to try to identify the reasons underlying the new imperial policy. But first we must try to establish the relationship which existed, during the first centuries of the Empire, between legal rules and social norms. In other words, we must try to understand the effective social and moral evaluation of homosexuality.

Tradition and Innovation

The tradition: The Carmina Priapea, *graffiti, satire*

For some time now, men had been sighing with love for boys, imploring their favours, suffering over their betrayals. What had become of the Roman males of yore, the tough conquistadores who grabbed what they wanted and never asked permission? Had they perhaps disappeared? Absolutely not. They had simply transferred elsewhere the manifestation of their virile superpotency. They had other opportunities to demonstrate what they were able to do. In order to clarify the nature of these opportunities, what better than to read the *Carmina Priapea*, a collection of poetry with different metres and subjects, dedicated, as their name suggests, to the god Priapus, the Phallus.

Priapus, the god of fertility, had been adopted in Rome as the protector of orchards and gardens, over which he presided in the crude representation of a tiny figurine equipped with enormous genitals. Priapus was the dedicatee of some dozens of poetical compositions, collected during the first century, of which the authorship was ascribed by the ancients to Virgil. This is a highly debatable attribution, like the other attribution which claims these contributions as the work of Tibullus, attributing the third poem in the series to Ovid. But for our purposes the interesting point is not the authorship of the *Carmina*;

they were probably written largely by unknown authors, although we cannot rule out the possibility that official poets like Martial amused themselves by cultivating this literary genre.[81] What is important is their content.

Priapus not only frightens away rapacious birds from orchards and gardens, but also scares off thieves. With what weapons or deterrents? The answer springs immediately to mind: with his phallus. He delivers the same threat which Catullus uttered against his enemies Furius and Aurelius. In the *Priapea* we read:

> Thief, I'll bugger you the first time.
> Try again, and you'll find it in your mouth.
> And if you come back a third time
> I'll try both penalties together
> you'll find it up your arse and down your throat.[82]

And let nobody think that these are empty threats:

> Don't think that what I say
> is said by way of jest or playfulness.
> When I catch a thief three or four times
> never doubt it, it goes in his mouth.[83]

There is a gradation in Priapus' punishments. For the first theft, the penalty is the one slyly alluded to in a mischievous pun by an unknown hand:

> The first of PEnelope with the next from DIdo
> then from CAdmus and finally from REmus.
> Put these together, thief caught in the act,
> in my orchard: this is how you'll pay for it.[84]

Pedicare, meaning buggery, is the sum of these parts. This is the basic penalty. For recidivists there is *fellatio*, the most shameful act which a man can be forced to perform. Let it be very clear, anyone undergoing punishment must not feel any pleasure in it:

> A softy, softer than the marrow
> of a goose's bones, came to steal, so as to suffer the punishment.
> Let him rob as long as he likes: I can't see him.[85]

Thus speaks Priapus, through whose mouth the Romans express their vision of virility. This is the same vision which inspires the unknown inhabitants of Pompeii who, on the walls of their city (obviously in what might be termed the less salubrious quarters of that city), were fond of boasting of their valour, reminding passers-by and future generations of how often, and with what success, they had performed the act which they felt would bring them glory: which obviously was none other than *futuere*.[86]

And so we get a record of the deeds of Earinus, Felix, Victor, Festus and a hundred other unknowns brought together by a single desire: to ensure that history should never forget that there, in that place, at that moment, they had completed the great performance which, depending on circumstances, had placed them on top of a woman or a man, quite without distinction. An act which they had often performed with their companions, in a reciprocal exhibition of manliness: Festus, for example, *hic futuit cum sodalibus* ('Festus fucked here with his mates').[87]

This act, valiantly carried out (and properly publicised) offered a guarantee against the risk of not being considered (and not being able to consider oneself) sufficiently male, and authorised the performer to jeer at the whole world from the height of his own virility. *Amat qui scribet, pedicatur qui leget* writes one Septumius, who unequivocally labels himself, with all due pride: 'pedicator'.[88] Another inscription threatens: *te pedicabo*.[89] A third: *pedicare volo*.[90] Generally, the intended victim is not indicated: this is the elementary crude expression of a desire to gain the upper hand, expressed (in words in this case) by means of an act which, by subjecting another person – woman or man – to the type of penetration considered most outrageous,[91] confirms that the person doing it, or capable of threatening it, is a real man. At the risk of being monotonous, the list could be extended. These graffiti confirm that popular poetry faithfully expresses the mentality and mind of the average citizen – and not only citizens of Pompeii.

In Rome, for example, about twenty years ago, scholars found and published some graffiti scratched on the walls of a building (the *paedagogium*) beside the Domus Augustiana built by the imperial family for the use of slaves; here again we read homosexual inscriptions inspired by exactly the same attitudes as the Pompeian inscriptions.[92]

In a combined school, gymnasium and barracks, built by Domitian and used by gladiators for training, one can make out (in area 41) a sketch of an ostrich, under which an unknown hand has written: *antea cucumeris non degerebas [digerebas], modo berpas [verpas] digeris*. (Once upon a time you could not digest cucumbers, but now you take them in, all the way.)[93]

If there are poets who sing of sweet and romantic loves, popular poetry and graffiti serve to re-establish a balance, showing that the ancient and glorious race of macho men has not passed away. The race has survived, held firm against the new softness, and is willing to stand out against it, almost as though to prove that in all events the Roman male is the same as he used to be. If he is in love, he may even dare to be sweet-natured, either with women or with men. But when necessary, he still knows how to wield his weapons.

Innovations: satire

Alongside the *Carmina Priapea*, in the first century AD, there is another literary genre which offers quite revealing sidelights on the mentality of the times, adding more detail to our picture of the Romans' attitudes to sex.

The genre in question is satire. In the works of Martial and Juvenal we find not only the sensibility and personal tastes of the authors, but also a varied world of characters whose features and defects – making all due allowance for the fiercely sarcastic and often excessive portrayal which satire paints – are indicative of the lifestyle, sexual habits and self-image of the virile Roman. We can see which factors reinforce their sense of virility, and which undermine it. One thing which cannot be numbered among those features which call virility into question, we quickly discover, is a propensity to have love affairs with *pueri*. (Indeed, such preferences had never been a threat to perceived virility.) The satirical poets have no problem in declaring their desire for boys. Let us start with Martial.

Martial

May I have a boy with a cheek smooth with youth, not with pumice, for whose sake no maid would please me.[94]

This is what Martial wants: a sweet, submissive little slave-boy – the perfect prescription as an alternative and antidote to women who had not the slightest intention of acting submissive.

In the first century AD Roman women became emancipated. Legally, if they are married, they no longer fall under the power (*manus*) of their husbands. Unlike the previous dispensation, a woman still belongs to her own original family after her marriage. Although not completely free, women are therefore less controlled than they used to be. At the very least, from the Augustan age onwards, they can no longer be killed by their husbands if caught in the act of adultery. True, they can be killed by their fathers, but the fathers are reluctant to exercise this right. Basically, having a lover is now much less dangerous than it used to be.

If a woman is *sui iuris* (meaning that she has no male relatives in the ascending line), there used to be a time-honoured rule that placed her for life under the director of a male tutor. But this wise restraint is no longer any use. If the tutor does not meet her requirements, she can replace him with a more complaisant one, leaving her practically her own mistress.[95] As if that were not enough, many women nowadays are rich and therefore claim the right to give orders. Just imagine: they are looking for parity. On this point, Martial has very clear ideas. It is simply not on.

'Why am I unwilling to marry a rich wife?' Do you ask? I am unwilling to take my wife as husband. Let the matron be subject to her husband, Priscus; in no other way do woman and man become equal.[96]

As for sexual behaviour, wives nowadays seem almost to be making a concession to their husbands if they agree to confine themselves to just one lover: 'My wife asks me, Gallus, to put up with a lover of hers, but only one. Am I not then, Gallus, to gouge out this fellow's two "eyes"?'[97] And poor Gallus, too, can hardly lay claim to a perfect wife:

Amongst Libyan tribes your wife, Gallus, has a bad reputation; they charge her foully with insatiate greed. But these stories are simply lies; she is not at all in the habit of receiving favours. What, then, is her habit? To give them.[98]

In this situation, what can a fellow do except hope to be left a widower with all due speed? 'All the friends she had, Fabianus, Lycoris has buried. May she become a friend to my wife!'[99]

And the other women, the ones who have not become wives? Sadly, they too have grown arrogant, sexually demanding and insatiable:

You bid my penis, Lesbia, to be always standing for you; believe me, one's prick is not the same as one's finger. You may urge me with toyings and wheedling words, but your face is imperious to defeat you.[100]

In the circumstances, one really is better off with boys. Some of them are still like Cestos, needing to consoled, because they weep in terror before excessive attempts at courtship: 'Often Cestos complains to me with overflowing eyes that he is pawed by your finger, Mamurianus.'[101]

With boys, one can still play the male part:

Kisses I reject save those I have ravished from reluctance, and your anger pleases me more than your face; so I often beat you, Diadumenus, to make myself solicit you often. I achieve this: you neither fear nor love me.[102]

Of course boys are sometimes capricious, like Didimus:

You seek me out, I run away; I look for you, you're off. This mess, Didimus, is my heart. If you want to, I don't want to, I want to when you don't want to.[103]

Deep down, Didimus' attitude is not unpleasing: it allows an old game to be played. Given the new assertiveness of women, it now becomes the responsibility of boys to reassure their lovers about their virility. They had better be careful, then. They had better not call it into question, as the women had done. They had better not challenge it, or make excessive demands. If they do that, they lose all their charm:

When thou sayest 'I haste; now is the time,' then, Hedylus, my ardour at once flags and weakens. Bid me wait: more quickly, stayed, shall I speed on. Hedylus, if thou dost haste, tell me not to haste![104]

At least boys should remain submissive. Otherwise, how can one be expected to love them?

You wish to be courted, Sextus; I wished to love you. I must obey you; as you demand, you shall be courted. But if I court you, Sextus, I shall not love you.[105]

Martial's attitude to sex is very clear. Fundamentally, so to speak, he is bisexual: he is attracted both to women and to men. If in practice he happens to prefer boys, the reasons are largely of a psychological kind. Women, with their treacherous attitudes, their shameless sexual behaviour, their refusal to take a subordinate role as they are supposed to, have become insufferable. They leave almost no choice for a man who wants to be a real man: they force him, inevitably, to opt for boys.

What emerges absolutely clearly from Martial is that bisexuality for him is no problem at all; it is so normal that it needs neither to be hidden nor to be boasted about. What the poet does boast about, the one part of his image that he cannot give up, is the role of the male who subjugates people. Hence his total and absolute scorn for sexually passive adult males:

You see that fellow with unkempt hair, Decianus, whose gloomy scowl you too fear, who prates of the Curii, and of the Camilli, champions of liberty? Don't credit his appearance; he was a bride yesterday.[106]

What a lot of *molles*, *cinaedi* and *pathici* Rome contains! Some, like Naevolus, try to hide their shame. But Martial pitilessly points them out for real men to laugh at: 'Seeing that the boy's prick is sore, and your backside, Naevolus, though I am no diviner, I know what you are up to.'[107]

Others, like Hyllus, lack all restraint:

Often in all your money-box, there is only one shilling, while this too is worn more than your arse, Hyllus. Yet it will be taken from you not by the baker, not by the barmaid, but by anyone who will be overbearing with a prick all too eager. Your poor belly gazes at the banquet of your arse; and the former is always hungry, while the latter gorges.[108]

Martial offers perfect confirmation of the values of traditional sexual ethics.[109] The fundamental contrast between different types of sexual behaviour still remains the active/passive dichotomy, not the hetero/homosexual one. Men continue to perform the virile role with both women and men. More precisely, they start to be real men when they make love to boys. During the first phase of their sexual life, women do not exist:

Enjoy feminine embraces, Victor; enjoy them, and let your poker learn an activity unknown to it. The red bridal veil is woven for the bride, the maid is got ready, and by now the newly wedded wife will crop close your boys. Now, she will grant sodomy just once to her wishful husband while she still dreads the first hurt of that strange new lance; nurse and mother will forbid it to be done more than once, and they will say 'She's a wife to you, not a boy.' Oh dear! What terrible worries, what awful troubles you'll have to put up with if a quim is going to be a stranger to you.[110]

In its own different way, the epigram picks up the topic of Catullus' poem 61. Marriage brings an end to the age of *pueri* – but only in theory. It is no accident that Victor's bride fears competition from boys; all wives fear these rivals, and are aware that it will be very difficult to freeze them out. Here is Martial sniggering at wives who think they can win their husbands' love by deploying, as one might say, the same arms used by boys:

Having caught me, wife, in a boy, in a harsh cross voice you rebuke me and tell me that you too have a backside. Juno said the same a lot of times to wanton Jupiter Thunderer! He none the less lies with grown-up Ganymede. Hercules of Tiryns put down his bow and bent Hylas over instead. Do you believe Megara had no buttocks? Phoebus Apollo was tortured by Daphne as she ran away; but a Spartan lad ordained that those passionate flames should depart.

Although Briseis lay a lot with her back turned, a clean-shaven boy-friend was closer to Achilles. So refrain from giving masculine titles to your things, wife, and believe you have two quims.[111]

The theme is not a new one: we have already seen it in the *Greek Anthology*.[112] The problem reappears in Rome in exactly the same terms, and is resolved in the same terms: women cannot claim to satisfy all of a man's requirements. They might as well accept this.

Juvenal

By the end of the first century AD Rome has become the sump of all debauchery; at least that is what Juvenal thinks. Corrupt, grasping, vulgar and ignorant, sometimes hypocritical and sometimes shamelessly exhibitionist, the characters in his satires seem to have touched the low point of all base behaviour. One of the most obvious aspects of their depravation is their sexual behaviour. All of them without distinction, men and women, rich and poor, young and old, indulge in every kind of licentiousness, having cast aside all restraint. As for women, what can be said of their wickedness?

The famous sixth satire, dedicated to women, presents a female world to which no variety of wickedness is unknown. Its 661 verses place women in the dock as a sex, apart from all differences of class, wealth or age. Messalina, dissolute wife of Claudius, prostitutes herself in a brothel.[113] But women from humbler backgrounds are not to be out-done: 'High or low their passions are all the same. She who wears out the black cobble-stones with her bare feet is no better than she who rides upon the necks of eight stalwart Syrians.'[114] They have got into the habit of switching husbands constantly; one woman has changed no fewer than eight times in five years.[115] They abandon themselves to homosexual lovemaking, even going so far as to do it in front of the altar of Chastity.[116] They are arrogant and presumptuous, and in order to be fashionable they even act Greek in bed.[117] They quote from Homer at table, reducing their fellow diners to silence with their exhibitions of learning.[118] They are not only debauched, but insufferable.

Not one woman escapes Juvenal's condemnation. His misogyny, it has to be said, borders on the pathological, and his accusations must clearly be taken with a pinch of salt.[119] But that is not the point which concerns us here. The interesting point is what he thinks and says about men – against whom he is equally scarifying. This time, though, it is not the entire male sex which is under the lash; merely some (well, actually, quite a few) individual specimens of the breed. When writing about men, Juvenal's scorn is no longer accompanied by sheer hatred; never-theless, his satire is fierce and pitiless just the same. We are thus compelled, once again, to cut his denunciations down to size. This does not detract from the fact that his accusations point to a trend, an attitude, a style of behaviour which is not only real but now openly recognisable. The practices he describes are undoubtedly less wide-spread than his works would suggest, but they are neither negligible, nor marginal, nor exceptional.

One characteristic feature of this behaviour is sexual depravity. Men have given up their virile role, some on account of vice, some for the sake of fashion, some for cash. As in the former case of Martial, they can be divided basically into two categories: the hypocrites, who speak out against the spread of vice while secretly abandoning themselves to it, and the shameless ones, who parade their vices without restraint. In the second satire, the one against male vices, both categories are accused with equal vehemence.

The hypocrites may rail against vice as much as they like, but their appearance inexorably betrays their guilty secret. They shower them-selves with perfume,[120] wrap kerchiefs around their foreheads and hang trinkets about their necks.[121] They are pathetic and ridiculous. The other homosexuals, the shameless ones, have cast aside all restraint. Dressed in female clothing, they celebrate the festival of the *Bona Dea*, formerly reserved for women.[122] They extend their eyebrows with soot, and paint their eyes,[123] gather up their long hair in golden nets.[124] Armed with mirrors, they rub bread pellets on their faces, to make the skin smoother.[125] Nor is this all: they conduct weddings with each other, imitating the rites of marriage in an outrageous farce, with a husband and a 'wife' who wears a veil and brings a dowry to the husband.[126] It will not be long, says Juvenal, until they apply to register their marriages in the town hall.[127] These new 'brides' suffer just one drawback: they cannot procreate and thereby bind their lovers to them-selves with children.[128]

Lastly, we have the men who prostitute themselves. Take Naevolus, protagonist of the ninth satire. Naevolus wanders around the city in a black temper. 'Why is this?' asks the poet, who pretends to meet him. Because Naevolus' owner, the man to whom he has sold his services, is a horrible, grim, miserable skinflint. Yet he is rich: he could reward Naevolus as he deserves, seeing that Naevolus has been a husband not only to him but to his wife as well. If it were not for Naevolus, that man would certainly have no children. Thanks to him, he has even been able to give proof of his non-existent virility. What is to be done? The poet consoles poor Naevolus in his desperate state of mind. Don't worry, he tells him, there are plenty of *pathici* about, and you will have no difficulty in finding a more open-handed one.

The interest and novelty of this satire is obvious. Male prostitution, as we know, had always been widespread in Rome. But in the old days, boys sold themselves to be subjected to sex like women. Their paymaster was still a real man. Now, everything has changed. Naevolus is an active homosexual. The Romans have sunk to such a level of depravity that they no longer pay to put somebody else underneath them – they now pay someone to go on top. The ideology, then, has not changed: a man is only a real man if he is gloriously active. But the facts show that real Roman males are getting rarer and rarer. Even allowing for the exaggerated description of current practices, offered both by Martial and by Juvenal, passive behaviour has kept on spreading in a worrying fashion. And as we shall see, it goes on spreading. Here is the great, intolerable novelty, the one against which the laws of the Roman Empire will take vigorous action, ushering in the age of savagely harsh repression.

7

The Empire

Practices

We have already seen the sexual practices of the Romans at the end of the Republic and during the reign of Augustus. Making love to boys, although theoretically punished by the *Lex Scatinia*, had become socially acceptable behaviour.

Relations between adults, on the other hand, were more problematical. Regulated by a typical form of double standard, they were only half acceptable, given that the passive adult male was considered effeminate and was sneered at and held in low esteem, which also affected his status as a citizen.

But despite this, during the Empire male passivity spread to the point where it caused considerable worries for legislators, inducing them to issue repressive measures which grew more and more severe as time went on. One factor determining the new policy was undoubtedly the Christian influence, but equally certainly, this policy was made necessary by the progressive and unstoppable spread of a habit which had always been reproved, but which it had obviously proved impossible to cut off. How did it happen that such an un-Roman activity found space to expand to the point where it was socially disquieting?

A not inconsiderable role was played by Hellenisation. As we saw earlier, passivity, while theoretically disapproved of in Greece, had become – if we are to believe Aristophanes – a mass custom, a cause of the decadence of the *polis* and a visible sign of that decadence. And the Romans experienced the influence of Greek culture when it was already going into decline. But perhaps the spread of effeminate behaviour was also influenced by another factor, within Roman history itself. To understand this it is necessary to take a step backwards in time, returning to the first century BC, where the sources begin to display a new and different attitude to the *molles* – or at least to some of them.

Some of the most prominent people in the political life of the city –

military generals and popular leaders, men whose virility was certainly not open to question on other counts – were behaving sexually like women. Or at least that is what was said and, in the last analysis, this is what counts. The attitude taken towards these people, the popular judgement of their character and power, the social assessment of their overall personality, was singularly ambiguous. On the one hand, they were the butt of ridicule; on the other hand they were loved, esteemed and admired. Their sexual passivity was not enough to have them ranked among the *molles*, the *cinaedi*, the *pathici*, who were by definition incapable of being credited with civic virtues. To some extent, their deviance was tolerated.

The Sexual Behaviour of the Powerful: Excuse or Example?

At the head of this series of personages stands Caesar, of course, who was celebrated in antiquity for having been the lover of Nicomedes, king of Bithynia.

His adventure with Nicomedes, in Rome, was very well known. Dolabella called him 'the Queen's rival and inner partner of the royal bed'. Curio the Elder called him 'Nicomedes' Bithynian brothel'. Bibulus, his colleague in the consulship, said that he was 'the Queen of Bithynia'. During a public assembly, Octavius had turned to Pompey, calling him king, and to Caesar, calling him 'queen'. Memmius said that he had been seen, with other *exoleti* (passive homosexuals), acting as a cup-bearer during a banquet given by Nicomedes, which had also been attended by Roman businessmen. In the Senate, when Caesar had pleaded the cause of Nysa, daughter of Nicomedes, recalling the benefits received from her father, Cicero had interrupted him with the exclamation: 'Enough of that, if you please! We all know what he gave you, and what you gave him in return.' As if all this were not enough, during the triumph held after the conquest of Gaul the soldiers sang: *Gallias Caesar subegit, Nicomedes Caesarem*. Caesar got on top of the Gauls, Nicomedes got on top of Caesar.[1]

Caesar, then, was publicly mocked. It was said of him that he wore his toga in such a way that it swished languidly along the ground, walking like a *mollis*.[2] Catullus, in his *carmen 57*, defines him bluntly as *cinaedus* (nancy-boy), and accuses him once again of effeminacy in *carmen 29*. How could the Romans, Catullus asks, put up with an infamous character like Mamurra? Yet they do put up with him. As for Caesar, he actually favours him. Who could do such a thing, if not an *inpudicus, et vorax et aleo* (a passive homosexual, a voracious gambler)?

According to Suetonius the allusions to Mamurra annoyed Caesar, so much so that the poet was forced to beg pardon.[3] But to accuse Caesar of being a *cinaedus* Catullus had no need to refer to his attitude to Mamurra. His lack of virility emerged from other evidence:

> nihil nimium audeo, Caesar, tibi velle placere
> nec scire utrum sis albus an ater homo.[4]

'There is nothing, Caesar, that I would like more than to please you, and to know whether you are white-skinned or dark.' Thus Catullus wrote to Caesar, once again questioning his virility. Like the Greeks, the Romans also believed that fair skin was a sign and a consequence of passivity.[5]

But leaving aside the problem of the relationship between Caesar and Catullus (which is, in the first place, a political problem),[6] what is interesting for our purposes is to try to understand the general reaction by Caesar to these reiterated public accusations.

According to Dio Cassius, Caesar was not in the least bothered by the scurrilous language of his soldiers, but if they alluded to Nicomedes, he reacted and even tried to justify himself.[7] But Suetonius recounts an episode showing that Caesar was not at all concerned by jibes about his sex life. Once, in the Senate, after boasting that he had got everything he had wanted, despite the opposition of his enemies, Caesar had declared that from then on he would be able to walk on their heads. And when a senator, to insult him, remarked that this would not be easy for a woman, Caesar had replied that Semiramis governed Syria, and the Amazons held almost the whole of Asia.[8]

The reply is anything but implausible. With Catullus, Caesar had been offended because the references to Mamurra were a political attack. But why should he worry when it came to personal questions? Leaving aside all else, he was well respected. Despite all, and for everybody including Catullus, he was 'the great Caesar'.[9]

To what did he owe this respect? There were two interlinked factors. Firstly his virility, although called into question by his adventure with Nicomedes, was guaranteed by his fame as an adulterer. According to Suetonius, Nicomedes was the only man with whom Caesar had adopted a passive role, or at least it was the only case of *inpudicitia* that could be held against him.[10] Perhaps not everyone believed this version; all the same, it was true that Caesar had a reputation as quite a ladies' man. He had been the lover of Servius Sulpicius' wife Postumia, Aulus Gabinius' wife Lollia, Crassus' wife Tertulla, and even Pompey's wife Mucia.[11] Not to mention what he had got up to in the provinces, as governor. Another song which was sung during the Gallic triumph reminded the public of his exploits and warned husbands to keep their wives out of sight.[12] As if all this were not enough, there were the queens. Cleopatra was certainly not the only one. Among other conquests, Caesar had seduced Eunoë, wife of King Bogudes of Mauritania.[13] It could truthfully be said of Caesar, then, that he was *omnium virorum mulier, omnium mulierum virum* ('wife to all men and husband to all women').[14] Caesar, then, offered the Romans an unusual sexual image: a man who remained virile even if he happened to assume the subordinate position now and again – a man who was such a he-man that he could afford to turn passive once in a while.

The second fundamental factor which undoubtedly helped – which, indeed, was of crucial importance – in allowing him to present this macho image, was of course his reputation as a soldier. For the Romans there was an inevitable link between prowess on the battlefield and sexual potency. Take a man who covered himself in glory in combat, who smashed his enemies and crushed the barbarians. How could such a paragon not be sexually potent? Manliness, as we have already seen, was the highest virtue of the citizen. And this was a complex quality, which involved and included physical strength, military superiority, character and sexuality. The comparison between the lover and soldier, in any case, was a literary commonplace for the Romans. *Militat omnis amans, et habet sua castra Cupido*, writes Ovid. Every lover is a soldier, and Cupid has his encampments.[15] A winner in war was a winner in bed. And Caesar was unbeatable as a warrior. He is the first in a line of conquerors, men of power, dominators who are not always exclusively dominant when it comes to sex. One example is Augustus, Caesar's nephew, adoptive son and successor.

Like Caesar, Augustus had a sexually disconcerting side. Pompey accused him of being effeminate. Mark Antony, his colleague in the triumvirate, was more explicit: he said that Caesar had forced Augustus to yield to him before adopting him. Suetonius reports this story, adding another tale from Lucius Antonius: Augustus, after losing his *pudicitia* with Caesar, had rented himself out to Aulus Hirtius in Spain for a consideration of 300,000 sestertii. Also according to Lucius Antonius, he used to rub red-hot walnut shells on his legs, to soften the hair.[16]

Just like Caesar, then, Augustus was considered *inpudicus*. Suetonius tells how one day, at the theatre, the audience heard a verse alluding to a priest of the goddess Cybele playing a timbrel with his fingers: *videsne ut cinaedus orbem digito temperat?* Taking this for a reference to Augustus, the audience responded with generous applause.[17] To understand the reasons for such popular enthusiasm, one must remember that

Cybele's priests (known as Galli or Archigalli) were ritually castrated.[18] Referring to the priest, therefore, the verse meant: 'Look, how this invert's finger beats the drum.' But *orbs* meant not only 'a circular drum' but also 'the world'. So in reference to Augustus the line defined him as 'the catamite who rules the world with his finger'.

Further proof of how widespread was the ruler's reputation as a passive homosexual (whether it was true or false in fact) comes from the inscriptions found on the so-called *glandes perusinae*, the lead shot used in slings by Roman soldiers during the siege of Perugia in 41–40 BC.[19]

Young Octavian (who was subsequently to become Augustus), then aged twenty-two, was fighting against Mark Antony and his brother Lucius. The lead pellets, which have luckily been found, tell us what the soldiers thought about him. Roman soldiers used lead shot not only to kill their enemies, but also to insult them. On this occasion, depending on whether they were fighting for Octavian or for Antony, they wrote down what they thought of the enemy commander. Basically, these were insults of a sexual nature, and as regards the future Augustus they are unequivocal. Contemptuously called Octavia – in the feminine form[20] – he is accused of fellatio (a charge which does not require further explanation)[21] and is variously described as *laxus* or *pathicus*.[22]

Are these mere crude soldierly jokes, which do not necessarily bear any relation to the truth? Of course. They are barrack-room jokes, as we would say today, which in the past, as nowadays, view lack of virility as the worst possible accusation and are evidence more of the mentality that goes into them than of any real fact. Antony, too, is defined as *calvus* – and baldness, for the Romans, was a sign of inadequate virility.[23] But the charges against Octavian are much more weighty and more frequent: his reputation as a *mollis* was clearly well consolidated.

However, exactly like Caesar, Octavian too survived this accusation. Like Caesar, he too was an adulterer.[24] After emerging from the years of his youth, his reputation changed radically. With the image of the political dominator, he also earned the reputation of a conqueror of women. This reputation was built not only on the basis of a life liberally sprinkled with marriages and extramarital affairs[25] but on a clever and effective public relations strategy implemented by himself. A trace of this is preserved in a poem by his own hand,[26] which provides skilful testimony (albeit quite vulgarly) of his great virility. A ditty recorded by Martial, probably composed during the siege of Perugia (which would explain the barrack-room tone, unexpected and unusual in Augustus), seems to present itself as an able and astute indirect response to the accusations made by the soldiery.[27]

> Quod futuit Glaphyram Antonius, hanc mihi poenam,
> Fulvia constituit, se quoque uti futuam.
> Fulviam ego ut futuam? quid si me Manius oret
> pedicem, faciam? Non puto, si sapiam.
> 'Aut futue aut pugnemus' ait. Quid quod mihi vita
> carior est ipsa mentula? Signa canant.

In just six verses, Augustus gives his detractors a singular version of the facts which led to the Perusine war. Why did the conflict break out, according to this version? Because Fulvia, wife of Mark Antony, who had betrayed her with Glaphyra, wanted to take revenge on her husband by becoming the mistress of Octavian. But Octavian had refused her offer, and Fulvia had issued an ultimatum, which in truth was not very becoming for a respectable married lady. *Aut futue aut pugnemus*, she said to Octavian. Fuck me or fight me. So they fought.[28] The war, then, was provoked by the virility of Octavian, object of the heavy-handed advances mentioned above, and at the same time by the virtue of the young general. Unlike Mark Antony, well known of his extramarital adventures, Octavian had refused to commit adultery – and with what dreadful consequences! Twice virtuous, this Octavian, in two very different senses: virile, and respectful of established morality. Exactly what one would expect from a legislator who shortly afterwards approved the *Lex Iulia de adulteriis*, already mentioned.

The series of emperors to whom the sources attribute sexual behaviour which does not correspond to the canons of received morality could be extended practically without limit. Suetonius' stories of the debauchery to which Tiberius abandoned himself in the last years of his life, during his stay on Capri, are too well known to be rehearsed here.[29] It is superfluous to speak of Caligula's depravity: after giving proof of his infamy by committing incest with all of his sisters, whom he used to rape in front of his wife, he continued his damnable career by indulging in all forms of unspeakable excess. Among other things, he had had sex both with Marcus Lepidus and with the pantomime actor Mnester, while Valerius Catullus boasted that he had had him, wearing out his groin in the process.[30] The same can obviously be said of Nero, who had Sporus castrated and then took him as his wife. Later he married the freedman Doryphorus, who had served him as a husband.[31] Galba liked mature, vigorous men.[32] Otho wore a little wig and massaged his face with a poultice of bread to prevent his beard from growing.[33] Vitellius, who had spent his childhood on Capri among

Tiberius' male harem, was called *spintria* (a very vulgar term, used to denote male prostitutes).[34] Even Titus, whom Suetonius calls 'an object of universal love and adoration',[35] was accused of abandoning himself to nightly orgies with a group of degenerates.[36] Of Domitian it was told that he offered himself for the night to Clodius Pollio,[37] and that he had had an affair with Earinus.[38] Hadrian was well known for his relationship with Antinoos,[39] after whose death, according to Aelius Spartianus, he abandoned himself of despair, weeping like a woman (*muliebriter*).[40] And according to Aurelius Victor, in addition to this, he was dedicated to all forms of lust.[41] Commodus is presented by Aelius Lampridius as *omni parte corporis atque ore in sexum utrumque pollutus.* ('Every part of his body, even his mouth, was defiled by intercourse with both male and female.')[42]

Heliogabalus, whose homosexuality was well known, is described, again by Aelius Lampridius, in the role of Venus, and according to Herodianus asked to be castrated so that he might be more like a woman.[43] Constantine was accused by Ammianus and by the anthologist of Ammianus of giving himself to love with the *spadones*,[44] meaning those eunuchs who had lost their procreative power but not their sexual capacity.[45] According to Aurelius Victor, Constans, author (with his brother Constantius) of a savage law against passive homosexuals, was himself a homosexual in private life.[46]

Only Claudius is exempt from criticism. Gibbon writes of him that out of the first fifteen emperors, he was the only one to confine his sexual relations solely to women.[47]

Clearly, when it comes to the reliability of imperial biographies, doubts may plausibly be entertained. Evildoing is part of the essential material for writing such a biography, and the stereotype of the tyrant demands that he should be devoted to all types of vice, with sexual vice taking pride of place. On the other hand, Suetonius in particular did have access to documentary archives in the imperial palace, and at least part of his information is reliable – just as the general picture of the milieu which he describes is reliable, in its broad outlines.[48]

At this point, on the basis of the information in our possession, it is inevitable that we should ask two questions. The first has to do with the discrepancy between the private lives of the emperors and the regulations they imposed, or at least tried to impose, on their subjects. But that is not a difficult problem to resolve: rules are always promulgated for those who are in a subordinate position. The people imposing the rules are above them, they do not believe that they are personally subject to them, and they do not intend to impose these rules on themselves as a moral imperative and code for living.

The second problem, a more complex one, has to do with the need to understand whether the sexual passivity of the powerful citizens served, for the Romans, as an example or as an excuse. Faced with accounts of imperial softness, one is almost inevitably led to ask: was passivity (obviously the type which was practised openly and on a large scale) perhaps a custom of aristocratic origin? Was it a luxury which was enjoyed by those who held power, and which only at a later stage became widespread among the people? Or should we conclude, on the contrary, that the example provided by the powerful citizens served merely as an excuse which allowed all those who were breaking the ancient precepts secretly (or were liable to all the consequences already mentioned if they did so openly) to come out of the closet, as it were, rendering visible a phenomenon which up to that time had been hidden, but which was nevertheless widely practised among those whose private lives have left no trace in the historical record? In all probability, although it is difficult to say with certainly, this was the actual position.

Historians obviously speak only of those who have made history. But sources of another kind do offer insights into the life of ordinary people, those of whom historians had no reason to speak. And while these sources are unfortunately later than the time in which the dominant classes started to set a bad example to the public, they nevertheless describe the behaviour of the Roman population well into the first century AD. They come from just a few decades after the Augustan age. And the sexual customs to which they allude obviously represent no novelty for the common people; they are not described as the prerogative of a few marginal deviants, but as widely practised customs, types of behaviour which had now joined the mainstream of society. If this had not been the case, they would not have deserved so much attention.

The nature of ordinary people's behaviour has already emerged from our reading of the *Satires* of Martial and Juvenal. Leaving aside the exaggerations inevitably linked with this literary genre, which describes and castigates their customs, the Romans at this time obviously cultivated habits which fell nothing short of those of their more powerful fellow citizens. Adult men, properly married with children, highly respected fathers of families, went so far as to pay other men to dominate them sexually. And we need to mention those who had themselves put down by slaves: 'Servus est minus qui foderit agrum quam dominum,' writes Juvenal:[49] the poor chap who has to plough the master's field is less of a slave than the chap who must 'plough' the master himself. Nor can we discount this as Juvenal's usual exaggeration. Seneca, for example, tells of a slave, already grown to adulthood, forced to dress up as a woman and shave his beard so as to seem like a *puer* when he took part in banquets, but in the bedroom forced to serve his owner as a husband.[50] Passivity was spreading to such a point that it had become quite a worrying phenomenon.

But we may return to the problem already raised: what was the role of the ruling class in this ever more explicit and visible change in sexual customs? In the light of what we have seen, it seems logical to suppose that the more powerful citizens of Rome set a new course, helping by their example to gain widespread acceptance of it. They were perhaps the first whose prestige and power made it possible to stop hiding what was considered the worst of vices in other citizens, without suffering the negative consequences of this revelation. In these citizens, private vice was compensated by undeniable manifestations of other virtues: the political and warlike virtues, in particular, which had always been a paradigm of manliness. The others, who were not themselves powerful, welcomed the exhibition of this behaviour as an excuse.

The popular attitude to Caesar, on closer examination, can be interpreted precisely in this way. Caesar, the conqueror, the soldier who straddled the world, had allowed himself to be put underneath at least once in his life. What better defence for anyone on whom infamy was heaped for doing the same thing? What better opportunity to prove, to oneself and others, that even somebody who went under another man sexually was none the less a real man?

The songs chanted during the Gallic triumph can be interpreted, I believe, in a different sense from the usual one. The verse which records that 'Gallias Caesar subegit, Nicomedes Caesarem' was in fact followed by two verses which went as follows: 'ecce Caesar nunc triumphat, qui subegit Gallias / Nicomedes non triumphat, qui subegit Caesarem.'[51] Now it is Caesar's turn to triumph, because he has put down the Gauls: not Nicomedes' turn, who put down Caesar. The soldiers are thus not mocking Caesar, but the King of Bithynia, clearly highlighting the fact that having played husband to Caesar had brought him no glory: Caesar was always the real man.

On reflection, one almost feels that even Caesar's reputation as an adulterer, a great conqueror of women, was to some extent constructed in order to develop an image which was seen by the soldiers (and obviously not only by them) as confirmation of their own virility, whatever personal concessions they might make to soft practices.

The song in which the soldiers, remembering Caesar's amatory exploits in the provinces, warn husbands to lock away their wives, goes as follows: 'urbani, serbate uxores, moechum calvum adducimus.'[52] Caesar, therefore, is the bald adulterer. It is no accident that, in boasting of his sexual potency, the soldiers emphasise his baldness: given that baldness was a synonym of passivity, they are letting it be known that a *cinaedus* can also be a seducer. This impression is confirmed by the popular enthusiasm for the theatrical joke about the priest of Cybele, which the audience referred to Augustus: the homosexual ruling the world with his finger.

What appears to emerge from the popular reaction to the 'deviancy' of the powerful is a sort of claim for personal autonomy, a confused and possibly subconscious desire to gain recognition, even in the midst of derisive laughter, for a very important principle: even a passive homosexual – the crowd seems to say – can be a man. Even if he is not Caesar; even if he is not Augustus.

Women and Homosexuality

Female homosexuality seen by men

Unlike the situation in Greece (for which, thanks to Sappho, we have at least one sample of female evidence concerning love between women) in Rome everything we know about this topic – absolutely everything – is filtered through the words of men, and they, obviously, tell it from their point of view. What point of view might one expect from a Roman, what attitude towards an aspect of female sexuality which, rejecting the necessary subjection to the male, took refuge in love affairs which excluded the male, and which inevitably called into question his image as the only possible dispenser of pleasure?

Female homosexuality was evaluated by a Roman male in a very different way from his view of the homosexual aspect of his own virile bisexuality. This is not only for the reasons already given, but also for another reason. Exactly like the Greeks, the Romans also saw woman as a dangerous being by her nature. Being incapable of governing herself, she needed to be controlled. And just like the Greeks, the Romans controlled their women, but in a different way. The Greeks shut women up in the house, and excluded them completely from social life. The Romans, on the other hand, used enculturation as the first line of control. They educated their women, making them participants in their life, admitting them to social gatherings, conversations, pastimes and a certain level of education. This was not done in a haphazard fashion: Roman women had been assigned a task which, if it was to be carried out properly, required that they should not perceive their condition as an inferior one. Like their menfolk, they had to be proud of being Roman.

The task of Roman women was not merely to reproduce life physically: it was to contribute to the formation of citizens. Unlike Greek women, they took personal charge of their sons, were connected to them by a powerful lifelong bond, and were supposed to transmit their fathers' values to them.[53] How could they fulfil this task if they were completely excluded from the life of the city?

Roman women had only the status and not the function of citizenship, as they did not participate either in legislative or in judicial assemblies, they could not be magistrates, and were excluded in general from the *virilia officia*.[54] But they did participate in the life of the city even if their gender ruled them out from some aspects of social life. At banquets, for example, they were only admitted up to a certain point – up to the moment when, during the second portion of the feast (known as *secundae mensae*), wine was served and the women had to go away. A strange habit, but only to our eyes. Wine, for the Romans, was a dangerous drink: it made people lose control. And women must never lose control. Their first duty was to keep themselves chaste, if unmarried or widowed, or faithful to their husbands, if married. Under the influence of drink, was there not a danger that, given their incapacity to govern themselves, they might fail in this duty?[55]

Over time, admittedly, things changed: the new permissiveness and the proliferation of bad behaviour undermined the ancient rule, so women also drank. None the less, such behaviour was unworthy of a respectable lady. In Petronius' *Satyricon*, for example, during the banquet in Trimalchio's house, we read that Fortunata and Scintilla (wives respectively of Trimalchio and Abinna) 'were giggling, slightly tipsy, and smooching together while talking about their domestic business, or about their husbands who amused themselves outside the house and neglected them'. Two women with drink on board are behaving with suspect effusiveness. And this is no accident. Although the reference to homosexuality in their relationship is not explicit, it shows through the words of Petronius, who describes them as 'they stand over there, all stuck together'.[56] An incidental reference, from which one really should not assume either disapproval or disdain, but we should not be led astray. Certainly Petronius does not condemn them, but in a work like the *Satyricon* a moral judgement would be unthinkable, even on something like female homosexuality. We are entitled to point out, however, that the two ladies who take some drink and then engage in these equivocal manifestations of affection are anything but respectable ladies. Pretentious and vulgar, grasping and ignorant, they are women whose past life is at least questionable. Fortunata, Trimalchio's wife, is in fact an ex-prostitute. These are the women who may be suspected of homosexuality.

But let us return to respectable ladies. Used to being with men and participating in their lives, Roman women do not feel frustrated, useless, inferior, exploited. Roman men did not exploit their women: they confined themselves to using them, and paid for their services with consideration and respect. It was a singular fate, that of Roman women. In order to be capable of passing on the paternal virtues to their sons, to teach them to be Roman citizens, with all the pride that this implied (*civis romanus sum!*), to fill them with the certainty that they belonged to a race of dominators, they had to enjoy a certain level of freedom; but the price of this freedom (within the limits allowed) was very high. One had to become a willing participant in the transmission of values firmly anchored to the idea of male superiority. This idea was precisely what they passed on to their offspring, perpetuating a culture which was not only patriarchal, but absolutely male centred.

Although this is a complex question, and a quick survey runs the risk of excessive simplification, in substance it can truly be said that the Romans made their women accomplices and collaborators in an operation which guaranteed the transmission over different generations of a culture which ruled out any autonomous life choices for the female sex. Between Roman men and Roman women, it could be said, a pact had silently been drawn up, guaranteeing advantages (obviously different advantages) to both sides. In exchange for giving up their personal power of choice (usually an unconscious sacrifice), Roman women obtained not only protection (the most frequent and banal of all exchanges between the sexes) but also recognition and honours which have not frequently fallen to the lot of mothers.

But having made these necessary points, it should be noted that, despite their privileged position in a certain sense (at least compared to the position of Greek women), Roman women were still subjected to rigorous control by men. Precisely on account of the importance of their given task, they had to be above suspicion, like Caesar's wife.[57] And when (as happened frequently at certain stages in Roman history) the women of Rome were no longer above suspicion, the situation changed radically: no more eulogies, honours, praise – nothing but scorn, sarcasm, violent and often vulgar accusations. If they were not to be models of every virtue, women must become unrestrained and uncontrollable creatures, prey to lustful passions and unnameable vices, adulteresses, ready to sell themselves to the highest bidder, inconstant and unfaithful. And, of course, homosexual (*tribades*, from the Greek *tribas*).

That homosexuality was the worst form of female depravity, in the eyes of the Romans, can be seen unequivocally from a simple reading of the evidence, which is sparse but explicit.

Female homosexuality, first of all, unlike the male variety, was 'against nature'. Thus we read in Ovid's *Metamorphoses*, where a woman who has fallen in love with another woman laments the un-natural quality of her love.[58] The story concerns Iphis, a girl born on the island of Crete, and brought up and dressed as a male ever since her birth. Before she was born, her father had decreed that if the baby were female, it would be killed. But Iphis' mother, acting on a suggestion by Isis, had hidden the sex of her child from everybody. The baby had been given a name which could also belong to a boy, and her mother had managed to deceive her husband, thus solving all problems for a number of years. But when Iphis reached a marriageable age, the situation became unsustainable. Her father betrothed her to the blonde Ianthe, with whom Iphis fell madly in love. The despairing girl bewailed her fate. Never had nature forced a human creature into such a monstrous love. Crete, her native land, had produced monsters. Most notoriously, it had given life to Pasiphae, but even the love felt by the daughter of the Sun had not been as monstrous as that of Iphis: at least Pasiphae had been in love with a male. This was Iphis' lament, and she howled about the horror of her fate: *meus est furiosior illo amor.*[59] My love is even madder than that of Pasiphae – who had fallen for a bull! As these torments went on, the wedding-day grew nearer. Although desiring it ardently, Iphis knew that she could not celebrate it. But at last the drama was resolved: invoked by Iphis and her mother, Isis transformed the unfortunate girl into a man.

The profoundly and radically different way in which the Romans evaluated male and female homosexuality can thus be clearly seen. Love between women is in the first place against nature, and in the second place criminal. Even though no law covers it, it is considered a crime: a married woman who has a homosexual relationship commits adultery.

In his first *Satire*, Martial speaks of Bassa, a woman on whose *pudicitia* no one would ever have dared to cast aspersions. She was a woman that no man had ever seen in male company, to whom nobody had ever attributed lovers. As befitted a respectable woman, Bassa went around only in the company of other women. And yet Bassa, whom Martial had seen as an absolute reincarnation of Lucretia, was a homosexual:

In that I never saw you, Bassa, intimate with men, and that no scandal assigned you a lover, but every office a throng of your own sex round you performed without the approach of man – you seemed to me, I confess, a Lucretia; yet, Bassa – oh, monstrous! – you were, it seems, a poker. You dare to bring together a couple of quims, and your portentous lust imitates man. You have invented a prodigy worthy of the Theban riddle, that here, where no man is, should be adultery!⁶⁰

Bassa's sexual behaviour gives rise to a riddle which not even Oedipus could solve: Martial's words, in the final verse, are as follows: *hic ubi vir non est, ut sit adulterium.*

But Bassa is not the only woman dedicated to this monstrous practice: there are others whose behaviour is no less disgusting, for example Philaenis, who is not satisfied merely with training like an athlete⁶¹ and vomiting at dinner after filling herself up with wine,⁶² as men used to do. Philaenis does much worse: 'When she is lustful, she does not suck (she thinks that is not manly) but simply guzzles on girls' middles.'⁶³ Given her behaviour, then, Philaenis is perfectly right when she defines the woman with whom she has a liaison as 'her mistress': 'Lesbian liberationist, Philaenis, you rightly call the woman you fuck "my mistress".'⁶⁴

The description of these women, who try in their monstrous and pathetic way to be men, returns in the sixth *Satire* of Juvenal. Here again, women devote themselves to athletic activities; here again they vomit at dinner.⁶⁵ The charge of homosexuality, which is not explicit in these verses, is stated openly later on in the same satire, when the poet describes the behaviour of Tullia and Maura, foster-sisters, who when passing by the ancient altar of Chastity, stop their litters. They 'befoul the image of the Goddess, playing their filthy pranks for the moon to witness'. The context in which this encounter takes place leaves no doubt as to the judgement it deserves: it is a deliberate outrage against the goddess, an exhibition of vulgar debauchery, provocatively committed on the very altar of Chastity. And Tullia and Maura are certainly not the only women who give themselves to these deplorable loves.

During the celebration of the mysteries of the *Bona Dea*, whose cult was reserved for *matronae*, women now became drunk and abandoned themselves to every type of debauchery:

> The flute stirs the loins and the Maenads of Priapus sweep along, frenzied alike by the horn-blowing and the wine, whirling their locks and howling. What foul longings burn within their breasts! What cries they utter as the passion palpitates within! How drenched their limbs in torrents of old wine! Saufeia challenges the slave-girls to a contest. Her agility wins the prize, but she has herself in turn to bow the knee to Medullina.⁶⁶

Martial and Juvenal obviously do not weigh very heavily in the scales of evidence. Their scorn for women is so strong that their words must be taken with quite a large pinch of salt. But they are not the only ones who refer to female homosexuality in a way which suggests that it was not an entirely exceptional practice.

Seneca, in his *Controversiae*, lays out for his pupils some cases where a legal solution could cause further problems: among these cases was the case of the husband who had caught his wife in the act of adultery with another woman.[67] Lucian, in his *Dialogues*, tells of the homosexual adventure of a courtesan.[68] In the *Amores* by pseudo-Lucian, Caricles affirms that if male homosexuality is permissible, then the female variety should also be allowed.[69] But as we have already seen, it would be a mistake to believe that he did not condemn it. He is a supporter of matrimony, and condemns male homosexuality: his speech, then, is a paradoxical one. Anyone who allows male homosexuality, to be consistent, should also allow female homosexuality – and who could ever stoop to such depths? Obviously, according to Caricles, not even men who felt entitled to have sexual relations with other men would support such an extreme position.

In the *Book of Dreams*, by Artemidorus of Ephesus (the manual of dream interpretation from the second century AD, to which we shall return) we find a classification of erotic dreams, divided into three categories: according to nature, custom and law; contrary to law; and contrary to nature. Relations between women, like those between men, are grouped among dreams 'contrary to nature'.[70]

Caelius Aurelianus, a doctor whose works we shall have occasion to consider again, writes as follows:

> These women are more desirous of lying with women than with men. In practice, they want women with male concupiscence, and when they are tired or temporarily satisfied in their passions they throw themselves, like victims of perennial intoxication, onto new forms of pleasure. Ensnared by this damnable style of life, they find pleasure in the use of their sexual powers. Like the *molles*, the 'tribades' are also affected by mental disease.[71]

The inexorably negative judgement of female homosexuality is thus constant, and becomes more frequent with Christianity.

Pagan morality, being the morality of a world of men, believed that, in the last analysis, female homosexuality was not important enough to deserve serious discussion. Christians had a different view of the world: women were people, exactly like men, belonging to a community. Preaching was aimed also at women, who were considered, like men, as hearers who must be taught not to commit sin. The sins which were to be rooted out included the sin 'against nature'. Among the causes which had provoked divine anger against the pagans, Paul cites the behaviour of pagan women, who replaced the natural practice of sex by an unnatural practice.[72]

Even dressing as a man is an action to be condemned. Jerome speaks of those women who 'in manly attire, having changed their habit, are ashamed of being women, as they are by nature. They cut their hair and impudently show off their eunuch faces.'[73] Like eunuchs, they are neither men nor women, and that is not allowed.

The Christian preoccupation with avoiding all occasions which could induce women to commit the sin against nature is clearly shown by a passage from Augustine, who addresses the following exhortation to nuns:

> The love between you, however, must not be earthly but spiritual. The things which women shamefully do even to other women, in low jokes and games, must be avoided, not only by widows and the chaste virgins of Christ, who live according to a holy rule of life, but also by married women and girls destined for marriage.[74]

But let us return to pagan society. Female homosexuality, which is spoken of very little (and which is not taken into consideration by the law, unlike the male variety), is nevertheless, as we have seen, a shameful custom which betokens depravity and unpardonable lust. The fact that women abandon themselves to this behaviour merely confirms their general tendency to vice. This is unforgivable.

By making love to other women they usurp a male prerogative: the right to dispense pleasure. It is no accident, in my opinion, that Roman men imagined sexual relations between women as an unnatural and almost caricatured reproduction of heterosexual intercourse. Their conception of sexuality did not allow them to envisage things differently. In the Roman imagination, female homosexuality could only mean an attempt by a woman to replace a man, and an attempt by another woman to derive from homosexual intercourse, quite unnaturally, the pleasure which only men were able to confer. That is how Martial imagines Bassa's relations with her lovers. That is how he imagines the sex life of Philaenis, who has assumed a virile role not only in the sexual field but also psychologically. Like males, she must always demonstrate her sexual power at all costs. To this end, she penetrates boys and possesses no fewer than twelve virgins a day: 'Boys buggered, virgins smashed by the dozen in a single day....'[75] As we have seen, Philaenis prefers cunnilingus to fellatio, because she thinks it is more manly.[76]

While it is true that this totally masculine vision of relations between women is taken to extreme limits of caricature by Martial, it is equally true that the same vision returns, albeit in a less extreme form, in very different authors. It seems to be the usual way of envisaging female homosexuality. In describing the sexual relations between the courtesan Leena and her lover Megilla, Lucian presents the latter woman disguised as a man, with an athlete's shaven head, and says that she makes love to Leena *hōsper andra*, like a man.[77] On reflection, one can see that the Christian writers adhere to the same line: homosexual women, according to Clement of Alexandria, are women who 'play the man against nature'.[78]

Given that pleasure could only be dispensed by men, love between women could be nothing other than a grotesque parody of the act of submission. And this is highly symptomatic: the most serious crime committed by lesbians was daring to think they could do without men. They were women who rejected the fundamental rule underlying relations between the sexes, the role of nature which had given men alone the power of sexual dominance, not only over women, but also over other men: inferior men, such as slaves; hated men, such as enemies; despised men, such as passive homosexuals. These lesbians were women who questioned the rule according to which men alone were entitled to rule and dominate the world.

Women faced with male homosexuality

One is forced inevitably to ask, faced with this male attitude, how the women of Rome reacted to the homosexual relationships of their menfolk.

It hardly needs to be said that Roman men, exactly like their Greek counterparts, very often continued to have homosexual liaisons even after getting married. Manlius Torquatus is certainly not the only one to be suspected (as Catullus says) of showing reluctance to accept the rule whereby he must forget *pueri* after his wedding-day.[79]

If we were to judge the facts on the basis of the insinuations advanced by Martial and Juvenal, we should be forced to conclude that the men obeying this rule were few in number. Not all went as far as Bassus, who squandered with *pueri* the possessions which his wife had brought him as a dowry.[80] Nevertheless, almost all men, unless they were *pathici*, loved boys – even when they were respectably married.

Of course, Martial and Juvenal were exaggerating. But the phenomenon of bisexuality in married men did exist, so women were forced in some way to face this problem and to deal with it. How exactly did they do this?

171

According to the sources, they coped by tormenting their husbands. Juvenal, for example, describes a woman who ballyrags her husband in bed, accusing him of unfaithfulness both heterosexual and homosexual.[81] Martial pokes fun at a wife who, after catching her husband with a boy, helps to compete with him by offering her husband the favours which she believes she can concede, just like a boy.[82] Fortunata, wife of Trimalchio, is jealous of the boys to whom her husband devotes his attention, and she does not fail to badger him about this.[83]

Given the tone in which the sources refer to this female attitude, one must point out that for the men who describe such behaviour it really is nothing more than yet another proof of how insufferable women are: as though their other faults were not enough, they nag their husbands over their innocent pastimes.

But what did the women really think about the situation? How did they assess, and how did they accept, their husbands' homosexual liaisons?

Clearly the situation was different for a woman, depending on whether her husband was a *pathicus* or, on the contrary, a virile seducer of boys. To have a *pathicus* for a husband must certainly have been embarrassing. Apart from the possibility that he might be totally lacking in virility, there was the problem of social disapproval which, while falling directly on the husband alone, must also presumably have caused a problem for his wife, whose status and image were dragged down by this deplorable situation.

The notion of an adult male being a *pathicus*, despite the gradual spread of immorality, was at least theoretically an exception. It was what might be termed a socially pathological hypothesis. The idea of a husband making love to *pueri* was much more normal. Not only was it more frequent, it was socially more accepted and acceptable: in some sense it formed part of the social physiology of sexual relationships. So how did women react to their men's adventures with boys?

In the total absence of any female testimony, we can only rely on logical speculation. What seems reasonable to suppose is that probably, as in Greece, *pueri* were not in practice particularly dangerous rivals, at least for wives. A wife's position was not imperilled by an extramarital love affair, which was not, and obviously could not be, an alternative to the matrimonial relationship. In social terms, the boys were non-existent rivals. As to whether Roman women suffered on the level of affection and passion, or how much they suffered, over having to share with the *pueri* and attentions, affection and sexual services of their husbands, that is something we can never know.

The Law

During the first centuries of the Empire, Roman law interested itself only marginally in the problem of homosexuality. The few provisions in this area deal with side issues, and do not touch the core of the problem.

What provisions are these? In the first place there is one, contained in the praetor's edict, by which passive homosexuals cannot *postulare pro aliis*, that is represent others in legal proceedings. This rule, reported by Ulpian (writing in the first decades of the third century) goes back to an earlier time. In reporting this provision the jurist states that, according to Pomponius, it does not apply to anyone who has suffered homosexual rape at the hands of bandits or enemies.[84] Given that Pomponius lived at the time of Hadrian, we can deduce that the rule dates from before that period. It is not a rule which will cause excessive surprise. If women lacked the capacity to represent others in court,[85] why should the *pathici* have it? The praetor who established this principle was basically doing no more than recognising that they had renounced their masculine prerogatives.

So far, there is nothing new. The innovation which can be noted during these centuries is merely the emergence of increasingly vehement hostility to male prostitution on the part of the imperial authorities.

Caligula appears to have banished the *spintriae* (male prostitutes) from the city of Rome. Suetonius reports that he could only be restrained with difficulty, after lengthy pleadings, from having them all thrown into the sea, and 'he drove them from the city'.[86] It is anything but certain that this provision ever came into force. But if it was enacted, this was certainly the first of a series of attempts to outlaw mercenary sexual relationships.

In the life of Alexander Severus by Aelius Lampridius (one of the *Scriptores Historiae Augustae*), we read that the emperor decreed that the taxes on pimps, prostitutes and *exoleti* should not be deposited in the public purse; instead, he ordered that these taxes should be used for restoring the theatre of Marcellus, the Circus Maximus, the amphitheatre and the stadium built by Domitian in the Campus Martius.[87] And the *exoleti* were, once again, the male prostitutes – although this term is sometimes used to indicate adult passive homosexuals (the literal meaning is 'grown up', from *exolescere*),[88] in this case the term refers only to male prostitutes, as is proved unequivocally by the fact that the targets of this provision were subject to special taxation.

Alexander Severus was thus anxious to show that male prostitution was a shameful business. He was even thinking of declaring it illegal, says Aelius Lampridius. But he did not do so. This step was later taken by Philip the Arab. Alexander decided that such a measure could prove counterproductive, and merely transform into a private vice something which was already a bad public custom (and, one is compelled to add, a considerable source of earnings for the state).

Confirmation of the fact that the activity of the *exoleti* was outlawed towards the middle of the third century by Marcus Julius Philippus, known as the Arab, comes from a story told by Aurelius Victor. Philip, says Aurelius, whose main source of information is Suetonius,[89] was induced to take this step by an extraordinary prodigy. One day, while victims were being burned, female organs were seen in the belly of a male pig. The soothsayers interpreted this phenomenon without hesitation: a terrible disaster was about to strike the Empire.

The emperor (who had been deeply struck one day be seeing a young male prostitute who looked like his own son) then outlawed the *usus virilis scorti*. How he forbade it, and what punishments he decreed against it, we do not know. But we do know for certain that this vice was not stamped out. In 390 the emperor Theodosius, to combat male prostitution, was forced to issue an extremely severe constitution, which we shall examine shortly. According to the historian Evagrius, the emperor Anastasius I, at the beginning of the sixth century, abolished a tax known as the *chrysargyron*, which was levied on male prostitutes among others.[90] According to Zozimus, this tax was introduced by Constantine, but Evagrius scornfully rejects that assertion.[91] What interests us is not so much to know who imposed the tax as to realise that male prostitution obviously continued to be widely practised, despite repeated attempts by the emperors to choke it off.

Still referring to prostitution, it should finally be remembered, in confirmation of the widespread nature of the phenomenon during the centuries of the Roman Empire, that a provision by Septimius Severus required the *praefectus urbi* to ensure that male slaves should not be forced by their owners to prostitute themselves.[92] Apart from these items, we know very little about the attitudes of the emperors in relation to homosexuality *per se* during the early centuries of the Empire. According to Christius, Alexander Severus increased the penalties for this type of behaviour.[93] In his view, the provisions reported in the *Pauli Sententiae* should be attributed to the intervention of this emperor. And the *Pauli Sententiae*, as we saw, bear witness to the fact that, at an unknown moment in time, passive homosexuality was punished by a heavier financial penalty than had been prescribed by the *Lex Scatinia* (more precisely, the confiscation of half of the offender's property, and the incapacity to make a will dealing with a larger portion of the property). We also know from the *Pauli Sententiae* that, once again at an unknown time, the death penalty was decreed for anyone corrupting a *puer*, with *deportatio in insulam* for the one who tried to corrupt him.[94]

It is highly problematical to assume that these innovations should be traced back to Alexander Severus. The only testimony which speaks of an initiative by this early third-century emperor in the field of homosexual behaviour comes from Aelius Lampridius, as we have seen. Alexander Severus, so far as we know, confined himself to imposing a tax on the *exoleti*. When, and by whom, the rules mentioned in the *Pauli Sententiae* were introduced, we therefore cannot be sure. As we are dealing with a textual source which was revised at least up to the middle of the fourth century, it is very difficult, given the lack of comparative evidence, to advance hypotheses with any degree of certainty. The first definite date in the history of imperial repression turns out to be the year 342, the year in which Constantius and Constans issued a new, savagely harsh provision, later included (and thus confirmed) in the Theodosian Code.

Constantius and Constans

In 342, on 4 December, in a constitution issued from Milan, Constantius and Constans issued the following statement:

> Cum vir nubit in feminam, femina viros proiectura quid cupiat? Ubi sexus perdidit locum, ubi scelus est id, quod non proficit scire, ubi Venus mutatur in alteram formam, ubi amor quaeritur nec videtur, iubemus insurgere leges, armari iura gladio ultore, ut exquisitis poenis subdantur infames, qui sunt vel qui futuri sunt rei.[95]

> When a man couples (literally 'marries') as though he were a woman, what can a woman desire who offers herself to men? When sex loses its function, when that crime which is better not to know is committed, when Venus changes her nature, when love is sought and not found, then we command that the laws should rise up, that the laws should be armed with an avenging sword, so that shameless ones today and tomorrow may suffer the prescribed penalties.

It is not difficult to work out who this constitution aims to strike: the emperors are condemning passive homosexuality. But the use of the verb *nubere*, in the opening phrase, has led to quite a few misunderstandings, and it has sometimes been interpreted as designed to punish marriages between men with death.[96]

Those who support this hypothesis point out that the sources frequently speak of marriages of this kind. This is true: apart from the parodic descriptions of these rites in Juvenal, one can recall, for example, the stories in Suetonius and Aurelius Victor of the wedding between Nero and Sporus, who brought a dowry to Nero in a ceremony which saw him dressed in a red veil (*flammeum*), like a bride.[97]

But it is clear that the law issued by Constantius and Constans does not allude to these marriages. The verb *nubere* is here used in a non-technical sense, which is a frequent use indicating the behaviour of a man who takes up a sexually passive role. Martial, as we saw, sneers at an apparently virile man who, however, *nupsit heri* – 'got married' yesterday – and he explains that he does not want a rich wife because *uxori nubere nolo meae* – 'I am unwilling to take my wife as husband'.[98] It may be added that marriages between men, evidence of which does survive in the sources, were clearly practised only by a minority of people, whose social status allowed them to provoke public opinion openly and brazenly to exhibit their homosexuality. The notion that imperial legislation would concern itself with such a custom, to the extent of punishing it with the death penalty, seems extremely strange. Even stranger is the hypothesis recently advanced, that Constantius and Constans punished homosexuals who married women.[99] This idea finds no support in the text.

The constitution, as was long ago pointed out by Gothofredus, was concerned with passive homosexuals,[100] and laid down that they must be subjected to *poenae exquisitae*.[101] What penalties, exactly? Those already in force, as argued by those who believe that this constitution is a simple call for repression?[102] Or were there new penalties, introduced by Constantius and Constans – more precisely, the death penalty, which most people think was inflicted by beheading the guilty parties?[103]

Gothofredus favours the hypothesis that Constantius and Constans introduced a new penalty, but he denies that the form of execution was by the sword. This constitution, he writes, does not provide for decapitation, as some people claim. The words *iubemus insurgere leges, armari iura gladio ultore* do not indicate the *poena gladii*, 'but the severity of the penalty', which according to Gothofredus was the *poena igni* – burning alive. The same penalty appears in a constitution of Theodosius I, dated 390, which we shall shortly examine, returning later to deal with the problem of the penalty laid down by Constantius and Constans. What this penalty might have been is more easily understood, perhaps, in the light of later constitutions.

Valentinian, Arcadius and Theodosius

On 6 August 390 Valentinian, Arcadius and Theodosius, in a constitution addressed to Orientius, vicar of the city of Rome, the text of which is preserved in the *Romanarum et Mosaicarum legum Collatio*, decreed as follows:

> Non patimur urbem Romam uirtutum omnium matrem diutius effeminati in uiro pudoris contaminatione foedari et agreste illud a priscis conditoribus robur fracta molliter plebe tenuatum coniucium saeculis uel conditorum inrogare uel principum, Orienti karissime ac iucundissime nobis. 2. Laudanda igitur experientia tua omnes, quibus flagiti usus est uirile corpus muliebriter constitutum alieni sexus damnare patientia, nihilque discretum habere cum feminis, occupatos, ut flagitii poscit inmanitas, atque omnibus eductos, pudet dicere, uirorum lupanaribus spectante populo flammae uindicibus expiabit, ut uniuersi intellegant sacrosanctum cunctis esse debere hospitium uirilis animae nec sino summo supplicio alienum expetisse sexum qui suum turpiter perdidisset. Prop. pr. id. Maias Romae in atrio Mineruae.

> We cannot tolerate the city of Rome, mother of all virtues, being stained any longer by the contamination of male effeminacy, nor can we allow that agrarian strength, which comes down from the founders, to be softly broken by the people, thus heaping shame on the centuries of our founders and the princes, Orientius, dearly beloved and favoured. Your laudable experience will therefore punish among revenging flames, in the presence of the people, as required by the grossness of the crime, all those who have given themselves up to the infamy of condemning their manly body, transformed into a feminine one, to bear practices reserved for the other sex, which have nothing different from women, carried forth – we are ashamed to say – from male brothels, so that all may know that the house of the manly soul must be sacrosanct to all, and that he who basely abandons his own sex cannot aspire to that of another without undergoing the supreme punishment.[104]

In this case, there is no doubt at all as to the punishment prescribed by Theodosius: death by fire. But there may be some doubt as to the people on whom this death is to be inflicted. Here again, the constitution has received different interpretations.

According to some scholars, it was designed to punish those who are today referred to as transvestites.[105] Others maintain that the new law punished active homosexuals and those who directed boys or men

177

towards homosexual prostitution[106] – people who condemned *another person's* manly body to a womanly sexual destiny. Yet others argue that this law punished those who used their *own* manly body for this purpose – meaning passive homosexuals. Within the group who opt for this latter interpretation, some believe that the constitution punished any manifestation of passivity, while others argue that it was aimed only at those who played the woman's part in brothels.

Which interpretation should we accept? The hypothesis that Theodosius set out to repress the phenomenon of *transvestism* gives rise to quite a few problems. It is true that for Roman men, dressing up as women was quite a widespread custom. But calling this *transvestism* means using a term which does not correspond to the modern meaning of the word. Wearing women's clothing, for the Romans, was not a sign of a pathological cast of mind, as the behaviour of transvestites is seen today. It did not come from the realisation of a dramatic conflict between a male body and a female sensibility and sexuality. Nor was it the extreme rejection of a maleness experienced as an 'unnatural' imposition, and a desperate attempt to assume the external trappings of the female sex. Proof of this comes from a case dealt with by the jurist Quintus Mucius, reported in Pomponius.

A senator had laid down in his will that a certain person should receive some items of female clothing as a legacy. But the senator in question was accustomed to dine in women's clothing. What was the legal situation? Should it be assumed that the legacy referred to the clothing in which the senator used to eat his dinner? Quintus Mucius rules this out.[107] Quite apart from the solution of this particular case, what is worth emphasising is the lack of surprise on the part of the jurist. Clearly, he was not in the least disturbed at the idea of a senator dining in drag.

This habit, while not exceptional, was not necessarily exempt from all social disapproval. Undoubtedly, cross-dressing showed a tendency towards 'softness'. Quintilian writes, for example, that dressing as a woman betokens a lack of virility, just like having a body which is *vulsum* (plucked hairless) and a gait which is *fractum* (effeminate): these habits and these attitudes, he writes, derive from *inpudicitia*.[108]

But there is no evidence that dressing as a woman was forbidden, or that those doing so were condemned to any penalty, however slight. In Seneca we read that a praetor can be accused of *crimen maiestatis* if he carries out his legislative functions in female or servile clothing.[109] But the fact that this charge could be brought in cases where the praetor wore a slave's outfit shows that the illegality of his behaviour was not linked to 'sexual transvestism', to use that term. The fault lay, more generally, in the exercise of a public function while dressed in a way which did not match the dignity of that function.

Dressing up as a woman, then, was a private habit which enjoyed relatively wide social toleration, and had no particular legal consequences. If Theodosius had aimed to punish 'transvestites' he would have been introducing a rule absolutely alien to the Roman tradition. Is it possible to imagine that, if he had decided on such a step, he would have inaugurated this new type of repression by prescribing nothing less than the penalty of being burned alive?

When Theodosius speaks of those who condemn a manly body to a sexual destiny which is not male, he is therefore alluding to those who condemn this body to undergo the sexual attentions of another man. And this brings us to the second problem: is he referring to those who condemn another person's manly body to a passive role, or should we conclude that he is prescribing the stake for those who condemn themselves to this fate? Basically, is he alluding to active homosexuals (and possibly those who organise male homosexual prostitution), or to passive homosexuals?

On a close reading of the text, the correct solution is the latter. The manly body to which the emperor refers is, obviously, the body of those whom he condemns to death: the body of those who, as he says, 'have nothing different from women' (*nihil discretum habent cum feminis*). In the light of this specification, it is impossible to imagine that he wanted to punish active homosexuals, and possibly pimps. He was thinking of passive homosexuals, but his intention was not to punish any passivity with fire: the stake is reserved for those who 'played the woman's part' in brothels (*occupatos ... atque omnibus eductos ... uirorum lupanaribus*). Theodosius' constitution is therefore directed to repressing the most intolerable form of passivity – the kind which most openly flouted the law as it already stood.

Clearly, the constitution of Constantius and Constans had not produced the desired effect. Imperial provisions (the text of Theodosius' constitution is clear) were being ignored. In particular, male homosexuals who prostituted themselves were openly breaching the law in an organised fashion, carrying on their trade in brothels. This type of behaviour, especially in the city of Rome, mother of all virtues, was absolutely intolerable. Male prostitutes must be publicly burned. Perhaps this would call a halt to corruption.

The question which inevitably arises, faced with the atrocious nature of this law, is whether it was implemented. The answer is by no means straightforward.

One line of reflection might cause us to assume that Theodosius hoped to frighten the population by threatening a terrible punishment, but that he really had no intention of applying it in an inexorable and rigorous way. The constitution (as we learn from the text contained in the *Romanarum et Mosaicarum legum Collatio*) is dated the Ides of May, but was only published in the month of August, as indicated in the Theodosian Code – where, as we shall see, it was included in an abbreviated form. Was Theodosius perhaps giving the prostitutes time to clear out of the brothels, thereby escaping death?[110] Although this hypothesis cannot be ruled out, the fact remains that in at least one case the imperial provisions were carried out. Under this legislation, the head of the militia in Thessalonica, a Goth named Butheric, arrested a famous protagonist of the circus games noted for his effeminacy – and this sudden arrest had dramatic consequences. The people, rising up in defence of their favourite, killed Butheric, provoking a reaction from the authorities. In the course of seven hours, after collecting them all in the circus, the Goths butchered 3,000 people. Writing about this episode, Glotz says that the popular reaction was an explosion of hatred against the German garrison.[111] This is a credible hypothesis: it is really quite difficult to imagine a popular uprising in defence of a homosexual's 'human rights'. But the episode is of considerable interest in any case: if the imperial provisions were applied in Thessalonika, why should we rule out the idea that they were also applied elsewhere?

If we have information about the Thessalonika case, this is obviously on account of its dramatic consequences.[112] The chronicles had no reason to speak of other cases (if, as is possible, such other cases existed).

The period of harshest repression, however, was yet to come. Progressively and inexorably, the cases of homosexuality punished by the stipulation of capital punishment grew more and more numerous.

Theodosius II and the Theodosian Code

In 438, the constitution of Theodosius the Great was inserted by Theodosius II in the Theodosian Code. It was quite significantly amended for this purpose. Although commentators sometimes confine themselves, oddly enough, to observing that the text was abbreviated, the cuts which were made in it were not dictated by a simple desire for concision. Deliberately shorn of its reference to prostitutes, the constitution now turned into an instrument for broader repression, and went so far as to state a new rule: from then on, all passive homosexuals would be condemned to the fire.[113] In its new version, the text went as follows:

Omnes, quibus flagitii usus est virile corpus muliebriter constitutum
alieni sexus damnare patientia, nihil enim discretum videntur habere
cum feminis, huismodi scelus spectante populo flammae vindicibus
expiabunt.

All of those who are accustomed to condemn their own manly body,
transformed into a womanly one, to undergo sexual practices reserved for the other sex, and who have nothing different from
women, will pay for this crime among the avenging flames, in front of
the people.[114]

In AD 506 the constitution was included in this form in the *Breviarium
Alaricianum*, the code issued by Alaric II, king of the Visigoths, to regulate the relationships between Roman citizens living in his kingdom,[115]
and we cannot prove that it did not continue in force, in the West, even
after the era of Justinian.

Isidore of Seville (who lived between 570 and 636) shows that he
does not know the legislative works of this emperor. In his *Etymologies*,
where he lists the great legislators known to him, from Moses to
Solon, from Lycurgus to Numa Pompilius, from the Decemviri to
Caesar, Isidore cites Theodosius II as the last great legislator. He does
not even mention Justinian. Strange though this may appear, it seems
that he did not know the *Corpus Iuris Civilis*. The hypothesis that the
Theodosian Code, through the *Breviarum Alaricianum*, continued to
be applied in the West, even after Justinian's time, can therefore not be
ruled out.[116] And it is quite significant that some summaries in the
Breviarium interpret the constitution of Theodosius II in a broad sense,
seeing it as prescribing the stake not only for passive homosexuals, but
also for active ones.[117]

And thus we turn to the innovations introduced by Justinian –
leaving aside the question of whether they were implemented to an
equal extent all over the Empire.

Justinian

Until the end of the fifth century, imperial policy in relation to homosexuality had respected the principles of ancient sexual ethics: the
only people condemned to die were passive homosexuals. Their active
counterparts were guaranteed to remain unpunished. But when Justinian
came to the throne, things changed radically.

In his *Institutions* (published in 533), we read that 'he who exercises
his shameful lust with a man is punished *gladio* on the basis of the *Lex
Iulia*'.[118] We are well aware that this reference to the *Lex Iulia* did not

correspond to the truth. But it served the emperor's purposes, in any case, by attributing authority – citing a non-existent classical precedent – to a newly introduced provision, which was totally contradictory to Roman tradition: punishment now struck active homosexuals as well. The text of the *Institutions* is crystal clear, and has a binding authority.

Although they were designed for school use (more precisely, composed to serve as the new textbook in law schools), Justinian's *Institutions*, inasmuch as they formed part of the *Corpus Iuris Civilis*, were a legal text. That is to say, the rules which they contained were to be applied. And Justinian's firm intention that they should be (including the area which interests us) emerges from the fact that, during the years following the publication of the *Institutions*, he dedicated two constitutions to this topic, confirming the death penalty for all homosexuals without distinction of role.

The first of these constitutions, dating from 538, deals with perjurors, blasphemers, and those who 'perform actions contrary to nature herself'. These acts against nature are homosexual relations, which the emperor deliberately associates with false swearing and blasphemy: homosexuality, for him, is a religious crime, and must be punished by divine will.

Those who commit these actions are ordered by the emperor to 'take into their souls the fear of God and the judgment to come, and abstain from these devilish and illicit lusts', so that divine anger, provoked by acts of this sort, may not fall upon them and their cities may not be destroyed, together with all their inhabitants.[119]

The thing that is to induce homosexuals to give up their behaviour is the memory of the well-known punishment of the people of Sodom, to which we shall return. But not only this: on account of their crime, Justinian points out, we have famine, earthquakes and plagues. Hence the injunction to abandon their infamous vice forthwith: 'We therefore warn them to abstain from the aforesaid crimes, so as not to lose their souls. Those who, even after this warning, continue to commit this crime, in the first place will render themselves unworthy of divine mercy, and in the second place will be subject to the penalties laid down by law.'[120]

Next comes the instruction to the competent authorities that these penalties must be rigorously applied:

We have ordered the most glorious prefect of the capital city to arrest those who persist in carrying on the aforesaid illicit and impious acts, even after our warning, and subject them to the extreme punishment [*eschatais timōriais* = *ultimis suppliciis*], so that their failure to deal with these sins may not endanger the city and the State on account of these vicious deeds. And if, after this warning of ours, still finding these individuals, they conceal them, they will also be condemned by God. And if the most glorious prefect finds people committing these crimes, and fails to punish them according to the laws, in the first place he will have to face divine judgment, and in the second place he will encounter our indignation.[121]

Homosexuality has been transferred into the field of crimes which offend the divinity: the punishment is now a double one, human and divine. The text constantly moves from the threat of earthly justice to the threat of punishment in the next world. Law is now a weapon of the church, it acts to realise the will of the Lord, to forestall the catastrophes which divine anger may cause. And it works by subjecting the sinner-criminals to the death penalty.[122] But *Novella 77* does not specify the way in which homosexuals are to die, and the later Edict 141, again dedicated to this burning question, is also silent on that point.

Clearly, the imperial warning had not produced the desired effect. In 559 Justinian issued a new provision, this time specifically addressed to those committing sins of lust against nature (*aselgainontes* or *luxuriantes contra naturam*):

The clemency and benevolence of God, which is always necessary, is particularly necessary at this present moment, in which we have provoked his anger in many ways, on account of the multitude of our sins. He has threatened and shown the penalties which we deserve for our faults, but he has acted with clemency and withheld his anger while awaiting our penitence, showing that he does not will the death of us sinners, but our conversion and our life. It is not right, therefore, that we should despise the benevolence, patience and indulgence of our clement God, drawing upon us the anger in the day of anger on account of our souls which are hard and far from repentance. We must all desist from all wicked habits and actions, especially those which have been contaminated by the abominable, wicked behaviour which is rightly odious to God: we speak of outrages committed by men, where they act most basely by abandoning themselves sinfully, men with men...[123]

It is clear that the behaviour outlawed here is the same as that banned in *Novella 77*. Once again we are dealing with any form of homosexual intercourse, quite independently of the role adopted. Once again, Justinian recalls the punishment of the people of Sodom, adding that homosexuality is condemned both by the apostle (Paul, as we shall see later on), and by the laws already in force. He goes on:

> All must abstain from the impious and wicked action which not even animals commit. Those who have never committed these actions should continue to abstain in the future. Those who have been contaminated by this attitude not only should abstain from it in the future, but should undertake the proper penitence, submitting themselves to God and reporting their disease to the most holy Patriarch, receiving the means of salvation, and carrying the fruits of penitence as it is written, so that a merciful God, in the abundance of his pity, may also bestow his clemency upon us.... We therefore proclaim that all those who are aware of having committed this sin, if they do not cease sinning and confess their disease before the most holy Patriarch, thinking of their own salvation, begging God's pardon for these impious actions before the feast days are over, must undergo the most severe punishment (*pikroteras timōrias* = *poenas acerbiores*), as they will not be worthy in future to receive any forgiveness.[124]

This constitution does not introduce any innovation in the system of repression. It confines itself to exhorting the emperor's subjects not to violate the divine and human laws, and exhorting the authorities to repress the abhorred behaviour, scrupulously applying the law against those who fail to profit by the imperial clemency. The repression, then, will begin only at the end of the period of grace allowed by the emperor to those who intend to mend their ways; they are permitted to escape punishment by promising the patriarch of the city, in confession, that they will no longer commit the sin that offends the Lord.[125]

The problem of the punishment to be inflicted on homosexuals thus remains open. Given the imprecise nature of the emperor's words, it is necessary to turn for clarification to literary sources, which report the outcome of trials actually held on this subject. And from the literary sources comes a surprise: in practice, the penalty for homosexuality is castration. That is what Malala says.[126] Procopius agrees, attributing the institution of this penalty to Justinian.[127] The same information comes from Theophanes, when he tells the story of Isaias and Alexander, bishops respectively of Rhodes and Diospolis in Thrace:[128] accused of pederasty, he says, these bishops were condemned to be castrated and were led in procession to be exposed to public derision, so that everyone could see what penalty was reserved for those who committed this crime. He goes on to add that after these events, Justinian laid down severe penalties for homosexuals, and there was great fear and trembling.

Apart from its contrast with the provisions in the *Corpus Iuris*, this information should not really be too surprising. Personal mutilation had been in use for some time in the Empire. For example, in 319, Constantine had decreed that informers should have their tongues cut out.[129] Constantine again, in 320, had decreed that molten lead should be poured into the mouths of nurses who, through their conversation, had encouraged *puellae* to be abducted – meaning that they ran away with men whom their parents did not consider desirable husbands.[130] Justinian's Code stated that a slave who tried to run away must have his foot cut off.[131] And in *Novella* 134, dating from 556, 'in consideration of the weakness of the human race', he decreed that corporal punishments should be mitigated, and forbade the amputation of both hands or both feet, as well as the infliction of punishments that broke joints.[132] While revealing that the emperor wanted to avoid the more disabling types of mutilation, this constitution clearly shows that this type of penalty did exist, and not only in practice: official law prescribed it and regulated its application.[133]

On close examination, then, nothing prevents us from believing the historians, not even the fact that the penalty prescribed for homosexuality in the *Corpus Iuris* was death: the trials to which they refer go back to the early years of Justinian's reign (more precisely, the year 529), when Justinian had not yet passed legislation in this area.[134] And, among other things, it cannot be ruled out that these trials were held against active homosexuals. Although this cannot be said with certainty, given the fact that he does not use words in a technical sense, it should be pointed out that Theophanes defines the bishops as 'pederasts'. Justinian may have punished those bishops for a type of behaviour which had not been repressed up to that time. If this is true, it would be unsurprising if he chose the penalty of castration to inaugurate this new repression.

The penalty prescribed for informers – having their tongues cut out – symbolically recalls the crime committed and strikes the part of the body involved; the molten lead in the nurses' mouths punishes a crime committed through speech; the amputation of a foot punishes the slave by depriving him of that part of the body with which he attempted to run away; similarly castration deprives the active homosexual of the organ which committed his crime. And even when the trials mentioned above were against passive homosexuals, the penalty would still have a clear, although different, symbolic value: castration deprived the *pathici* of the manliness they had criminally rejected, leaving them no better than women.

During the early years of Justinian's reign, before the publication of the *Corpus Iuris*, the penalty for homosexuality was thus castration. And it certainly cannot be ruled out – although there are no documents to attest it explicitly – that this penalty had been in use for some time, perhaps since the constitution of Constantius and Constans which, in 342, had established that homosexuals must suffer the *poenae exquisitae*. What penalty could be more *exquisita* – more suitably devised, appropriate, specifically suited – for the punishment of a homosexual? But castration was not confirmed as an official punishment in the *Institutions* and the *Novellae*: when he legislated in this area, officially extending punishment to active homosexuality, Justinian decided that the penalty should be death.

The stages in imperial repression, if what I have described is accurate, may thus be mapped out as follows: in 342 Constantius and Constans stated that the law must arm itself with an avenging sword, and punish passive homosexuality with a specially decreed penalty – presumably castration. In 390 Theodosius I decreed that passive homosexuals who prostituted themselves in brothels should be burned alive. In 438 the Theodosian Code extended the penalty of burning alive to all passive homosexuals. With Justinian, lastly, the condemnation was extended to all active homosexuals, and the penalty for all was death (although we do not know in what form).[135]

What were the causes underlying the escalation of imperial repression? For many centuries, homosexuality had not only been tolerated but, if active, considered a sign of virility. How and why did this wholesale condemnation and pitiless repression come into being?

Inevitably, one seeks an explanation in Christian teaching, to which Justinian explicitly links his condemnation, where, as we saw, he defines homosexuality as a sin which offends the Lord. By Justinian's time, the patristic writers had worked out a theology of sexuality which condemned relations between persons of the same sex as being 'against nature'. But while this is true, it is equally true that during the first centuries of the Empire, pagan sexual morality had undergone a deep and radical transformation, which had led to a vision of sex in many ways the same as the Christian one, or at least less incompatible with the Christian view than the older morality had been.

To understand the real reasons that determined imperial policy, it is necessary, before going on to analyse the terms of Christian teaching, to try to delineate the internal metamorphoses of pagan morality, at least in outline.

8

The Metamorphoses of Sexual Ethics in the Ancient World

Metamorphoses Within Pagan Belief

Paul Veyne writes that between the age of Cicero and the century of the Antonines, Rome saw a sea-change in sexual relations, by the end of which pagan morality was identical to the future Christian morality of marriage. And this transformation, he argues, happened quite independently of any Christian influence.[1] When Christian morality emerged, in this view, it merely reiterated (one might say took over) the new late pagan morality.

According to Veyne, there were two factors in this transformation: the first was the move from a 'competitive aristocracy' to an 'aristocracy of service'; the second was the phenomenon which Veyne defines as 'reactive self-repression' on the part of the plebs.

During the first two centuries of the Christian era, Veyne observes, the Roman ruling class underwent profound change. The heads of the different family groups (which for centuries had led groups opposed to each other, each of which saw its prestige and power in its ability to impose its will on others) became in substance servants of the prince. Their prestige and success now depended on their ability to maintain good relations with their peers. And this brought a far-reaching change in their psychological attitudes and behaviour.

Formerly, the head of the family group – whose sexuality was based on rampant aggression – had no problems or remorse in subjecting his wife, female slaves and male slaves to his will. The new nobleman was no longer capable of such behaviour. Outside the family, in society, he was part of a network of equal relations, and dealt with people whom he was necessarily obliged to respect. In this new situation, his morality changed completely. Being no longer in command, no longer giving orders to others, he was no longer capable of giving orders even to himself. He had to adopt a set of rules to live by, so he took on the rule of respectability. The new morality was thus determined by a psychological reaction to changed social conditions. And the new rules were reinforced and generalised by the second factor, also determined by a psychological reaction: the reaction of the lower classes.

Free citizens of a less exalted condition tried to compensate for their social subjection by taking on personal dignity through repression: self-repression, more precisely. Socially inferior and subject to commands from on high, the plebeians reacted to oppression in such a way that 'secondary benefits' were extracted from it. By repressing their own behaviour, they acquired dignity in the eyes of the nobility, the gods and themselves. By taking on a repressive moral code, they thus confirmed their status as free beings, citizens, persons capable of self-determination. And from this they derived the 'symbolic' benefits mentioned above.

These, therefore, were the paths followed by the transformation of pagan morality. Before Christianity became widespread, Veyne concludes, Roman sexual morality had changed from bisexuality, based on aggressive gratification, into heterosexuality based on reproduction. Late pagan sexuality, in other words, was in principle limited to matrimonial intercourse. Chastity (outside marriage) had become a virtue. Marriages had multiplied. Marital relations had changed: husbands and wives were supposed to love each other, and discord in the home was not tolerable. In short, the 'morality of couples' had come into being.

But within this more general framework, let us turn more specifically to the problem of homosexuality. Plebeian self-repression, sexual moralising in the style of Juvenal, Veyne writes, led to the creation of a different view of homosexuality and heterosexuality (which obviously gave the advantage to the latter).[2]

Only the upper classes failed to carry through this repressive process in full, or at least it did not reach the same degree as with the less exalted social groups. Among the nobility, the imbalance in morality was a great deal less broad. As they had not yet invented the theory of sexuality against nature, they confined themselves to jeering at the *molles*. But the ancient recognition of male bisexuality was disappearing in any case: the new rule was heterosexuality based on reproduction.

Christian preaching then took its place in this framework, and found that the ground had been made still more fertile by Stoic teaching, which exhorted individuals to control their passions, dominate their impulses, and channel their sexuality towards procreation. Within a vision of life where the spirit, in order to be free, had to dominate the flesh, sexuality could only be understood in this manner, and homosexuality was therefore condemned.

The causes which modified pagan sexual ethics were therefore internal ones. Veyne is not the only one to argue this; in a different perspective, Aline Rousselle has also attributed the causes of this change to factors other than the Christian influence.[3]

Between the first and the second century, she observes, sexual activity was perceived as a danger to health. Medical theory was extremely significant in this regard: to avoid losing one's physical fitness (or to regain it, if lost) there was really nothing better than abstinence. Every emission of semen is harmful, writes Soranus, and sexual intercourse is damaging. Men who control their sexual impulses are bigger and stronger than their incontinent brethren.[4]

The same opinion is advanced by Rufus, Galen and Oribasius: their works clearly reveal that the symptoms reported by their patients were as follows: complete lack of energy, constant tiredness, a general state of unease and discomfort. The doctors urged them to fight these symptoms by leading a healthier life involving physical exercise, careful dieting, and especially sexual abstinence.

But what were the causes of this exhaustion, this general widespread weakness in the ruling classes (the people whom the doctors address, as their advice has been sought by members of that class)?

The reason for their debility was because the life of an official working for the prince was unhealthy and stressful, requiring a commitment of time which limited, or even wiped out, the time available for looking after one's own bodily health. The Roman nobleman no longer lived in the open air, no longer took part in sports, was continually tied up in meetings, negotiations and sedentary activities which made him lazier and heavier, tired him mentally and put pressure on his nervous system, giving rise to anxieties and tensions.

The problem experienced by these men, according to Aline Rousselle, was to control their desires, avoid excesses, and regulate their physical well-being. The psychological reaction mentioned by Veyne, which impelled the Roman nobility to self-repression, seems in view of these observations to match up with health requirements: the new sexual rule is thus continence, if not abstinence. In the light of all this, should we conclude that asceticism came into being in Rome quite independently of the Christian influence?

It is clear that the aspiration to self-control, detachment from the flesh, and the sublimation of desires was not summoned into being by Christianity. Asceticism is a component found in pagan culture, as far back as the Greek world before the Romans.[5]

In Orphism and Pythagorean thought, in the philosophy of Plato and especially in Neoplatonic culture – leaving aside the admittedly major

189

differences – it is possible to discern a shared attitude, represented by the conviction that man must free his soul from the limitations of the body, struggle against desire, and resist temptation. And the influence of Neoplatonic culture on Christianity is so well known that it needs little explanation here.[6]

It may be added that, for different reasons, sexual desire was regarded with suspicion also by the Epicureans, the Cynics and the Stoics. Unlike the Orphics, the Pythagoreans and Plato, who believed that the control of impulses is a prerequisite for the immortal soul, confined to the earthly world, to reach the world beyond the senses to which it naturally belongs, the Epicureans concerned themselves only with earthly happiness. But even in this perspective, sex could be dangerous.

Epicurus believed that the wise man should not marry, except in special circumstances. He also believed that pleasure is not sensuality: sexual relations do not make life happy.[7] And the Epicurean school also had some followers in Rome. Lucretius, his most famous disciple, went so far as to say that desire was a disease which sexual relations could not cure, and that 'the wise man should avoid this folly, which prevents us from achieving serenity.'[8]

From a different starting point, the Cynics too had reached a very cautious attitude towards sex. Diogenes, for example, praised those who did not marry. Asked what was the right age to contract matrimony, he replied: 'As a young man, not yet. As an old man, never.'[9]

The position of the Stoics, lastly, although less extreme, involved a partial acceptance of sex for purposes outside itself. Zeno and his followers believed that reproduction concerned not only the body but also the soul. Marriage was therefore allowed; but what distinguished man from the animals was still his ability to control his impulses with his reason.[10]

In the first century AD Musonius Rufus taught that sexual relations were reprehensible even in marriage, unless they had a reproductive purpose. For the same reason – the fact that it was sterile – homosexual intercourse was to be condemned.[11]

The rhetorician Seneca, also a Stoic, declared that a wise man must love his wife with moderation, not with passion. He must control his impulses and not allow himself to be drawn easily into coitus. Those who engage in union with their wives to generate children in the interest of the state and of humanity, he argued, should imitate the animals, and when their wives are pregnant should avoid destroying their offspring.[12]

The idea of a contrast between flesh and spirit, reason and impulse, the material and immaterial components of the human being, is thus not a Christian innovation. Differently formulated, it appears in pagan culture, right through its history. In Rome, the aspiration towards continence, if not asceticism, took root and spread during the first two centuries of the Christian era, becoming a fundamental part of the dominant culture. Through the teachings of medicine this value became not only a moral imperative but also a means of health maintenance and therapy.

The Christians, it has been said, did not make the world ascetic. Rather, it was the world in which Christianity found itself at work which made Christianity ascetic.[13] Having said that, can we assume that the Christian sexual ethic, and in particular the Christian condemnation of homosexuality, are nothing more than a rationalisation and theorisation of late pagan ethics?

To examine this hypothesis we must analyse not only Christian teaching, but also its Jewish roots before drawing any conclusions.

The Judaeo-Christian Tradition

The New Testament

The fact that Christian teaching condemned homosexuality from the beginning is a fact which (although sometimes denied)[14] emerges with absolute clarity from a reading of the sources.

Although not very frequent, the references to homosexuality in the New Testament are crystal clear. In the letter to the Romans, describing the reasons which have brought God's anger down on the pagans, Paul writes:

> Their women exchanged natural relations for unnatural, and the men likewise gave up natural relations with women and were consumed with passion for one another, men committing shameless acts with men and receiving in their own persons the due penalty for their error.[15]

To argue, as has been done, that Paul is here condemning only male prostitution, not homosexuality in itself, is really very difficult.[16] In the first place, the reference to prostitution appears only where he is speaking of male homosexuality. When he speaks of female homosexuality obviously to condemn it, he does so in global terms, without any limitations or reserves, basing his condemnation on the contention that it is 'against nature'. This same contention underlies the condemnation of male homosexuality, so we are not entitled to limit Paul's field to mercenary relationships. In addition, there would be an obvious

191

incongruity if he had issued an assymetrical condemnation, which would justify some types of intercourse between men, but none between women.

To this we may add that there is no reference to prostitution in the first letter to the Corinthians, in which, among those who 'will not inherit the kingdom of God', along with the fornicators, idolaters, adulterers, thieves, misers, drunks, backbiters and graspers, we find the *malakoi* and the *arsenokoitai*[17] (in Jerome's translation, respectively the *molles* and *masculorum concubitores*). In other words, the homosexuals – indicated with good reason by two different terms: the *malakoi* being the passive homosexuals, and the *arsenokoitai* the active ones.

Paul, then, condemns each and every form of homosexuality. But despite the clarity of his language, the text is sometimes interpreted in a much more restricted sense than a simple reading reveals. Paul, it is maintained, condemned only a specific and precisely identified type of homosexual relations – pederastic relations – which had now degenerated to the point where, in practice, they amounted to mere bullying of young boys, whom the apostle therefore wished to protect.[18] In support of this hypothesis, it is asserted that *malakoi* is a word which indicated the boys who were subjected to such treatment (thus pejoratively defined because quite frequently they sold their services), while *arsenokoitai* indicated those adults who took advantage of these youths, or who paid them for their services.[19]

But this hypothesis is clearly unacceptable for a number of reasons, the first being a matter of vocabulary. To maintain that *malakoi* referred to passive homosexuals of a youthful age (excluding adults) means falsifying the meaning of the term (which Jerome was not mistaken in translating into Latin with the word *molles*, the meaning of which we know well). The Greek word *malakia* indicates, exactly like *mollities*, the lamentable passivity of an adult. For proof of this, it is enough to think of what Dionysius of Halicarnassus says about Aristodamantes, whose nickname was *malakos*: the reason for this nickname, Dionysius says, is not absolutely certain. Some people think that it may be due to Aristodamantes' effeminacy (*thēludria*); others maintain that it is attributable to his sweetness of behaviour.[20]

Obviously, then, the term, which had originally meant 'soft' in the sense of sweet or mannerly, had taken on the negative value of 'effeminate'. And for the ancient world, an effeminate person only meant a passive adult male. A boy could not be such, because he lacked the prerequisites of softness. How could a boy who was not yet a man become effeminate, despising his manliness? Intellectually still weak, like women, legally incapable of acting, also like women, sexually indeterminate, because he was not yet capable of fertilising anybody, the boy, by definition, could not be described as effeminate. So the *malakoi* to whom Paul alludes are not boys. They are passive homosexuals, whom Paul defines by using a term which, in Greek, alludes only to adults, but which he obviously uses to indicate all those who take on an 'effeminate' role, without distinction of age. And along with those, he also condemns the *arsenokoitai*: a term which literally means a man who shares his bed with another man, but which Paul is clearly associating with *malakoi* to include active homosexuals also in his condemnation. And there is nothing in the text to limit his condemnation to adults who took advantage of boys. If Paul's aim had been to protect *paides* from exploitation and abuse, among other things, he would presumably have levelled his condemnation only at the abusers, and not at their victims as well.

In short, as can clearly be seen from a reading of the two passages devoted to this topic, Paul condemned homosexuality on a global basis, whatever its manifestations.[21] This is a not inconsiderable innovation. It immediately shows the Christian attempt to introduce a different sexual ethic, which replaced the old contrast between activity and passivity with a new, fundamental dichotomy between heterosexuality and homosexuality. The novelty of this principle is underlined, if it needs underlining, by a consideration which is by no means of negligible or secondary importance: in his letter to the Romans, as we saw, Paul condemns not only male but also female homosexuality. For him, clearly, the problem is not the typical one experienced by Roman law and ethics in the era before Justinian, of how to proclaim the principle that a man must be manly. His concern is to impose respect for a rule which is for the first time defined as natural, which demands that men should always and only couple with women, and vice versa. In Paul, the expressions *kata physin* and *para physin*, unlike the situation in previous times, signalled the imperative and inescapable rule of heterosexuality, and the abnormality of any practice which moves away from it. Paul's preaching, then, lays the foundations for a new sexual ethic, which Christian writers in the following centuries were to repeat with decisive constancy, without any concession or hesitation. This new morality returns, not only in the New Testament, but also in another text, which is usually overlooked, but is no less significant than the previous ones: a pastoral letter written to Timothy at an unknown date, but which it is believed can be dated to the early years of the second century.[22] The topic is 'the law': and Paul, in listing those who break the law, includes *pornoi*, *arsenokoitai* and *andrapodistai*.[23]

The reference to the *malakoi* (*molles*) has disappeared, and condemnation now falls not only on male prostitutes (*pornoi*) and those who trade in slaves (this is the meaning of *andrapodistai*: in practice, those who reduce a free man to a state of slavery with a view to making a prostitute of him). Condemnation falls on all homosexuals, without distinctions of role (*arsenokoitai*).

What is the source of these principles? Are they perhaps the first statements in a new ethical system which was then beginning to form in the Christian world, or are they inherited from a cultural tradition different from the old pagan one, but no less ancient: the Hebrew tradition?

Relations with the Jewish tradition

Like the texts from Paul, the references to homosexuality contained in the Old Testament have been the subject of much debate, receiving different interpretations. Jewish culture, according to some scholars, did not condemn homosexuality in itself: it merely condemned prostitution and violence.[24] But these are forced interpretations, which do not hold up against an examination of the sources.

The extract quoted in support of the view that the condemnation only covered prostitution is a celebrated passage from Deuteronomy which reads: 'There shall be no cult prostitute of the daughters of Israel, neither shall there be a cult prostitute of the sons of Israel. You shall not bring the hire of a harlot, or the wages of a dog, into the house of the Lord.'[25] It is blindingly obvious that these words do not contain a condemnation of homosexuality in itself: the type of intercourse condemned is the mercenary kind, whether homosexual or heterosexual. The passage is not decisive for the present argument, but it does pose some problems which demand closer examination.

The Hebrew term translated by the word 'prostitute' (*porneuōn*, in the Septuagint, *scortator* in the Vulgate) is *qādēsh*, and *qādēsh* is a sacred male prostitute, who pays over the income from his work to the temple. On the basis of this consideration, some have argued that the only type of prostitution forbidden was the sacred kind.[26] But on closer examination, it is difficult to accept this interpretation: the text, after saying that there shall be no cult prostitute either among the sons or the daughters of Israel (*qādēsh* and *qēdēshāh*), says that the temple is not to receive money from the *zōnāh* and the *kelev*. The *zōnāh* and *kelev* (literally a dog) are simply people, of the female and male sex respectively, who sell their bodies, *tout court*, with no religious implications.[27] Deuteronomy is therefore condemning any sort of prostitution, whether male or female, sacred or profane.

The question of whether the type of male prostitution condemned was homosexual, as most people believe,[28] or heterosexual, as some people believe, is something which does not have to be decided here.[29] For present purposes it is enough to note that the condemnation of relations between men, quite independently of whether or not these are mercenary relations, appears explicitly in Leviticus, where we read: 'You shall not lie with a male as with a woman; it is an abomination.'[30] Proof that this condemnation does not merely strike at passive homosexuality comes from another passage, also from Leviticus, which states the penalty for the behaviour mentioned above: 'If a man lies with a male as with a woman, both of them have committed an abomination; they shall be put to death, their blood is upon them.'[31]

Even when faced with such an explicit text, some scholars have observed that the lack of any reference to female homosexuality means we are not dealing here with a condemnation of homosexuality in itself, and that in any case the condemnation of male homosexuality which the text contains (about which very little argument is possible) is the only condemnation of this type to be found in the Old Testament.[32] The proof of how forced this interpretation is comes from the celebrated story of the people of Sodom. Dispatched by the Lord into the city whose inhabitants had forgotten divine precepts and abandoned themselves to all types of depravity, two angels were invited into the house of Lot, who offered them hospitality. But during the night the people of Sodom surrounded the house and demanded that Lot should put the foreigners out in the street 'so that we may know them'. Lot tries in vain to offer them his two virgin daughters instead, so that they can abuse them (as Jerome translates: *abutemini eis sicut vos placebit*). The Sodomites do not want Lot's daughters: they want the foreign visitors.

This is their sin, and the punishment is proverbial: the Lord destroys the city, burying it under a rain of fire and sulphur. Only Lot, led by the angels up into the hills, survives the massacre. His wife, who was also going to be saved, makes the mistake of turning around to see what is happening, disobeying the angels, and she is transformed into a pillar of salt.[33]

Despite the fact that this account really seems to leave little room for doubt, some scholars have not accepted the most widespread interpretation (the one accepted by post-biblical tradition) of the nature of the Sodomites' sin: that they wanted to rape the foreign visitors. According to their alternative interpretation, the behaviour of the Sodomites is meant in the first place to symbolise every guilty thing that could be done and imagined, and in the second place their last, most serious sin (the one for which they were destroyed when they tried to commit it) was the violation of the demands of hospitality towards the visiting angels.[34]

In support of this hypothesis it has been pointed out that none of the biblical condemnations of homosexuality (which we have already examined) refers to the story of Sodom, and that the passages alluding to the Sodomites and the destruction of their city do not specify which sin earned them punishment.[35] Alternatively, if the biblical passages do allude to Sodom, they confine themselves to speaking in general terms of arrogance, meanness, lack of pity for the poor, and the fact that the Sodomites committed 'abominable' acts.[36]

As for the hypothesis that the last and decisive sin of the Sodomites was their violation of hospitality, it is argued that in Scripture the verb *yāda'* (which indicates their intentions towards the angels) normally indicated the social act of 'getting to know someone', and much less frequently the metaphorical meaning of 'having sexual intercourse.'[37]

But it seems very difficult to argue that the type of knowledge which the Sodomites wished to have of the angels was purely of a 'social' kind. If this had been the case, why on earth should Lot have tried to stave it off by offering his daughters to be raped? The offer of his daughters is clearly aimed at placating the desires of the Sodomites by offering them an alternative outlet. Clearly, homosexual rape was a much more infamous act than heterosexual rape. Confirmation of this comes from a comparison with the story of the atrocity at Gibeah, related in the Book of Judges.[38] A Levite who lived near the hill country of Ephraim had married a woman of Bethlehem, who had left him to return to her father. The Levite, who wanted to be reconciled with his wife, did not give up: he went to Bethlehem, where his father-in-law had no difficulty in handing him back his wife. But the road home was long, and as evening fell the Levite decided to stop at Gibeah, where he was given hospitality in the house of an old man. During the night (exactly as in Sodom) the men of Gibeah beset the house, demanding that the stranger should be handed over to them, 'so that we may know him' – *hina gnōmen auton*, as the Septuagint translation says. But Jerome explicitly translates: '*ut abutamur eo*', 'so that we may abuse him'. What was to be done?

The old man, trying to ward off this misdeed, spoke to his fellow citizens: I have a virgin daughter, he says, and the stranger has a woman. I will give them to you, instead of the stranger, I am so determined that you must not commit such an act of madness.

The word which I have translated as madness is the Hebrew word *nevālāh*,[39] translated by the Septuagint as *aphrosynē*, and by Jerome explicitly as *scelus contra naturam*. But even though the explicit reference to the unnaturalness of the desire of the people of Gibeah appears only in Jerome, very little doubt is possible about the fact that they wanted to violate the stranger. Exactly as with the men of Sodom, in this case too they are offered the chance to 'know' women instead of the stranger. And while here it is not the Lord who intervenes to prevent a misdeed, nevertheless in this case too the wicked deed is not done. The Levite cleverly resolves the difficult situation. He opens the door of the house, and shoves his woman out, handing her over to those who were so anxious to 'know' him, so that they can do whatever they like with her (*et eis tradidit illudendam*, says Jerome). Which is exactly what the men of Gibeah do all night, until at dawn the woman is abandoned in front of the door of the house. Here the Levite finds her, when he goes out to resume his journey. 'Get up, we must be off,' he says to the dead woman, who is stretched out on the ground with her hands on the threshold; but the woman makes no reply. The Levite then loads her on to his donkey and carries her off. Here, taking a knife, he cuts her corpse into twelve pieces which he then dispatches throughout the territory of Israel. Those who are charged with delivering the remains have to ask the addressees if they have ever seen such a crime. The Israelites, obviously, want to know what happened, and the Levite tells them that the inhabitants of Gibeah wanted to kill him, and had raped his woman. The Israelites then decide to take action, so that this wicked deed should not go unpunished. Four hundred thousand of them make their way to Gibeah and destroy it, killing men and beasts alike. Twenty-five thousand people are massacred.[40]

A singular story, indeed, deserving a lengthy analysis; but here we shall limit ourselves to the point most directly at issue. Once again, as in the case of the Sodomites, and perhaps even more explicitly, an attempt at homosexual violence is considered so intolerable as to legitimise the behaviour of a man who, without any hesitation, sacrifices (or would be disposed to sacrifice, in Lot's case) his daughters or his woman. It seems very difficult to deny that the biblical account, in both cases, should be taken to mean that homosexuality is an execrable type of behaviour. At this point, what can be said of the hypothesis whereby the identification of the sin of Sodom with homosexuality is a late interpretation – more precisely a Palestinian interpretation, dated not earlier than the second century BC, inspired by Jewish hostility towards Greek customs and Greek homosexuality?[41]

Leaving aside the observations made so far, the fact remains that the explicit sexual interpretation, although late, is not only Palestinian but, as we shall see, also a Greek interpretation. In that case, obviously, it cannot be merely inspired by hatred of the Greeks. Finally it should be pointed out that the sexual interpretation gains credibility within Scripture from the explicit condemnation contained in Leviticus.

It therefore seems beyond doubt that the Old Testament condemns homosexuality in all its manifestations. It would be wrong to consider the story of the friendship between Jonathan and David, sometimes seen as a love story, as evidence to the contrary.

To take just one example, T. Hörner writes in this connection that since the Scriptures do not condemn that relationship, we must deduce that they reveal two standards of judgement and two different positions in relation to homosexuality. On the one hand, there is 'good' homosexuality, born of love (such as the relationship of David and Jonathan). On the other hand, we have 'wicked' homosexuality: that of the Sodomites. Scripture condemns only the second variety, which means, basically, only homosexual violence, and not homosexuality in itself.[42] But in the light of what we have seen, this interpretation is unacceptable. The condemnation of homosexuality is already present in the Bible, and will be confirmed by the post-biblical tradition, both Palestinian and Greek.

As regards the Palestinian tradition, it is enough to recall that in the *Mishnah* (the first text which, around AD 200, fixes the teachings in written form), we read that homosexuality is punished by stoning:[43] the biblical condemnation is thus upheld. The *Mishnah* further specifies that capital punishment is appropriate only for those who commit the act voluntarily,[44] that when the act involves a minor, only the adult involved is to be put to death, and that if it takes place between two people one of whom is asleep, the death sentence is only to be pronounced against the partner who was awake at the time.[45]

In the Talmud, the topic is developed further.[46] The rabbis discuss the regulations contained in Leviticus and Deuteronomy. Leviticus 18:22 states: 'You shall not lie with a male as with a woman.' The expression 'to lie', they believe, alludes to the act of one who takes the dominant position sexually. This passage therefore condemns only active homosexuality. Leviticus 20:13, which uses the same verb, confirms that the ban only covers a person who possesses another man; but after saying 'if a man lies with a male as with a woman...' it goes on to prescribe 'they shall be put to death'. Obviously, then, passive homosexuality is also prohibited. Where can we find the condemnation of this behaviour, as we do not read it in Leviticus? The solution comes from the passage in Deuteronomy condemning male prostitution: the prostitute is a man who sells himself 'like a woman'. The Scriptures therefore condemn any manifestation of homosexuality.[47]

Even on the briefest reflection, the procedure adopted by the rabbis is surprising. To condemn passivity they rely on a passage the original meaning of which is different from the one they attribute to it. They are induced to do this by the need to extend to passive homosexuals a condemnation which they have not read, because they have given the expression 'to lie with a male' an interpretation which rules it out.

One might consider, then, that for the rabbis the most reprehensible type of homosexuality, the sort that immediately sprang to mind when they thought about this sin, was the active variety. Or at least one feels that the condemnation of passive homosexuality was not their primary preoccupation. We shall return to this question further on. For the moment, the important thing to point out is that the rabbinical inter-pretation, in any case, confirms the biblical condemnation of homo-sexuality in all its manifestations.

We now turn briefly to female homosexuality, of which both the Scriptures and the rabbis are substantially unaware. The very small amount that we know about it seems to show that it did not give rise to particular concern. The fact that two women were carrying on a rela-tionship between themselves, one feels, was something which concerned only them, and left the community practically indifferent.

That is what one would be led to feel, in particular, by the discussion which saw the two schools of Hillel and Shammai ranged in opposing positions. The problem was this: the law demanded that a woman marrying a priest should be a virgin. What should be said about a woman who, before her marriage, had had sexual relations with another woman? Could she marry or not? The school of Shammai saw homosexual intercourse as equivalent to heterosexual intercourse, and ruled that the marriage could not take place. But the school of Hillel maintained that there was nothing to prevent this woman from getting married (to the priest).[48]

We shall also return to this topic, after a quick examination of the evidence which gives us some idea of the Greek tradition: Philo of Alexandria and Flavius Josephus.

In the work of Philo (a philosopher and theologian born about 20 BC) we read some significant references to the story of Sodom. Philo had absolutely no doubt that the sin of the Sodomites was a sexual one. In this city, he writes, 'men mounted males without respect for the sex nature which the active partner shares with the passive,'[49] and on account of this they became sterile. In Philo, the condemnation of homosexuality is linked to the reproof for wastage of seed, and the sterility of relationships *para physin:* 'had Greeks and barbarians joined together in effecting such unions,' he writes, 'city after city would have become a desert, as though depopulated by a pestilential sickness.'[50]

Philo's judgement on homosexuals is all the more severe as he is forced to admit that the vice, far from disappearing, has been spreading. He writes: 'In former days the very mention of it was a great disgrace, but now it is a matter of boasting not only to the active, but to the passive partners.'[51]

In these words one seems to read an echo of the Greek evaluation of homosexuality which, as we saw, was socially deprecated only if passive. But it is only an echo. Philo is a Greek, and it is almost inevitable that he should consider the passive role as more shameful. But he is also a Jew, and therefore condemns the active role too. And as a Jew, he is anxious to emphasise a fundamental difference between Jews and Gentiles. The Gentiles break the laws with impunity. The Jews, however, are not free to do this: 'If you are guilty,' he says to his co-religionists, 'of pederasty or adultery or rape of a young person, even of a female, for I need not mention the case of a male, similarly if you prostitute yourself or allow or purpose or intend any action which your age makes indecent, the penalty is death.'[52]

It is by no means sure that all the types of behaviour indicated by Philo were actually punished with death. Although he knew the law, Philo was not particularly interested in the interpretation of legal regulations: his preoccupation was not law but morality.[53] Despite this, there emerges from his work – and this is essentially the point which interests us – a condemnation of each and every type of homosexual relationship; the same unshaken general condemnation which emerges from the work of Flavius Josephus, author of a history of the Jewish people, probably written after the revolt against the Romans which was crushed in AD 66–70.[54]

In commenting on the Torah, Flavius Josephus, exactly like Philo, has no doubts at all: the Sodomites tried to use homosexual violence against the angels.[55] His view of homosexuality emerges from his description of the sexual customs of the Greeks (in particular, Josephus speaks of the peoples of Sparta, Elis and Thebes), who coupled *para physin* and, to justify their actions, even dared to attribute their own depravity to the gods.[56]

What is interesting to observe, both in Philo and in Flavius Josephus, is their insistence on the fact that homosexuality is a pagan vice, not a Hebrew one. It is even more interesting to find the same insistence in the Palestinian tradition.

In the *Mishnah* we read that an unmarried man must not be the teacher of a boy, nor can a woman act in that capacity. Rabbi Judas says that 'an unmarried man cannot look after a flock, nor can two unmarried men sleep under the same mantle. But the Sages permit this.'[57]

Obviously, the rule was intended to ensure that the unmarried man would not find himself exposed to temptation. But the Sages (who represent the dominant opinion) maintained that this worry was excessive. To explain the reason for their position, we can read a comment in the *Tosefta*: 'Israel is not suspected' (neither of homosexuality nor of bestiality, obviously).[58] The question of whether this comment corresponded to reality is not particularly important for present purposes. It is obviously unthinkable that homosexuality (to confine ourselves to the problem that concerns us) could be totally unknown to the Jews. The extent of the 'vice' is difficult to gauge. One piece of evidence, however, seems to indicate that in the second century BC the Jews had been contaminated by pagan example.

The Testaments of the Twelve Patriarchs, a work written between 153 and 109 BC, and translated into Greek before AD 50,[59] clearly reveals a certain preoccupation with this question. In the *Testament of Levi* (third son of Jacob and Leah) we read a prophecy: 'priests will be idolaters, adulterers, moneygrubbers, lascivious and violators of children *(paidophthoroi)*.'[60]

In the *Testament of Naphtali* (eighth son of Jacob and Bilhah) is the following exhortation: 'You, my sons, must not be thus [i.e., like the Gentiles]. Recognising the Lord in the firmament, the earth, the sea and all creation, do not become like Sodom, which changed the natural order [*taxin physeōs*].'[61] And later on: 'I have read in the writings of Enoch that you will wander away from the Lord, adopting all the sins of the Gentiles, and committing the sin of Sodom.'[62] And the sin of Sodom is homosexuality. If the *Testament of Naphtali* speaks in general terms of the Sodomites' *anomia* (meaning an unspecified violation of the law on their part), the *Testament of Benjamin* (twelfth son of Jacob and Rachel) is much more detailed: 'And I believe that there will be a demon amongst you, from the words of Enoch the just, and you will fornicate with the fornication [*porneia*] of Sodom and you will perish.'[63]

As already noted, the point of interest for us is not the extent to which homosexuality was practised among the Jews, but the judgement passed by the Hebrew tradition on this behaviour. If what has just been shown is correct, that judgement was always, from the outset and without concession, both in the Palestinian and in the Greek tradition, a condemnation firmly smiting the sin 'against nature'.

At this point it is difficult to avoid thinking, inevitably, that the Christian condemnation of homosexuality in itself, starting with Paul,

finds its basis in the Jewish religion. Recent attempts to argue that the
Bible (with Paul following in its wake) confined itself to condemning certain types of homosexual behaviour (the violent and mercenary
types, and those involving the exploitation and abuse of young boys)
seem to be refuted by the existence of a centuries-old tradition, constant
and coherent, the traces of which go back at least as early as the sixth
century BC. And the reason for the Jewish aversion to sexual relations
between men has an explanation which accounts for its firmness, when
one thinks of how intolerably criminal any wastage of male seed was
for the Jews.

The sexual act, for the Jews, was only lawful if it ended with the
semen being deposited in the female uterus. Any emission of semen
outside this context was a contamination. In Leviticus we read: 'If a
man has an emission of semen, he shall bathe his whole body in water,
and be unclean until the evening. And every garment and every skin on
which the semen comes shall be washed with water, and be unclean
until the evening.'[64] The Book of Genesis contains the famous story of
Onan, punished with death not only – and not so much – for having
broken the law of the levirate, by which he was supposed to marry his
brother's widow, but also, and especially, for having evaded this rule by
committing an act which was criminal in its turn: that of spilling his
seed on the ground.[65] In the Jewish tradition, masturbation was to
remain a very serious sin.[66]

The duty of the Jews was to procreate and fill the earth. The absolute
need to 'increase and multiply', for a people like the Jewish people, is in
any case perfectly clear when one thinks about their history. After the
Diaspora this need became still stronger, on account of their desire to
preserve their racial identity, to avoid disappearing as a group, to
preserve and pass on their beliefs and customs. It is no accident that the
sense of horror over the wastage of semen returns in the most varied
sources, from the Torah to Philo.

The Jewish aversion to homosexuality, then, derives from a perception of the need (obviously vital for any people, but particularly and
dramatically felt by the Jews) to concentrate their efforts on procreation.[67] If this is true, as appears to be the case, one can perhaps
understand why in the Jewish world (unlike the Greek and Roman
world) condemnation is directed also – and perhaps primarily – against
the active partner. He is the one who wastes his seed. He is at the root
of the guilt which also falls on his accomplice. In this context one can
also understand the relative indifference shown by the Jews towards
female homosexuality: as it did not threaten the propagation of the
race, why worry about it?

The Christian synthesis

After trying to delineate the attitude of the Judaeo-Christian tradition – necessarily more briefly than is required by the complexity and importance of the topic – the time has come to return to the problem from which we started, and to try to understand whether and to what extent the policy of the Christian emperors in the area of homosexuality was determined by changes internal to pagan sexual morality, or whether and to what extent it was dictated by the desire to conform to Christian teaching. But to answer this question it is not enough to refer to the framework of the new pagan morality, which we have so far described in its general outlines, without going into more detail, in particular on its assessment of sexual relations between men. It is now necessary to try to understand, more specifically and precisely, the late pagan attitude towards those relationships which Christianity defined as 'against nature'. On closer examination, it emerges that the pagans did not share the Christian view.

Undeniably, for some time the pagan world had also contained some authorities who believed that sexual relations between men should be, if not avoided, at least limited. But whatever the reasons, this was not because the relations were between people of the same sex. Lucretius, for example, when he said that desire is a disease which sexual intercourse cannot succeed in curing (although he certainly did not think that it should be avoided on that account), placed sexual relations between men and those with women on the same level. All that can be said is that Lucretius highlights the problems which arose from sexuality, but homosexuality was not, for him, a source of special concern.[68]

The trend towards continence, self-control, sometimes even abstinence, undoubtedly caused sexual relations between men to be regarded with a certain degree of concern. Musonius Rufus, for example, disapproved of them. But not because they were 'against nature': simply because they were not directed towards reproduction. Consequently he disapproved in exactly the same way of non-procreative heterosexual intercourse.[69]

Only medical precepts, at first sight, seem to display a specific aversion to homosexual intercourse, advising against it more strongly than its heterosexual counterpart. But medical opinion did this for health reasons: 'Intercourse between men is more violent than that with women', writes Rufus of Ephesus, 'and thus it is more tiring.'[70] No moral condemnation, then. Nor could one infer a negative moral judgement from the fact that Soranus saw homosexuality as a disease. His approach to the question clearly shows that the disease does not consist in the fact of being attracted by somebody of the same sex. The disease of which Soranus speaks is not homosexuality, but passivity. Caelius Aurelianus, who translated his work into Latin, summarising it, explains the nature of the problem in the following terms: for some people, it is difficult to believe that effeminate men (*molles sive subacti*) can exist. But some people have unlimited desires, and therefore some men adopt the gait, clothing and other characteristics of women. These people have a disease which, Soranus says, does not strike the body, but the mind: their desires are the product of a corrupt mind (*malignae ac foedissimae mentis passio*). As for the causes of this disease, there are different opinions. According to Parmenides, some people are attracted by people of the same sex on account of the circumstances in which they were conceived; they are neither true men nor true women. Others maintain that the disease is hereditary and is transmitted through the semen, and so they believe that anyone affected by this disease can do nothing to be cured of it. The disease, furthermore, unlike other hereditary diseases, grows worse with the passage of time, for the following reason:

> When the body is still strong and can perform the normal functions of love, the sexual desire [of these persons] assumes a dual aspect, in which the soul is excited sometimes while playing a passive role and sometimes while playing an active role. But in the case of old men who have lost their virile powers, all their sexual desire is turned in the opposite direction and consequently exerts a stronger demand for the feminine role in love. In fact, many infer that this is the reason why boys too are victims of this affliction. For, like old men, they do not possess virile powers; that is, they have not yet attained those powers which have already deserted the aged.[71]

Nothing could be more symptomatic than this diagnosis: in perfect coherence with the principles of sexual morality in the ancient world, disease is seen as a lack of virility.

Homosexuality in itself, in late pagan ethics, is not yet an expression of unacceptable sexuality. When it manifests itself in the assumption of an active role, it still belongs to the laws of desire; it is only worrying and deplorable when it comes out as effeminacy. Proof of this comes from a reading of the *Book of Dreams* by Artemidorus.

Born in Ephesus, in Asia Minor, this 'interpreter of dreams' lived in the second century after Christ. As a practitioner and theoretician of dream analysis, Artemidorus set out his science in a textbook which sums up all the Greek wisdom on this topic. Yet he lives and writes under the Roman Empire, around which he travels, and the habits, mentality and values of which he knows and shares.[72] His *Book of Dreams* emerges from an experience of life that is intrinsically Roman; it is addressed to the citizens of the Empire, and teaches them how to interpret their own dreams. Naturally, these include erotic dreams, which Artemidorus classifies and divides into three categories: those which follow nature, custom and law; those which are against the law; and lastly those which are against nature. Homosexual dreams are included among the dreams 'according to nature'.[73]

As for their significance, this varies depending on whether the partner involved is a free man or a slave: to possess a slave is good luck, to be possessed by him is not. Similarly, different meanings can be taken from the dream of being possessed by an outsider: if the stranger is older and richer, the dream is favourable, if he is younger and poorer it is unfavourable.

Then there are some homosexual dreams that are against the law: more precisely, the dream of raping one's own son. In this case too, the meaning is different depending on the circumstances: if the son is a minor, the dream is unfavourable, but if he is an adult it is favourable.

It would certainly be interesting at this point, within the division of homosexual dreams into favourable and unfavourable (and if a dream is lucky it must be socially acceptable, or so we may well think), to devote a little space to the undeniable innovations which this classification reveals.

Consider, for example, the dream of having intercourse with a slave: to possess him is good luck, to be possessed by him is bad luck. The ancient rule whereby active homosexuality receives a positive evaluation, while the passive type is given a negative value, is here once again confirmed. But when one moves to the dream about intercourse with a free man, the old principles seem to have lost their value: to be possessed by an older and richer stranger is a favourable dream. The field of allowable homosexual relationships seems to have undergone extension rather than restriction. Is it possible to see this as an adaptation of popular morality to behaviour which in practice (if what we have seen is correct) saw an ever-increasing number of adult men practising and often exhibiting passive behaviour? Artemidorus, in this connection, seems to confirm that hypothesis, and offer at least partial justification for imperial policy. The emperors were reacting to the spread of a 'vice' which was imperilling the very image of Rome: to try to stamp out this vice was, for them, a social and political duty, whatever their personal habits. But people like Artemidorus did not share these worries: dream analysis was a professional practice (as well as a theoretical field of knowledge) which had no political duties. That is why Artemidorus can take a different attitude. The imperial constitutions set forth and tried to impose official morality, while Artemidorus reflects popular morality – and popular morality accepted sexual relations between men. But above and beyond these considerations, one fact is certain: for Artemidorus, homosexuality in itself is not against nature.

The only unnatural homosexual relationship in the *Book of Dreams* is one between women (placed in this category alongside sexual activity with oneself).[74] This classification fits perfectly into the male vision which sought to repress female sexuality, on which we have already dwelt. By identifying only intercourse between women as 'unnatural', this approach confirms once more – as if there were any need – that sexual relations between men were not unnatural. We may add, in conclusion, that Artemidorus is not the only source bearing witness to this view. Confirmation that th∫ was a widespread opinion can be gained from a reading of two works which I have already examined in the first part of the present book, but which, given the time when they were written, bear witness – like Artemidorus' book – to the sexual morality shared by all subjects of the Empire, whether Greek or Roman. These works are the *Amatorius* of Plutarch and the *Amores* of pseudo-Lucian. In neither of them, as we have seen, is homosexuality rigorously and definitively condemned as such.

In pseudo-Lucian, true, Caricles (who supports the superiority of love for women) declares that loving people of the same sex is *para physin*.[75] In the first place he believes that homosexuality is against nature because, by practising it, men 'cast their seed upon the rocks'. Just like Plato – and it is no accident that he uses the same image[76] – he thus identifies heterosexuality with intercourse directed towards procreation. This allows us to speculate that for pseudo-Lucian (as for Plato, who says so explicitly) non-procreative heterosexual intercourse is also 'against nature'. In the second place, Callicratidas, who speaks up for the love of boys, replies to Caricles by saying that, while it is true that heterosexuality is natural (as shown by the fact that animals couple with animals of a different sex), it is also true that man is superior to animals because he has created culture: and homosexuality (precisely because it is a cultural feature) is superior to heterosexuality.[77]

Late pagan morality, then, is certainly different from earlier pagan morality, for all the reasons which I have tried to point out. There can be no doubt that internal changes had taken place. The spread of Christian morality would be incomprehensible if one had to imagine it clashing with a radically different style of life and set of philosophical principles. To some extent, the new morality had to satisfy requirements felt by pagan society, responding to needs which were certainly complex and difficult to define, but undeniably real. Christianity was clearly able to give an adequate response to these needs.[78] One of the responses which managed to meet these requirements was undoubtedly the church's theory of continence as a moral value, abstinence as a higher state of life, closer to the Lord, an instrument for winning the prize in the life to come.

'To the unmarried and the widowed I say that it is well for them to remain single as I do. But if they cannot exercise self-control, they should marry. For it is better to marry than to be aflame with passion.' Thus writes Paul in his first letter to the Corinthians.[79] Marriage was beginning to appear to the Christians as a lower state than chastity. This was the interpretation given to one phrase used by Christ. Christ had explained to his disciples that one must not repudiate one's wife, and that it was adulterous to marry a repudiated woman, just as it was adultery to remarry after repudiating one's wife.[80] The disciples had then asked him whether, if that was the position, it might not be better to avoid marriage altogether. And Christ had replied: 'Not all men can receive this precept, but only those to whom it is given. For there are eunuchs who have been so since birth, and there are eunuchs who have been made eunuchs by men, and there are eunuchs who have made themselves eunuchs for the sake of the kingdom of heaven. He who is able to receive this, let him receive it.'[81]

For Christ, therefore, virginity was an alternative to marriage, but not necessarily superior to it. However, his statements were given a different interpretation. In Greek, the phrase translated as 'he who is able to receive this, let him receive it' runs as follows: '*ho dynamenos chōrein chōreitō*'. And *chōrein* means to understand with one's intellect. Jerome translated: '*qui potest capere, capiat*', and the expression was taken to mean: 'He who is able to do this, let him do it' – in other words, 'he who is able to keep himself chaste, let him remain chaste'. Paul was not the only one to interpret Christ's words in this way. Justin in the second century, to offer the pagans an example of Christian continence, tells of a young man who, in order to avoid temptation, asked the prefect of Alexandria to allow a doctor to emasculate him. The doctors of the city maintained that they could not carry out this operation without the consent of the authorities. The prefect, however, disallowed the application. And Justin comments: 'This did not prevent the young man from sticking to his proposal.'[82] The rejection of sexuality, in short, was a very strong component in Christian culture,[83] and fitted in perfectly with the late pagan trend towards asceticism.

A close examination shows that in this field Christianity was closer to late pagan morality than to Jewish morality. The Jewish tradition gave sex more importance than was allowed by Christian ethics. I am speaking here, obviously, of heterosexual relations; we have already discussed the Jewish condemnation of homosexuality. But when it comes to heterosexual intercourse, Jewish culture was certainly less repressive than Christian culture. For example, while a bride's virginity was highly prized, premarital sex was not prohibited. Sexual intercourse was allowed even during pregnancy and breastfeeding. With the proviso that all sexual intercourse should end up with the semen being deposited in the womb, one can basically state that sexuality in the Jewish world was not only tolerated, but recognised.[84]

In this area, then, the Christian exaltation of continence was closer to late pagan than to Jewish ethics. None the less, Christianity was preaching new and different principles – and one of these principles was its condemnation of homosexuality in itself, considered (in this case following the Jewish tradition) as an abominable and perverse form of sexuality, offensive to the Lord, and one which, whatever its manifestations, could not be tolerated because it was always and everywhere 'against nature'. These new principles encapsulate – in the sexual area – the differences between late pagan morality and Christian morality: Christianity adds to the pagan disapproval of male sexual passivity the Hebrew disapproval of active homosexuality (as well as the passive variety), and goes so far as to issue a global condemnation of all sexual intercourse between people of the same sex.

Falling within a more general framework of the rejection of the 'pleasures of the flesh' (which were later demonised by the Fathers of the Church),[85] this condemnation further restricted the space allowed for sexuality, definitively and drastically limiting the sphere of lawful intercourse to marital sex for procreative purposes.

It is difficult, in the light of these observations (returning to the problem of imperial policy), to avoid thinking of Christianity as one of the causes, not to say the fundamental and decisive cause, of the change in legislative policy, its gradual hardening, and especially the extension of the range of types of homosexual behaviour to be punished.

This hypothesis, however, may encounter the following objection: to conform to the Christian ethic, the emperors would also have had to punish active homosexuality. And as we know, this happened only with Justinian. Up to the sixth century (meaning three whole centuries after the proclamation of Christianity as the state religion),[86] repression was directed only against the passive role. But this objection may be met by considering that the imperial authorities found themselves legislating in a world which for many centuries had not only accepted, but respected and admired active homophilia. To conform completely to Christian teaching could be unadvisable for various reasons. What success could be hoped for from a legislative initiative which was in total, open and irremediable contrast with popular morality? The decision to repress passivity, and only passivity, with ever-increasing severity, could well have been an attempt at a compromise, reconciling the new moral precepts with a custom too long established to be suddenly wiped out from on high, avoiding conflict with a sexual ethic which was still basically inspired by the love of virility, understood as the ability to subject other people to one's power.

In this climate, imperial legislation would have been almost certainly ignored and disobeyed completely. The attempt to introduce the new morality had to proceed slowly, cautiously, gradually: the increasing cruelty of the punishment inflicted on the *molles* was a measure which, obviously, stood a much better chance of being accepted by popular opinion than a sudden and unacceptable condemnation of active homosexuality. If all this is true, the reasons why Constantius and Constans, Theodosius I and Theodosius II confined their attention to the *molles* can be readily understood. By so doing, while they signalled their obedience to the state religion, the emperors avoided a showdown which would probably have led to ignominious failure.

On closer examination, imperial policy in the area of homosexuality is comparable to their actions on divorce. This is no coincidence.

The idea that the marriage bond could be dissolved purely at the wish of the parties was profoundly rooted in the mentality and practice of Rome. In this case too, therefore, a sudden switch to Christian teaching (which, needless to say, condemned divorce) would have been unthinkable. Again imperial policy proceeded gradually, hampering the right to divorce more and more, without ever abolishing it.[87] The emperor who had the nerve to introduce laws which fully conformed to Christian principles was, once again, Justinian, who in 542 instituted penalties against divorce *communi consensu* (a divorce decided by common agreement between the married couple, without either having committed a fault, or without external factors powerful enough to warrant the decision: for example, the husband's impotence occurring after the marriage).[88] This law was so unpopular that Justinus II, Justinian's successor, was forced to withdraw it in 566.

Imperial policy in the area of homosexuality, then, seems in reality orientated and determined by the desire to impose Christian morality. This was done at first with a certain degree of caution: while laying down severe penalties for passive homosexuals, the first imperial constitutions in this area safeguarded the ancient principles of Roman morality. Then, with Justinian, all hesitation was cast aside: homosexuality must disappear, without distinctions, without any escape even for those who, while practising homosexuality, did so with full regard for the ancient rules. Every manifestation of homosexuality must now be wiped out because, always and everywhere, intercourse 'against nature' offended the Lord.

Conclusions

Nullus liber erit, si quis amare volet
(Propertius)

The pagan world considered sexual relations between men as an integral part of a sexuality which not only did not rule out relationships with women, but considered them necessary and dutiful (as well as desirable). This same model of sexuality considered, on the other hand, that intercourse between women was a foul coupling, a sign of unthinkable debauchery. That is the general framework within which the conclusions of the present study must be set. As we have seen, male homosexual relationships were experienced differently in Greece and Rome, and the Greek and Roman mentalities were quite far apart in this area. Hence, inevitably, our conclusions must be subdivided and differentiated. Some conclusions are only valid with reference to the Greek world; others apply only to the Roman world; yet others, more general, can be drawn from a consideration of some shared underlying features (leaving aside internal differences) between the Greek sexual ethic and its Roman counterpart. These show the deep and radical changes which pagan ethics underwent on coming into contact with Christian culture.

As regards Greece, everything that we have seen confirms that for a Greek man, from the earliest times that the sources allow us to examine, homosexual relationships were part of a life experience regulated by a series of social norms which laid down the time scales and etiquette of these relationships, and their alternation with heterosexual relationships. This obviously means that this experience was perfectly legitimate, both socially and legally. The only legal regulations in the area of homosexual relationships were designed to ensure that pederasty should not degenerate from being a stage in the cultural formation of younger people, as it was intended to be, to become instead an indiscriminate and anti-educational promiscuity, morally and socially dangerous.

211

But from this observation we cannot conclude that the sexual ethic of Greece was not repressive. Firstly, the Greek view of female homosexuality was very different from that of male homosexuality. From their point of view, the Greeks had very strong underlying reasons for giving a negative judgment on the 'tribades'. Female pleasure, in their view, was something which had to be controlled. Women (as shown by the story of Tiresias) experience more pleasure than men in sexual intercourse. Moreover, they are incapable of controlling themselves. Even before their social lives, what needed controlling was their sexual lives: more precisely, what might be called their autonomous sexuality, the kind which would have led them to experience pleasure outside the function for which they were destined – in other words, any female sexuality which was not at the service of men.

The Greek sexual ethic, which was worked out in detail and not particularly interested in the idea of sex being 'natural' (where naturalness means heterosexuality), was therefore based on a double standard. Or rather, like all cultural factors in Greece, it took men alone as its point of reference. Women were considered only indirectly, as instruments of reproduction or pleasure; for them there was no recognition of bisexuality – the sole, ineluctable rule of their sexual lives was to be subjected to the power of a man.

But having pointed out once more the extent to which Greek society was made to measure for man, another consideration demands a further correction of the image of the supposed sexual freedom of the Greeks, even if one confines one's attention to male sexuality alone.

The Greeks were certainly aware that men, besides their heterosexual impulses, also had homosexual leanings; and this awareness clearly underpinned the cult of bisexual divinities in many areas of Greece.[1] We all know the story of Hermaphroditus, the lovely boy who at the age of fifteen, loved by a nymph who did not want to be separated from him, was united with her in a bisexual being.[2] Equally significant, although more complex in their interpretation, were the numerous rituals where men and women exchanged clothes and roles. Every year in Argos there was a festival (*hybristika*) during which men wore women's clothing and women wore men's clothing.[3] In Sparta wives received their husbands, on the first night of their marriage, wearing male clothes and shoes, and with their heads shaven.[4] In Cos, husbands dressed as women to receive their wives.[5] Leaving aside the other possible meanings of rituals inverting sexual roles, the traces of an androgynous vision of the human person can be clearly discerned.

But this did not mean that the Greeks were entitled to free expression of their bisexuality – even if they were male. Even men were not allowed to display their feelings and follow their individual impulses. The Greek man had to go through his homosexual experiences at the right moment, with the right people and according to the right rules. And these rules involved the assumption of a series of roles which were not always necessarily congenial to those who had to take them on, at the prescribed moment.

For a start, being the passive partner in a homosexual relationship was not necessarily the dream of every adolescent boy. And while it is true that in the age of the cities taking on this role was neither indispensable nor inevitable (obviously the position had been different in the pre-city age and in relation to homosexuality as initiation, which was a necessary duty), it is also true that it must have been anything but easy for a Greek boy to avoid this type of relationship if it did not happen to match his personal leanings.

To be courted, flattered and praised must have been a very gratifying experience, both psychologically and socially. As we have seen, to be courted was a recognition of one's beauty and virtue, and it conferred social value. Boys were inevitably induced to want to be courted, and to behave in such a way that they would be courted. But perhaps not all boys were equally happy to take part in the intercourse desired and sometimes demanded by their adult lovers. Greek boys (at least those belonging to the élite) were taught to accept sexual intercourse in the same way that respectable Victorian ladies were taught to put up with it: not as a pleasure, but as a duty. Thus, in practice, it could happen that a relationship would be accepted by somebody who did not really desire it, on account of a sort of social duty or conditioning, while people who really did desire these relationships went through them with a pretence of detachment, modesty and chilly reserve which inhibited the free expression of desires, but which were indispensable in order to save a *pais* from being classified as 'too easy'.

But leaving aside this aspect of the problem also, we may turn to the more general aspect determined by the need to observe the ineluctable rule of the change of role.

On reaching the age of majority, the Greek boy had to take on the active role of a lover, with both women and boys. In other words, a Greek male in the space of a few short years underwent two sexual initiations of contrary kinds. The first of these taught him to learn and assume a role which the second initiation, a few years later, enjoined him to forget.

Without question, the fact that the change of role was a fundamental general social rule must have made this stage less traumatic than it might appear to our eyes. Despite this, it must presumably have been a difficult experience, especially for those who, in their adolescent years, playing the part of the young 'beloved', had discovered an exclusive or at least predominant tendency towards passivity within themselves. To give up the role of the 'beloved' after experiencing it (and what is more, in a culture which attached great importance to this role) must have been as difficult as trying to resist a necessarily repressed homosexual impulse in a rigorously heterosexual society.

To say that the Athenian man was allowed all sexual possibilities is to give an image of Greek sexuality which has very little to do with reality. The idea of a Greece where men moved without the slightest difficulty from one sexual role to another, so that male bisexuality caused none of the 'anxiety' provoked by homosexual experience in the modern world, is in fact a highly dubious notion.[6]

It can be presumed that the change from the role of lover of a *pais* to that of lover of a woman (and vice versa) caused no particular problems. It is also true, however, that the need to change at a certain moment in one's life from the role of desired love object to the role of desiring subject, must have caused, at least in a certain proportion of the male population, not only 'anxiety' but quite considerable problems, both psychological and sexual. The Greeks were aware of all these difficulties – or at least some of them were. In the light of the considerations advanced so far, we can perhaps find an explanation of statements by authors like Plato, Xenophon and pseudo-Lucian, who, as we saw, spoke of the disgust felt by young love objects, their humiliation and rancour against their lovers. These authors seem to refer – generalising from individual cases which were certainly not general – to those boys who essentially put up with homosexual intercourse as some kind of social necessity. And we can also understand, perhaps, why Aristotle (referring to passive homosexual experience at a youthful age) observes that 'the memory of pleasure experienced provokes the desire to renew the union which accompanied it'.[7] He seems to be referring to the difficulty of assuming an active role if, in one's youth, one has discovered a tendency towards passivity which is not merely transitory.

But there is one other observation to be made in this connection. Neither Plato, nor Xenophon, nor Aristotle (nor the philosophers in general) can be considered as a mirror reflecting popular attitudes towards sex. They express a sense of unease which certainly existed to some extent but, equally certainly, it was perceived only by a minority – by that élite (or perhaps more precisely, by part of that élite) for whom keeping the rules guaranteed their membership of the 'best' society.

It has been rightly pointed out that on the one hand we have the philosophical theories, whatever they might be, and on the other hand we have the mass practice, the everyday sexual life and the love relationships of a predominantly illiterate population, which probably showed absolutely no concern for the ethical and pedagogical value of their sexual relationships.[8] Pederastic relations were viewed as morally problematical in theory, and perhaps also in practice, only by a minority. And this minority's judgement on homosexuality was not generally a negative one.

Statements which are often taken as condemning homosexual relationships can more properly be seen as expressing an awareness that it was not always easy to cope with this experience. This being so, the fact that there were many people who disregarded the condemnations was no accident. Similarly, it was no accident that Aristophanes believed that the mass violation of these rules was a sign of the decadence of his city. Sexual ethics in Athens expressed a norm which was simultaneously moral, social, cultural and political. If this norm was generally flouted, the very survival of the city was placed in peril. Hence the need for the rules to be observed, regardless of individual feelings. Given this situation, it is clear that one has to speak with a certain degree of caution, in the Greek context, about the free expression of bisexuality.

On mature reflection, it must be said that the attitude of classical scholars to Greek homosexuality has been quite strange. At first there was an embarrassed refusal to recognise a fact which called into question the mythical image of a world which these scholars loved and admired unreservedly as the place of all perfection. Later the scholars constructed a different world, where what might have been seen as a 'vice' was remade into a myth. The awareness of human bisexuality, denied elsewhere, was allowed to express itself happily in a free Greece. And even the most fully informed observers, who pointed out the existence, even in Greece, of repressive rules (albeit obviously different from the modern ones) basically gave some credit to this overvalued image of liberty.

When Michel Foucault, for example, interprets Greek sexual morality as the expression of an individual moral code, a rule of continence, measure and self-control which was independently and freely chosen by individuals, he transforms a kind of censorship into an expression of freedom. The Greeks, according to Foucault, took on a moral code of sexual austerity without repressive institutional instruments: self-control (which is nothing more than a respect for the rules) developed in Greece precisely on account of the absence of external coercive rules, and served at the same time as an instrument of domination and as the

215

exercise of freedom. To dominate others, one has to control oneself first of all. Hence the need to draw up a code of pleasures which made it possible – thanks to the exercise of 'moderation' – to avoid losing control of one's passions. And the instrument of this operation was 'free censorship': voluntary repression, austerity, carefully moderate use of pleasures.

But the Greek homosexual code (even in the absence of legal rules) was not *purely* an internal code. The absence of legal rules did not mean an empty space, a territory open to the expression of freedom.[9] The fact that the law did not punish homosexuality did not mean that homosexuality could be expressed without restraint: the restraints had been in place for centuries, sinking their roots into the pre-city past of Greece (when they had served as institutional restraints), while in the age of the cities they changed into a rigorous and detailed social code, imposing from the outside a very precise and detailed paradigm of experience, and limiting its freedom. Not even in the freedom of Greece was sexuality experienced in a world without frontiers.

The Greeks were certainly bisexual, in the sense that when they were boys they were loved by a man, while in the first years of their own adulthood they preferred to make love to adolescent boys. Later in life they chose women, and even when they were married they were allowed to have their *paidika*. But theirs was not a free bisexuality. In this connection Foucault asserts that the Greeks' possibility of choosing between the two sexes was not based on a double, ambivalent, bisexual structure of desire. For the Greeks, he argues, what caused people to desire a man or a woman was 'simply the appetite that nature had implanted in man's heart for "beautiful" human beings, whatever their sex might be'.[10] But it is reasonable to wonder whether things really worked out that way. It is difficult to imagine that in all Greeks the bisexual impulse was so well balanced as to ensure that a desire for somebody of one's own sex was exactly the same as the desire for people of the opposite sex. Perhaps it was like that for some people, but even in Greece, inevitably, there were men whose impulses were directed decisively if not exclusively towards a single sex (whether the female or the male).

In this sense and in this perspective, I think that it makes some sense to speak of Greek homosexuality as an 'opaque area'[11] – meaning that it is one of those aspects of the Greek world which is particularly difficult to understand, and above all more problematical than has normally been assumed. To be 'homosexual' (in the modern sense of the term, which rules out relations with women) cannot have been easy in Greece. And being bisexual – given the rigour of the moral and social code which regulated these relationships – must also have been, albeit in a different way and to a lesser extent, something that imposed choices which were not always easy.[12]

Standing, at least theoretically, at the centre of the formation of the citizen (despite the absence of legal rules), pederasty was a form of sexual relationship which concerned the city more than any other. It was a social institution, in the broadest sense of the term, and one which was entrusted with the task of making Greeks into the best of men. But the costs of this institution, in terms of freedom, could be very high. For pederasty to work not only control and self-discipline were needed: at times, what was required was no less than the annihilation of individual impulses.

Let us now turn to Rome. Like the Greeks, the Romans also felt that is was normal for a man to have sexual relations with other men as well as with women. But their ethic was very different from the Greek one. Only one rule was common to the two moralities: the rule which stated that virility meant taking the active role in sex. However, unlike the Greeks, the Romans did not believe that it was educational for boys to be passive partners in a homosexual relationship. In certain ways, they too thought of boys as being equivalent to women: for example, because they were incapable of free will, and thus, in legal terms, without the power to act. But sexually boys were men, albeit only potential men, and as such they should never be placed in a position of subjection. Never, during their entire lives – and especially, for obvious reasons, during a delicate period such as adolescence.

The sexual mentality of the Roman male (in perfect agreement with his political ethics) was that of an aggressive dominator – who was fully convinced, among other things, that when he forced other people to submit he held the prerogative of dispensing pleasure (even though, in practice, he paid little heed to the wishes of those whom he subjected to his powers). So it is no accident that we can read under a bas-relief of an erect phallus the inscription *hic habitat felicitas*, 'here dwells happiness'.[13] This deep-rooted conviction of the Roman male provides the fundamental reason for his absolute inability to imagine that there could be women who preferred being loved by other women. Deprived of those attributes which 'conferred happiness', the 'tribades', in his view, were nothing but poor mad girls, or sick females who tried vainly and outrageously to usurp the male prerogatives. This being the mentality of the adult male, it is clear that the sentimental education of a Roman boy (if one may call it that) could not even remotely resemble that of his Greek counterpart. To say nothing of the fact that, in Rome, adolescence was a short-lived period of life: at fourteen, a boy was already considered an adult. If he was *sui iuris* (meaning a *paterfamilias*), he acquired the ability to exercise his rights without the involvement of a tutor, and he was entitled to take a wife.[14]

As has correctly been observed, iconography represents boys (and even children of two, three or four years of age) as grave, composed, serious persons. Even in their clothing, they were practically miniature adults.[15]

In this framework, it is clear that the formation of a Roman boy not only could not envisage, but absolutely had to exclude, homosexual relationships, in which he would inevitably have been the passive partner. That type of experience would have gravely endangered his moral and political formation. That is why in Rome, unlike Greece, there were provisions against pederasty from the Republican period onwards. These rules were first enforced administratively, and later by legislation, under that *Lex Scatinia* which, as we saw, laid down a financial penalty for anyone who outraged a *puer ingenuus* (even if the boy in question had given his consent), and which at the same time punished adults who failed in their duty as males and allowed themselves to be placed in a subordinate position.

But the existence of these rules did not mean that homosexuality was forbidden as such. The Roman male had to be able to express, whenever and however he wished, his sexual exuberance, which could not be satisfied solely by intercourse with women. To this end he had two categories of available men: prostitutes and slaves. Unlike the situation in Greece, male prostitution (we are speaking now of the early centuries) was not forbidden. And as for slaves (so long as they were not other people's slaves) it was understood as a matter of course that they were obliged to satisfy their owner's desires.

Roman homosexuality, then, was purely and simply, not to say brutally, a matter of bullying and violence, a manifestation of the social and sexual power of the stronger over the weaker, the master over the slave, the victor over the vanquished. Given this fact, it was exclusively an active form of homosexuality (or at least it was supposed to be exclusively so). Much less complex and sophisticated, entirely lacking in the moral tension which characterised its Greek counterpart, the sexual life of a Roman had only one basic rule: being a male and proving you were a male, never undergoing the humiliation of serving others, making sure that others 'served' you, the proud victor, the soldier and the lover who always and everywhere swept all before him, in love as in war.

This, in very brief summary, was the native Roman code, the one which matched the psychology and political ethics of the city during the first centuries of its existence. But with Hellenisation, things changed. The Romans discovered the love of boys (perhaps even of free-born lads, sometimes even nobly born) who could be loved and courted like women, and who like women, had learned to feign resistance, to hold out, and finally to yield. The Romans had become sentimental: they loved their *pueri*, and were no longer content merely to possess them. The ancient code was now accompanied by another code, but this was Hellenic only in its form and exterior aspects. In a world where pederasty had no cultural roots, where making love to a boy never meant educating him and shaping him, where the pre-city past included no traces of homosexuality for initiation purposes,[16] loving boys meant something quite unlike what it meant in Greece. It had no political and moral overtones. Courtship did not mean overcoming the resistence of a youth, who tested the intentions of his lover: the modesty of the *pueri* was merely a ploy designed to raise the price, to build up desire. The Romans to some extent (at least those who practised it, meaning the exponents of the most cultivated class) merely *played* at the pederastic relationship. This did not mean that they did not love their *pueri*: from one point of view, it was natural for them to love them. Albeit in a different way, they had always been bisexual. On the other hand, perhaps, they also loved them because, with the *pueri*, the game of courtship was more gratifying than with women, who by now had become too emancipated, liberated and arrogant. The boys, who had learned the art of being courted and who pretended to hold out, basically allowed one to feel more of a real man.

Admittedly, courtship was not a very 'Roman' thing, but this was compensated by the fact that in the end, by yielding, the *puer* reinforced the virility of the man who had conquered him. In a different fashion from the crude and hasty style of the early centuries, the Roman male could go on thinking of himself as a dominant figure. The love of boys had not transformed him into a peace-loving man: he was still fighting a war, and winning it. Among other things, he continued at all events to bugger his enemies (or at least to threaten such action). He was thus fully entitled to hold the same self-image that he had always held. But one problem quickly arose, and it was extremely embarrassing. Sometimes the soldier did not win his war. Passive homosexuality was beginning to be a visible fashion, spreading among unsuspected people, and turning into a mass vice (at least if one listens to Juvenal and Martial).

Customs had changed, but the mentality had changed very little. Was this too an effect of Hellenisation? The customs of the Greeks, when the Romans came into contact with them, had lost their former morality. Homosexuality no longer solely meant pederasty: the *katapygones* laughed at by Aristophanes were numerous. Is it possible to imagine that, as well as the sweetness of loving young men, the Romans also learned from the Greeks the 'softness' of passivity?

It is more probable that the Greek example simply helped them to abandon themselves with greater ease and fewer problems to personal tendencies which, within the original framework, had had to be rigorously repressed, but which emerged and showed themselves with ever-increasing frequency during a period of general crisis in values. This was the time when Rome was getting ready to become an empire: a multitude of foreigners had invaded the city, freed slaves were becoming an ever more important element, social classes were mixing, big estates were disappearing, the services sector was growing out of all proportion, and hordes of unemployed wandered around the capital city. Family morality was in a state of crisis, and with it the virility of the head of the family, that male who had formerly had no doubts at all about his political, economic, social, family and sexual role.

The disorientation was all-embracing. Whatever his own sexual behaviour, the Roman male could not admit that he was not a real man: he continued to brand as *cinaedi* all other men who abdicated their 'manhood', but he could not even conceive of being like them.

If the Greek male was not fully free to express his sexuality, neither was his Roman counterpart. In a very different way, the Roman sexual ethic (as indeed happens with any code) forced Roman men to take on a demanding model, albeit a crude one. Though he was not forced to make a transition from object to subject of desire, the Roman man was forced to maintain throughout his life a self-image which perhaps, when the city was founded, had truly reflected the 'national character' (so that presumably there were only marginal problems of inability or refusal to match the stereotype). But, over time, this image had become increasingly unreal, increasingly less well matched not only to the sexual habits, but also and perhaps primarily to the psychological attitudes and social practices of the majority of the population.

To some extent, the Roman male was condemned to a life of maleness – the maleness of a sexual thug who, by imposing his desires on women and *pueri*, his enemies and those who had wronged him, proved his sexual potency, indomitable character and social muscle to himself and to others. Obviously, it was not so easy to give up this image: not even to himself could a Roman man admit that he did not match the image. And to avoid admitting it, he had to prevaricate with himself, and find an excuse – the example of the powerful people who made no secret of their sexual passivity.

Caesar had been the lover of Nicomedes, as everybody knew – yet

Caesar was the invincible soldier who conquered the world, the great seducer whom no woman could resist. He was therefore a real man, and could afford to be passive if that was what he wanted. What did it matter if sometimes he had surrendered his weapons in the battles of love, given that in war he used to carve up his enemies with his weapons of steel? And Caesar's manliness belonged to Rome, to every Roman citizen. But for his excuse to be valid, the ideal model had to remain the same as it always had been: on the ideological level, there could be no compromise. Individual transgression was compensated by contempt for other people's lack of manliness.

The individual excuse – the one which allowed a *mollis* to reconcile his idea of virility with his own behaviour – had no value on the political level. Those in charge of the Empire could not allow Rome to become a city where adult men prostituted themselves in brothels, where vice was rampant, where men were no longer really men. All the more so because the new customs ran counter not only to ancient pagan ethics: they were even more contrary to Christian ethics.

Christianity had introduced a new way of looking at sex, which came from the Hebrew tradition. It had introduced the principle of 'naturalness', which was exclusive to heterosexual intercourse. The pagan contrast between activity and passivity, which identified manliness with the assumption of the active sexual role, either with women or with men (and which had informed the morality of the Greeks as well as of the Romans, albeit in completely different ways), was contrary to the new state religion, which condemned homosexuality in all its manifestations.

The emperors, in order to be fully consistent, should also have condemned it. But doing this would have meant clashing with an ethic which for centuries had been inspired by a concept of masculinity which, at least in theory, had never faded. Legislative policy could not avoid taking account of it. What could be done at once – and what was done – was in the first place a sort of compromise: an extremely harsh condemnation of passive homosexuality alone. From 342 onwards, with Constantius and Constans, repression got under way. Theodosius I, in 390, returned to the topic, and in 438, at the behest of Theodosius II, all passive homosexuals were condemned to be burned alive.

But respect for Christian morality demanded much more: homosexuals, whether passive or active, committed the unforgivable, unnamable sin which more than any other was offensive to the Lord. It was necessary to ensure that all those who abandoned themselves to practices 'against nature' should be punished. And Justinian did precisely that: all homosexuals, independently of which role they assumed, were condemned to death by him. The concept of nature had changed.

Conclusions

For many centuries it had been 'according to nature' for women to be put down, while it had been 'according to nature' for men to put down both women and other men. Now, nature no longer allowed them any alternative choices: the only act 'according to nature' was heterosexual intercourse.

Notes

CHAPTER 1: THE BEGINNINGS,
THE GREEK DARK AGE AND THE
ARCHAIC PERIOD

1. fr. 130 Lobel-Page, translated
    by David A. Campbell, Loeb
    Classical Library, 1982, p. 147.
2. Significantly, the effects of Eros
    on the human spirit were de-
    bated particularly keenly by
    those who, in different contexts,
    speculated on how to establish
    the conditions under which
    human actions were voluntary,
    and, if an action were illicit,
    whether the person committing
    it was to be considered guilty.
    Leaving aside the first references
    in Homer (for which see my
    article 'Aitios. Archeologia di un
    concetto', in *Studi C. Grassetti*,
    Milan, 1980, p. 209, and with
    modifications in *Norma e
    sanzione in Omero*, Milan,
    1979, p. 273 ff.), the first explicit
    treatment of the problem is
    found in Gorgias who, in his
    Encomium for Helen, analyses
    the possible causes of Helen's
    flight with Paris, arguing that
    in no sense can Helen be con-
    sidered guilty. All the possible
    causes which induced her to run
    away with her lover, he says, are
    such as to render this action
    involuntary: and these causes
    include, precisely, Eros (Gorgias,
    Helena = Diels-Kranz, *Vs.* 82 B
    116).
3. E. Bethe, 'Die dorische Knaben-
    liebe, ihre Ethik, ihre Idee', in
    Rhein. Mus., n. F. 62 (1907),
    p. 438 ff.
4. H.I. Marrou, *Histoire de l'édu-
    cation dans l'antiquité*, Paris,
    1948; English translation, *A
    History of Education in Anti-
    quity*, London, 1956, 3rd impr.
    1981, p. 27.
5. *Od.* VI, 48–315.
6. *Il.* VI, 369–493.
7. See, for example, A. van
    Gennep, *Les rites de passage*,
    Paris, 1909, translated into
    English by Monika B. Vizedon
    and Gabrielle L. Caffee as *Rites
    of Passage*, Chicago 1961; and
    A. Brelich, *Paides e Parthenoi*,
    Rome, 1969.
8. H. Jeanmaire, *Couroi et couretes*,
    Lille, 1939; Louis Gernet, *Anthro-
    pologie de la Grèce ancienne*,
    Paris, 1968, English translation
    by John Hamilton and Blaise
    Nagy, *The Anthropology of
    Ancient Greece*, Baltimore and
    London, 1981; A. Brelich, *Paides
    e parthenoi*, Rome, 1969; P.
    Vidal-Naquet, *Le chasseur noir:
    Formes de pensée et formes de*

société dans le monde grec, Paris, 1981, p. 151 ff.; J. Bremmer, 'An Enigmatic Indo-European Rite: Paederasty', *Arethusa*, 13, 1980, p. 2 ff.; H. Patzer, *Die Griechische Knabenliebe*, Wiesbaden, 1982; B. Lincoln, *Emerging from the Chrysalis*, Cambridge, Mass., 1981, and Bernard Sergent, *L'homosexualité dans la mythologie grecque*, Paris, 1983; English translation by Arthur Goldhammer, *Homosexuality in Greek Myth*, London, 1987 (on this study see E. Cantarella, in *Dialogues d'histoire ancienne*, 10, 1984, p. 420 ff.) and *L'homosexualité initiatique dans l'Europe*, Paris, 1986.

9. Sergent, *Homosexuality in Greek Myth*. On pp. 262–5 of the English edition (to which reference is made from now on), there is a summary table of the different homosexual myths, with their areas of origin.

10. Strabo, 10, 4, 21 (= Eph., *Fgrhist* 70 F. 149, 21).

11. Plut., *Lyc.*, 7, 1 (cf. *Ages*. 2, 1) and Xen., *Resp. lac.*, 2, 12, ff. On this topic see P. Cartledge, 'The Politics of Spartan Paederasty', *Proceedings of the Cambridge Philological Society* 201, 1981, p. 17 ff. Cartledge believes that pederasty was institutionalised in this city.

12. See respectively F. Hiller von Gaertringen, *Die Insel Thera in Altertum und Gegenwart*, Berlin, 1899–1909 (see also the same author's article 'Gymnopaidien', in PWRE VII, 1912, cols 2087–9), and R. Carpenter, 'The Antiquity of the Greek Alphabet', *AJA* 37 (1933), p. 26. Carpenter's dates are accepted by D.M. Robinson and E.J. Fluck in *A Study of the Greek Love-Names. Including a Discussion*

of *Paederasty and a Prosopographia*, Baltimore, 1937, p. 21 ff.; these authors, however, believe that the Thera inscriptions can be considered as contemporaneous with the inscriptions in Athens, at the beginning of this period, which described the boy beloved by the person commissioning a vase as *kalos* (beautiful). We will return to this later.

13. *I.G.*, XII, 357.

14. Marrou, *Histoire*, p. 367 n. 10.

15. Ael., *Var. hist.*, III, 12.

16. Callim., fr. 169 68 Pfeiffer Theocr., XII, 13 and Alcm., fr. 34. On the meaning of the verb *eispnein* see also C. Diano, *Saggezza e poetiche degli antichi*, Vicenza, 1968, p. 167 ff. (*L'eros greco*), and in particular p. 169. On the change from the physical to the metaphorical meaning of the verb see P.G. Maxwell-Stuart, 'Strato and the *Musa puerilis*', *Hermes* 100 (1972), p. 216 ff., in particular pp. 224–5. The metaphorical meaning (spiritual inspiration) is documented for example in Xen., *Symp.*, 4, 15. Further terminological information can be found in Cartledge, 'Politics of Spartan Paederasty', p. 31 n. 18. Against this hypothesis, however, one may now consult Sergent, *L'homosexualité initiatique*, pp. 218–19.

17. Eva C. Keuls, *The Reign of the Phallus. Sexual Politics in Ancient Athens*, New York, 1985, pp. 276–7.

18. 'Fluidity' of institutions is the expression used by one of the greatest scholars of the Homeric world, M.I. Finley, in *The World of Odysseus*, New York, 1977, 2nd edition.

19. On the much-debated problem of the birth of the *polis*, and on

the period when one can begin to speak about a political organisation (obviously different from the Mycenaean one) see V. Ehrenberg, 'When did the Polis Rise?' in *Zur griechischen Staatskunde*, ed. F. Gschnitzer, Darmstadt, 1969, p. 3 ff. and also the literature cited by Cantarella in *Norma e sanzione* p. 287 ff., to be supplemented by W.C. Runciman, 'Origins of State: The Case of Archaic Greece', *Comparative Studies in Society and History* 24, 1982, p. 351 ff.

20. For an overall up-to-date account of the period in question, see *Origini e sviluppo della città. I. Il medioevo greco* by various authors, in *Storia e Civiltà dei Greci*, I, edited by R. Bianchi Bandinelli, Milan, 1983.

21. The proof that the Homeric poems, although set in the Mycenaean era, really reflect the conditions of life in the centuries of the so-called Greek Dark Age, is to be found in Finley, *World of Odysseus*. For further bibliographical information see Cantarella, *Norma e sanzione*, p. 7 ff., which also contains bibliographies on the destruction of the Mycenaean palaces, its possible causes and its dating.

22. This point is made, for example, by R. Flacelière, *L'amour en Grèce*, Paris, 1950, p. 213, who believes that the reason for this absence lies in the fact that pederasty, caused by the lack of women or by their inaccessibility, would have no reason to exist in a society where women were free, as in Homeric society.

23. The 'deadly anger' of Achilles, with all that follows from it, is therefore not provoked by sexual jealously. What he cannot toler-

ate, in Agamemnon's behaviour, is the outrage implicit in the removal of 'goods' belonging to him, which is what female prisoners of war, in practice, amounted to.

24. Hom., *Il.*, XXIV, 128–30.
25. W.M. Clarke, 'Achilles and Patroclus in Love', *Hermes* 106, 1978, pp. 381–96.
26. Cf. *Il.*, XVIII, 22–7, 32–4 (Antilochus holds his hands, fearing that he wishes to kill himself); 86–7, 120, 333–5; XIX, 4–5.
27. fr. 135 Nauck. Cf. Plut., *Amat.*, 751 c. See also Ps. Luc. *Amores*, 54.
28. Cf. G. Perrotta, *Sofocle*, Messina-Milan, 1935, p. 36.
29. Aesch., *Against Timarchus*, 142.
30. Ath., XIII, 601 a.
31. Plato, *Symp.*, 180 a.
32. Cf. *ARV*, 21, 1.
33. The passages in Homer do not provide much help in resolving this question: whereas the speech of Thetis to Achilles gives the impression that Achilles was the *erastēs*, in a passage from Book XVI (verses 786–7) we read that Patroclus was older than his friend.
34. *Od.*, III 399–403. See Sergent, *Homosexuality in Greek Myth*, p. 311, n. 29. The relationship between Telemachus and Pisistratus is also considered as a proof of the existence of homosexuality in the poems by Robinson and Fluck, *A Study of the Greek Love-Names*, pp. 18–19. On this topic see also M. Oka, 'Telemachus in the Odyssey', *Journal of Classical Studies* 13, 1965, p. 33 ff.
35. *Od.*, IV, 302–5.
36. *Od.*, XV, 4–5 and 44–5.
37. Cf. Sergent, *Homosexuality in Greek Myth*, pp. 255–8.

38. Thus Diog. Laert., I, 62. On Solon's archonship see Aristot., *Ath. pol.*, 13, 1. On the character and his work see A. Masaracchia, *Solone*, Florence, 1958 and A. Martina, *Solon Testimonia veterum*, Rome, 1968.
39. Plut, *Sol.*, 1.
40. 'The Dialogue on Love', adapted from the translation by W.C. Helmbold, Plutarch, *Moralia*, Loeb Classical Library, IX, 1961, p. 321.
41. fr. 384 Lobel-Page.
42. Cf. Cic., *De nat. deorum* I, 28 (the sight of a boy's flanks delighted him); Cic., *Tusc.* IV, 71 (*quae de iuvenum amore scribit*). On this subject see D. Page, *Sappho and Alcaeus*, Oxford, 1955, p. 294, and now M. Vetta, 'Il P. Oxy. 2506 fr. 77 e la poesia pederotica di Alceo', *Quad. Urb.* 39, 1982, p. 7 ff.
43. fr. 368 Lobel-Page.
44. fr. 23 (Gent.) = 402(a) (Loeb). The English translations are taken from David A. Campbell's edition, *Greek Lyric*, II, Loeb Classical Library, 1988.
45. fr. 43 (Gent.) = 407 (Loeb)
46. fr. 148 (Gent.) = 471 (Loeb). Cf. Horat, *Ep.*, XIV, 9–10: 'Not otherwise enamoured of Samian Bathyllus, do they say, was Teian Anacreon.'
47. fr. 26 and 71 (Gent.) = 414 and 347 (Loeb).
48. fr. 5 (Gent.) = 359 (Loeb).
49. fr. 14 (Gent.) = 357 (Loeb).
50. fr. 83 (Gent.) = 378 (Loeb).
51. fr. 35 (Gent.) = 400 (Loeb).
52. fr. 25 (Gent.) = 413 (Loeb).
53. fr. 22 (Gent.) = 402(c) (Loeb).
54. The episode is in *Schol.* Pind. *Isthm.* 2, 1b (III, p. 213 Drachm.). Gentili's comment is in *Poesia e pubblico nella Grecia antica*, Bari, 1984, p. 126.
55. *Suid.*, s.v. *Ibykos*, cf. Cic. *Tusc.*, IV, 33, 71.
56. fr. 288 Page. Translation from J.M. Edmonds' 1924 *Lyra Graeca*, Loeb Classical Library, p. 89 (Ibycus 6).
57. Theognis, *Elegies*, II, 1235–8; on homoeroticism in symposiastic poetry, especially that of Theognis, see M. Vetta, *Theognis. Elegiarum liber secundus*, Rome, 1980, p. xxxvii ff.
58. II, 1243–4.
59. Ibid., 1295–8.
60. Ibid., 1299–1311.
61. Ibid., 1312–18.
62. Ibid., 1337–41.
63. Ibid., 1367–8.
64. Ibid., 1369–72.
65. Gentili, *Poesia e pubblico*, p. 177.
66. fr. 123 Sn.-Maehl.

CHAPTER 2: THE CLASSICAL AGE

1. On the rules of courtship see Kenneth Dover, *Greek Homosexuality*, London, 1978, esp. p. 81 ff. and Michel Foucault, *L'usage des plaisirs (Histoire de la Sexualité*, Vol. II), Paris, 1984, English translation by Robert Harley, *The History of Sexuality, Vol. 2: The Use of Pleasure*, London, 1986, p. 196 ff. On a particular aspect of courtship, the gifts given by lovers, see also G. Koch-Harnack, *Knabenliebe und Tiergeschenke. Ihre Bedeutung in päderastischen Erziehungssystem Athens*, Berlin, 1983.
2. H. Kelsen, 'Die platonische Liebe', *Imago. Zeitschrift für Psychoanalytische Psychologie* 19, 1933; Italian translation, *L'amor platonico*, Bologna, 1985, p. 47 ff.

3. Plato, *Symp.*, 180 c–185 c. On this passage, and in particular on the relationship between gratifying lovers on the part of the beloved – we shall return to the practical meaning of this – and *philosophia*, see H. Reynan, 'Philosophie und Knabenliebe', *Hermes* 95, 1967, p. 308 ff.

4. D. Cohen, 'Work in Progress: the Enforcement of Morals. A Historical Perspective', *Rechtshistorisches Journal* 3, 1984, p. 114 ff. (esp. pp. 116–19) and 'Law, Society and Homosexuality in Classical Athens', *Past and Present* 117, 1987, p. 3 ff. According to Cohen, the attitude of the Greeks in relation to male homosexuality was more complex and contradictory than is usually allowed. Relations between two adults, he argues, were not punished by the law (which believed that the sector of private morality lay outside its purview), but they were disapproved of, if not by the whole population, then at least by part of it. The acceptable rules of behaviour, in his view, censured not only those who took a passive role in the relationship (as is usually maintained), but also the active partner. Greek attitudes to homosexuality, in short, were full of tensions and contradictions; and relations with boys, in particular, were regulated by a series of legal provisions, substantially directed towards preventing them, or at least limiting them. We will return to this question. Also see Cohen's new book, *Law, Society and Sexuality: the Enforcement of Morals in Classical Athens*, Cambridge, Mass., 1991.

5. Cf. Kenneth Dover, 'Eros and Nomos', *Bulletin of the Institute of Classical Studies* 10, 1964, p. 31 ff. (In *Greek Homosexuality*, p. 89 ff., one can find a somewhat different position, and a specification of the differences between the two types of courtship). Parallels between modern-day heterosexual courtship and pederastic courtship (as mentioned in the text) reappear in Cohen, 'Law, Society and Homosexuality'.

6. Cf. Eileen Power, *Medieval Women*, Cambridge, 1975, p. 24 ff.

7. R. Nelli, *La vie quotidienne des Cathares en Languedoc au XIIe siècle*, Paris, 1969, p. 79 ff.

8. See ibid., p. 95. On the relationship between the troubadours and their objects of inspiration, see another contribution by R. Nelli, 'L'éthique des troubadours', thesis, University of Toulouse, 1963 (later Paris, 1975, 2 vols), and J. Solé, 'I trovatori e l'amor-passione' in *L'amore e la sessualità*, ed. Georges Duby, Bari, 1986, p. 71 ff. (*L'amour et la sexualité*, Paris, 1984).

9. On this point see Foucault, *The Use of Pleasure*, p. 207 ff. Foucault recalls, *inter alia*, that in his *Eroticos* (or LXI) Demosthenes refutes the thesis of those who maintain that a boy is dishonoured by yielding.

10. Plato, *Symp.*, 184 a–b.

11. Ibid., 182 a.

12. Ibid.

13. On the social composition of popular tribunals see K. Dover, *Greek Popular Morality in the Time of Plato and Aristotle*, Oxford, 1974, pp. 34–5. In Dover's view, the way in which orators addressed juries shows

Dover's view, the way in which orators addressed juries shows either that most jurors were fairly prosperous, 'or, if they did not belong to the prosperous class, they liked to be treated as if they did' (Dover thinks this second hypothesis less probable). He observes that in any case juries were certainly not really rich people; court orators quite frequently exploited the feelings of resentment that wealth aroused in their hearers. This means, in substance, that the juries belonged to the Athenian middle class.

14. Aesch., *Against Timarchus*, 139.
15. Thus in para. 132.
16. The praise of ancient lovers is in paras 140–53. The praise of more recent lovers and of the most beautiful *paides* in contemporary Athens is in paras 155–7.
17. Cf. *Il.*, XIV, 312. Elsewhere, it also means the desire for food (*Il.*, I, 469) or for tears (*Il.*, XXIV, 227).
18. See Liddell-Scott-Jones, under this heading. And also (with reference to all this terminology) see Dover, *Greek Homosexuality*, p. 52 ff.
19. Xen., *Symp.*, 8, 2; 8, 8 and Lys., *c. Symp.*, 3, 39.
20. Cf., for example, Plato, *Symp.*, 182 a, 217 a, 218 d; *Phaedr.*, 233 d–e; 231 c; 232 d; 234 b.
21. Hes., *Op.*, 59 ff. and *Theog.*, 570 ff.
22. Plato, *Symp.*, 213 c–d, translated by Walter Hamilton, Penguin Classics, Harmondsworth, 1951, pp. 103–4.
23. Ibid., 217 c–d.
24. Ibid., 219 b–c–d.
25. J.D. Beazley, 'Some Attic Vases

in the Cyprus Museum', *Proceedings of the British Academy* 33, 1947, p. 195 ff. (especially p. 199). This gesture, however, appears also in scenes of heterosexual courtship, as pointed out by C. Reinsberg, *Ehe, Hetaerentum und Knabenliebe*, Munich (Beck's Archaeologische Bibliothek), 1989, pp. 190–1. There is a collection of vases with courtship scenes in C.A. Shapiro, 'Courtship Scenes in Attic Vase Painting', *AJA* 85, 1981, p. 133 ff.

26. Dover, *Greek Homosexuality*, p. 96 ff.
27. On the iconographical representation of heterosexual relations see G. Arrigoni, 'Amore sotto il manto e iniziazioni nuziali', *Quad. Urb.*, n.s. 15, 3, 1983, p. 7 ff. On the representation of women in general, see D. Williams, 'Women on Athenian Vases: Problems and Interpretations', in *Images of Women in Antiquity*, ed. A. Cameron and A. Kuhrt, Detroit, 1983, p. 92 ff., where (p. 105, n. 1) the publication of an iconographic research project by I. Jenkins on marriage and death is described as forthcoming. The idea that anal penetration was one of the erotic manifestations envisaged by the pederastic relationship is also maintained by M. Sartre, 'L'omosessualità nell'antica Grecia', in *L'amore e la sessualità*, p. 33 ff.
28. E.g., Plato, *Symp.*, 184 d.
29. *I.G.*, XII, 357.
30. Lex. Gort., II, 1–20.
31. A. Richlin, *The Garden of Priapus. Sexuality and Aggression in Roman Humor*, New Haven and London, 1983, p. 35 ff.

32. *Greek Anthology*, XII, 40 (anonymous).
33. Ibid., 204 (Strato).
34. Ibid., 36 (Strato): 'Anus (*prōktos*) and gold (*chrysos*): the number of letters is the same, counting them up candidly, I made this discovery.'
35. Ibid., 38, translated by W.R. Paton, *The Greek Anthology*, IV, Loeb Classical Library, 1979. All translations from the *Greek Anthology* are taken from this source.
36. Ibid., 37.
37. Ibid., 22.
38. Ibid., 11. See also XII, 216 and 240. Astyanax, son of Hector and Andromache, was thrown from the ramparts of Troy by Ulysses. On Strato of Sardis see P.G. Maxwell-Stuart, 'Strato and the *Musa puerilis*', *Hermes* 100, 1972, p. 216 ff., showing that the interest in *paides* is not only aesthetic, but also sexual.
39. It is universally accepted that the law was really not written by Solon, but dated from a later period. As a representative view, see M.P. Nilsson, *Die hellenistiche Schule*, Munich, 1955, Italian translation, *La scuola nell'età ellenistica*, Florence, 1973, p. 16, which dates the legislation to the fourth century.
40. Aesch., *Against Timarchus* 12, translated by Charles Darwin Adams, Loeb Classical Library, 1911, repr. 1968, p. 13.
41. The text of this law, which was already known in 1949, was published by J.M. MacCormack, *Ancient Macedonia*, II, Thessaloniki, 1977, pp. 139–49 and later by L. Robert, in 'Bulletin épigraphique', *Revue des études grecques*, 91, 1978, p. 385 ff. With the amendments

proposed by Robert, it is now contained in *SEG* XXVII, 261. The lines recorded in the text are from B, 26–9.
42. This interpretation is put forward by L. Moretti, 'Sulla legge ginnasiarchica di Berea', *Rivista Italiana di Filologia Classica* 110, 1982, p. 45 ff. On this point, in particular, see p. 52.
43. *SEG*, XXVII, 261, B 13 ff.
44. Aesch., *Against Timarchus*, 10.
45. For a review of the different interpretations of the term *neaniskoi* and the most recent inscriptions containing it, see G. Sacco, 'Sui neaniskoi dell'età ellenistica', *Rivista Italiana di Filologia Classica*, 107, 1979, p. 39 ff.
46. On the ephebic state see C. Pelekides, *Histoire de l'éphébie attique des origines à 31 avant Jésus-Christ*, Paris, 1962 and later P. Vidal-Naquet, *Le chasseur noir. Formes de pensée et formes de société dans le monde grec*, Paris, 1981.
47. Diog. Laert., VIII, 10.
48. Nauck, p. 48.
49. Aristoph., *Acarn.*, 685.
50. Aesch., *c. Ctesiph.*, 154 (cf. Plato, *Menex.*, 249 B as well as Thuc., II, 46).
51. Again in Aeschines, in the oration *Against Timarchus* we read of a widow who was so demented that her *neaniskos* son took charge of the management of the household (para. 171). It is clear that this circumstance was surprising. As it was quite normal in Athens for the adult sons of widowed mothers to take charge of the family inheritance, we may deduce that the son in question was a minor.
52. Plut., *Agis*, 4, 1; 7, 4; 10, 1; 19, 6; 19, 8.

53. Plato, *Symp.*, 198 a.
54. For *aphrōn*: Hyperid., 6, 28. On this topic cf. Dover, *Greek Popular Morality*, p. 197 ff.
55. Aesch., *Against Timarchus*, 18; 39; 139; Isaeus, *de Astyph. hered.*, 20.
56. Xen., *Symp.*, 4, 15.
57. Aesch., *Against Timarchus*, 9.
58. *Greek Anthology*, XII, 219; Loeb Classical Library, 1979, p. 219.
59. Ibid., 187. The words 'Lambda and Alpha' are annotated by W.R. Paton, the translator (p. 378): 'Probably, as the commentators explain, having some sort of sexual meaning. There is double meaning in all the rest of the epigram, but it is somewhat obscure and had best remain so.'
60. Ibid., 222.
61. Ibid., 206.
62. Ibid., 34.
63. Aristot., *Ath. Pol.*, 56.
64. Plato, *Lysis*, 203 a–205 a, translated by W.R.M. Lamb, *Plato* Vol. III, Loeb Classical Library, 1925, repr. 1975, p. 13.
65. Lysias, *On the Murder of Eratosthenes*, 32, translated by W.R.M. Lamb, *Lysias*, Loeb Classical Library, 1930, p. 19. On this topic see S.G. Cole, 'Greek Sanctions against Sexual Assault', *Cl. Phil.* 79, 1984, p. 97 ff.
66. On the lack of legal knowledge among jury members, and the problems raised by the speakers' habit of citing laws in a form suited to their own interests, see H.J. Wolff, 'Methodische Grundfragen der Rechtsgeschichtlichen Verwendung attischer Gerichtsreden', in *Atti II Congr. Int. Soc. ital. Storia dir.*, Florence, 1971, p. 1125 ff.
67. H.I. Marrou, *A History of Education in Antiquity*, London, 1956, 3rd impr. 1981, p. 27.
68. Aristot. *Pol.*, V (VIII), 1339.
69. Marrou, *History of Education*, p. 102.
70. Nilsson, *La scuola nell'età ellenistica*, p. 50.
71. *Greek Anthology*, XII, 4.
72. Ibid., 186.
73. Ibid., 31.
74. Ibid., 35.
75. Ibid., 33.
76. Ibid., 176.
77. Ibid., 39.
78. Ibid., 36.
79. Ibid., 178.
80. Ibid., 9.
81. Ibid., 10.
82. Plut., *Amat.*, 770 c.
83. Plato, *Prot.*, 309 b. The verb 'to pursue' (*diōkein*), to indicate the attempt at conquest, is typical of the vocabulary of courtship, together with the verb 'to flee' (*pheugein*) to indicate the beloved's resistance. Cf. Plato, *Symp.*, 184 a.
84. *Greek Anthology*, XII, 4.
85. Ibid., 22.
86. Plato, *Symp.*, 181 c–d.
87. *Greek Anthology*, XII, 228.
88. Ibid., 205.
89. Plut., *Lyc.*, 17.
90. As shown by, among other things, the funeral inscriptions: cf. U.E. Paoli, *La donna greca nell'antichità*, Florence, 1953, p. 132, n. 25. On the age at which girls reached puberty in Greece, see D.W. Amudsen and C.J. Diers, 'The Age of Menarche in Classical Greece', *Human Biology* 41, 1969, p. 125 ff., according to whom this age, on average, fell between thirteen and fourteen.
91. Plato, *Laws*, VI, 785 b.
92. Aristot., *Pol.*, VII, 1135 a. But in Xenophon's *Oeconomicus*,

for example, Ischomachus marries a 14-year-old girl.

93. The fact that in the ancient world even very young people were considered suitable to undergo sexual relations is confirmed by the Roman custom of giving in marriage girls who had not yet reached puberty. On this problem see M. Durry, 'Le mariage des filles impubères à Rome', in *Comptes rendus de l'Académie des Inscriptions*, 1955, p. 84 ff., and 'Autocritique et mise au point', *RIDA* 3, 1956, p. 227 ff. – both articles now collected in *Mélanges Durry, Revue des Etudes Latines* 47 bis (1969), p. 16 and p. 27 ff. respectively; also see K. Hopkins, 'The Age of Roman Girls at Marriage', *Population Studies* 18, 1965, p. 309 ff.; D. Gourevitz, *Le mal d'être femme*, Paris, 1984, p. 109 ff.; and J.P. Neraudau, *Etre enfant à Rome*, Paris, 1984, p. 256 ff.

94. Thus, for example, J. Henderson, *The Maculate Muse. Obscene Language in Attic Comedy*, New Haven and London, 1975, p. 204 ff. On the multiplicity of Greek men's relations with women (wives, concubines, courtesans and prostitutes) see E. Cantarella, *L'ambiguo malanno. Condizione e immagine della donna nell'antichità greca e romana*, Rome, 2nd edition, 1985, p. 75 ff.; English translation, *Pandora's Daughters*, Johns Hopkins University Press, 1987, p. 48 ff.

95. Athenaeus, 603 f.

96. On Plato's sexuality, with different points of view, see Kelsen, 'Die platonische Liebe', and D. Wender, 'Plato: Myso-

gynist, Paedophile, and Feminist', *Arethusa* 6, 1, 1973, p. 75 ff. This topic will be developed later in the book.

97. On the poet's life see G. Perrotta, *Sofocle*, Messina and Milan, 1935, p. 1 ff., and A. Dain, *Introduction à Sophocle*, I, Paris, 1955.

98. Athenaeus, 603 f–604 c. On this episode see M. Lefkowitz, *The Lives of the Greek Poets*, Baltimore, 1981, pp. 81–2.

99. Plut., *Per.*, 8 (cf. Cic., *De officiis* 1, 40).

100. Athenaeus, 604 D.

101. Thus F. Buffière, *Eros adolescent. La pédérastie dans la Grèce antique*, Paris, 1980, p. 149, n. 1. On Agathon see P. Lévêque, *Agathon*, Paris, 1954.

102. Lysias, *Against Simon* [5 ff.].

103. Thus Strato in *Greek Anthology*, XII, 228.

104. Cohen, 'Law, Society and Homosexuality' and *Law, Society and Sexuality*.

105. Lysias, *On the Murder of Eratosthenes*, 32.

106. Aesch., *Against Timarchus*, 15–16.

107. On this topic see E. Ruschenbusch, 'Hybreōs graphē', *ZSS*, R.A. 82, 1965, p. 302 ff. and subsequently D.M. McDowell, 'Hybris in Athens', *Greece and Rome* 23, 1976, p. 16 ff.; N.R.E. Fisher, 'Hybris and Dishonour: I,' *Greece and Rome* 26, 1979, p. 32 ff.; E. Cantarella, 'Studi sul lessico giuridico greco: *hybris* in Omero', *Incontri Linguistici* 7, 1977, p. 19 ff.; M. Gagarin, 'The Athenian Law Against Hybris', in *Arktouros: Hellenic Studies Presented to B.M. Knox on the Occasion of his 65th Birthday*, Berlin and New

York, 1979, p. 229 ff.
108. Dem., *Meidias*, 45–50.
109. This question is asked, for example, by D.M. Robinson and E.J. Fluck, *A Study of the Greek Love-Names*, Baltimore, 1937, p. 35.
110. The man was punished as an adulterer (*moichos*) quite independently of the fact that he was married, if he had relations with one of those women of whom the city demanded, thoughout their lifetimes, that they should have no sexual contact outside marriage (the daughters, sisters, wives and mothers of citizens), or with other men's concubines. If he was careful to avoid these categories of women, an Athenian man was free to engage in extramarital affairs even if he was married.
111. Aristoph., Frogs, 52 ff.
112. In the light of these observations, it seems quite odd that R. Scroggs can state (*The New Testament and Homosexuality*, Philadelphia, 1983, p. 35) that he finds no traces in these texts of homosexual relationships between adults, apart from cases of prostitution.
113. On this, see the views of A.M. Komornincka, 'Sur le langage érotique de l ancienne comédie attique', *Quad. Urb.* 38, 1981, p. 55 ff. (especially p. 69).
114. Aristoph., *Clouds*, 961–1103.
115. Thus, most recently, Cohen, 'Law, Society and Homosexuality', and Cohen, *Law, Society and Sexuality*.
116. Cf. Aesch., *Against Timarchus*, 113 and 126, as well as *On the Embassy*, 99.
117. *Birds*, 716 and 843; *Knights*, 721; *Clouds*, 1084 (referring to the punishment known as

raphanidōsis, consisting in a tit-for-tat punishment inflicted on male adulterers, using a horse-radish); again *Clouds*, 1090–9; *Wasps*, 1070; *Thesmophoriazusae*, 200.
118. Phot., s.v.
119. *Knights*, 719 ff.
120. *Birds*, 104.
121. *Clouds*, 1330.
122. This is the meaning of the term in *Clouds*, 529; and see also *Birds*, 664 and *Clouds*, 909. In other cases, it is decidedly homosexual: cf. *Birds*, 79, *Knights*, 638 ff.; *Clouds*, 1023; *Wasps*, 84 and 687; *Thesmophoriazusae*, 200. It is sometimes used also of women: cf. *Lysistrata*, 137 and 776.
123. See Henderson, *Maculate Muse*, pp. 211–12.
124. *Melanpygoi* already appears in Archil. 178, and later in Herod., 7, 216; Ps. Luc., 32. For *lasioi*, see Aristoph., *Clouds*, 349.
125. *Clouds*, 1014–18.
126. Ibid., and *Frogs*, 1070.
127. Hence derives the noun *Katadaktulikos*: cf. *Knights*, 1381 and Schol. *Knights*, loc. cit.; *Peace*, 549. The gesture was also in use, with the same meaning, in Rome, where the middle finger was called *digitus inpudicus* for this reason (Mart., 6, 70, 5), and where the gesture in question was described by the phrase *medium unguem ostendere* (Juven., 10, 53). See A. Richlin, 'Sexual Terms and Themes in Roman Satire and Related Genres', Ph.D. dissertation, Yale University, 1978.
128. *Birds*, 444; *Peace*, 549.
129. *Clouds*, 653–4.
130. *Kikinnos* in *Wasps*, 1068 is a synonym of *eupruprōktia*.

131. Agathon in *Thesmophoriazusae*, 191, 216–48; Cleisthenes in *Knights*, 1373 ff., *Thesmophoriazusae*, 235, 575.
132. Cf. *Thesmophoriazusae*, 130 ff.
133. Aesch., *Against Timarchus*, 21. On this law, and more particularly the *atimia* (deprivation of citizen rights) of male prostitutes in the general framework of the loss of civic rights as a legal penalty, see the recent contribution by J.M. Rainer, 'Zum Problem der Atimie als Verlust der bürgerlichen Rechte insbesondere bei männlichen homosexuellen Prostituierten', *RIDA* 3s., 3, 1986, p. 90 ff. (especially pp. 106–14).
134. Aesch., *Against Timarchus*, 119. On the law, as well as on the cultural images of manhood and on popular evaluation of it see J.J. Winkler, *The Constraints of Desire. The Anthropology of Sex and Gender in Ancient Greece*, New York and London, 1989, p. 45 ff., chapter 2: 'Laying Down the Law: The Oversight of Man's Sexual Behavior in Classical Athens'. An abridged version is contained in D.M. Halperin, J.J. Winkler and F.I. Zeitlin, *Before Sexuality. The Construction of Erotic Experience in the Ancient Greek World*, Princeton, 1990, p. 171 ff.
135. See E. Cantarella, 'Prostituzione (diritto greco)', in *Novissimo Digesto Italiano*, Torino, XIV, 1967, p. 225 ff.; with bibliography and sources.
136. Dem., *Against Aristocr.*, 53. On the concept of *moicheia*, understood on the basis of this law (the provisions of which are reproduced later) as meaning sexual relations with a woman other than one's own

wife or concubine (unless this woman were a courtesan or prostitute), see E. Cantarella, *Studi sull'omicidio in diritto greco e romano*, Milan, 1976, p. 131 ff. (with bibliography) and D. MacDowell, *The Law in Classical Athens*, London, 1978, pp. 124–5 and D. Erdmann, *Die Ehe im alten Griechenland*, New York, 1979. For a different interpretation of the term *moicheia*, taken as meaning only sexual relations with the wife of another citizen, see D. Cohen, 'The Athenian Law of Adultery', *RIDA* 3s., 32, 1981, p. 147 ff. and the same author's *Law, Society and Sexuality*; it is not possible to discuss Cohen's thesis here.
137. Lys., *Against Theomn.*, 19.
138. Aesch., *Against Timarchus*, 130 and 159.
139. Ibid., 29.
140. M. Montuori, 'Su Fedone di Elide', *Atti Accad. Pontaniana*, n.s. 25, 1975, and 'Nota su Fedone di Elide e S. Kenneth Dover', *Corolla Londinensis* 2, 1982, now reprinted in *Socrate, un problema storico*, Naples, 1984, at p. 355 ff. and p. 374 ff. respectively.
141. Dover, *Greek Homosexuality*, p. 26 ff.
142. Paras 72 and 87.
143. The law is summarised but not quoted at para. 13.
144. Foucault, *The Use of Pleasure*, and P. Veyne, 'L'homosexualité à Rome', *Communications* 35, 1982, p. 26 ff., collected in *Sexualités occidentales*, edited by Philippe Ariès and André Béjin, Paris, 1982 (translated into English by Anthony Forster as *Western Sexuality*, Oxford, 1985). Reservations on this point, with emphasis on the

importance of the homosexual/ heterosexual contrast, can be found in Cohen, 'Law, Society and Homosexuality' and *Law, Society and Sexuality*, arguing, as already mentioned, that a *pais* accepting a sexually passive role in his relations with the *erastēs* thereby lost his honour.

145. The possibility of discerning a link between the initiation idea of homosexuality and the idea of it in the Classical age is also pointed out by S. Durup-Carré, 'L'homosexualité en Grèce antique: tendance ou institution?', *L'homme* 97–8, 1986, p. 371 ff.

146. Aesch., *Against Timarchus*, 110–11, translated by Charles Darwin Adams, Loeb Classical Library, 1968, pp. 91–3.

147. Aesch., *Against Timarchus*, 185 (pp. 147–9).

148. Aeschines' speech leaves no doubt that being a kept man was no better than extracting a fee for each individual encounter. Among the arguments which he puts up in support of his assertion that Timarchus was a prostitute, he includes a list of lovers from whom he alleges Timarchus had received maintenance or benefits (paras 40–76).

149. Ibid., 183.

150. Ibid. Cf. [Dem.], *Against Neaera*, 87.

151. Aesch., *Against Timarchus*, 21.

CHAPTER 3: HOMOSEXUALITY AND HETEROSEXUALITY COMPARED IN PHILOSOPHY AND LITERATURE

1. H. Kelsen, 'Die platonische Liebe', *Imago* 19, 1933.

2. Xen., *Mem.*, I, 3, 13.

3. See W.K.C. Guthrie, *Socrates*, Cambridge, 1971, p. 70 ff. On the sexuality of the philosopher see also O. Kiefer, 'Socrates und die Homosexualität', in *Jahrbuch für Sexuelle Wissenschaften*, Vol. IX, 1908, which speaks of a probable sublimation of the philosopher's bisexuality.

4. Xen., *Symp.*, 8, 2.

5. Plato, *Men.*, 76 c.

6. Plato, *Charm.*, 155 c–e, translated by W.R.M. Lamb, Loeb Classical Library, 1927, pp. 15–17. Guthrie, *Socrates*, p. 74, observes appropriately that 'the rest of the dialogue is devoted to a treatment of *sophrosynē*, self-control or temperance'.

7. Plat., *Symp.*, 219 b–c–d.

8. Fr. 11 c in H. Dittmar, *Aischynes von Spettos: Studien zur Literaturgeschichte der Sokratiker*, Berlin, 1912, p. 273. Cf. Plat., *Prot.*, 309a; *Gorg.*, 481 d., and *Alcib.* I, beginning.

9. Guthrie, *Socrates*, p. 75.

10. Plato, *Alcib.* I, 131 c.

11. Xen., *Symp.*, 8, 23.

12. Ibid., 2, 8–9.

13. Xen., *Oec.*, III, 12.

14. On Aspasia, see the longer treatment in E. Cantarella, *L'ambiguo malanno*, pp. 81, 84; English translation, *Pandora's Daughters*, pp. 53–5.

15. Xen., *Oec.*, III, 14–15.

16. Plato., *Phaed.*, 60 a.

17. Plato., *Tim.*, 42 b–c, translated by H.D.P. Lee, Harmondsworth, 1965.

18. Ibid., 90 e.

19. Ibid., 76 e.

20. That, at least, is what Epictetus says (Arrian, *Epict.*, fr. 15).

21. Plato, *Republic*, V 451 c–457 d, and also 466 e–467 e. On female guardians, 'desexualised' by Plato, see A.W. Saxonhouse, 'The Philosopher and the Female

in the Political Thought of Plato', *Political Theory* 9, 2, 1976, p. 195 ff.

22. This point is argued by D. Wender, 'Plato: Misogynist, Paedophile, and Feminist', *Arethusa* 6, 1, 1973, p. 213 ff. (especially p. 214), who explains Plato's feminism as a consequence of his paedophilia and misogyny. Hating women, and not wanting a family, he had nothing to lose personally from female emancipation. As an alternative explanation, Wender puts forward the possibility that as a homosexual Plato was less frightened of women than other (bisexual) men: not being sexually attracted by them, he did not fear, as other men did, that unless they were kept 'in their place', women would get the better of him. Lastly, as a third possible reason, consideration should be given to the fact that homosexuals, given the nature of their sexual relationships, are less drawn than other men to identify what is natural with what is right; and therefore they would be less convinced of the 'natural' necessity to keep women down (pp. 225–7). The last hypothesis presupposes that the ancient Greeks had the same idea as ourselves about what is 'natural', which, as we shall see later, is highly debatable. A view of Plato as less misogynistic than the men of his time appears, albeit incidentally, in M.C. Horowitz, 'Aristotle and Women', *Journal of the History of Biology* 9, 1976, p. 183 ff. Also incidentally, J. Morsink, 'Was Aristotle's Biology Sexist?' ibid., 12, 1979, p. 83 ff., writes that Plato 'can be considered feminist for his day' (p. 83 n. 2).

23. Plato, *Laws*, V, 742 c; VI, 444 a–773 b; 774 a–b; 783–5 b; VII, 720 a–d; 808 a–b; XI, 923 c–925 d; 930 a–d; 937 a.

24. Ibid., VI, 780 a–1d; VII, 789–90b.

25. U. von Wilamowitz-Möllendorff, *Platon, sein Leben und seine Werke*, Berlin, 5th edition, 1959, pp. 312–13 and 573.

26. *Ep.*, 1 Page. The fragment for Aster is number 14. Number 7, on the other hand, is dedicated to Dion. Diogenes Laertius (III, 29) also speaks of two boys loved by the philosopher. Aulus Gellius (*Attic Nights*, 19, 11) reproduces a whole poem of love for a *pais*, which he attributes to Plato.

27. Plato, *Symp.*, 181.

28. Ibid., 189 d–192 e, translated by Walter Hamilton, Harmondsworth, 1951.

29. An aversion to physical relations between men, as a reaction to homosexuality against which Plato had himself struggled, is the theory put forward by Kelsen, 'Die platonische Liebe'.

30. Plato, *Phaedr.*, 240 c–d–e.

31. Ibid., 231 b–232e.

32. Plato, *Laws*, 636 c.

33. P. Veyne, 'Homosexuality in ancient Rome', in *Western Sexuality: Practice and Precept in Past and Present Times*, edited by Philippe Ariès and André Béjin, translated by Anthony Forster, Oxford, 1985, pp. 26–35 (pp. 26, 27).

34. Plato, *Laws*, 838 e–839 a.

35. Ibid., 839 b.

36. Veyne, 'Homosexuality in Rome', p. 24.

37. Plato, *Laws*, 874 c.

38. Xen., *Symp.*, 8, 19.

39. Ibid., 8, 21–2.

40. On the relationship between Xenophon's *Symposium* and

Plato's *Symposium* see Bruns, 'Attische Liebenstheorien', *Neue Jahrbuch für das Klassische Altertum* 5, 1900, p. 26, and W. Kroll, *Freundschaft und Knabenliebe (Tusculum-Schriften, IV)*, Munich, 1927; idem, 'Knabenliebe', PWRE XI, I Stuttgart, 1921, col. 897.

41. Xen., *Oec.*, VII–X, translated by E.C. Marchant, Loeb Classical Library, 1923.

42. In particular, according to him, women had the same ability as men to practise self-control. See Xen., *Oec.* VII, 26–7.

43. D.M. Robinson and E.J. Fluck, *A Study of the Greek Love-Names*, Baltimore, 1937, p. 35 ff.

44. Thuc., II, 53 ff.

45. Robinson and Fluck, *Study of the Greek Love-Names*, p. 43.

46. Ath., 566 e. On Aristotle's family life, about which we know little, see A.-H. Chroust, *Aristotle: New Light on his Life and on Some of his Lost Works*, Notre Dame, 1973, I, ch. 5 and 15.

47. On this topic, in greater detail and with bibliographical information, see E. Cantarella, *L'ambiguo malanno*, p. 80 ff.; English transl., *Pandora's Daughters*, p. 52 ff.

48. Aesch., *Eum.*, vv. 658–661, translated by Herbert Weir Smyth, *Aeschylus*, II, Loeb, 1988, p. 335.

49. Aristot., *De generat. animalium*, 728a, 17 ff. On this topic see M. Vegetti, *Il coltello e lo stilo*, Milan, 1979, p. 125 ff., and later, devoted specifically to this topic, G. Sissa, 'Il corpo della donna, lineamenti di una ginecologia filosofica' in S. Campese, P. Manuli and G. Sissa, *Madre Materia, Sociologia e biologia della donna greca*, Turin, 1983; Horowitz, 'Aristotle and Women', p. 183 ff., and (in response to Horowitz, taking a different position) Morsink, 'Was Aristotle's Biology Sexist?', p. 83 ff. On the animal aspect and negative characteristics which the philosopher attributed to women, see also S. Saïd, 'Féminin, femme et femelle dans les grands traités biologiques d'Aristote', in *La femme dans les sociétés antiques*, ed. E. Lévy, Strasbourg, 1983, p. 93 ff.

50. Aristot., *Pol.*, 1254 b, translated by H. Rackham, Loeb Classical Library, 1932.

51. Ibid., 1260 a.

52. Ibid., 1259 b.

53. Ibid., 1254 b. See also I(A), 12, 1259 b. On women's domestic position in Aristotle see S. Campese, 'Donna, casa, città nell'antropologia di Aristotele', in *Madre Materia*, p. 15 ff.

54. Aristot., *Pol.*, 1269 b. On the condition of women in Sparta see J. Redfield, 'The Women of Sparta', *Classical Journal* 73, 1977–8, p. 146 ff. and P. Cartledge, 'Spartan Wives: Liberation or Licence?', *Classical Quarterly* 31, 1981, p. 84 ff.

55. The story is told as an *exemplum* in J. Greven, *Die Exempla aus den Sermones Feriales et Comunes de Iakob von Vitry*, Heidelberg (*Sammlung mittellateinischer Texte*, 9), 1914, no. 15 (a collection made between 1229 and 1240). The *exemplum* is also found in the *Tractatus de diversis materiis predicabilibus* by Etienne de Bourbon (completed between 1250 and 1261), kept in the Bibliothèque Nationale in Paris, Latin manuscript 15970, fo. 507 vo a.

56. H. d'Andeli, *Le lai d'Aristote de Henri d'Andeli publié d'après tous les manuscrits par*

Delbouille, Paris, 1951 (Bibl. Fac. Philos. et Lettres de Liège, 123). On the anecdote and its iconographic fortunes, see Horowitz, 'Aristotle and Women,' pp. 189–90, who comments that Aristotle, thanks to this legend, has got what he deserved from womankind (p. 213).

57. On this problem see H.H.E. Meier and R.L. de Pogey Castries, *Histoire de l'amour grec dans l'antiquité*, Paris, 1952, p. 292 ff. This is a translation of a work by Meier published in Leipzig in 1837, in the *Allgemeine Encyclopädie der Wissenschaften und Künsten*, edited by J.S. Ersch and G. Grüber, sect. 39, IX, p. 149 ff., adapted by De Pogey Castries.

58. Aristot., *Pol.*, 1972.

59. Aristot., *Nic. Eth.*, VII, 6, 1148 b.

60. *Hist. Anim.*, VII, 581 b.

61. *Quaest.*, IV, 26.

62. Arist., *Nic. Eth.*, VII, 6, 1148b.

63. *Ibid.*, 5, 3–5.

64. For the titles of the works of Aristotle's pupils, and for the sources through which we know about them, see Winckelmann's edition of Plutarch's *Amatorius*. For a more precise dating of this work, which could come from any year between 96 and 127 (death of Plutarch) see R. Flacelière, 'Notice' in Plutarch, *Oeuvres morales*, X, Paris, 1980, p. 80.

65. Plut., *Amat.*, 750 c, translated by W.C. Helmbold, Loeb Classical Library, 1961.

66. Ibid., 750 d.

67. Ibid., 751 f–752 a.

68. Ibid., 760 e–f. [Loeb = 761 a–b].

69. Ibid., 766 d–767 e.

70. Ibid., 766 d–e.

71. Plut., *Pelop.*, 18.

72. *Greek Anthology*, XII, 7, translated by W.R. Paton, Loeb Classical Library, 1979.

73. Ibid., V, 277.

74. Ibid., 278.

75. *Achillis Tatii alexandrini, de Clitophontis et Leucippis amoribus libri octo*, 2, 35–8: see R. Merkelbach, *Roman und Mysterium in der Antike*, Munich and Berlin, 1962, p. 114 ff.; and Achilles Tatius, *The Adventures of Leucippe and Clitophon*, with an English translation by S. Gaselee, Loeb Classical Library, 1917.

76. On the dating of this work, and its chronological relationship to that of Achilles Tatius, from which it seems to take some topics, see the introduction to the dialogue in the Loeb Classical Library edition (1967) by M.D. Macleod (Luc., VIII, pp. 147–8).

77. Ibid. The arguments of Caricles are set forth at paras 19–20.

78. Ibid., para. 20.

79. The two verses cited at para. 25 come from Euripides, *Phoenissae*, 529–30.

80. *Amores* paras 25–6.

81. As we know, Tiresias, the Theban soothsayer, having lived – according to the legend – as a woman as well as a man, is supposed to have declared that the sexual pleasure experienced by women was nine times higher than the male variety (Hes. fr. 275 M.W.; Ovid, *Metamorphoses*, 3, 316–38). The argument on reciprocal pleasure is developed in *Amores* para. 27.

82. Ibid., para. 27.

83. Ibid., para. 28.

84. The Callicratidas speech takes up paras 30–49 of *Amores*.

85. Ibid., para. 33.

86. Ibid., para. 35.

87. Ibid., para. 36.

88. Ibid., para. 38.
89. The animals in question are monkeys. The denunciation of women takes up paras. 39–49.
90. *Amores*, para. 48.
91. On this topic see E. Cantarella, *L'ambiguo malanno*, p. 94 ff.; English transl., *Pandora's Daughters*, p. 63 ff.
92. *Amores*, para. 51.
93. Ibid., para. 54.

CHAPTER 4: WOMEN AND HOMOSEXUALITY

1. On the life of Sappho see R. Cantarella, *Letteratura greca* Milan, 12th ed., 1972, p. 203 ff.
2. Plut., *Lyc.*, 18, 9.
3. Thus, for example, R. Flacelière, *L'amour en Grèce*, Paris, 1950, p. 88 ff.
4. R. Merkelbach, 'Sappho und ihr Kreis', *Philologus* 101, 1957, p. 1 ff.
5. See B. Gentili, 'Le vie di Eros nella poesia dei tiasi femminili e dei simposi' in *Poesia e pubblico nella Grecia antica*, Bari, 1984, p. 101 ff., and 'La veneranda Saffo', ibid., p. 285 ff.
6. *Suid.*, s.v. Sappho.
7. Sappho, fr. 55, Lobel-Page, translated by David A. Campbell, Loeb Classical Library, 1982 (*Greek Lyric I*).
8. Sappho, fr. 22, vv. 9–14.
9. Sappho, fr. 168 Voigt (omitted from Lobel-Page).
10. Sappho, fr. 94, vv. 1–20.
11. Sappho, fr. 47.
12. Sappho, fr. 130.
13. Sappho, fr. 31, Loeb, *Greek Lyric I*, pp. 79–81.
14. G. Devereux, 'The Nature of Sappho's Seizure in fr. 31 LP as Evidence of her Inversion', *Classical Quarterly* 20, 1970, p. 17 ff. By the same author, see also 'Greek Pseudo-homosexuality and the "Greek Miracle",' *Symbolae Osloenses* 42, 1967, p. 70 ff. On the fragment by Sappho, and on the debate occasioned by Devereux's theories, see G.A. Pritivera, 'Ambiguità, antitesi, analogia nel fr. 31 LP di Saffo', *Quad. Urb.* 8, 1969, p. 37 ff.; F. Manieri, 'Saffo, appunti di metodologia generale per un approccio psichiatrico', *Quad. Urb.* 14, 1972, p. 46 ff., and C. Calame, *Les Choeurs de jeunes filles en Grèce archaïque*, I, Rome, 1977, p. 430 and n. 160.
15. Devereux, 'The Nature of Sappho's Seizure', p. 31.
16. Alcm., fr. 3 Calame. On the parthenion, see B. Gentili, 'Il partenio di Alcmane e l'amore omoerotico femminile nei tiasi spartani', *Quad. Urb.* 22, 1976, p. 59 ff., and 'Le vie di Eros', p. 101 ff.; M. Vetta, 'Recenti studi sul primo partenio di Alcmane', *Quad. Urb.* 39, 1982, p. 127 ff. On female initiations, see A. Brelich, *Paides e parthenoi*, Rome, 1969, p. 229 ff.; Calame, *Choeurs de jeunes filles*, p. 420 ff.; 'Hélène (le culte d') et l'initiation féminine en Grèce', in *Dictionnaire des Mythologies*, Paris, 1981; 'Il primo frammento di Alcmane', in *Rito e poesia corale in Grecia*, Rome, 1977, p. 101 ff.; B. Lincoln, *Emerging from the Chrysalis*, Cambridge, Mass., 1981; I. Chirassi Colombo, 'Paides e gynaikes. Note per una tassonomia del comportamento rituale nella cultura attica,' *Quad. Urb.*, n.s. I, 1979, p. 25 ff.
17. Alcm. fr. 3 Calame, vv. 70–7.
18. Alcm. fr. cit., vv. 78–82.
19. A. Griffiths, 'Alcman's Parthenion: The Morning After the Night

Before', *Quad. Urb.* 14, 1972, p. 7 ff.

20. Himer., *Or.* 9, 4 Colonna = Sapph. Test. 194 Voigt.

21. Aristaenet., *Ep.*, 1, 10 = Sapph. ad fr. 71 Voigt. On all of this see the fuller treatment in Gentili, 'Le vie di Eros,' pp. 106–7.

22. With reference to Sappho, C. Mossé speaks of female 'pederasty' in 'Saffo di Lesbo', in *L'amore e la sessualità*, ed. Georges Duby, Bari, 1986, p. 51. But when one reflects more widely on the experience of the *thiasoi*, in the light of what we have just seen, this expression seems inappropriate.

23. The possible nature of the ritual symbolising sexual intercourse is discussed by E. Cantarella, 'Dangling Virgins: Myth, Ritual and the Place of Women in Ancient Greece', *Poetics Today* 6, 1985, p. 91 ff., now in *The Female Body in Western Culture*, Cambridge, Mass., 1986.

24. Plut., *Lyc.*, 18, 9.

25. Cf. J. Bremmer, 'An Enigmatic Indo-European Rite: Pederasty', *Arethusa*, 13, 1980, p. 279 ff. (in the Appendix on 'Initiation and Lesbian Love', pp. 292–3).

26. On Homeric society as a preliterate society cf. E.A. Havelock, *Preface to Plato*, Cambridge, Mass., 1978, and *The Greek Concept of Justice from its Shadow in Homer to its Substance in Plato*, Cambridge, Mass., 1978; L.E. Rossi, 'I poemi omerici come testimonianza di poesia orale', in *Origini e sviluppo della città. Il medioevo greco* (in *Storia e civiltà dei Greci*, I, Milan, 1983). With reference to the oral aspects of culture in the centuries of lyric, see Gentili, *Poesia e pubblico*.

27. Cf. J.P. Vernant, 'Marriage', in *Myth and Society in Ancient Greece*, translated by Janet Lloyd, New York, 1988, p. 55 ff.

28. On the importance in Sappho's poetry of the period of change in which she lived (which can be perceived, among other things, in the appearance in her poetry of the hypotactic construction of phrases, replacing the paratactic construction typical of Homeric poetry) see Page de Bois, 'Sappho and Helen', in *Women in the Ancient World*, p. 95 ff. On Sappho's way of feeling and describing love and eroticism (unlike the male variety), see E.S. Stigers, 'Sappho's Private World', in *Reflections of Women in Antiquity*, ed. H.P. Foley, New York, 1981, p. 45 ff., and J. Winkler, 'Gardens of Nymphs: Public and Private in Sappho's Lyrics', ibid., p. 63 ff.; see new version entitled 'Double Consciousness in Sappho's Lyrics', in *The Constraints of Desire. The Anthropology of Sex and Gender in Ancient Greece*, London and New York, 1989, p. 162 ff. On the more general social and political situation in Lesbos, see S. Mazzarino, 'Per una storia di Lesbo nel VI secolo a.C.', *Athenaeum*, n.s. 21, 1943, p. 38 ff.

29. K. Dover, *Greek Homosexuality*, London, 1978, p. 181.

30. Anacr., fr. 6.

31. Anacr., fr. 8.

32. Anacr., fr. 48.

33. Anacr., fr. 132.

34. Anacr., fr. 13, translated by D.A. Campbell, Loeb, 1988.

35. In support of the reading *allon*, proposed by Barne, the arguments put forward have included the decorum of the poems, and the consideration

that it is very unlikely that Anacreon would interpret *lesbis* in the sense that the word *allēn* would require (cf. A. Davison, 'Anacreon fr. 5 Diehl', TAPHA 90, 1959, p. 45 ff.). This consideration has been superseded by the hypothesis of Bruno Gentili that *allēn* does not allude to a girl, but to another thing of a female gender (which we shall see below). See a recent contribution to the question by M. Wigodsky, 'Anacreon and the Girl from Lesbos', *Cl. Phil.* 57, 1962, p. 109.

36. See D. Page, *Sappho and Alcaeus*, Oxford, 1955, p. 142 ff.

37. B. Gentili, 'La ragazza di Lesbo', *Quad. Urb.*, 16, 1973, p. 124 ff. and 'Eros nel Simposio', in *Poesia e Simposio nella Grecia antica*, ed. M. Vetta, Bari, 1983, later expanded in 'Le vie di Eros', p. 101 ff. On this question see also G. Giangrande, 'Anacreon and the "Fellatrix" from Lesbos', *Museum Philolog. Lond.* 4, 1981, p. 15 ff.

38. Theopomp. com., fr. 35 Kock. Cf. Aristoph., *Eccl.*, 920 and Pherecr. fr. 149 Kock.

39. On this point see especially Gentili, 'Eros nel Simposio', pp. 90–1.

40. Cf. A. Cassio, 'Post-classical Lesbiai', *Classical Quarterly* 33, 1983, p. 296 ff. and H.D. Jocelyn, 'A Greek Indecency and its Students: *laikazein*', in *Proc. Cambridge Phil. Soc.* 206, 1980, p. 12 ff. On *tribas* meaning homosexual see W. Kroll, 'Lesbiche Liebe', in PWRE XII, 2, Stuttgart, 1925, col. 2102.

41. U. von Wilamowitz-Möllendorff, *Sappho und Simonides*, Berlin, 1917, p. 72.

42. Gentili, 'Eros nel Simposio',

p. 91; 'Le vie di Eros', pp. 131–3.

43. Eustat., 762, 62.

44. Alciphr., *Ep.*, 4, 14, 4, translated by F.H. Fobes, Loeb, 1959.

45. Dover, *Greek Homosexuality*, p. 171.

46. Eur., *Med.*, 249.

47. Xen., *Symp.*, IV, 12.

48. Xen., *Hell.*, 4, 37.

49. On the thirteenth Idyll of Theocritus, see R. Pretagostini, *L'Ila di Teocrito: mito e attualità. Ricerche sulla poesia alessandrina. I. Teocrito, Sotade*, Rome, 1984, p. 89 ff., and, for a parallel with what happened in Rome, with reference to the comparable problem of young love objects reaching the age of loving women, see M.S. Celentano, 'Licida: la passione degli uomini, l'amore delle donne (Hor., *Carm.*, 1, 4, 19–20)', *Quad Urb.* 47, 1984, p. 127 ff.

50. It is enough to recall the uncontrollable disturbance felt by Socrates at the sight of the hidden nakedness of Charmides (despite, or because of, the philosopher's reluctance to allow any space for sex in his pederastic relationships), or the descriptions of Plato and even Xenophon (one of the few supporters of conjugal love) of the lover who, drunk with love, contemplates his beloved, incapable of controlling the desire which drives him to touch him and try to have constant physical contact with him (respectively Plato, *Charm.*, 155 c–e; *Phaedr.*, 240 c–d–e; and Xen., *Symp.*, 8, 21–2).

51. Eur., *Med.*, 263–6, translated by A.S. Way, Loeb, 1980.

52. On this point see E. Cantarella, *L'ambiguo malanno*, pp. 100–1,

with further considerations on the second meaning of the 'bed', the word which also indicates the (very parlous) link between woman and naturalness, which will be dealt with shortly; English transl., *Pandora's Daughters*.

53. Theocr., *Id.*, VII, 120 ff. (translated by Dover, in *Greek Homosexuality*, p. 171).
54. Lucian, *Dialogues of the Courtesans*, 289.
55. Ibid., 290–2.
56. Ibid., 292.
57. Ibid., 289.

CHAPTER 5: THE ARCHAIC PERIOD AND THE REPUBLIC

1. Horace., *Ep.*, II, 1, 156.
2. Cic., *Tusc.*, IV, 33, translated by J.E. King, Loeb Classical Library, 1927.
3. Plin., *Ep.*, VII, 4.
4. Virg., *Aen.*, VI, 851–3.
5. P. Veyne, 'La famille et l'amour sous le Haut-Empire romain', in *Annales E.S.C.* 33, 1978, p. 36 ff.
6. Seneca, *Controversiae*, 4 preface 10.
7. P. Veyne, 'Homosexuality in ancient Rome', pp. 28–9. On homosexuality in Plautus see J. Jachmann, *Plautinisches und Attisches*, Berlin, 1913, p. 58 n. 2, who advances the hypothesis that Plautus' allusions to this custom were Roman; J.M. Cody, 'The "senex amatorius" in Plautus' *Casina*', *Hermes* 104, 1976, p. 453 ff.; S. Lilja, 'Homosexuality in Plautus' Plays', *Arktos* 16, 1982, p. 57 ff., where there is a review of relevant passages, among which we may merely cite

Asinaria, 703; *Captivi*, 867; *Mostellaria*, 847; *Pseudol.*, 785 and 1189.

8. The problem of derivation from external models has raised, for example, the problem of deciding whether the legal rules to which Plautus alludes are Roman or Greek, and there is no doubt that in many cases we are dealing with rules of Greek law. On this point see U.E. Paoli, *Comici latini e diritto attico*, Milan, 1962 (*Altri Studi di diritto greco e romano*, Milan, 1976, p. 31 ff.). A different view is taken by E. Costa, *Il diritto romano nelle commedie di Plauto*, Turin, 1890, repr. Rome, 1969.
9. Plut., *Quaest. Rom.*, 101.
10. *Gai. Inst.* 3, 220–1.
11. *Materfamilias*, in practice, had more than one meaning. In Justinian's *Digesta* (*Dig.*, 47, 10) we read three of them: a respectable woman (as in the case with which we are dealing), a woman in her own right (*sui iuris* – meaning that she had no male ancestors) and *uxor in manu* (meaning a wife subject to the personal power of her husband or of her husband's *paterfamilias*, known as *manus*). On this point see W. Kunkel, s.v. in PWRE XIV, 2, 1930, p. 2183 ff. and W. Wolodkiewicz, 'Materfamilias', *Czasopismo Prawno-Historyczne* 16, 1, 1964, p. 103 ff.
12. Edward Gibbon, *Decline and Fall of the Roman Empire*, 1776–88, argues that homosexuality was introduced to Rome by the Etruscans, who are described by Theopompus as devoted to this type of love and guilty of corrupting the young Romans who, as Livy

says, used to go and study in Etruria, and also by the Greeks, on whose homosexuality – Gibbon comments – many things could be said, but 'scelera ostendi oportet dum puniuntur, abscondi flagitia' – 'crimes should be revealed, provided they are punished, vices hidden' (Vol. V, edited by Felipe Fernandez-Armesto, London, 1987, p. 297). According to E. Royston Pike (*Love in Ancient Rome*, London, 1965, p. 254), 'the odious vice', as Gibbon calls it, arrived in Rome from Greece through the Etruscans.

13. Val. Max., 8, 1, 8 *damn.* Cf. Liv., VIII, 45, 180. On the gravity of the crime see Ael., *Var. hist.*, XII, 35; Plin., *N.H.*, VIII, 45, 70.

14. Liv., XXXIX, 45, 2 ff. It should be noted that in Liv., XLIII, 1, the story returns in a different version (the same as that recorded in Val. Max., 2, 9, 3), according to which Flaminius' lover was a female prostitute. But, as already mentioned, we are not so interested in the truthfulness of the episodes as in the indication which can be drawn from them about the customs and morality of the time.

15. Plut., *Titus*, 18–19. On this episode see F. Le Corsu, *Plutarque et les femmes*, Paris, 1981, pp. 175–6.

16. *CIL* I, 2, p. 317.

17. Polyb., 31, 24 ap. Ath., VI, 21.

18. On the condition of female prostitutes in Rome see C. Salles, *Les bas fonds de l'antiquité*, Paris, 1982.

19. Val. Max., 8, 1, 12. *absol.*

20. On disapproval of *pueri* as luxury items see *De finibus* II, 3. For the particular condemnation drawn forth by the sexual use of other people's slaves, see *Pro Sexto Roscio Amerino*, 120. On this passage see F. Gonfroy, 'Homosexualité et idéologie esclavagiste chez Cicéron', *Dialogues d'histoire ancienne* 4, 1978, p. 219 ff. (especially p. 221).

21. On this topic see R. Martin, 'La vie sexuelle des esclaves', in J. Collard et al., *Varron. Grammaire antique et stylistique latine*, Paris, 1978, p. 113 ff., as well as Gonfroy, 'Homosexualité et idéologie'.

22. Cf. *Gai. Inst.*, 1, 84 and 160; *Just. Inst.*, 3, 12, 1 and *Just. Cod.*, VII, 24, 1.

23. Cf. Catull., 15, 18 'quem, attractis pedibus, patente porta, percurrent raphani mugilesque' ('a grisly fate / Awaits you. Feet chained, through the open gate / Of your own flesh you'll suffer, for your sins, / The thrust of radishes and mullet's fins.' *The Poems of Catullus*, translated by James Michie, London, 1981.) Obviously these were domestic punishments, expressions of family power involving no intervention by the city authorities.

24. Cf. Val. Max., 6, 1, 13, where we read of C. Attienus and Pontius emasculated by Vibienus and L. Cerennius, who had surprised them with their respective wives. See also Horace, *Sat.* I, 2, 44–6; Mart., 2, 60, 2 and the *Carmina Priapea* (passim), to which we shall return.

25. Mart., 2, 83; 3, 85.

26. On the meaning and use of this term see J.N. Adams, *The Latin Sexual Vocabulary*, London,

1982, pp. 130–2 and passim. For the meaning of *irrumare* (as well as Adams, pp. 125–30) see A. Richlin, 'The Meaning of *irrumare* in Catullus and Martial', *Cl. Phil.* 76, 1981, p. 40 ff. The fact that *irrumare* a man and forcing him to perform *fellatio* was the most outrageous way of humiliating him emerges, among other sources, from Catullus (16, 1; 14; 21, 13; 28, 10; 37, 8; 74, 5) and the *Carmina Priapea* which we shall read further on.

27. Horace, *Sat.*, I, 2, 41–6.
28. Cat., in Gell., *Attic Nights* 10, 23, and once again Val. Max. 6, 1, 13, where we read about C. Gellius, killed with whiplashes by S. Musca and L. Octavius, punched to death by C. Memmius.
29. On the provisions of the *Lex Iulia*, and the innovations they introduced, see E. Cantarella, 'Adulterio, omicidio legittimo e causa d'onore in diritto romano', in *Studi sull'omicidio in diritto greco e romano*, Milan, 1976, p. 163 ff. More generally on the *Lex Iulia*, see D. Daube, 'The *Lex Iulia* concerning Adultery', *The Irish Jurist* 7, 1972, p. 373 ff.; P. Csillag, *The Augustan Laws on Family Relations*, Budapest, 1976; A. Richlin, 'Approaches to the Sources on Adultery at Rome', *Women's Studies* 8, 1981, p. 225 ff. (*Reflections of Women in Antiquity*, ed. H.P. Foley, New York, 1981, p. 379 ff.) and J.F. Gardner, *Women in Roman Law and Society*, Bloomington and Indianapolis, 1986, and London, 1986, p. 121 ff. On actions open to a slave-owner against somebody who had had

intercourse or relations with his slave, see D. Dalla, '*Ubi Venus mutatur*'. *Omosessualità e diritto nel mondo romano*, Milan, 1987, p. 44 ff.

30. Val. Max. 6, 1, 9. A substantially identical episode is found in Livy, III, 8, 27 (to which we will return), and Dion. Hal., *Rom. Ant.*, 16, 19.
31. *Dig*, 48, 5, 35 (34).
32. Liv. 3, VIII, 27.
33. J. Christius, *Historia Legis Scatiniae*, Magdeburg, 1727, p. 7, points out that Veturius' story is dated four years after the abolition of slavery for debt.
34. Val. Max., 6, 1, 11.
35. Val. Max., 6, 1, 10.
36. Plut., *Caius Marius*, 14, 15.
37. Cic., *Pro Mil.*, 4, 9; Val. Max., 6, 1, 12; Quintil, *Inst. Orat.*, III, 11, 4 and *Decl. Min.*, 3, 3b; Dion. Hal., *Rom. Ant.* 16, 4, 8.
38. On the Vestals see G. Giannelli, *Il sacerdozio di Vesta*, Florence, 1913; F. Guizzi, *Aspetti giuridici del sacerdozio romano. Il sacerdozio di Vesta*, Naples, 1968; M. Beard, 'The Sexual Status of Vestal Virgins', *JRS* 70, 1980, p. 12 ff.; T. Cornell, 'Some Observations on the "crimen incesti"', in *Le délit religieux dans la cité antique*, Rome, 1981, p. 27 ff; and also (with specific reference to burial) A. Fraschetti, 'Le sepolture rituali nel foro Boario', ibid., p. 51 ff. (on the Vestals, p. 72).
39. On Roman military law see V. Giuffré, *Il 'diritto militare' dei romani*, Bologna, 1980, with bibliography on p. 89 ff., and M. Carcani, *Dei reati, delle pene e dei giudizi militari presso i romani*, with an introductory note by V. Giuffré,

Naples, 1981 (*Antiqua*, 11).

40. The pages here dedicated to the *Lex Scatinia*, like all the following ones dedicated to the legal repression of homosexuality, represent a reworking of a seminar which I gave in February 1987 at the Max Planck Institut für europäische Rechtsgeschichte. The text was originally published in *Rechtshistorisches Journal* 6, 1987, p. 263 ff. As regards the real name of this law, I prefer the reading *Scatinia* to *Scantinia*, as it is sometimes called. The reasons for this preference may be found in the arguments put forward by Christius, *Historia* p. 1 ff. *Scantinia* is preferred by G. Stroppolatini, 'Lex Scatinia o Lex Scantinia?' *Annuario Istituto storia del diritto romano di Catania* VII, 1899–1900, p. 4 ff., recently followed by Dalla, '*Ubi Venus mutatur*' p. 71 ff.

41. Cic., *Fam.*, 8, 12, 3.

42. Ibid., 8, 14.

43. Suet., *Dom.*, 8.3.

44. Aus., *Epigr.*, 91; Tertull., *De Monog.*, 12; Prud., *Peristeph.*, 10, 204.

45. The text actually says *leges et iura*; and *iura* are not sentences but legal opinions.

46. Juven., 2, 36 ff., translated by G.G. Ramsay, Loeb Classical Library, 1979. We shall return later on to the word *cinaedos* (synonymous with *mollis* or effeminate).

47. Gibbon, *Decline and Fall* (1987), II, p. 1716.

48. Cic., *Pro Cnaeo Plancio*, 12, 30.

49. Cic., *Cat.*, II, 7.

50. Ibid., 10.

51. Ibid., 23.

52. Ibid., I, 26; II, 7; 10.

53. Cic., *Post reditum in Senatu*, 4.

54. Ibid., 12.

55. Cic., *Pro Cnaeo Plancio*, 87; *De domo sua*, 62; *Pis.*, 20.

56. Plut., *Marc.*, 2, 2–4.

57. Val. Max., 6, 1, 7.

58. Cic., *Phil.*, III, 16, 16.

59. Christius, *Historia*, p. 9.

60. T. Mommsen, *Römisches Strafrecht*, Leipzig, 1889; French translation *Le droit pénal romain* (T. Mommsen, J. Marquardt and P. Krüger, *Manuel des antiquités romaines*, XVII), Paris, 1900, p. 431 and n. 5.

61. Val. Max., 6, 1, 10. On this topic see Dalla, '*Ubi Venus mutatur*', p. 73 ff.

62. Cf. F. Gonfroy, 'Un fait de civilisation méconnu: l'homosexualité masculine à Rome', doctoral thesis, Poitiers, 1972, which I was fortunate to be able to read thanks to the Ecole Française de Rome and the keeper of its library, Mme Noëlle de la Blanchardière, to whom I offer my grateful thanks. On this point, in particular, see p. 103.

63. Thus, for example, G. Rotondi, *Leges publicae populi romani*, Milan, 1912, p. 91 n. 1; W. Kunkel, *Untersuchungen des römischen Kriminalverfahrens in Vorsullanischen Zeit*, Munich, 1962, p. 72; J. Bernay-Vilbert, 'La Répression de l'homosexualité masculine à Rome', *Arcadie* 250, 1974, p. 443; Gonfroy, 'Un fait', p. 303, Veyne, 'Homosexuality in Ancient Rome,' p. 29.

64. P. Oxy. IV, 668, col. V.

65. E. Kornemann, *Die neue Livius-Epitome aus Oxyrhynchus. Text und Untersuchungen*, Aalen, 1963 (Klio, Beiheft 2). The name 'Scantius' appears, for example,

in Livy, X, 46, 10, while 'Scantia' is found in Cic., *Pro Mil.*, 75.

66. The various conjectural readings are reported by O. Rossbach, *Periochae omnium librorum, Fragmenta Oxyrhynchi Reperta...*, Leipzig, 1910.

67. C. Ferrini, 'Esposizione storica e dottrinale del diritto penale romano', in *Enciclopedia del diritto penale romano*, Milan, 1904, p. 361. S. Lilja (*Homosexuality in Republican and Augustan Rome*, Helsinki, 1983, p. 112 ff.), after analysing the various possible hypotheses, concludes that the dating of this law is uncertain.

68. Christius, *Historia*, p. 8 ff.

69. Cf. Livy, XXIII, 21.

70. M. Voigt, 'Über die Lex Cornelia sumtuaria', *Berichte über die Verhandlungen der Kön.-Sachs Gesellschaft der Wissenschaften zu Leipzig*, *Phil.-Hist. Kl.* 42, 1890, p. 243 ff. (especially p. 275).

71. This position is adopted by Christius, *Historia*, p. 10, and by Veyne, 'Homosexuality in ancient Rome,' p. 29. It is less easy to understand the position taken by Mommsen, *Le droit pénal*, II, p. 431. After stating that the law punished pederasty, he speaks of a sanction against those who took advantage of a freeborn youth, without specifying whether this has to be a *puer*. This makes it look as if he is using the term 'pederasty' in a non-technical sense.

72. Thus Ferrini, 'Esposizione storica', p. 361, speaking of abuses *inter ingenuos*; E. Weiss, in PWRE XII 2, col. 2413, refers to *stuprum cum masculo*; Bernay-Vilbert, 'La répression', p. 443, believes

that the law allowed for cases of varying gravity, and threatened the death penalty for corrupting minors (this hypothesis is certainly mistaken). On the other hand, A. Richlin (*The Garden of Priapus*: *Sexuality and Aggression in Roman Humour*, New Haven and London, 1983, Appendix 2: 'The Circumstances of Male Homosexuality in Roman Society of the Late Republic and Early Empire,' p. 220 ff.) feels that *ingenui* of any age who agreed to take a passive role in sex incurred a penalty (see, in particular, p. 224).

73. Christius, for example, writes of a punishment for the violator alone. Mommsen does not rule out the possibility that the passive partner might also be liable to penalties. Richlin speaks of punishment for the passive partner alone. The references are those cited in the previous note. Lastly, Dalla, '*Ubi Venus mutatur*', p. 94 ff., thinks that penalties followed both pederasty and passivity.

74. See the section on the *Lex Iulia de adulteriis*, p. 142 ff.

75. Juven., 2, 36–48. At verses 49–50 we further read: 'Clodia does not lick Cluvia, nor Flora Catulla; but Ispones gets under young men and is turned pale by double vice.'

76. On the meaning of the term *mollis* see Gonfroy, 'Un fait', p. 272 ff., and A. Richlin, 'Sexual Terms and Themes in Roman Satire and Related Genres', Ph.D. diss., Yale University, 1978, p. 295 ff.

77. Sen., *Contr.*, 4 preface 10. Seneca adds that it was customary to joke about the fact that a freedman had to

submit to his master's sexual urges, as a moral duty or service (*officium*). Jokes included lines like *non facis mihi officium* ('you aren't doing your duty by me'), or *multum ille huic in officiis versatur*, 'he gets in a lot of duty from him'. On the meaning of *inpudicitia* see Veyne, 'Homosexuality in ancient Rome,' p. 30.

78. Auson., *Epigr.*, 92.
79. On the *Lex Titia* see M. Voigt, 'Über die Lex Cornelia sumtuaria', p. 257 ff., and R. Taubenschlag, 'Lex Iulia et Titia', in PWRE XII col. 2392 ff.
80. Quintil., *Inst. Orat.*, IV, 2, 69. See also *Inst. Orat.*, VII, 4, 42. The form taken by a judgment *ex lege Scatinia* is a further question which has been widely discussed. For the hypothesis that it took the form of a criminal trial, see A.H.M. Jones, *The Criminal Courts of the Roman Republic and Principate*, Oxford, 1972, p. 57 ff., and Dalla, '*Ubi Venus mutatur*', pp. 92–4, which discusses the various hypotheses on this topic.
81. *Dig.*, 48, 5, 30 (29) (Ulp., 4 *de adult.*).
82. *Dig.*, 48, 6, 3, 4 (Marc., 14 Inst.).
83. *Paul. Sent.*, 2, 26, 5.
84. J. Coroï, *La Violence en droit criminel romain*, Paris, 1915, p. 214. As regards the sponsor of this legislation, Mommsen (*Le droit pénal*, Vol. II, pp. 385–6) believed that it had been passed by Julius Caesar. This hypothesis has recently been accepted by Gardner, *Women in Roman Law and Society*, p. 118. Most scholarship, however, maintains that this law was passed under

Augustus. For an early exposition of this view see F. Lanfranchi, *Il diritto nei retori romani*, Milan, 1938, p. 463.

85. Christius, *Historia*, p. 10, where the text of the law is reconstructed as follows: 'si quis ingenuum puerum stupraverit, aut appellaverit de stupro, aut ea causa comites corruperit, nomen eius ad populum defertor, poena decem milium esto.'
86. Cf. J.P. Néraudau, *Etre enfant à Rome*, Paris, 1984, pp. 148–9 and 226–8.
87. *Dig.*, 47, 10, 15, 22 and 23.
88. The praetor's edict (in the definitive form given to it in AD 130, at the behest of the emperor Hadrian, by the jurist Salvius Julianius) has been reconstructed by O. Lenel (*Das Edictum perpetuum*, Leipzig, 3rd edition, 1927). The edict *de adtemptata pudicitia* is found on p. 400 (tit. XXXV, para. 192). As to whether the title of the edict really was 'de adtemptata pudicitia', some questions are put forward by A. Guarino, 'Le matrone e i pappagalli', in *Inezie di giureconsulti*, Naples, 1978, p. 165 ff.
89. *Dig.*, 47, 10, 15, 16–18.
90. *Dig.*, 47, 10, 15, 19.
91. *Dig.*, 47, 10, 15, 20.
92. The incorporation of *adtemptata pudicitia* within the sphere of *iniuria* can be seen from Dig., 47, 10, 14 ff. On the crime of *iniuria*, see P. Huvelin, 'La notion de l'*iniuria* dans le très ancien droit romain', in *Mélanges Appleton*, Lyons, 1903, especially p. 21 ff.; G. Pugliese, *Studi sull'iniuria*, Milan, 1941 and A.D. Manfredini, *Contributo*

allo studio dell'iniuria in età repubblicana, Milan, 1977, p. 184 ff.

93. Paulus writes (*Dig.*, 47, 10, 10): 'adtemptari pudicitia dicitur, cum id agitur ut ex pudico inpudicus fiat.'

94. The addressees of the edict are aptly described as *pappagalli* (literally, 'parrots' – a beautifully expressive contemporary Italian term for showy young men who whistle after women in the street) by Guarino, 'Le matrone e i pappagalli'.

95. Plaut., *Curc.*, 35–8, translated by Paul Nixon, Loeb, 1959.

96. Christius, *Historia*, p. 12, and Richlin, *The Garden of Priapus*, p. 222, who observes that the passage implies that any love affair is permissible, so long as the beloved *puer* is not freeborn, and seems in his turn to link the passage to the *Lex Scatinia*.

97. *Dig.*, 50, 16, 204 (Paulus, 2 *Epitomarum Alfeni*). The slave is a *puer* whatever his age, because, unlike the *puer liber* (whose incapacity is only temporary), he is excluded from the *civitas* throughout his life (or at least until he is set free). On this topic see Néraudau, *Etre enfant à Rome*, p. 48 ff.

98. *Etymologies*, XI, 2.

99. Censor., *De die nat.*, XIV, 2.

100. Cf. *Gai. Inst.*, 1, 196.

101. On the problems posed by the dating of this comedy see Plaute, *Comédies*, III, Paris, 1935, edited and translated by A. Ernout, p. 61.

CHAPTER 6: THE LATE REPUBLIC AND THE PRINCIPATE

1. Cic., *Brutus*, XXXV, 132, and *De orat.*, II, 7, 28, translated by J.C. Rolfe, Loeb, 1928.

2. Gell. *Attic Nights*, 19, 9, translated by J.C. Rolfe, Loeb Classical Library, 1928.

3. On the life and poetry of Catullus see M. Lenchantin de Gubernatis, *Il libro di Catullo*, Turin, 1950, Introduction (pp. v–xli). On Lesbia's identity (she was probably Clodia, wife of Q. Metellius Celeris) see p. xxix, n. 6.

4. Cat., 48: 'Mellitos oculos tuos Iuventi / siquis me sinat usque basiare / usque ad milia basiem trecenta / nec numquam videar satur futurus / non si densior aridis aristis / sit nostrae seges osculationis'. (English translation from Guy Lee, *The Poems of Catullus*, Oxford, 1990, p. 49).

5. See, for example, B. Arkins, *Sexuality in Catullus* (*Altertumswissenschaft Texte und Studien*, VIII), Hildesheim, Zurich and New York, 1982.

6. For a critique of the 'fiction' thesis, with arguments in favour of an inescapable link between poetry and life, both in general and with reference to homosexual love, see J. Griffin, 'Augustan Poetry and the Life of Luxury,' *JRS* 66, 1976, p. 87, and 'Genre and Real Life in Latin Poetry,' *JRS* 71, 1981, p. 39 ff. A further treatment of the theme may be found in R. Whitaker, *Myth and Personal Experience in Roman Love-Elegy*, Göttingen, 1983.

7. This is correctly argued by Veyne, *L'élégie érotique romaine, l'amour, la poésie et l'occident*, Paris, 1983, p. 20 ff., translated into English as *Roman Erotic Elegy: Love, Poetry and the West*, Chicago, 1988.

8. Ibid., p. 85 ff.
9. On the identity of Juventius cf. E.T. Merrill, *Catullus*, Cambridge, Mass., 1951 (repr. 1983), p. xxix, and introductory note to poem 15. According to Merrill, Juventius was a noble man from Verona, sent to Rome by his family and entrusted to Catullus, who started a relationship with him to comfort himself for Lesbia's betrayals. According to L. Richardson·Jr, 'Furi et Aureli, comites Catulli,' in *Cl. Phil.* 58, 1963, p. 93 ff., although it is difficult to establish whether Juventius was free-born and noble, one could speculate whether *mellitus*, 'sweet as honey' (the adjective which Catullus uses more than once to define Juventius), might not perhaps be the surname of this family (given that the family name *Melittus* is attested, for example, in *CIL* III, 3538). Alternatively, it could be a pun on his real name, which might be something like *Mela* or *Melissus* (cf. p. 96 and notes 11 and 13 on p. 106). According to Arkins, *Sexuality in Catullus*, Juventius' name (and he says there really was a Juventius, even though the story of his love affair with Catullus was a literary fiction) was Marcus Iuventius Talna, attested in Cic., *Att.*, 13, 28, 4 and Cat. 38.
10. Cat., 99: 'Subripui tibi dum ludis mellite Iuventi / saviolum dulci dulcius ambrosia / Verum id non impune tuli namque amplius horam / suffixum in summa me memini esse cruce / dum tibi me purgo nec possum fletibus ullis / tantillum vestrae demere saevitiae / Nam simul id factum est multis deluta labella / guttis abstersisti omnibus articulis / ne quicquam nostro contractum ex ore maneret / tamquam commictae spurca saliva lupae / praeterea infesto miserum me tradere Amori / non cessasti omnique excruciare modo / ut mi ex ambrosia mutatum iam foret illud / saviolum tristi tristius elleboro / Quam quoniam poenam misero proponis amori / numquam iam posthac basia subripiam.' (English translation from Lee, *Poems of Catullus*.)
11. More precisely, a 'little kiss' (*saviolum*). On the Roman terminology of kisses see Ph. Moreau, 'Osculum, basium, savium,' *Revue Philologique* 52, 1978, p. 87 ff.
12. Cat., 16: 'Pedicabo ego vos et irrumabo / Aureli pathice et cinaede Furi / qui me ex versiculis meis putastis / quod sunt molliculi parum pudicum / Nam castum esse decet pium poetam / ipsum versiculos nihil necessest / qui tum denique habent salem ac leporem / si sint molliculi ac parum pudici / et quod pruriat incitare possunt / non dico pueris sed his pilosis / qui duros nequeunt movere lumbos / Vos quei milia multa basiorum / legistis male me marem putatis? / Pedicabo ego vos et irrumabo.' On Furius and Aurelius and their relations both with Catullus and Juventius, cf. Richardson 'Furi et Aureli'. (English translation from Lee, *Poems of Catullus*.)
13. Cf. Lucil., 32 and 1138–40. I refer to the edition of F. Marx, C. *Lucilii Carminum Reliquiae*, 2 vols, Leipzig, 1904–5, repr. Amsterdam, 1963. On Lucilius' attitude to homosexuality see

A. Richlin (*The Garden of Priapus. Sexuality and Aggression in Roman Humour*, New Haven and London, 1983, p. 164 ff.), who observes that just as Catullus invented the vocabulary for kisses Lucilius invented one for pederasty (p. 168). To the terms used by Lucilius we may add *catamitus*, from the Greek *Ganymedes*, the name of the boy loved by Zeus. Cf. J.N. Adams, *The Latin Sexual Vocabulary*, London, 1982, p. 228 n. l.

14. Cf. P. Veyne, 'L'homosexualité à Rome', in *Sexualités occidentales*, Paris, 1982, p. 43, and A. Richlin, 'Sexual Terms and Themes in Roman Satire and Related Genres', Ph.D. diss., Yale University, 1978, p. 310 ff., and *The Garden of Priapus*, p. 27 and passim. The meaning of *irrumare* has already been explained. On the meaning of *pedicare* see M. Negri, 'Paedicare o pedicare?' in *Rendiconti Istituto Lombardo di scienze e lettere, Classe di Lettere, Scienze Morali e Storiche, cl. lettere*, 112, 1978, p. 220 ff.

15. Cat., 21: 'Aureli pater esuritionum / non harum modo sed quot aut fuerunt / aut sunt aut aliis erunt in annis / pedicare cupis meos amores / Nec clam: nam simul es iocaris una / haeres ad latus omnia experiris / Frustra nam insidias mihi instruentem / tangam te prior irrumatione / Atque id si faceres satur tacerem / nunc ipsum id doleo quod esurire / mellitus puer et sitire discet / Quare desine dum licet pudico / ne finem facias sed irrumatus.' (English translation by Lee, *Poems of Catullus.*)

16. Sometimes it was performed by the bridegroom himself: cf. *Catulli Veronensis liber*, recensuit A. Baehrens, nova editio a K.P. Schulze curata, Lipsiae, 1893, p. 310. In antiquity there were various interpretations of this ritual: cf. Servius, *Ad Verg. ecl.*, 8, 30, who recalls, among others, the view that it marked the end of the bridegroom's homosexual activities: '... nam meritorii pueri, id est catamiti, quibus licenter utebantur antiqui, recedentes a turpe servitio nuces spargebant id est ludum pueritiae ut significarent se puerilia cuncta iam spernere.'

17. Cat., 61, vv. 122–31: 'ne diu taceat procax / Fescennina iocatio, / Neu nuces pueris neget / desertum domini audiens / concubinus amorem / Da nuces pueris iners / concubine satis diu / lusisti nucibus lubet / iam servire Talasio / Concubine, nuces da.' (English translation by Lee, *Poems of Catullus.*)

18. Cat., 61, 134–43: 'Diceris male te a tuis / unguentate glabris marite / abstinere sed abstine / Io Hymen Hymenaee io / Io Hymen Hymenaee / Scimus haec tibi quae licent / sola cognita sed marito / ista non eadem licent / Io Hymen Hymenaee io / Io Hymen Hymenaee.' (English translation ibid.)

19. On this see Veyne, *L'élégie érotique romaine*, (chapter V: 'La *mauvais société*', p. 78 ff.). Translated into English as *Roman Erotic Elegy: Love, Poetry and the West*, Chicago, 1988, p. 67 ff.

20. Cat., 56: 'O qui flosculum es Iuventiorum / non horum

modo, sed quot aut fuerunt /
aut posthac aliis erunt in
annis...'. (English translation
by Lee, *Poems of Catullus*.)

21. Cat., 81: 'Nemone in tanto
potuit populo esse Iuventi /
bellus homo quem tu diligere
inciperes / praeterquam iste
tuus moribunda ab sede Pisauri
/ hospes inaurata pallidior
statua? / Quid tibi nunc cordi
est? quem tu praeponere nobis /
audes et nescis quid facinus
facias?' (English translation
ibid.)

22. According to Richardson ('Furi
et Aureli', p. 93), the unknown
homo bellus could be Aurelius.

23. Cat., 40.

24. Cat., 21 (already reproduced in
the text); and see n. 15 above.

25. E.A. Havelock, *The Lyric
Genius of Catullus*, Oxford,
1939, p. 113 ff.

26. Ep., IV, 6–7. On Tibullus' life
see E. Paratore, *Storia della
letteratura latina*, Florence,
1950, p. 459 ff.

27. For example, Paratore, *Storia
della letteratura latina*, p. 470.

28. Veyne, *L'élégie érotique
romaine*, p. 60 ff. Translated
into English as *Roman Erotic
Elegy: Love, Poetry and the
West*, Chicago, 1988, p. 50 ff.

29. Tib., I, 8, translated by Philip
Dunlop, *The Poems of Tibullus*, Harmondsworth, 1972.

30. Tib., I, 9, ibid.

31. Dictynna is another name for
Diana, goddess of the hunt.
Minerva was noted for beautiful hair.

32. This name for the Muses
comes from Pieria, a region in
Thessaly.

33. We do not know the identity of
this Titius, who, according to
Tibullus, is obviously guilty of
depriving himself of the joys of

loving boys because he is under
his wife's thumb. This seems to
confirm Tibullus' preference for
homosexual love, a topic to
which we shall return.

34. Tib., I, 4.

35. Cf. Veyne, *L'élégie érotique
romaine*, p. 63. Translated into
English as *Roman Erotic Elegy:
Love, Poetry and the West*,
Chicago, 1988, p. 53.

36. Cf. Apul., *Apol.*, 10. Others
believe that Apuleius' text is
corrupt and that the name in
question was Roscia. On this
problem see J.P. Sullivan,
Propertius, A Critical Introduction, London, New York
and Melbourne, 1976, p. 77 ff.,
including chapter 3 ('Cynthia
prima fuit') dedicated to an
examination of 'romantic' love
in the elegiac poets and their
relations with the new emancipated women whom they
celebrated. For a feminist
interpretation of Propertius'
attitude to Cynthia, see J.P.
Hallet, 'The Role of Women in
Roman Elegy: Countercultural
Feminism,' *Arethusa* 6, 1973,
p. 103 ff. On Propertius' concept of love see also H.P. Stahl,
Propertius. 'Love' and 'War',
Berkeley, Los Angeles and London, 1985, especially chapter
2 ('Love: a Peace not won
through Arms').

37. Elegies X and XIII of the first
book are also addressed to
Gallus.

38. Lucil., 678–9. On the limited
amount of affection contained
in conjugal relationships, see
J.P. Hallet, *Fathers and
Daughters in Roman Society.
Women and the Elite Family*,
Princeton, 1984, p. 219 ff.
('Uxor et maritus').

39. Gellius, *Attic Nights*, 1, 6, 2,

translated by J.C. Rolfe, Loeb, 1928.

40. Ibid., 1, 6, 4–6.
41. Lucr., *De rerum natura*, IV, 1052–6.
42. Ibid., 1052–5: 'Sic igitur Veneris qui telis accipit ictus / sive puer membris muliebribus hunc iaculatur / seu mulier toto iactans e corpore amorem / unde feritur eo tendit gestitque coire / et iacere umorem in corpus de corpore ductum.'
43. Horace., *Sat.*, I, II, 116–19, translated by H. Rushton Fairclough, Loeb Classical Library, 1926.
44. Ov., *Amores*, 1, 1, 20.
45. Ov., *Ars amat.*, II, 683–4: 'Odi concubitus qui non utrumque resolvunt / (hoc est cur pueri tangar amore minus).' English translation by A.D. Melville, Ovid, *The Love Poems*, Oxford University Press, Oxford, 1989.
46. Ov., *Ars amat.*, II, 687–8: 'Quae datur officio, non est mihi grata voluptas; / officium faciat nulla puella mihi.' On the basis of these beliefs of Ovid's, one might wonder whether his relations with women were, so to speak, more advanced than those of his fellow citizens. But in this connection Sullivan (*Propertius*, p. 88) observes that on consideration, the opinion which the poet had of the female sex was anything but favourable. As can be seen from the first book of the *Ars amatoria*, he believed that at their best, women were human beings, while at their worst they were degenerate creatures like Pasiphae. Apart from some sexually advanced attitudes, Ovid's notion of the relations between the sexes was ab-solutely classical.
47. Ov., *Met.*, 3, 316–38.
48. Cf. Chapter 3, n. 81, p. 237.
49. Ov., *Ars amat.*, II, 719–28: 'Cum loca reppereris quae tangi femina gaudet / non obstet tangas quo minus illa pudor / adspicies oculos tremulo fulgore micantes / ut sol a liquida saepe refulget aqua / accedent questus accedet amabile murmur / et dulces gemitus aptaque verba ioco. / Sed neque tu dominam velis maioribus usus / desine nec cursus anteeat illa tuos / ad metam properate simul! tum plena voluptas / cum pariter victi femina virque iacent.' English translation by A.D. Melville. The originality of Ovid's position with regard to theories of pleasure in the ancient world is pointed out by Veyne in *L'élégie érotique romaine*, p. 131 and p. 144 n. 74.
50. Horace, *Odes*, I, 4, 29–30. English translation from James Michie, *The Odes of Horace*, London, 1963, revised edition 1987, p. 27.
51. Cf. M.S. Celentano, 'Licida: la passione degli uomini, l'amore delle donne (Horat., Carm., 1, 4, 19–20)', *Quad. Urb.* 47, 1984, p. 127 ff., showing how Horace's verses describe the 'physiological moment' of the move from homosexual to heterosexual love. I would call this, more precisely, the shift from a passive to an active role (not necessarily heterosexual).
52. Horace, *Odes*, IV, 10, translated Michie, *Odes of Horace*, p. 247.
53. Horace, *Ep.* II, 11, 1–4, translated by C.E. Bennett, Loeb, 1968.

54. Horace, *Sat.*, II, 3, 325.
55. Horace, *Ep.*, II, 11, 23–8, translated by Bennett.
56. Ibid.
57. Ibid., XIV, 9–16.
58. Virgil, *Aen.*, IX, 182 ff. and X, 433 (death of Euryalus). On the relationship between the two youths see F. Gonfroy, 'Un fait de civilisation méconnu: l'homosexualité masculine à Rome', doctoral thesis, Poitiers, 1972, p. 36.
59. Virgil, *Ecl.*, II, 7 and 15–16, translated by H.R. Fairclough, Loeb, 1935.
60. His readers in the ancient world had no doubts on this point: cf. Mart., 5, 16.7, 55 and 8, 69; Apul., *Apol.*, 10, 5 and Serv., *ad Aen.*, II, 1 and II, 15, who among other things emphasises the homosexual nature of the relationship between Corydon and Alexis by highlighting an example of Virgilian wordplay, on which see B. Weiden Boyd, 'Virgilian Word-Play and Allusion', *Harvard Studies in Classical Philology* 87, 1983, p. 169 ff. The wordplay works as follows: in *Ecl.*, II, 51 Corydon includes among his gifts to Alexis some apples, covered in soft down (*ipse ego cana legam tenera lanugine mala*). Servius comments that the apples in question are really quinces, which the Romans called *cydonea mala*. But the apples to which Virgil alludes are really those defined by the Romans as *struthea*. The reference to the down covering these apples gives rise to a pun, based on the fact that *mala* means both apples (plural of *malum*) and a cheek (*mala-malae*). And the cheeks of *pueri*

like Alexis were covered by soft down, like the apples (*struthea*) which Corydon wishes to give him. On top of this wordplay by Virgil, Servius further adds a *double entendre* linked to the word *cydonea*. Cydon, in the *Aeneid* (X, 324–7), is one of the two young Rutilian lovers killed by Aeneas, and his name (which points to his homosexuality) derives from the name of the city of Cydonia, situated on Crete, a place which was famous for the widespread extent of love between men. For the identity of Alexis (possibly the young slave Alexander, belonging to Maecenas), see Gonfroy, 'Un fait', p. 149 ff. Lastly, as regards Virgil's attitude towards homosexual love, see the recent contribution by L. Canali, *Vita sesso morte nella letteratura latina*, Milan, 1987, p. 33 ff. Canali argues that after the tale of the love between Corydon and Alexis (and the barely hinted reference to the relationship between Euryalus and Nisus), the theme of homosexuality, ill suited to the great 'Augustan' poet, disappears from the work of Virgil: 'but hostility to women and heterosexual love remains and in fact grows stronger' (p. 34).

61. On this see most recently E. Cantarella, *L'ambiguo malanno*, p. 168 ff.; English transl., *Pandora's Daughters*.
62. Cf. *Paul. Sent.* 2, 26, 11; *Dig.* 25, 7, 1, 2 (Ulp. 2 *ad leg. iul. et Pap.*).
63. *Dig.*, 50, 16, 101 (Mod., 9 *diff.*) and *Dig.*, 48, 5, 6, 1. (Ulp., *de adult.*).
64. *Dig.*, 48, 5, 35 (34) (Mod., 1 *reg.*).

65. J. Christius, *Historia Legis Scatiniae*, Magdeburg, 1727, pp. 14–15; T. Mommsen, *Le droit pénal, romain*, Paris, 1900, Vol. II, p. 432.

66. Cf. Gonfroy, 'Un fait', p. 308 ff.; P. Csillag, *The Augustan Laws on Family Relations*, Budapest, 1976, p. 181; Richlin, *The Garden of Priapus*, Appendix 2, p. 224; and D. Dalla, *'Ubi Venus mutatur'* Milan, 1987, who argues that the *Lex Iulia*, while not abrogating the *Lex Scatinia*, modified it.

67. *Paul. Sent.* 2, 26, 12–13. Cf. *Mos. et Rom. Legum Coll.*, V, II, 1–2.

68. *Inst.*, 4, 18, 4.

69. More precisely, we are dealing with a work probably written in the time of Diocletian, given official recognition by Constantine in AD 327–328 (cf. *Cod. Theod.*, 1, 4, 2), and revised up to the middle of the fifth century. Cf. J. Gaudemet, *La formation du droit séculier et du droit de l'Eglise aux IVe et Ve siècles*, Paris, 1978, p. 95.

70. On the repression of violent *stuprum*, as well as what has already been noted in the text, see the widespread coverage in J. Coroï, *La Violence en droit criminel romain*, Paris, 1915, and some observations by Gonfroy, 'Un fait', p. 311 ff.

71. Cf. Cantarella, *L'ambiguo malanno*, p. 168 ff., with bibliography; *Pandora's Daughters*.

72. E. Cantarella, 'Adulterio, omicidio legittimo e causa d'onore in diritto romano', in *Studi sull'omicidio in diritto greco e romano*, Milan, 1976, p. 163 ff.

73. *Dig.*, 48, 5, 9 (Pap., 2 *de adult.*).

74. For this see C. Ferrini, 'Esposizione storica e dottrinale del diritto penale romano', in *Enciclopedia del diritto penale romano*, Milan, 1904, p. 367. According to Dalla, on the other hand, the expression was coined by the *Lex Iulia* (cf. *'Ubi Venus Mutatur'*. *Omosessualità e diritto nel mondo romano*, Milan, 1987, pp. 106–7).

75. Mommsen, *Le droit pénal*, Vol., II, p. 427, n. 4.

76. Suet., *Dom.*, 8, 3.

77. Juven., 2, 36–48.

78. Tertull., *De monog.*, 12.

79. Aus., *Epigr.*, 91.

80. Prud., *Peristeph.*, 10, 204.

81. On the *Carmina Priapei*, see H. Herter, *De Priapo*, Giessen, 1932 (*Religionsgeschichte Versuche und Vorarbeiten*, XXIII); M. Coulon, *La poésie priapique dans l'antiquité et au Moyen Age*, Paris, 1932; and especially V. Buchheit, *Studien zum Corpus Priapeorum* (*Zetemata*, 28), Munich, 1962, p. 108 of which gives the different theories on the dating of the poems. Buchheit admits the unitary nature of this poetry, which he attributes to an anonymous author dating from slightly later than AD 100. For the attribution to Martial of poems generally attributed to Virgil, Tibullus and Ovid, and the almost totality of the collection, see L. Herrmann, 'Martial et les Priapées,' *Latomus* 22, 1963, p. 31 ff. The edition forming the basis of the translations given in the text comes from I. Cazzaniga, *Carmina Ludicra Romanorum-Pervigilium Veneris-Priapea*, Turin, 1959.

82. *Carmen 35*; cf. 28, 35.

83. *Carmen 44*.

84. *Carmen 67*. Among others, M.

Negri, '*Paedicare o pēdĭcāre?*' in *Rend. Istit. Lomb.* 112, 1978, bases himself on this pun to resolve the dilemma of the etymological derivation of the verb sometimes written as *paedicare* (as preferred by those who derive it from the Greek *paidikos, ta paidika*) while others write it *pedicare* (from *scindere podicem*). There are no variations of the name Penelope with *Pae*; hence the pun would be impossible if the correct spelling were *paedicare*. It may be added that the verb is also used to indicate a sexual act performed on adult men and on women, which would be meaningless if it came from paidika. The correct spelling, therefore, is *pedicare*.

85. *Carmen 64.*
86. The graffiti in question are collected in the fourth volume of the *Corpus Inscriptionum Latinarum*, from which they will be quoted henceforth, as well as in E. Diehl, *Pompeianische Wandinschriften und Verwandtes*, Berlin, 1930. On this topic see G. della Valle, 'L'amore in Pompei e nel poema di Lucrezio', *Atene e Roma*, 39, 1937, p. 139 ff.; H. Tanzer, *The Common People of Pompeii: a Study of the Graffiti,*, Baltimore, 1939; Richlin, *The Garden of Priapus*, p. 81 ff. S. Lilja, *Homosexuality in Republican and Augustan Rome*, Helsinki, 1983, p. 97. On the meaning and use of *futuo* cf. Adams, *Latin Sexual Vocabulary*, p. 118 ff.
87. CIL IV *Supplementum*, 3935. See also 3942, where a similar group enterprise is carried out by Ampliatus Afer.
88. CIL IV, 4008.

89. CIL IV, 2254.
90. CIL IV, 2210.
91. *Pedicare*, we saw, is a word indicating sodomy either of a man or a woman. It is used thus for example in Mart., 11, 104. Cf. Negri, '*Paedicare o pēdĭcāre?*', p. 222 and Adams, *Latin Sexual Vocabulary*, p. 123.
92. Cf. V. Väänänen, (gen. ed.), *Graffiti del Palatino*, 2 vols (*Acta instituti romani Finlandiae*, III–IV), Helsinki, 1966–70. In the first volume, under numbers 121, 230, 232 and 363, we see some significant references to *pedicatio*. Obviously, after what we have seen of the Pompeian inscriptions, it is not possible to explain away these references by arguing that we are dealing only with the customs of slaves: cf. W. Kroll, 'Römische Erotik', *Zeitschrift für Sexualwissenschaft* 17, 1930–1, p. 157.
93. Cf. *Ludus Magnus*, ed. A.M. Colini and L. Cozza, Rome, 1962, p. 47, fig. 67. *Verpa* is a term indicating the male genitalia. Cf. Cat., 28, 12 and Mart., 11, 46, 2.
94. Mart., 14, 205, translated by Walter Ker, Loeb Classical Library, 1919.
95. Cf. E. Cantarella, *L'ambiguo malanno*, p. 184 ff.; English transl., *Pandora's Daughters*, and later J.F. Gardner, *Women in Roman Law and Society*, Bloomington and Indianapolis, 1986, p. 5 ff.
96. Mart., 8, 12.
97. Mart., 3, 92.
98. Mart., 2, 56.
99. Mart., 4, 24. In fact, it would appear that Martial was not married. On this point, see J.P. Sullivan, 'Was Martial Really

Married? A Reply', *Classical World* 72, 1979 p. 238 ff., and 'Martial's Sexual Attitudes', *Philologus* 123, 1979, p. 288 ff., especially p. 292.

100. Mart., 6, 23 (I, p. 371). Other epigrams on the vices of women: 1, 62; 1, 87; 6, 31; 6, 39; 6, 67; 10, 41; 10, 69; 12, 58. The only praise which Martial offers to the ladies is directed to *matronae* of unquestioned integrity and heroism such as that of Portia, who on hearing of her husband's death, decided to kill herself. As all weapons had been hidden from her, she swallowed live coals (1, 42). Another paragon was Arria, who to encourage her husband, who was showing a certain reluctance to commit suicide, plunged a sword into her own breast, saying: 'My wound does not hurt, believe me, but yours that you are about to inflict does hurt me' (1, 14). Cf. 7, 21 and 7, 23 for Polla Argentaria, Lucan's widow.

101. Mart., 1, 92, vv. 1–2.
102. Mart., 5, 46.
103. Mart., 5, 38. The motif is Ovidian: 'What follows, I fly; what flies, I follow in turn' (*Amores*, II, 19, 36–7; translated by Grant Showerman, Loeb Classical Library, 1977).

104. Mart., 1, 46 (I, p. 57). The masculine name Hedyle is amended by some scholars (Bentley, Schneidewin) into the feminine Hedyli. But Hedyle appears in other epigrams, as the name of a passive homosexual (cf. 4, 52 and 9, 37). The emendation is not acceptable (as argued by Sullivan, 'Martial's Sexual

Attitudes,' p. 295, n. 3).
105. Mart., 2, 55.
106. Mart., 1, 24. The final sentence, 'nupsit heri', translated as 'he was a bride yesterday', has sometimes been interpreted as a reference to marriages between males, allegedly celebrated in Rome: cf. John Boswell, *Christianity, Social Tolerance and Homosexuality. Gay People in Western Europe from the Beginning of the Christian Era to the Fourteenth Century*, Chicago and London, 1980, p. 122. Clearly, however, what we have here is an allegation that the hairy soldier, apparently above suspicion, took on a passive womanly role. We shall return to the topic of marriages between homosexuals.
107. Mart., 3, 71.
108. Mart., 2, 51. Other epigrams on passive homosexuals: 2, 28; 3, 73; 3, 74; 6, 37. On the impotent (another butt of rabid contempt) see 3, 75.
109. On the poet's personality, predilections and sexual attitudes see Sullivan, 'Martial's Sexual Attitudes,' and Richlin, *The Garden of Priapus*, p. 39 ff.
110. Mart., 11, 78.
111. Mart., 11, 43.
112. *Greek Anthology*, XII, 7.
113. Juvenal, 6, 115–35.
114. Juvenal, 6, 349–51, translated by G.G. Ramsay, Loeb, 1979.
115. *Ibid.*, 229–30.
116. *Ibid.*, 306–11.
117. *Ibid.*, 187–91.
118. *Ibid.*, 434–37.
119. On Juvenal's attitude to women, see R.P. Bond, 'Antifeminism in Juvenal and Cato', in *Studies in Latin Literature and Roman History*, I, ed.

C. Deroux, Brussels, 1979, p. 418 ff.
120. Juvenal, 6, 40–42.
121. *Ibid.*, 83–5.
122. *Ibid.*, 87–90.
123. *Ibid.*, 93–5.
124. *Ibid.*, 6, 96.
125. *Ibid.*, 6, 104–7.
126. *Ibid.*, 6, 117–42.
127. *Ibid.*, 6, 117–36.
128. *Ibid.*, 6, 137–8.

CHAPTER 7: THE EMPIRE

1. Suet., *Div. Iul.*, 49–50. It is interesting to note that the charges of homosexuality are minimised by O. Kiefer, *Kulturgeschichte Roms unter Besonderer Berucksichtigung der Römischen Sitten*, English translation by G. and H. Highet, *Sexual Life in Ancient Rome* London, 1953, p. 297 ff. When one considers that this book does not devote a single paragraph to homosexuality, this is of course not too surprising. On the figure which he defines as the 'energetic mollis', see Veyne, *L'élégie érotique romaine.* [*La poesia, l'amore, l'occidente*], Paris, 1983, p. 265 ff., who identifies in the exhibition of 'softness' a contradiction which was pleasing to the nobility but which was 'a secret between initiates, and one which the common people were not to know about'. This is certainly true as regards the intentions of the nobility, who felt it quite inappropriate for the lower orders to be inspired by this model, but in my opinion, as we shall see later on, the populace (completely aware of these practices) saw in this 'paradox' a heaven-sent opportunity to justify their own 'softness'.

2. Macr., *Sat.*, II, 3, 9. Cf. Dio. Cass., 43, 43.
3. Suet., *Div. Iul.*, 73.
4. Cat., 93.
5. A. Richlin, 'Sexual Terms and Themes in Roman Satire and Related Genres', Ph.D. diss., Yale University, 1978. p. 298.
6. On this see W.C. Scott, 'Catullus and Caesar (c. 29),' *Cl. Phil.* 66, 1971, p. 17 ff. After speculating whether the attack in *carmen 29* also involves Pompey, who had also protected Mamurra, Scott speculates on what foundation there might be to the accusations against Caesar, concluding that their truthfulness is highly debatable. His reputation as a dice-thrower, in particular, might be based simply on the phrase 'alea iacta est'! The charge of *inpudicitia* is different, however, as it receives abundant support from the sources.
7. Dio. Cass., 43, 20.
8. Suet., *Div. Iul.*, 22, 3.
9. Cat. 11, 10.
10. Suet., *Div. Iul.*, 49.
11. Ibid., 50.
12. Ibid., 51.
13. Ibid., 52.
14. Ibid., 49.
15. Ov., *Amores* 1, 9, 1. Cf. *Ars amat.* II, 233 f and 674. The theme is a Greek one, to be found as far back as Sappho. Cf. L. Rissam, 'Love as War. Homeric References in the Poetry of Sappho,' Königstein, Ts., 1983 (*Beitr. z. klass. Phil.*, 157). In Latin literature it may be found in the works of Plautus, Terence, Propertius and Tibullus, besides those of Ovid. Cf. P. Murgatroyd, 'Militia amoris and the Roman Elegists', *Latomus* 34, 1975,

pp. 59–79.

16. Suet., *Aug.*, 68. But Cicero defends him from this charge: cf. *Phil.*, III, 6–15. Suetonius also says that as a young man he underwent various *infamiae* (68–71).

17. Suet., *Aug.*, 68.

18. According to Festus, s.v., the term *galli* is derived from the river Gallus, famous because people who immersed themselves in its water, when they were seized by fury, deprived themselves of their manhood. On this topic see D. Dalla, *L'incapacità sessuale in diritto romano*, Milan, 1978, p. 41 ff. For the use of the term *gallus* as an insult see Plaut., *Miles glor.*, 1417 and 1420, as well as *Priapeia*, 55, 6.

19. The inscriptions were published by C. Zangemeister in *Ephemeris Epigraphica* VI (*Glandes plumbeae latine inscriptae*), Rome and Berlin 1885, and are found in the CIL XI, 6721. On the war of Perugia see Emilio Gabba, 'The Perusine War and Triumviral Italy', *Harvard Studies in Classical Philology* 75, 1971, p. 139 ff.

20. CIL XI, 6721, 7.

21. Ibid., 9a.

22. See respectively CIL XI, 6721, 10 and 39. Mommsen interprets the word *laxe* as *de culo pandendo*: cf. Zangemeister, *Ephemeris*, p. 58. The insult *laxus* is found again in *Priapeia*, 17, 3; 18, 2; 31, 3 and 46, 1.

23. CIL XI, 6721, 13 and 14. On baldness as a sign of diminished virility, see Plaut., *Amphitr.*, 462 and Mart., 3, 74, 5–6 and 16, 67.

24. Suet., *Aug.*, 69, Cf. Dio. Cass., 54, 19 and 56, 43.

25. Augustus' wives were, in chronological order, Claudia, Scribonia and Livia (Suet., *Aug.*, 62). For his reputation as an adulterer see Suet., *Aug.*, 69.

26. The view that this poem was really written by Augustus is advanced by E. Malcovati, *Imperatoris Augusti operum fragmenta*, Turin, 3rd edition, 1948, XII, n. 3; H. Bardon, 'Rome et l'impudeur', *Latomus*, 24, 1965, p. 495 ff.; E. Gabba, *Appiani Bellorum civilium liber quintus*, Florence, 1970, XLIII–XLIV. On the other hand, W. Teuffel, *Geschichte der Römischen Literatur*, Leipzig, 7th edition, 1920, II, 13, insists that such vulgar verses could not possibly be the work of a ruler known for his work on behalf of public morality.

27. This is the opinion of J.P. Hallet, 'Perusinae Glandes and the Changing Image of Augustus', in *American Journal of Ancient History* 2, 1977, p. 154 ff.

28. Mart., 11, 20: 'Because Antony pokes Glaphyra, Fulvia has appointed this penalty for me, that I, too, should poke her. I to handle Fulvia? What if Manius were to implore me to treat him as a sodomite? Am I to do it? I trow not, if I be wise. "Either poke me or let us fight," she says. And what that my poker is dearer to me than my very life? Let the trumpets sound.' (Translation by Walter C.A. Ker in the Loeb Classical Library, Martial, *Epigrams*, II, 1920, p. 253.)

29. Suet., *Tib.*, 42–4.

30. Suet., *Calig.*, 24 and 36.

31. Suet., *Nero*, 28 and 29.

32. Suet., *Galba*, 22.
33. Suet., *Otho*, 12.
34. Suet., *Vit.*, 3. Cf. Dio. Cass., 63, 4, 2. The term *spintria* (from the Greek *sphinktēr*) appears in Petr., *Satyr.*, 113, 11. Cf. Richlin, 'Sexual Terms,' p. 303.
35. Suet., *Divus Titus*, 1, translated by R. Graves, Penguin, Harmondsworth, 1957, repr. 1979.
36. Suet., *Divus Titus*, 7.
37. Suet., *Dom.*, 1.
38. Mart., 9, 11–13 and 19, 16; Dio. Cass. 67, 2, 3.
39. Dio. Cass., 69, 11.
40. Spart., *Hadr.*, 14.
41. Aur. Vict., *De Caes.*, 14.
42. Hel. Lampr., *Comm. Ant.*, 5, 2–3.
43. Respectively Hel. Lampr., *Elag.*, 2, 4, 8, 10 and Herod., V, 2, 9 and V, 5, 3–4.
44. Amm., 21, 16, 2 and Epit., 42, 19.
45. Cf. Dalla, *L'incapacità sessuale*, p. 29 ff. On the role of eunuchs at court see R. Turcan, *Vivre à la Cour des Césars*, Paris, 1987, p. 83 ff.
46. Aur. Vict., *De Caes.*, 41, 24.
47. E. Gibbon, *Decline and Fall of the Roman Empire*, 1776–88, II. The problem is tackled by V. Bullough, *Sexual Variance in Society and History*, New York, 1976 (chapter 6: 'Roman Mythology and Reality,' p. 127 ff.) and more briefly, by the same author, in *Sex, Society and History*, New York, 1976, p. 1 ff. ('Sex in History: a Virgin Field'). According to Bullough, the Romans were always hostile to homosexuality, which only spread in Rome on a temporary basis, in special situations, owing to external influences and at times of moral collapse. The author therefore tends to argue that homosexuality was less widespread than we could infer from reading the lives of the emperors. This is probably true. But that certainly does not mean that homosexuality was contrary to the Roman mentality. The Romans, as we know, were against passivity, but active homosexuality formed part of their customs and ideology. Equally questionable is Bullough's statement that homosexuality was severely punished in Rome from Republican times onward.
48. On this problem see A. Richlin, *The Garden of Priapus, Sexuality and Aggression in Roman Humour*, New Haven and London, 1983, p. 88 ff. On the reliability of Suetonius, his methods, the intentions of his biographical enterprise, and its consequences, see J. Cascon, *Suétone Historien*, Rome, Befar, 1984.
49. Juven., 9, 45–6. On the metaphorical use of the verb *fodio* (which returns in Martial 1, 92, 11–12 and in *Carmina Priapea*, 52), see Richlin, *Sexual Terms*, p. 301, and J.N. Adams, *The Latin Sexual Vocabulary*, London, 1982, pp. 151–2.
50. Sen., *Ep.*, XLVII, 7.
51. Suet., *Div. Iul.*, 49.
52. Ibid., 51.
53. On the mother–son relationship in Rome, see J. Hallet, *Fathers and Daughters in Roman Society. Women and the Elite Family*, Princeton, 1984.
54. Cf. E. Cantarella, *L'ambiguo malanno*, p. 220 ff.; English transl., *Pandora's Daughters*.
55. On the different interpretations

(both ancient and modern) of the ban on women drinking wine, see again Cantarella, *L'ambiguo malanno*, p. 161 ff.; English transl., *Pandora's Daughters* and also *Tacita Muta*, Rome, 1985, p. 52 ff.

56. Petr. *Satyr.*, 67. On sexuality in the *Satyricon* see J.P. Sullivan, 'The *Satyricon* of Petronius. Some Psychoanalytic Considerations', *The American Imago* 18, 1961, p. 357 ff., and the same author's *Realism and Satire in Petronius*, London, 1963, as well as *The Satyricon of Petronius*, London, 1968, chapter 6, 'The Sexual Themes of the Satyricon'. According to Sullivan, the scopophilia and exhibitionism which can be seen as occurring in the pages of the book reflect the sexual behaviour or fantasies of its author. A different position is taken by G. Gill, 'The Sexual Episodes in the Satyricon', *Cl. Phil.* 68, 1973, p. 172 ff., who sees the whole thing as literary exhibitionism. Lastly, see M.A. Cervellera, 'Omosessualità e ideologia schiavistica in Petronio,' *Index*, 11, 1982, p. 221 ff.

57. Suet., *Div. Iul*, 6: Caesar divorced Pompeia because Clodius had got into her house dressed as a woman, during a religious rite which was being celebrated there, and the people consequently suspected an adulterous liaison between Clodius and Pompeia.

58. Ov., *Met.*, 9, 666–797. On this story see J. Foster, *Sex Variant Women in Literature*, London, 1958, p. 26 ff.

59. Ov., *Met.*, 9, 737–8.

60. Mart., 1, 90: cf. J.P. Sullivan, 'Martial's Sexual Attitudes', *Philologus* 123, 1979, p. 293.

61. Mart., 7, 67, 5–8.

62. Mart., 7, 67, 9–10.

63. Mart., 7, 67, 14–15. A woman called Philaenis also appears in 2, 33. She is red, bald and squinty-eyed: anyone kissing a similar woman, says Martial, *fellat*. Could she be the same woman? Cf. Richlin, *The Garden of Priapus*, p. 67.

64. Mart., 7, 70.

65. Juven., 6, 225–35 and 246–64. Some scholars maintain that Juvenal is adapting some passages from Martial, 7, 67 to his own satire. Cf. Richlin, *The Garden of Priapus*, p. 134.

66. Juven., 6, 305 ff.; see C. Gnilka, 'Maura Maurae collactea. Zu Juv., Sat. 6, 306–308', *Rivista di Filologia e di Istruzione Classica*, 96, 1968, pp. 47–54.

67. Sen., *Contr.*, 1, 2, 23.

68. Luc., *Mer.*, V.

69. Ps. Luc., *Amores*, 28.

70. Artemid., I, 80.

71. Caelius Aurel., *Tard. pass.*, IV, 9, 132–3 in *On Acute Diseases and on Chronic Diseases*, ed. I.E. Drabkin, Chicago, 1950.

72. Paul, *Rom.*, 1:26.

73. Jerome, *Epist.*, XXI, 27.

74. August., *Epist.*, CCXI.

75. Mart., 7, 67, 1–3.

76. Mart., 7, 67, 14–17. On the significance and practice of cunnilingus see Adams, *Latin Sexual Vocabulary*, pp. 80–1 and 136.

77. Luc., *Mer.*, V, 1.

78. Clem. Alex., *Paidag.*, III, 3, 21, 3.

79. Cat., 61. Similar theme in Mart., 11, 68.

80. Mart., 12, 97.

81. Juven., 6, 268–72.

82. Mart., 11, 43.

83. Petr., *Satyr.*, 69 and 74–5.

84. *Dig.*, 3, 1, 1, 6, (Ulp., 6 *ad edictum*).

85. *Dig.*, 3, 1, 1, 5. (Ulp., 6 *ad edictum*). Only some capacities that women lacked were also removed from the *molles*: political capacity, which women never had, was never brought into question in their case.

86. Suet., *Cal.*, 16.

87. Hel. Lampr., *Alex. Sev.*, 24, 3–4.

88. Other meanings of the term are given in Richlin, *Sexual Terms*, pp. 290–1.

89. Aur. Vict., *De Caes.*, 28, 6. Cf. H.W. Bird, 'Aurelius Victor on Women and Sexual Morality', *Class. Journ.* 78–9, 1982–4, p. 44 ff.

90. Evagrius, *Hist. Eccl.*, III, 39.

91. Ibid., 40–1.

92. *Dig.*, 1, 12, 1, 8 (Ulp., *lib. sing de off. praef. urbi*).

93. J. Christius, *Historia Legis Scatiniae*, Magdeburg, 1727, p. 18 ff.

94. As well as *Paul. Sent.* II, 26, 13, already discussed, see *Paul. Sent.* V, 4, 14 (cf. *Dig.*, 47, 11, 1, 2). With reference to this, D. Dalla, '*Ubi Venus mutatur*'. *Omosessualità e diritto nel mondo romano*, Milan, 1987, p. 98, speaks of penalties against an active male homosexual having relations with a *puer*. The particular behaviour punished is that of a person who outrages or attempts to outrage a *puer*, by means of tricks such as removing or corrupting the boy's escorts. We are therefore dealing with a different type of behaviour from the one identified by Dalla. On the meaning of the term *flagitium*, found in *Paul. Sent.* V, 4, 14, see E. Volterra, '*Flagitium* nelle fonti giuridiche romane,' *Archivio giuridico* 11,

1934, p. 39 ff.

95. *Cod. Theod.*, IX, 7, 3. The constitution is also found in *Just. Cod.*, IX, 9, 30 (31). The translation of *femina viros proiectura* (elsewhere given as *porrectura*) by 'a woman who offers herself to men', given in the text, is preferable to a translation as 'a woman who refuses men', proposed by C. Pharr, *The Theodosian Code*, Princeton, 1952, pp. 231–2, and to the translation 'a woman who is about to abandon men', proposed by Dalla in '*Ubi Venus mutatur*', p. 167.

96. As argued by J. Boswell, *Christianity, Social Tolerance and Homosexuality*, Chicago and London, 1980, p. 119 ff.

97. Suet., *Nero*, 28, already cited. Cf. also Aur. Vict., *De Caes.*, 5.

98. Mart. 1, 24 and 8, 12. On this topic see Sullivan, 'Martial's Sexual Attitudes', p. 301.

99. D. Grodzinski, 'Tortures mortelles et catégories sociales,' in Y. Thomas (ed.), *Du Châtiment dans la cité* (Coll. Ecole Française de Rome, 79), Rome, 1984, p. 361 ff., especially p. 378 n. 50.

100. D. Gothofredus, *Codex Theodosianus cum perpetuis commentariis. Editio nova in VI tomos digesta*, III, Mantua, 1714, p. 62 ff., *ad C. Th.*, IX, 7, 3. A completely unacceptable view is advanced by D. Bailey, *Homosexuality and the Western Christian Tradition*, London, 1955, repr. Hamden, Conn., 1975, p. 71, who claims that this constitution was aimed at stamping out prostitution.

101. This does not mean 'refined' penalties, as translated by M. Lever, *Les Bûchers de Sodome*, Paris, 1985, p. 34 and Dalla,

'*Ubi Venus Mutatur*', p. 167; it means the penalties which are 'sought' in the sense of specially prescribed.

102. J. Bernay-Vilbert, 'La répression de l'homosexualité masculine à Rome', *Arcadie* 250, 1974, p. 451.

103. F. Gonfroy, 'Un fait de civilisation méconnu: l'homosexualité masculine à Rome', doctoral thesis, Poitiers, 1972, p. 320. On the expression *gladius ultor* in imperial legislation see G. de Bonfils, 'Sulla legislazione di Costanzo II e Costante,' in *Accad. romana Constantiniana, Atti V Congr. Internaz.* 1981, Città di Castello, 1983, p. 299 ff., especially p. 306.

104. *Mos. et Rom. Legum Coll.*, V, 3.

105. D. Manfredini, 'Qui commutant cum feminis vestem,' *RIDA*, 3s. 32, 1985, p. 257 ff. An unreliable interpretation is put forward by E. Costa, *Crimini e pene da Romolo a Giustiniano*, Bologna, 1921, p. 167, who claims that Theodosius punished *stuprum cum masculo* by burning alive.

106. This is argued by Bailey, *Homosexuality*, pp. 71–3.

107. *Dig.*, 34, 2, 33 (Pomp., 4 *ad Quintum Mucium*).

108. Quintil., *Inst. Orat.*, V, 9, 14.

109. Sen., *Contr.*, IX, 25, 17.

110. Bernay-Vilbert, 'La répression,' p. 443 ff., especially p. 452.

111. G. Glotz, *Histoire générale* IV, 2, p. 223, Paris, 1939. On this episode see C. Picard, *La Carthage de Saint Augustin*, Paris, 1965, p. 157 ff.

112. These consequences led in turn to a highly significant 'diplomatic' incident. When news of the massacre came to Milan, Theodosius was not

in town. When he did return, Ambrose, then bishop of Milan, went away so as not to meet him, refused to receive him, and refused him communion. To obtain forgiveness, after long negotiations, the emperor was forced to do penance and suspend the execution of capital sentences for thirty days. That, at least, is what Theodoretus writes. But on the reliability of his account see Van Otroy, 'Les vies grecques de St. Ambroise et leurs sources', *Ambrosiana*, 1897, p. 25 ff.

113. Dalla, '*Ubi Venus mutatur*', p. 183, observes in this connection that the cuts involve substantial variations. Whereas in its original form the law struck at prostitution, in the abbreviated form the constitution punished sexual submission and 'the assumption of the appearance of the other sex by transvestite means' (which I do not think is an accurate reading). Slightly later (again on p. 183), Dalla adds that the regulation served in the fifth century 'to repress passive homosexuality in general'. Manfredini, 'Qui commutant cum feminis vestem,' p. 268, speaks of 'variants of little significance'.

114. *Cod. Theod.*, IX, 7, 6.

115. *Brev.* VIII, 4, 5.

116. Isid., *Etym.*, V, 1, 1–7. The hypothesis comes from F. Patetta, 'Il Breviario Alariciano in Italia,' *Archivio Giuridico* 47, 1891, reprinted in F. Patetta, *Sulle fonti giuridiche medievali*, Torino, 1967, p. 601 ff., *Sulle fonti giuridiche medievali*, p. 601 ff., and is also considered by E. Volterra, 'Intorno alla

formazione del Codice Teodo-
siano,' *BIDR*, 3s., 22, 1983,
p. 109 ff.

117. Cf. *Epit. Suppl. lat. 215* and
Epit. S. Gall (ed. Haenel).

118. *Inst.*, 4, 18, 4.

119. *Nov.*, LXXVII, *caput* 1, pr.

120. Ibid., *caput* 1, 1.

121. Ibid., *caput* 1, 2.

122. On the terminology of punishments (*summum, extremum,
ultimum*) and its meaning
see J.P. Callu, 'Le jardin des
supplices au Bas Empire,' in *Du
Châtiment*, pp. 338–9. See
also Grodzinski, 'Tortures
mortelles', ibid.

123. *Nov.*, CXLI, pr.

124. Ibid., *caput* 1.

125. The period by which the disease must be confessed is
Easter, which that year fell on
13 April (cf. Gonfroy, 'Un fait',
p. 320). The constitution dates
from the Ides of March.

126. *Johannis Malalae Chronographia*, ed. Dindorf, Bonn,
1931, p. 436.

127. Procop., *Historia Arcana* XI,
ed. J. Haury and G. Wirth,
Leipzig, 1963.

128. *Theophanis Chronographia*,
ed. C. de Boor, 2 vols, Leipzig,
1883–5, I, p. 177 (AM 6021).

129. *Cod. Theod.*, X, 10, 2.

130. Ibid., IX, 42, 1 = Brev., IX,
19, 1.

131. *Just. Cod.*, VI, 1, 3. (This rule
dates from 317).

132. *Nov.*, CXXXIV, *caput* 13.

133. On this whole question see
E. Patlagean, 'Byzance et le
blason pénal du corps', in *Du
Châtiment*, p. 405 ff.

134. Cf. A.M. Jones, *The Proso-
pography of the Later Roman
Empire*, II, Cambridge, 1971. It
should be noted that, according
to Procopius, the bishops were
tried on the basis of an existing

law (issued by Justinian). Cf.
Dalla, '*Ubi Venus mutatur*',
p. 195 ff.

135. In this connection R. Bonini
correctly observes that whereas
Nov. LXXVII speaks of a
death penalty, *Nov.* CXLI is
vague on the indication of
penalties, so it is difficult to
draw precise conclusions from
its provisions. See 'L'ultima
legislazione pubblicistica in
Giustiniano (543–565),' in *Il
mondo del diritto nell'epoca
giustinianea*, Ravenna, 1985,
p. 139 ff., especially p. 167 ff.
This observation is certainly
correct, although I believe that
the expressions contained in
Nov. CXLI, on a close reading,
can be taken as referring to a
penalty which could be death,
albeit as an alternative to
castration.

CHAPTER 8: THE
METAMORPHOSES OF SEXUAL
ETHICS IN THE
ANCIENT WORLD

1. P. Veyne, 'La famille et l'amour
sous le Haut-Empire romain',
in *Annales E.S.C.* 33, 1978,
p. 36 ff. See the section on the
Roman Empire, also by Veyne,
in Philippe Ariès and Georges
Duby, (general editors) *A
History of Private Life*. I, *From
Pagan Rome to Byzantium*,
Cambridge, Mass., and London,
1987. On sexual morality, in
particular, see pp. 33–49,
59–69.

2. Veyne, 'La famille', p. 38.

3. A. Rousselle, *Porneia*, Paris,
1983, translated into English by
Felicia Pheasant: *Porneia. On
Desire and the Body in Antiquity*, Oxford, 1988.

4. Soran., I, 30–1.

5. E. Dodds (*The Greeks and the Irrational*, Berkeley and Los Angeles, 1951) writes that the Greeks took asceticism to theoretical extremes, in the chapter on 'The Shamans and the Origin of Puritanism' (p. 204).
6. Cf. E. Hoffmann, *Platonismus und Christliche Philosophie*, Zurich and Stuttgart, 1960.
7. Diog. Laert., X, 119 and 132.
8. Lucr., *De rerum natura*, IV, 1058–120.
9. Quoted by M.I. Finley, *Aspects of Antiquity. Discoveries and Controversies*, New York, 1968, p. 94.
10. Cf. F. Adorno in *La cultura ellenistica*, by various authors (in *Storia e civiltà dei greci*, Milan, 1983), p. 69 ff.
11. *Musonius Rufus and Greek Diatribe*, ed. D.L. Hijamans Jr, Assen, 1963, pp. 71–7.
12. Fragm. 85 in *Opera*, ed. F.G. Haase, Teubner, 1853. The passage is found in Jerome, *Against Jovinian*, 1, 30.
13. Thus M.S. Enslin, *The Ethic of Paul*, New York, 1930, p. 180. On the relationship between Greek thought and Christianity, maintaining the derivation of the latter from the former, at the end of the last century, see A. von Harnack's *Lehrbuch der Dogmengeschichte*, 3 vols, Freiburg, 1886–9, 4th edition, Tübingen, 1909–10; E. Hatch, *The Influence of Greek Thought on Christianity*, 1888, new edition with updated bibliography by F.C. Grant, New York, 1957; J.W. Swain, 'The Hellenic Origins of Christian Asceticism', Ph.D. thesis, Columbia University, privately published in New York, 1916; J. Leipoldt, *Griechische Philo-*

sophie und Frühchristliche Askese, Berlin, 1961, p. 60 ff.; and lastly V. Bullough, *Sexual Variance in Society and History*, New York, 1976, p. 159 ff.: 'Classical Sources of Christian Hostility to Sex'.

14. Cf. D.S. Bailey, *Homosexuality and the Western Christian Tradition*, 1955, repr. Hamden, Conn., 1975; J. McNeill, *The Church and the Homosexuals*, Kansas City, 1976; and J. Boswell, *Christianity, Social Tolerance and Homosexuality*, Chicago and London, 1980. A different position is taken by R. Scroggs (*The New Testament and Homosexuality*, Philadelphia, 1983, pp. 99–122), who argues that the New Testament, while not condemning homosexuality in itself, condemns pederasty. We shall return to his argument later. For a bibliography on the Jewish and Christian tradition in relation to homosexuality see T. Hörner, *Homosexuality and the Judeo-Christian Tradition: an Annotated Bibliography*, New York, 1981.
15. Paul, Rom., 1: 26–7. RSV, Catholic edition.
16. Cf. Bailey, *Homosexuality* and Boswell, *Christianity*, p. 107 and 341.
17. Paul, I Cor.: 6, 9.
18. Thus Scroggs, *New Testament*, pp. 101–9.
19. On this point see Boswell, *Christianity*, p. 106 ff., and p. 139 ff., as well as Scroggs, *New Testament* pp. 62–5 (for *malakos-malakia*) and pp. 106–7 for *arsenokoitai*.
20. Dion. Hal., *Rom. ant.*, 7, 2, 4. See also Plut., *Caius Gracc.* 4, 3, where Caius Gracchus accuses an adversary of *malakia*.

21. See also V.P. Furnish, *The Moral Teaching of Paul*, Nashville, 1979, p. 58 ff., who maintains that homosexuality was a problem of no interest to Paul, as shown by the fact that he refers to it briefly and incidentally, without ever making it the subject of specific ethical teaching. Quite unacceptable, lastly, is the opinion of Boswell (*Christianity*, p. 109), according to whom Paul (especially in the letter to the Romans), only condemns homosexual acts performed by heterosexuals.

22. Cf. Scroggs, *New Testament*, p. 66. On Timothy and on the bishops more generally, see A. von Harnack, *Die Mission und Ausbreitung des Christentums in den ersten drei Jahrhunderten*, Leipzig, 1902.

23. I Tim. 1: 9–10. On the list of sins see Scroggs, *New Testament*, p. 118 ff.

24. As well as the sources cited in note 14, see T. Hörner, *Sex in the Bible*, Tokyo, 1974 and *Jonathan Loved David. Homosexuality in Biblical Times*, Philadelphia, 1978.

25. Deut., 23: 17–18. It is difficult to say from what period the rules contained in Deuteronomy can be dated. It is usually argued that this code was laid down during the reforms of Josiah, in 612 BC. But the rules contained in it are not necessarily newly introduced.

26. Cf. Scroggs, *New Testament*, p. 71.

27. Unable to check the Hebrew sources for this ban personally, I am sincerely grateful to Richard D. Hecht, Professor of Religious Studies in the University of California at Santa Barbara, for his expert advice.

28. Hörner, *Jonathan Loved David*, p. 65, and McNeill, *The Church*, p. 57. According to R. Wood ('Homosexual behaviour in the Bible', *One Institute Quarterly* 16, 1962, p. 10 ff.), cult prostitution was a fertility rite, performed by both men and women.

29. Cf. Boswell, *Christianity*, p. 99, Bailey, *Homosexuality*, p. 52 and Scroggs, *New Testament*, p. 71.

30. Lev., 18: 22.

31. Lev., 20: 13. The passage is reproduced in the *Mos. et Rom. Legum Coll.*, which uses a different Latin version of the Vulgate. In substance, the two translations are, however, identical. We read in the *Collatio: Moyses dicit: qui manserit cum masculo mansione muliebri, aspermamentum est: ambo moriantur, rei sunt* (*Coll.*, V, 1).

32. Cf. Scroggs, *New Testament*, pp. 70–5.

33. Gen., 19: 4–11.

34. Cf. Bailey, *Homosexuality*, 1–28. McNeill, *The Church*, pp. 42–50 and Boswell, *Christianity*, p. 94.

35. Cf. Deut., 29: 23; Gen., 13: 19; 18: 20.

36. 'Abominable acts' is the translation of the Hebrew phrase *tō'ēvāh*, in Ezech., 16: 49–50. For an analysis of all the biblical references to Sodom (which come to 33 in all), see Wood, 'Homosexual Behaviour', p. 11 ff.

37. Of the 943 times that it appears, this verb has a sexual connotation only 15 times. However, R.D. Hecht has pointed out to me that this numerical fact is not decisive, as the verb has a different meaning depending on whether it alludes to knowledge of

things and facts or to inter-
personal knowledge. In the
latter case, it does have a
sexual value. For a list of
the passages where the verb
appears, see F. Brown, R.
Driver and C.A. Briggs, *A
Hebrew and English Lexicon
of the Old Testament*, Oxford,
1952.

38. Judges, 19: 1–30.

39. Judges, 19: 23. On the meaning
    of the word *nevālāh*, see C.F.
    Burney, *The Book of Judges*,
    1903, repr. New York, 1970,
    p. 469. Burney argues that the
    English word that best translates
    the Hebrew term is 'impious'
    (meaning a type of behaviour
    contrary to *pietas*, in the Roman
    sense of the term). With par-
    ticular reference to 'impiousness'
    in interpersonal relationships,
    Burney further maintains that
    the most appropriate English
    term is 'churl'. The translation
    'madness', 'senseless thing'
    (which perfectly matches the
    Greek word *aphrosynē*) was
    suggested to me as the best
    translation by R.D. Hecht.

40. The narrative continues in
    Judges, 20: 1 ff.

41. Thus Bailey, *Homosexuality*,
    followed by Bullough, *Sexual
    Variance*, p. 83.

42. Hörner, *Jonathan Loved
    David*, pp. 26–46, who also
    considers the relationship be-
    tween Ruth and Naomi as a
    homosexual one. The same
    view is taken by J.H. Foster,
    *Sex Variant Women in Litera-
    ture*, London, 1958, pp. 22–3.

43. *Sanhedrin*, 7, 4. The translation
    used here comes from H.
    Danby, *The Mishnah*, Oxford,
    1933; the introduction of this
    book gives information on the
    purposes and characteristics of
    this text (pp. xiii–xxxii).

44. *Keritoth*, 1, 2.

45. Ibid., 2, 6.

46. The oral tradition continues
    after the *Mishnah* was written
    down, and is collected around
    AD 600 in the Talmud, which
    expounds both the *Mishnah*
    and the Holy Scriptures. See J.
    Neusner, *The Oral Torah. The
    Sacred Book of Judaism*, San
    Francisco, 1986.

47. Thus in the Babylonian Talmud,
    Sanhedrin 54a–54b. Cf. Bailey,
    Homosexuality, pp. 61–3, and
    Scroggs, *New Testament*,
    pp. 77–9. The translation used
    here is the one from the four-
    volume edition by various
    authors, edited by I. Epstein,
    London, 1936.

48. Thus in the Palestinian
    Talmud, *Gittin* 49 and 70. On
    the marriages of priests see
    L.M. Epstein, *Marriage Laws
    in the Bible and the Talmud*,
    Cambridge, 1942, p. 308 ff.

49. Philo, *De Abrahamo*, 133.

50. Ibid., 136.

51. Philo, *De spec. legibus*, III,
    36–7.

52. Philo, *Hypot.*, 7, 1.

53. See C. Siegfried, *Philo von
    Alexandria als Ausleger des
    Alten Testaments*, 1875, repr.
    Amsterdam, 1970.

54. On Flavius Josephus and his
    work see P. Vidal-Naquet,
    *Flavius Josèphe ou du bon
    usage de la trahison*, Paris,
    1977.

55. Joseph., *Antiq. Jud.*, I, 200–1.

56. Joseph., *C. Apion*, II, 273–5.

57. *Kiddushin*, 4, 13–14. The ban
    on women teaching, as well as
    being a logical consequence
    of the fact that women were
    normally excluded from the
    teaching of the texts, could also
    have been inspired by the need
    to protect young men from
    their advances. For example,

Bullough (*Sexual Variance*, p. 76 ff.) maintains that the Jews considered women sexually avid and enterprising. On the condition of Jewish women, see J. Pirenne, 'Le status de la femme dans la civilisation hébraïque', in *Recueils Société J. Bodin*, Brussels, 1959, Vol. XI, p. 107 ff.

58. *Tosefta Kiddushin*, 5, 16. The *Tosefta*, which contains the teaching that was not transcribed from the *Mishnah*, was compiled around AD 400. The translation used here comes from J. Neusner, New York, 1979.

59. According to R.H. Charles (*The Greek Versions of the Testaments of the Twelve Patriarchs*, Oxford, 1908, repr. Oxford and Darmstadt, 1960, 2nd edition 1966, pp. xlii–xliv), the original was in Hebrew. Others maintain that it was written in Aramaic: cf. A. Hultgård, *L'eschatologie des Testaments des Douze Patriarches*, 2 vols, Uppsala, 1977 and 1982 (*Acta Univers. Upsalensis, Historia Religionum*, 7). After the edition by R.H. Charles, a new edition of the Testaments (partly based on new manuscripts) was made by M. de Jonge, *Testamenta XII Patriarcharum*, Leiden, 1970. More recently, on the work and the problems which it poses, see H.W. Hollander and M. de Jonge, *The Testaments of the Twelve Patriarchs*, Leiden, 1985.

60. *Test. Levi*, XVII, 11.

61. *Test. Naphtali*, III, 4.

62. Ibid., IV, 1. The writings of Enoch, alluded to by the author of the Testament, probably refer to a Hebrew work which has been lost, and which provided the basis for some passages in the *Book of the Secrets of Enoch*, compiled in Egypt during the first half of the first century AD. See W.R. Morfill and R. Charles, *The Book of the Secrets of Enoch*, Oxford, 1896.

63. *Test. Ben.*, IX, 1.

64. Levit., 15: 16–18.

65. Gen., 38: 7–10.

66. Bullough, *Sexual Variance*, p. 78 ff.

67. Thus, for example, J.A. Symonds, *A Problem in Modern Ethics*, privately published, London, 1986, p. 6, and Bullough, *Sexual Variance*, p. 86.

68. Lucr., *De rerum natura*, IV, 1052 ff.

69. *Musonius Rufus and Greek Diatribe*, pp. 71–7.

70. On this topic and on the text see Rousselle, *Porneia*, p. 12.

71. Caelius Aurel., *Tard. pass.*, IV, 9, 131–7 ('de mollibus sive subactis, quos graeci malthacos vocant'), in *On Acute Diseases and on Chronic Diseases* ed. I.E. Drabkin, Chicago, 1950, pp. 900–05. On his interpretation of homosexuality see H.P. Schrijvers, *Eine medizinische Erklärung der männlichen Homosexualität aus der Antike* (*Caelius Aurel., de morbis chronicis*, IV, 9), Amsterdam, 1985.

72. On this character see D. del Corno's introduction to Artemidorus, *Il Libro dei Sogni*, Milan, 1975.

73. Artemid., I, 78.

74. Artemid., I, 80.

75. Ps. Luc., *Amores*, 20.

76. Plat., *Leges*, VIII, 7, 839a.

77. Ps. Luc., *Amores*, 35.

78. On the internal and external conditions which allowed the spread of Christianity see von Harnack, *Die Mission und*

Ausbreitung, p. 12 ff.
79. Paul, I Cor., 7: 8–9.
80. Matt., 19: 9 and Mark, 10: 11.
81. Matt., 19: 10–11.
82. Justin., *Apol. I pro Christ.*, 29.
83. On this point, see the longer treatment in E. Cantarella, *L'ambiguo malanno*, p. 221 ff., with bibliography; English transl., *Pandora's Daughters*, p. 161 ff.
84. See L.M. Epstein, *Sex Law and Customs in Judaism*, New York, 1948 and Bullough, *Sexual Variance*, p. 74 ff. ('The Jewish Contribution').
85. The great Christian text on sexuality is Lactantius' *Divine Institutions* (for specific reference to homosexuality see VI, 23, 10, where passive homosexuals are compared to those who kill their own fathers). See also, obviously, Augustine's *Confessions* (on homosexuality: III, 8) and Tertullian's *De pudicitia*.
86. Cf. *Cod. Theod.*, XVI, 1, 17 (where Constantius declares Arian Christianity the state religion), and *Cod. Iust.*, I, 1, 1 (Theodosius I declares Catholicism the state religion).
87. The policy limiting the freedom to divorce begins with Constantine, in AD 331 (*Cod. Theod.*, III, 16, 1), and carries on with Honorius and Constantius (*Cod. Theod.*, III, 16, 2), with Theodosius II (*Nov. Theod.*, 12) and finally with Justinian (*Just. Cod.*, V, 17, 11).
88. *Nov.*, CXVII, 10.

CONCLUSIONS

1. A contribution which remains fundamental in this area is M. Delcourt, *Hermaphrodite. Mythes et rites de la bisexualité dans l'antiquité classique*, Paris, 1958, and later *Hermaphroditea* (Collection Latomus, 86), Brussels, 1966.
2. Ovid, *Met.*, 4, 285. See also Theophr., *Char.*, 16.
3. Plut., *De mult. virt.*, 245 E.
4. Plut., *Lyc.*, 15, 5.
5. Plut., *Quaest. Graec.* 304 E.
6. This hypothesis is argued, for example, by J.H. Henderson, *The Maculate Muse. Obscene Language in Attic Comedy*, New Haven and London, 1975. p. 206.
7. Aristot., *Quaest.*, IV, 26 (879b–880a).
8. For this view see the observations by Mary Lefkowitz, 'Sex and Civilisation' (review of Michel Foucault's *History of Sexuality*) in *Partisan Review* 52, 4, 1985, p. 460 ff.
9. On Foucault's 'over-valuation' of Greek freedom, in a different perspective, see M. Vegetti, 'Foucault et les anciens', *Critique* 471–2, 42, 1986, p. 925 ff.
10. M. Foucault, *The History of Sexuality. 2, The Use of Pleasure*, London, 1986, p. 187 ff.
11. This is argued by D. Cohen, 'Law, Society and Homosexuality in Classical Athers', *Past and Present* 117, 1987.
12. For a comparison between attitudes towards homosexuality in Western and non-Western cultures (with limits set by an analysis ranging from Islam to Melanesia, from China to North America, and from Japan to Saharan Africa, but with interesting observations), see R. Trumbach, 'London's Sodomites. Homosexual Behavior and Western Culture in the 18th Century,' *Journal of Social History* 11, 1977, p. 1 ff.

13. The phallus, made of stone, is preserved in the museum of Naples, and reproduced in J. Marcadé, *Roma Amor*, Geneva, Paris and Munich, 1964, plate 94.

14. On this topic see B. Sergent (*L'homosexualité initiatique dans l'Europe*, Paris, 1986, p. 213), who argues that the lowering of the age for acquiring citizenship was due to a prehistoric 'reform', which modified the relationship between boys and adults, which had been similar to those which survived in Greece, before the reform. But Sergent's hypothesis, arguing that initiation-based pederasty was an Indo-European institution, is designed to explain the lack of all traces of this institution in Rome, and as Sergent himself admits, there is no evidence for it in the sources.

15. Cf. J. Néraudau, *Etre enfant à Rome*, Paris, 1984, p. 261 ff.

16. The attempt by Sergent to imagine a prehistoric past when in Rome too there were homosexual rites of initiation, apart from finding no echoes in the sources, does not correspond in the slightest degree to the characteristics of Roman homosexuality, no matter how far back one moves in time. I therefore believe that we should discard this theory absolutely.

Abbreviations

AJA	*American Journal of Archaeology*
Annales E.S.C.	*Annales (Economies, Sociétés, Civilisations)*
A.P.	*Anthologia Palatina*
Arch. Giur.	*Archivio Giuridico*, Modena
ARV	J.D. Beazley, *Attic Red-Figure Vase Painters*, Oxford, 2nd edition, 1963
Beitr. z. klass. Phil.	*Beiträge zur klassischen Philologie*, Königstein
BIDR	*Bullettino dell'Istituto di Diritto romano 'Vittorio Scialoja'*
Brev.	*Breviarium alaricianum seu lex romana visigothorum ... cum epitomis*, G. Haenel, ed, Leipzig, 1848; repr. Aalen, 1962
CIL	*Corpus inscriptionum Latinarum*
Cl. Phil.	*Classical Philology*
Cod. Theod.	*Theodosiani libri XVI cum constitutionibus sirmondianis*, Th. Mommsen and P. Krüger, eds, Berlin, 3rd edition, 1954–62
Colonna	*Himerii declamationes et orationes*, A. Colonna, ed, Rome, 1951

Diels-Kranz	*Fragmente der Vorsokratiker*, H. Diels and W. Kranz, eds, Zurich and Berlin, 12th edition, 1964
Dig.	*Digesta iustiniani Augusti*, in *Corpus iuris civilis, I. Institutiones*, P. Krüger, ed; *Digesta*, Th. Mommsen, ed, revised by P. Krüger, Berlin, 16th edition, 1954
Drachm.	*Scholia vetera in Pindari Carmina*, A.B. Drachmann, ed, III, Leipzig, 1927
Epit. S. Gall.	See under *Brev.*
Epit. Suppl. lat. 215	See under *Brev.*
Fgrhist	*Die Fragmente der griechischen Historiker*, F. Jacoby, ed, Berlin, 1923
Gai. Inst.	*Gai institutionum commentarii quattuor*, in *Fontes iuris romani antejustiniani*, S. Riccobono, C. Ferrini, J. Furlani, V. Arangio-Ruiz, eds, second revised and enlarged edition, Florence, 1968
Gent.	B. Gentili, *Anacreon*, Rome, 1958
I.G.	*Inscriptiones Graecae*, Berlin, 1873
JRS	*Journal of Roman Studies*
Just. Cod.	*Corpus iuris civilis*, II. *Codex Justinianus*, P. Krüger, ed, Berlin, 12th edition, 1959
Just. Inst.	*Corpus iuris civilis*, I (see under *Dig.*)
Kock	*Comicorum atticorum fragmenta*, Th. Kock, ed, Leipzig, 1880–8
Lex. Gort.	*Inscriptiones Creticae opera et consilio F. Halbherr collectae. IV. Tituli Gortynii*, curavit M. Guarducci, ed, Rome, 1950
Liddell-Scott-Jones	H.G. Liddell and R. Scott, *A Greek English Lexicon*, rev. by H. Stuart Jones and R. McKenzie, Oxford, 1940

Lobel-Page	E. Lobel and D. Page, *Poetarum Lesbiorum Fragmenta*, Oxford, 1955
Mos. et Rom. Legum Collatio	*Mosaicarum et Romanarum legum collatio*, in *Fontes iuris romani antejustiniani*
Museum Philolog.	*Museum Philologicum Londiniense*, Amsterdam
Nauck	A. Nauck, *Tragicorum graecorum fragmenta*, suppl. B. Snell, Hildesheim, 2nd edition, 1964
Nov.	*Corpus iuris civilis*, III. *Novellae*, R. Schöll and G. Kroll, eds, Berlin, 6th edition, 1954
Nov. Theod.	*Leges Novellae ad Theodosianum pertinentes*, P.M. Meyer, ed, Berlin, 3rd edition, 1962
Page	*Poetae melici Graeci*, D.L. Page, ed, Oxford, 1962
Page, Ep.	*Epigrammata graeca*, D.L. Page, ed, Oxford, 1975
P. Oxy	*The Oxyrhynchus papyri*, B.P. Grenfell and A.S. Hunt, eds, Oxford, 1898
Paul. Sent.	*Sententiarum receptarum libri quinque qui vulgo adhuc Paulo tribuuntur*, in *Fontes iuris romani antejustiniani*
Pfeiffer	*Callimachus I fragmenta*, R. Pfeiffer, ed, Oxford, 1949
PWRE	A. Pauly and G. Wissowa, *Real-Encyclopädie der klassischen Altertumswissenschaft*, Stuttgart, 1894
Quad. Urb.	*Quaderni urbinati di cultura classica*
Rhein. Mus.	*Rheinisches Museum*
RIDA	*Revue internationale des droits de l'Antiquité*
SEG	*Supplementum epigraphicum Graecum*, Leiden, 1923

SIG	W. Dittenberger, *Sylloge inscriptionum Graecarum*, Leipzig, 1920–4
Sn.-Maehl.	*Pindari Carmina cum fragmentis*, B. Snell and H. Maehler, eds, Leipzig, 4th edition, 1975
Suid.	A. Adler, *Suidae Lexicon*, Leipzig, 1967
TAPHA	*Transactions and Proceedings of the American Philological Association*
Voigt	*Sappho et Alceus. Fragmenta*, E.-M. Voigt, ed, Amsterdam, 1971
West	M.L. West, *Iambi et elegi graeci ante Alexandrum cantati*, II, Oxford, 1972
ZSS	*Zeitschrift der Savigny-Stiftung für Rechtsgeschichte, romanistische Abteilung*

Select Bibliography

Adams, N.J., *The Latin Sexual Vocabulary*, London 1982.

Bailey, D., *Homosexuality and the Western Christian Tradition*, London, 1955, repr. Hamden, Conn., 1975.

Beazley, J.D., 'Some Attic Vases in the Cyprus Museum', *Proceedings of the British Academy* 33, 1947.

Bernay-Vilbert, J., 'La répression de l'homosexualité masculine à Rome', *Arcadie* 250, 1974.

Bethe, E., 'Die dorische Knabenliebe, ihre Etic, ihre Idee', *Rhein. Mus.* n. F. 62, 1907.

Boswell, J., *Christianity, Social Tolerance and Homosexuality. Gay People in Western Europe from the Beginning of the Christian Era to the Fourteenth Century*, Chicago and London, 1980.

Brelich, A., *Paides e parthenoi*, Rome, 1969.

Bremmer, J., 'An Enigmatic Indo-European Rite: Paederasty', *Arethusa* 13, 1980.

Buffière, F., *Eros adolescent. La péderastie dans la Grèce antique*, Paris, 1980.

Bullough, V., *Sexual Variance in Society and History*, New York, 1976.

—— *Sex, Society and History*, New York, 1976.

Calame, C., *Les Choeurs de jeunes filles en Grèce archaïque.* I, *Morphologie, fonction religieuse et sociale.* II, *Alcman*, Rome, 1977.

Cantarella, E., 'Mythes grecs et homosexualité', compte rendu de B. Sergent, *L'homosexualité dans la mythologie grecque*', *Dialogues d'histoire ancienne* 10, 1984.

—— *L'ambiguo malanno. Condizione e immagine della donna nell'antichità greca e romana*, 2nd edn., Rome, 1985; English translation, *Pandora's Daughters: The Role and Status of Women in Greek and Roman Antiquity*, Johns Hopkins University Press, 1987.

Cartledge, P., 'The Politics of Spartan Paederasty', *Proceedings of the Cambridge Philological Society* 201, 1981.

Celentano, M.S., 'Licida: la passione degli uomini, l'amore delle donne (Horat., Carm. 1,4, 19–20)', *Quad. Urb.* 47, 1984.

Cervellera, M.A., 'Omosessualità e ideologia schiavistica in Petronio', *Index* 11, 1982.

Christius, J., *Historia Legis Scatiniae*, Magdeburg, 1727.

Clarke, W.M., 'Achilles and Patroclus in Love', *Hermes* 106, 1978.

Cohen, D., 'Work in Progress: the Enforcement of Morals. A Historical Perspective', *Rechtshistorisches Journal* 3, 1984.

—— 'Law, Society and Homosexuality in Classical Athens', *Past and Present* 17, 1987.

—— *Law, Society and Sexuality: the Enforcement of Morals in Classical Athens*, Cambridge, Mass, 1991.

Cole, S.G., 'Greek Sanctions against Sexual Assault', *Cl. Phil.* 79, 1984.

Dalla, D., *L'incapacità sessuale in diritto romano*, Milan, 1978.

—— *'Ubi Venus mutatur'. Omosessualità e diritto nel mondo romano*, Milan, 1987.

Delcourt, M., *Hermaphrodite. Mythes et rites de la bisexualité dans l'antiquité classique*, Paris, 1958.

Devereux, G., 'Greek Pseudo-Homosexuality and the "Greek Miracle"', *Symbolae Osloenses* 42, 1967.

—— 'The Nature of Sappho's Seizure in fr. 31 LP as Evidence of her Inversion', *Classical Quarterly* 20, 1970.

Dover, K., 'Eros and Nomos', *Bulletin of the Institute of Classical Studies* 10, 1964.

—— *Greek Homosexuality*, London, 1978.

Durup-Carré, S., 'L'homosexualité en Grèce antique: tendance ou institution?', *L'homme* 97–8, 1986.

Epstein, L.M., 'Sex, Law and Customs', in *Judaism*, New York, 1948.

Flacelière, R., *L'amour en Grèce*, Paris, 1950.

Foster, J., *Sex Variant Women in Literature*, London, 1958.

Foucault, M., *Histoire de la sexualité, 2, L'usage des plaisirs*, Paris, 1984; *Le souci de soi*, Paris, 1984; English translation, *Vol. II: The Use of Pleasure*, New York, 1985; *Vol. III The Care of The Self*, New York, 1986.

Furnish, V.P., *The Moral Teaching of Paul*, Nashville, 1979.

Gentili, B., 'La ragazza di Lesbo', *Quad. Urb.* 16, 1973.

—— 'Il paternio di Alcmane e l'amore omoerotico femminile nei tiasi spartani', *Quad. Urb.* 22, 1976.

—— 'La veneranda Saffo', in *Poesia e pubblico nella Grecia antica*, Bari, 1984.

—— 'Le vie di Eros nella poesia dei tiasi femminili e dei simposi', in *Poesia e pubblico*.

Gonfroy, F., 'Un fait de civilisation méconnu: l'homosexualité masculine à Rome', doctoral thesis, Poitiers, 1972.

—— 'Homosexualité et idéologie esclavagiste chez Cicéron', *Dialogues d'histoire ancienne* 4, 1978.

Griffin, J., 'Augustan Poetry and the Life of Luxury', *JRS* 66, 1976.

—— 'Genre and Real Life in Latin Poetry', *JRS* 71, 1981. Both articles are contained in Griffin, *Latin Poets and Roman Life*, London, 1985.

Guarino, A., 'Le matrone e i pappagalli', in *Inezie di giureconsulti*, Naples, 1978.

Halperin, D.M., *One Hundred Years of Homosexuality and Other Essays in Greek Love*, New York, 1989.

Halperin, D.M., Winkler, J.J. and Zeitlin, F.I., *Before Sexuality. The Construction of Erotic Experience in the Ancient Greek World*, Princeton, 1990.

Henderson, J., *The Maculate Muse. Obscene Language in Attic Comedy*, New Haven and London, 1975.

Hiller von Gaertringen, F., *Die Insel Thera in Altertum und Gegenwart*, Berlin, 1899–1909.

Hörner, T., *Jonathan Loved David, Homosexuality in Biblical Times*, Philadelphia, 1978.

—— *Homosexuality and the Judeo-Christian Tradition: an Annotated Bibliography*, New York, 1981.

Kelsen, H., 'Die platonische Liebe', *Imago. Zeitschrift für Psychoanalytische Psychologie* 19, 1933.

Keuls, E., *The Reign of the Phallus. Sexual Politics in Ancient Athens*, New York, 1985.

Kiefer, O., 'Socrates und die Homo-sexualität', in *Jahrbuch für sexuelle Wissenschaften* 9, 1908.

Koch-Harnack, G., *Knabenliebe und Tiergeschenke. Ihre Bedeutung in päderastischen Erziehungssystem Athens*, Berlin, 1983.

Kroll, W., 'Knabenliebe', PWRE XI, 1, Stuttgart, 1921.

—— 'Lesbische Liebe', PWRE XII, 2, Stuttgart, 1925.

—— *Freundschaft und Knabenliebe* (*Tusculum Schriften*, IV), Munich, 1927.

Lefkowitz, M., 'Sex and Civilisation', *Partisan Review*, 54,2, 1985.

Lilja, S., 'Homosexuality in Plautus' Plays', *Arktos* 16, 1982.

Manfredini, D., 'Qui commutant cum feminis vestem', *RIDA* 3s., 32, 1985.

Marrou H.I., *Histoire de l'éducation dans l'antiquité*, Paris, 1948; English translation *A History of Education in Antiquity*, London, 1956, 3rd impr., 1981.

Maxwell-Stuart, P., 'Strato and the *Musa puerilis*', *Hermes* 100, 1972.

McNeil, J., *The Church and the Homosexuals*, Kansas City, 1976.

Meier, H.H.E. and Pogey-Castries (de), R.L., *Histoire de l'amour grec dans l'antiquité*, Paris, 1952.

Merkelbach, R., 'Sappho und ihr Kreis', *Philologus* 101, 1957.

Negri, M., '*Paedicare o pēdĭcāre*', *Rendiconti Istituto Lombardo di scienze e lettere, Classe di Lettere, Scienze Morali, e Storiche*, 112, 1978.

Oka, M., 'Telemachus in the Odyssey', *Journal of Classical Studies* 13, 1965.

Patzer, H., *Die Griechische Knabenliebe*, Wiesbaden, 1982.

Rainer, J.M., 'Zum Problem der Atimie als Verlust der bürgerlichen Rechte inbesondere bei männlichen homosexuellen Prostituierten', *RIDA* 3s., 33, 1986.

Reinsberg, C. *Ehe, Hetaerentum und Knabenliebe im antiken Griechenland*, Munich (Beck's Archaeologische Bibliothek), 1989.

Reynan H., 'Philosophie und Knabenliebe', *Hermes* 95, 1967.

Richlin, A., 'Sexual Terms and Themes in Roman Satire and Related Genres', Ph.D. diss., Yale University, 1978.

—— *The Garden of Priapus. Sexuality and Aggression in Roman Humour*, New Haven and London, 1983.

Robinson, D.M. and Fluck, E.J., *A Study of the Greek Love-Names. Including a Discussion of Paederasty and a Prosopographia*, Baltimore, 1937.

Rousselle, A. *Porneia*, Paris, 1983; English translation by Felicia Pheasant, Oxford, 1988.

Schrijvers, H.P., *Eine medizinische Erklärung der Männlichen Homo-sexualität aus der Antike (Caelius Aurelianus, de morbis chronicis, IV, 9)*, Amsterdam, 1985.

Scroggs, R., *The New Testament and Homosexuality*, Philadelphia, 1983.

Sergent, B., *L'homosexualité dans la mythologie grecque*, Paris, 1983; English translation by Arthur Goldhammer, *Homosexuality in Greek Myth*, London, 1987.

—— *L'homosexualité initiatique dans l'Europe*, Paris, 1986.

Shapiro, C. 'Courtship Scenes in Attic Vase Painting', *AJA* 85, 1981, p. 133 ff.

Stroppolatini, G., 'Lex Scatinia e Lex Scantinia', *Annuario dell' Istituto di Storia del diritto romano di Catania*, 7, 1899–1900.

Sullivan, J.P., *The Satyricon of Petronius*, London, 1968.

—— 'The Satyricon of Petronius. Some Psychoanalytic Considerations', *The American Imago* 18, 1961.

—— 'Martial's Sexual Attitudes',

Philologus 123, 1979.

Vegetti, M., 'Foucault et les anciens', *Critique* 471–2, 1986.

Vetta, M., *Theognis Elegiarum liber secundus*, Rome, 1980.

—— 'Recenti studi sul primo partenio di Alcmane', *Quad. Urb.* 39, 1982.

—— 'Il P. Oxy 2506 fr. 77 e la poesia pederotica in Alceo', *Quad. Urb.* 39, 1982.

Veyne, P., 'La famille et l'amour sous le Haut-Empire romain', *Annales E.S.C.* 33, 1978.

—— 'L'homosexualité à Rome', in *Sexualités occidentales*, Paris 1982. English translation, 'Homosexuality in Ancient Rome', in *Western Sexuality*, P. Ariès and A. Béjin, eds, Oxford, 1985.

—— *L'élégie érotique romaine, l'amour, la poésie et l'occident*, Paris, 1983. English translation, *Roman Erotic Elegy: Love, Poetry and the West*, Chicago, 1988.

—— 'L'impero romano', in *Histoire de la vie privée I. De l'Empire romain à l'an mil*, ed. P. Ariès and G. Duby, Paris, 1985.

—— 'The Roman Empire', in *A History of Private Life*. I, *From Pagan Rome to Byzantium*, general editors Philippe Ariès and Georges Duby, Cambridge, Mass. and London, 1987.

Vidal-Naquet, P., *Le chasseur noir. Formes de pensée et formes de société dans le monde grec*, Paris, 1981 (1983). English translation *The Black Hunter*, Johns Hopkins University Press, 1986.

Voigt, M., 'Über die lex Cornelia sumptuaria', in *Berichte über die Verhandlungen in der Köln-Sachs. Gesellschaft der Wissenschaften zu Leipzig*, Phil. Hist. Kl. 42, 1890.

Wender, D., 'Plato: Misogynist, Paedophile and Feminist', *Arethusa* 6,1, 1973.

Whitaker, R., *Myth and Personal Experience in Roman Love-Elegy*, Göttingen, 1983.

Winkler, J.J., *The Constraints of Desire. The Anthropology of Sex and Gender in Ancient Greece*, London and New York, 1989.

Wood, R., 'Homosexual Behaviour in the Bible', *One Institute Quarterly* 16, 1962.

Index

Index

Index

Index

Index

Index

Index